THEORIES
OF
MASS
COMMUNICATION

THEORIES
OF
MASS
COMMUNICATION

FIFTH EDITION

Melvin L. DeFleur

John Ben Snow Professor
S. I. Newhouse School of Communications
Syracuse University

Sandra J. Ball-Rokeach

Professor
The Annenberg School of Communication
University of Southern California

Longman

Theories of Mass Communication, 5th edition

Longman, 10 Bank Street, White Plains, N.Y. 10606

Associated companies:
Longman Group Ltd., London
Longman Cheshire Pty., Melbourne
Longman Paul Pty., Auckland
Copp Clark Pitman, Toronto
Pitman Publishing Inc., New York

Executive editor: Gordon T. R. Anderson
Production editor: Camilla T. K. Palmer
Text design: Jill Francis Wood
Cover design: Paul Agule
Text art: Hal Keith
Production supervisor: Kathleen Ryan

Library of Congress Cataloging-in-Publication Data

DeFleur, Melvin L. (Melvin Lawrence),
    Theories of mass communication / Melvin L. DeFleur, Sandra J. Ball-
Rokeach.
      p. cm.
    Includes index.
    ISBN 0-582-99870-0
    1. Mass media—Social aspects—History. 2. Mass media—Social
aspects—United States—History. I. Ball-Rokeach, Sandra.
II. Title.
HM258.D35 1988
302.2°34—dc19

ISBN 0-582-99870-0 (p)   88-9245
ISBN 0-8013-0007-X (csd)   CIP

10-MA-9594

Table of Contents

Preface

The present fifth edition of *Theories of Mass Communication* is a much revised version. Although the chapters dealing with the historical development of the several media have been retained relatively unchanged from earlier editions, the remaining chapters have been either significantly modified or are completely new to this edition.

Several completely new theoretical perspectives are offered as frameworks for interpreting the influence of communications on individuals, society, and culture. For example, the first chapter contains a theory of transitions in human communication. It is intended to narrow the gap between the study of human communication as a general process and the specific study of mass communication. It focuses very broadly on what happens to people and society when completely new forms of communication are introduced. Other new perspectives are included in chapters that follow.

In Chapters 2, 3, and 4 numerical data on the adoption, spread, and use of the various traditional media have been brought up to date. Additional information has been added to describe the origins and development of newer media, such as cable television and the video cassette recorder, now important components of our media systems.

Chapter 5 continues to focus on the mass media as social systems. It ties their structure and functions to the theoretical perspectives offered in Chapter 1 and shows that mass communication and the several media currently operating in the United States constitute a deeply institutionalized system that is tightly integrated with the American society as a whole. In particular, the analysis shows why it is unlikely that the media will discontinue their production of popular culture and their emphasis on content of a relatively unsophisticated level in the near future.

Chapter 6 has been somewhat revised from earlier editions. It provides an important background for understanding the type of society in which the media emerged and why the earliest interpretations of their influences and effects took the particular direction that they did. The idea of a "mass" society continues to play a part in much thinking about the media, but the earliest theoretical perspectives derived from such considerations have become less relevant to modern analyses. Nevertheless, this chapter provides an important starting point in understanding the unfolding development of mass communication theory as this took place in the basic social sciences and in the discipline of communication itself.

Chapter 7 provides a newly prepared perspective on three important concepts: (1) The study of individual differences developed as a result of an early emphasis on learning in psychology; (2) differences in social characteristics among various categories of people grew out of sociological studies of the heterogeneous composition of contemporary urban industrial societies; and (3) the influence of social relationships became evident in the early days of research into the mass communication process itself. Each of these—individual differences, social differentiation, and social relationships—continues to play an important part in understanding the short-term selective influence of mass communications.

Chapter 8 focuses the role of mass communications in the long-term process of socialization. In its discussion of modeling theory from psychology it reviews the way in which mass communications serve as a source for acquiring patterns of behavior that have been demonstrated by media presentations. Individuals can adopt these as means of coping with their personal environment. The chapter also develops a new theoretical perspective, the social expectations theory, that emphasizes the importance of mass communications as a source of information about social norms, roles, ranking, and social control. It is these psychological and sociological aspects of media content that are at the heart of the indirect socialization functions of mass communications.

A completely new perspective on the construction of meaning is offered in Chapter 9. It shows that although a focus on the social construction of meaning is relatively new to many media scholars, it is one of the oldest intellectual concerns in western society. From Plato to the present, philosophers, theorists, and researchers in various fields have probed the questions of the nature of reality, how we know that reality, and how our subjective conceptions of the objective world have influenced our behavior. Theories devoted to understanding the role of the media in the social construction of individual and shared meanings are now moving to the forefront of mass communication research.

Chapter 10 ties together the theoretical perspectives advanced in Chapters 7, 8, and 9 with a review of the role of basic theories in developing applied strategies for modifying the behavior of audiences. This is one of the least understood issues in communication studies and may be by far the most difficult problem to understand in the context of the mass media. Enormous expenditures are made daily in the world of advertising, political campaigning, and public persuasion efforts. However, little in the way of reliable guidelines have emerged from academic research and mass communication theory for predicting when a particular persuasion strategy will succeed or fail. This remains a relatively uncharted research frontier.

Chapter 11 is a new chapter that presents what has come to be called media system dependency theory. It articulates the basic concepts, assumptions, and hypotheses of this ecological theory and its roots in the basic theoretical paradigms set forth in Chapter 1. Discussion of the special nature of the media system as an information system in control of resources that individuals, groups, organizations, and societies require to attain their respective goals, lays the groundwork for an examination of macro and micro processes of media effects. Above all, it shows why the resources controlled by the media create dependency relations at all levels of modern society, relations that account for the media system's central roles in the organization of personal, group, and social life. This statement takes media system dependency theory beyond its application as a theory of media effects to make it a theory of mass communication. It affords us an understanding of why mass communication has become so necessary to our and our society's struggles to understand, act, and, even, play in our complex and ever-changing modern world. In a sense this theory seeks to provide the same kind of insight that might be gained were we to wake one morning to find that the media, for some mysterious reason, had vanished leaving us and our society with the problem of organizing daily life, not to speak of surviving, without mass communication.

Chapter 12 is necessarily a new chapter because it concerns some of the more important developments in communications technologies that have already altered the nature of mass communication and are likely to continue to do so in the future. Present and future implications of computer, cable, and interactive communication technologies are discussed. Various successful and some unsuccessful efforts to adapt these technologies for use in media systems are examined, including direct broadcast satellite systems, telephone- or television-based interactive systems, and videotex. Also discussed is the importance of examining emerging media systems in the context of our rapidly changing information service economy, and how all such developments may force the dominant mass communication systems of today to adapt to these changing environments to insure their survival. This discussion thus brings us full-circle back to the history of the development of mass communication and how systems of old, like systems of today, have to change not only how they do things technologically, but also change what they do by way of their mass communication roles in the organization of personal and social life.

Sandra Ball-Rokeach   Melvin L. DeFleur
Los Angeles, California   Syracuse, New
                                                       York

THEORIES
OF
MASS
COMMUNICATION

PART I

The Origins of Mass Communication

CHAPTER 1

Stages in the Development of Human Communication

Our impressive ability today to send messages instantaneously across vast distances, and to arouse similar meanings in millions of people simultaneously, is so familiar to us all that it is easy to regard it with nonchalance. In the perspective of human life as it existed in earlier times, however, what we do today when we open our newspaper, tune in our radio, go to a movie, or view our television set represents a change in human communication behavior of truly extraordinary magnitude.

In spite of the painstaking research and the best analytic efforts of communication scholars over the last half century, we are not sure what this change means, how it influences us individually or collectively, or how it will shape our future. In other words, the implications, influences and consequences of the soaring growth of our mass media are as yet incompletely understood. However, it does seem clear at this point that our mass media *do* influence their audiences, and indeed the society as a whole. What we do not fully understand is *how* and to what *extent*. The central task of this book is to present in overview the major formulations that have emerged thus far to try to provide answers to those two problems. In other words we seek to understand (1) how mass communication takes place and (2) what consequences it has for both individuals and the social order.

One way to begin such a task is to provide at the outset a broad perspective across time within which the rapid appearance of our current mass media can be understood as one among several radical advances that have taken place in the ability of *homo sapiens* to communicate. As we will see, previous revolutionary changes in the capacity of people to share meanings with others have had truly powerful influences on the development of thought, behavior, and culture. Understanding these changes and their consequences will make it easier to appreciate an important aspect of our contemporary mass media: Even though they have only recently arrived, they are already so central to our daily lives that they may help shape the destiny of our species in the future.

While previous experience is no certain guide to the future, there is value in looking backward to see what happened at several important points when people became capable of communicating in drastically different ways. It seems appropriate, therefore, to begin at the beginning and trace in brief overview where and when human communication began, how it improved suddenly at various times in the long course of prehistoric and historic development, and how those changes had profound implications for the lives of ordinary people.

THE BEGINNINGS

According to fossil records painstakingly accumulated by paleo-anthropologists over more than a century, the evolutionary process that eventually resulted in contemporary humankind goes back some 70 million years. They have identified a certain small ratlike creature (*proconsul*) that lived during the period of the dinosaurs as our remote ancestor. It was from this inauspicious beginning that the order *Primata*—mammals with flexible hands and feet, each with five digits—would eventually evolve. However, millions of years would elapse before the first monkeylike animals would inhabit sub-Saharan Africa, the probable place of origin of the human family.

Various primate forms evolved over succeeding eons. Most were quite small and lived in the trees. After additional eons, one species about the size of a house cat began to adapt to life on the ground as well as in the forest. It wasn't the only one able to move around on the ground, but it had an important characteristic: its brain to body ratio was somewhat larger than that of most of its contemporaries. This kind of brain capacity, which is roughly correlated with learning ability, would be a critical factor in the evolution of human beings.

Many ancient primate forms survived for a time but eventually lost out in the competition for food or territory and became extinct. At one point, however, contemporary human beings and modern primates—such as chimpanzees and gorillas—shared a common ancestor (dry-

opithecus). The animal was no larger than an average dog, but it had arms, legs, hands, and feet, all of which were similar to those of the monkey and ape families as we know them now.

Somewhere between 14 and 5 million years back, an apelike animal *(ramapithicus)* lived in what we now call Africa and Europe. Evidence is sketchy at this point, and there is controversy among experts concerning its appearance and behavior. We are not even certain that it walked upright, but it may have been the first member of the family *Hominidae* (manlike creature).

Less debate surrounds a somewhat later creature *(australopithecus africanus)* whose remains have recently been found in the Olduvai Gorge in Africa. Australopithecus lived between 5.5 and one million years ago and is generally accepted as the first primate that can truly be classified as a hominid—within the human family. The term "australo" means "southern" (Africa) and has nothing to do with Australia (which gets its name from the same source, however).

Little is known of the way of life led by australopithecus. It did walk upright, occupying rock shelters and living in family units. It was probably less than three feet tall on the average, but in overall appearance it was still very apelike. It was not an aggressive hunter, and it probably lived by scavenging. While it may have used sharp rocks or pointed bones to hack meat off dead animals it found, there is no evidence that it made such tools.

Overlapping somewhat with australopithecus were a series of two-legged proto-human creatures who walked upright, occupying various parts of Europe, Africa, and the Near East for more than a million years. Their mode of communication, if any, is totally unknown. However, brain capacity increased among these various hominids as time went by.

Eventually, about two million years ago, one of our early ancestors *(homo habilis)* appeared. These were important in human development. They were not very large. Remains of a recently discovered adult female indicate that she was about three and a half feet tall. Also, her arms hung down as far as her kneecaps, indicating that she could still swing through the trees as monkeys and chimps do today. However, there was one truly important difference between these beings and other species: They had begun to make tools! Within about a million years or so the mastery of fire followed; our first evidence of hearths comes from China. This development was important because distinctions between the survival techniques of the earliest human beings and those of other primates now started to become more pronounced. These early innovations—crude stone tools and the taming of fire—could be interpreted as the first halting steps in the development of human *culture.* We can tentatively define culture rather broadly as solutions to problems of living that are passed on to following generations. The tool-making and fire-use of our primitive ancestors definitely set them apart from other animals of their time. Eventually, human civilization as we know it would emerge from this elementary base.

Improvements and additions to the tool culture came very slowly, but by about 1.6 million years ago still another hominid *(homo erectus)* was using finely chipped, two-edged hand axes and other cutting tools fashioned from stone and eventually from flint. These early human beings were bigger—nearly our size—and they had shorter arms, as we do, with straight fingers and toes. They could not easily have swung through trees. Furthermore, the brain to body ratio had increased. *Homo erectus* averaged about 600 cc of brain volume; we average about 1,500 cc. Nevertheless, they were developing and passing on modes of survival that no other species had mastered. They were very capable hunters and gatherers, but we know little beyond that.

Still later, perhaps half a million years ago, the ancestral chain split into two separate lines. One resulted in a very stocky and muscular people, much stronger than we are today although not quite as tall on the average. They had big, powerful teeth for efficient chewing of tough meat, relatively large brains, heavy brow ridges, little or no forehead, and a receding chin. It was from this line that Neanderthal people descended *(homo sapiens, neanderthalensis).*[1] They began to occupy the European area and parts of the Near East some 150 to 125 thousand years ago, and from there they spread widely into Africa and Asia. The Neanderthals were considerably more advanced than any of the earlier species. Not only were they excellent hunters, they buried their dead ceremoniously, and they cared for the sick and old. They lasted until about 35,000 years ago and then mysteriously became extinct! No one knows why. There is no evidence of warfare, plague, or anything else that would have brought about such extinction in a relatively short time. They simply vanished.

The other line apparently developed somewhat later. No one knows quite how this happened, but a new kind of human being spread across the range that had been occupied by the Neanderthal and replaced them. These were the Cro Magnon *(homo sapiens, sapiens),* who first appeared in parts of Europe and the Near East somewhere between about 90,000 and 40,000 years ago. Eventually, they occupied virtually all parts of the old world and Asia. It is hypothesized that about 10,000 years ago their descendants crossed land bridges then existing and spread into what are now the Americas. There may have been more than one type of people, as there are today, but contemporary human beings are their direct descendants. The Cro Magnon, who lived in both caves and temporary shelters, were outstandingly successful hunters and gatherers. They made complex tools and had a relatively elaborate social organization. By making effective clothing and learning basic food preservation, they were able to survive in a harsh environment, even near the great glaciers of the last Ice Age, in places where the weather was much like that of northern Siberia today. Early in their existence the Cro Magnon established an artistic tradition with carvings and cave paintings. Eventually they domesticated animals, began to use metals, took up agriculture, and established fixed communities.

The Cro Magnon were virtually identical in appearance and brain capacity to contemporary human beings. They tended to be somewhat more muscular and robust, but that was probably so because of their vigorous way of life and healthier diet. If they could be brought forward in time and dressed in modern clothing, they would seem no different from anyone one might meet on the street. They were the end product of a 70 million-year evolutionary process.

A THEORY OF TRANSITIONS

All of these considerations of the evolution of humankind are a prelude to certain critical questions that are central to the concerns of this book. As we noted earlier, our overall goal is to try to grasp the consequences of the great changes in communication that have taken place in recent times as a result of the invention and spread of mass media. As we also noted above, one way in which the implications of today's communication revolution can be appreciated is to look at what has happened earlier to humanity when equally sweeping changes took place in the ability to share meanings.

The early experience of human species on our planet is often described by archaeologists and other scholars in terms of *ages*. Examples are the Old, Middle, and New Stone Ages, or the Bronze and Iron Ages. These names refer to periods—some rather short and some of many centuries—during which ancient people made tools from different materials or developed different technologies for solving their problems in producing food or constructing weapons. Those intervals and their numerous subdivisions (Paleolithic, Mesolithic, Neolithic, etc.) are undoubtedly helpful for tracing the growth of tool-making and technology, but they fail utterly to focus on a far more basic aspect of human existence—the ability to *communicate*.

A far more significant manner in which to look at human development is to define a series of "ages" in which our ancestors, both primitive and modern, made successive advances in their ability to exchange, record, recover, and disseminate information. It was, after all, precisely those abilities that enabled the succession of hominid forms that emerged during eons of evolution increasingly to think about, invent, accumulate, and transmit to others unique solutions to problems of living.

Viewing the development of humankind from the standpoint of increasingly sophisticated ages of communication does not imply that other issues are unimportant. It is useful to identify the ages during which one type of people or another bashed animals with stone versus flint, or bashed each other with axes made of bronze versus iron. However, the significant and sharply accelerating advances in civilization achieved by *homo sapiens, sapiens* during the last 40,000 years have depended more on their mastery of communication systems than upon the materials they used to fashion tools. While it is not easy to make inferences about the human cultural condition from old bones and physical artifacts, it is vastly more difficult to reconstruct how people communicated and what doing so meant to their way of life. Nevertheless, it is the mastery of communication systems used for information storage, exchange, and dissemination that represents the critical points of change in human history and even prehistory. It was the increasing ability to communicate fully and accurately that led to the escalating development of complex technology, and to myths, legends, explanations, logic, mores, and the complex rules for behavior that make civilization possible.

The story of human existence, then, should more properly be explained by a theory of transitions—that is, explained in terms of *distinctive stages in the development of human communication*, each of which had profound consequences for both the individual and collective social life. Briefly, these were eras associated with the development of signaling, speaking, writing, printing, and communicating with mass media as we know them today. Understanding the consequences of making the transitions from earlier to later stages will provide an important background for developing an appreciation of the significance and consequences of the stage that humankind entered at the beginning of this century.

In overview, the first of these stages was probably the *Age of Signs and Signals,* starting very early in the progression of pre-hominid and early proto-human life, long before our primitive ancestors walked upright. At first, such prehuman beings communicated as do other mammals. Inherited or instinctual responses played a significant role in such communication, and learned communication behavior was at a minimum. As brain capacity slowly increased, that importance was reversed. Literally millions and millions of years passed before it became possible to adopt at least some standardized—that is, learned and shared—gestures, sounds, and other kinds of signals that could be used by succeeding generations to engage in the basic exchanges needed for a social life. But this was not speech. Many animals use cries, shrieks, and bodily postures to signal danger, the presence of food, availability for mating, and coordinated hunting. As learning capacity evolved over millions of years of prehuman development, systems of communication based on signs and signals undoubtedly became increasingly elaborate, conventionalized, and, indeed, effective.

A radical change occurred, probably rather suddenly (in terms of the sweep of time we are considering), when human beings moved into the *Age of Speech and Language*. Compelling evidence now exists that this era began rather recently with the sudden appearance of the Cro Magnon, a new form of *homo sapiens*. Although this conclusion is not universally shared, it appears that these, our most immediate ancestors, *began* to talk somewhere between 90,000 and 40,000 years ago. By about 35,000 years ago, language was in use. The implications of living in a society where the fundamental communication process is speech are not a mystery to us. There are still societies today that are not literate and remain in the oral tradition. Obviously, all people today live in an oral society, but most have passed beyond the limitations of this stage by adding writing, print, and modern media.

In more recent times the pace quickened dramatically. It was only about 5,000 years ago that human beings made the transition into the *Age of Writing*. This great tool for the development of human capacities was independently invented in more than one part of the world. The Chinese and the Maya specifically developed writing completely independently, but the earliest transition took place among the Sumerians and the Egyptians in the old Fertile Crescent, in what is now parts of Turkey, Iraq, Iran, and Egypt.

Much more recently, we entered the *Age of Print*. We can fix an exact time (1455, in the city of Mainz). While crude approximations of printing can be found far back into history, the first book was produced by a printing press using movable type cast in metal only a few decades before Columbus made his famous voyage. Almost overnight the technology had spread all over Europe. From there it went to other parts of the world and revolutionized the way we develop and preserve our culture.

Finally, we entered the *Age of Mass Communication*. This was a transition that in some ways began early in the nineteenth century, with the emergence of newspapers for the common person and electric media such as the telegraph and the telephone. However, the newspaper was an extension of the age of print, and the other media were never used by huge numbers of people. More realistically, the Age of Mass Communication started at the beginning of the twentieth century with the invention and widespread adoption of film, radio, and television by large populations. It was these media that began the great transition that we continue today.

The nature and implications of these most recent changes in human communication processes are the principal subject of this book. But human evolution and cultural accumulation continue. We have recently lurched quite unprepared into the *Age of Computers*. No one is sure what this age implies for communication, but already computers are turning us into what has come to be called an "information society." Furthermore, computers and related technologies are reshaping and extending our mass media. Undoubtedly they will continue to alter virtually all of our communication processes in the years ahead. Although the implications of these changes are by no means clear at present, we will address them here as best we can.

It should be kept in mind that this theory of transitions is one of *accumulation* rather than an account of serially arranged but distinct periods. That is, our primitive ancestors learned to use signs and signals very early, and we still use them rather widely. Speech and language were added. Then writing was added, followed by printing and mass communications. Computer use is now spreading. Thus, the history of human communication has been one of compounding communication systems rather than simply a passing from one to another.

To gain a better understanding of the profound impacts these communication systems had on human existence during their respective eras, each needs to be discussed in somewhat more detail. As will become clear, people's daily activities during each age were deeply influenced by the communication systems that were in place during their lifetimes. Thus, an important principle to understand is that *the nature of a society's communication processes is significantly related to virtually every aspect of the daily lives of its people.* That principle is as true in an age of television as it was during the time when our prehistoric ancestors hunted wooly mammoths with spears at the edge of great glaciers.

Obviously, we assume that as human beings evolved, their ability to communicate also evolved. The more elaborate it became, the easier it was for them to invent, to borrow solutions from others, and to accumulate a body of lore and knowledge that aided in survival. On the other hand, we do *not* assume that the processes of evolution in communication was a smooth and gradual one that began with an elementary system of grunts and gestures and resulted in millions watching the Super Bowl via satellites and television. Just as there were distinct points at which new biological forms emerged, there were relatively sudden advances in the capacity to communicate.

Before we attempt to describe these transitions, a note of caution is in order. Solid evidence for the inferences we will make about the psychological and sociological implications of the ages of communication varies from none to meager for the earliest periods to considerably more abundant for the later ones. Therefore, much of our analysis is by necessity extrapolations from a variety of sources and scholarly disciplines. It would be difficult to verify with certainty some of our conclusions, especially those concerning the earliest hominids. Yet, wherever possible, those conclusions have been based on evidence revealed in the fossil record, the findings of biochemists, physicists, and other specialists, some of which is very recent. On the other hand, our purpose is not to provide a meticulous chronology of human communication systems that will serve for all time. It is merely to offer a broad synthesis—a theory of transitions that contrasts what we have today with earlier forms of communication and the limitations they placed on the human condition.

The Age of Signs and Signals

We suggested earlier that the earliest hominid species, even before the first tool-makers, probably communicated in ways similar to that of complex animals today, that is, with noises and bodily movements that constituted mutually understood signs and signals. At some point, learning undoubtedly began to play an increasingly significant role in their acquiring the ability to understand and participate in the local systems of signs and signals worked out by each family or band. The capacity to learn increased as the ratio of brain mass to body mass increased, but whatever their limitations on inventiveness and cultural accumulation, there are adequate grounds for concluding that our remote ancestors did not use spoken languages requiring the formation of subtle sound combinations.[2]

What seems most likely from the sketchy evidence we have is that the earliest human forms communicated through a limited number of sounds that they were physically capable of producing, such as growls, grunts, and shrieks, plus body language, probably including hand or arm signals, and larger movements and postures. Then, over eons of time, those capacities were developed to good advantage into increasingly complex and relatively efficient modes of communication based on shared rules for interpretation. Those modes did not progress into language/speech systems of the kind we are familiar with, however. Furthermore, if we are correct in our inferences, they did not allow either rapid communication or elaborate cultural development. The complexity of the messages that these early human beings could transmit interpersonally was limited. Perhaps even more important, these people were limited in terms of the way such a system could be used for *internal* communication—that is, conceptualization and thinking.

To illustrate, it is clearly possible to communicate with arm and hand signals that do not depend on spoken words. We see it done all the time on television when the football referee gives arm signals to indicate "off sides," "clipping," "time out," and so forth. One can easily imagine prehistoric people using similar gestures to coordinate a hunt, or to indicate their plans, conclusions, and judgments.

But why, one must ask, didn't they simply talk? They could, after all, make sounds. The answer to that question has only recently come to light in the work of paleoanthropologists who study the skulls and other remains of prehistoric people. Essentially what has been found is that early hominids shared certain anatomical features with other primates; their voice box, or larynx, was virtually identical to that of apes, chimpanzees, and other primates that we know today. Precise measurements of the skulls of early hominids along with computer models of tongue length and the configuration of associated soft tissues have shown that the locations of the larynx and voice box did not allow them to make the incredible range of sounds that are needed to develop human speech.[3] In other words, they did not talk because *they were physically unable to do so.* The same is true of primates today. Apes and chimps cannot be taught to imitate human speech. Their neurological and anatomical structure is not adequate to the task.

That is not to say that apes today cannot communicate, or that early hominids were unable to do so in their time. Both engage (or engaged) in relatively elaborate communication behavior. Most likely early human beings *exceeded* by a considerable margin the communication limits that characterize today's primates. They could make sounds and they could use hand signals, facial expressions, bodily movements, and various postures to encode ideas according to shared rules of meaning and interpretation. Yet, even at best, this was a slow and primitive mode of communication compared with human speech based on language. Furthermore, complex and lengthy communication was probably not possible for reasons that we will explain.

To illustrate some of the limitations of a communication system based on signs and signals, we can easily imagine two kinds of early human beings trying to communicate the same message content—one group who could use speech and language and one who could use only sounds and bodily gestures. A person in the first group, with full command of speech and language, could encode and say the following in about eight seconds:

I saw a young hunter yesterday;
he was wearing a parka and carrying a long spear;
he was running toward a deer near the water hole.

A listener who was familiar with the words, syntax, and grammar of the speaker would have no difficulty grasping the encoded meaning of that message in an instant. It would be understood with no appreciable delay, even as it was spoken; that is, reception and understanding would be virtually simultaneous with the speaker's report.

In contrast, a communicator from a group still in the Age of Signs and Signals would have to encode the above message in a far more cumbersome way. Using bodily gestures, grimaces, and noises as signals for each separate idea, that person would have to break down the content into discrete steps. Message delivery would be rather like the way people communicate as they play "charades" in modern times. Receiving the message would also take place in discrete steps. The process would probably proceed something like the following, with separate noises and movements for each part, and with a pause at the end of each segment to be sure that it was understood:

I saw a hunter
I saw him yesterday
he was young
he was wearing a parka
he was carrying a long spear
the hunter was running
he was running toward a deer
the deer was at the water hole.

There is no question that a well-developed system of signs and signals could handle such message. However, note that it would take much longer to encode and decode, one segment at a time, making the overall rate of transmission and reception significantly slower. This would not be much of a problem with a message such as the above because it is quite short. However, long and complex accounts, reports, or stories would be particularly troublesome for a communication system that proceeded in this segmented manner. Specifically, the problem would be *short-term memory.* Psychologists know today that people have difficulty (and presumably had equal difficulty in earlier periods when the brain was smaller) in remembering the beginning elements of a long, slowly delivered message. By the time the last part is transmitted, they have trouble remembering the early parts. The longer the message, the greater the difficulty.

Generally, then, people who lacked speech had an important limitation on their ability to transmit and receive long and complicated sets of meanings. This is a very important inference because it is just such messages that make up legends, myths, complex instructions, interpretations of the physical world, and so forth. What this implies is that the development of a relatively complex culture was not really possible in an age of signs and signals.

We can dismiss the idea that hand- and finger-signing systems such as those used by deaf people today were available to early hominids as substitutes for spoken language. Signing systems are contemporary adaptations based on alphabets, extensive vocabularies, rules of syntax, and configurations of grammar drawn from institutionalized languages. Speech and language came first, and sign language substitutes came later to assist people who could not speak or hear the words.

What all of this means is that people in the Age of Signs and Signals had to keep their messages simple, and they had to communicate them slowly. Thus, just as their tools were primitive, their modes of communication were inefficient and cumbersome by comparison with language systems. This limitation has important implications for the nature of their social life (which could not be elaborate) and particularly for their *thought* processes. It has been well established that the techniques we use to communicate with others are the same as those with which we communicate within ourselves. In other words, *the rules of thinking parallel the rules of talking.* Thought and reasoning are internal manipulations of language.[4]

It seems inescapable, then, that people who were not able to use speech/language communication for interpersonal exchanges were also unable to store and recall the kinds of ideas needed for intrapersonal communication—the internal processes of abstracting, classifying, synthesizing, inducing the general from the specific, and reasoning from premises to conclusions. Thus, their mental life must have been restricted to elementary conceptualizations based on their systems of signs and signals. This was a truly serious limitation and an important clue as to why their culture developed so slowly. Thus, there was an enormous time span, perhaps several million years, during which various hominids who existed prior to *homo sapiens* were locked into sign and signal communication systems. During that long period elements of human culture did develop, but they were trivial by later standards, and they came at a glacial pace.

Yet even the earliest hominids had advantages over other animals. For one thing, they had the hand, with its opposable thumb, plus a brain that provided an ever-increasing level of learning capacity, at least compared with that of other animals. Bit by bit, tools and technologies were invented and those solutions were passed on to the next generation and adopted by nearby groups. However, it took literally millions of years for significant changes to take place.

Here, then, we see one of the earliest "effects" of communication. In spite of the increasing differences that were occurring between human and other animal forms, communication processes that did not go beyond rudimentary sounds, gestures, body language, and the like placed significant and inescapable limits on the ability of early people to think and innovate. The result was that the pace and scope of cultural advancement was slow indeed.

The Age of Speech and Language

Far more is known about the Cro Magnon than about any other of the early people we have discussed. In their early period they made beautifully crafted tools of flint and stone. For the first time, human culture began to include art. They carved elaborate representations of animals and human beings from bone, stone, ivory, and other materials. Perhaps more important, they left beautiful paintings on the walls of the numerous caves in the areas in which they lived. Hundreds have been found in Spain and Southern France; some are truly masterpieces of composition and color that compare favorably with the best products of contemporary artists. These people depicted bison, reindeer, and other animals that they hunted. They made clothing of leather and had discovered the technique of hardening clay by fire. Cro Magnon paintings may well have been the first attempts to store information—the forerunners of writing.

More important, the Cro Magnon had a skull structure, tongue, and voice box that are just like ours today. Obviously, they had the capacity to speak and there seems little doubt that they did so. Thus, speech and language appear to have originated some time between 35,000 and 40,000 years ago among people who physically resembled human beings today.

What were some of the consequences of this transition to the Age of Speech and Language? For one thing, we noted earlier that when the Cro Magnon first appeared in the region, Neanderthal people were already well established in the same area. Physically, the Neanderthal were more robust, so they should have had a competitive edge for survival. There is little doubt that they were capable hunters and were intelligent; they produced very effective tools; they buried their dead with artifacts (suggesting shared beliefs in an afterlife). In short, they were well on their way in the evolutionary chain and could easily have become our ancestors. But the Neanderthal people became extinct.

The question is why did the Cro Magnon flourish and the Neanderthal die out? Some have suggested that they interbred, but there is little evidence that this happened. It is also unlikely that there was systematic warfare between the two; no evidence survives suggesting any such state of affairs. A far better inference is that when Cro Magnon people developed speech and language, it gave them a huge advantage over their neighbors. Because they could reason with language the Cro Magnon were able to plan and conceptualize, hunt in a more coordinated way, defend themselves more effectively, and better exploit the hunting regions that the Neanderthals had previously had to themselves. They invented and passed on ways to preserve food, keep warm in winter, and generally overcome obstacles to surviving in a harsh environment. Meanwhile, the Neanderthal remained in the Age of Signs and Signals, with its consequent limitations. Then as the climate changed drastically at the end of the Ice Age, the Neanderthal did not adapt to the new conditions.

The Cro Magnon continued to prosper as the centuries moved on. The area in which they originally lived became increasingly dry, and the hunting and gathering way of life was more and more difficult. They retreated to the Fertile Crescent along the Tigris and Euphrates Rivers, westward to the shores of the Mediterranean, and as far south as the Nile. At first they gathered wild grains and survived by foraging, as they always had. But further alterations in the climate made that way of life increasingly difficult. Then, slowly, beginning about 10,000 B.C., they invented the various elements needed to survive as farmers. At first it was simply a matter of natural plant husbandry—scattering seeds and coming back later to gather whatever had grown. The domestication of animals took place during the same period. That was also a haphazard process. Dogs were first, then horses, sheep, goats, and eventually poultry. During the early part of the period they alternated between agriculture and roaming. Then, starting about 6500 B.C., permanent farming and fixed village life began. Human existence became increasingly stable, predictable, and safe. People lived longer and populations expanded.

Cultural development took place at an increasing pace. Ancient cities and the remains of prehistoric civilizations abound in the area of the Fertile Crescent. People not only learned to work the land, raise animals, and worship gods, they developed an increasingly elaborate technology, including the use of metals, weaving, the wheel, pulleys,

and pottery. They had time for leisure, for innovation, and for con-
templation. However, they could not yet write. Language itself became
increasingly diversified. New ways of speaking were constantly developed as people spread into new regions where they faced and overcame new problems. Older languages were modified over the generations. Modern linguists, however, have identified large numbers of
words in some fifty prehistoric vocabularies and in numerous modern
languages that can be traced back as far as about 5000 B.C. (some 7,000
years ago) to a proto-Indo-European "common source."[5] It can be suggested that this common source ultimately led back to the language
originally developed by the Cro Magnon people. In any case, there is no
question that the development of speech and language had made possible great surges in human development.

In summary, the significant lesson to be learned from our brief look
at the development of speech and language is that this form of human
behavior had profound consequences for both individuals and society.
The ability to use language did not *cause* great changes, but it certainly
made it possible for human existence to take giant strides forward.
Words, numbers, and other symbols, plus the rules of language and
logic, enabled human beings to cope with their physical and social
environments in ways that were completely out of the question during
the previous era of signs and signals. By mastering symbolic systems,
individuals could classify, abstract, analyze, synthesize, and speculate.
They could remember, transmit, receive, and understand messages of
far greater length, complexity, and subtlety than was possible with the
use of earlier forms of communication. In short, the change to speech
and language communication made possible breathtaking modifications of human existence as societies in various parts of the world made
the transition from a hunting-gathering way of life to the development
of great classic civilizations. While language alone did not bring this
about, such changes would have been impossible without it.

The Age of Writing

It took millions of years for our species to acquire the ability to use
language. It took many centuries for writing to become a reality, but this
was a comparatively shorter time span. The story of writing is one of
moving from pictographic representation to phonetic systems, from
representing complex ideas with pictures or stylized drawings to using
simple letters to imply specific sounds. The earliest attempts to record
information so that it could be recovered later were elaborate representations of animals and hunting scenes on stone, which was the first
medium. We noted earlier that Cro Magnon people produced beautiful

paintings on the walls of caves. They may have used other media, but if so, those did not survive.

Conventionalized Pictographs. Even pictures of events represent an advance over mere unaided recall as long as those who prepared or used them could decode the meanings that they were intended to arouse. This was an idea that did not come easily. It may have taken thousands of years. If pictures have no agreed-upon encoded interpretations or meanings, they are of little value as an aid to communication. The key, of course, was to develop standardized meanings for the pictographic representations.

Standardization of meanings of pictures, then, was the first step in the development of writing, but it did not begin until well after agriculture had been established. An important stimulus to the development of such systems was that people needed ways to record land boundaries and ownership. Also, as commercial activity and trading increased contacts between unlike people, they needed records of the buying and selling. There were many other needs that had to be met in an agricultural economy. For example, it was important to keep track of the rise and fall of rivers (as in the case of the Nile) and the movements of the heavenly bodies, which determined the planting and harvesting seasons. It is not surprising, therefore, that writing first began in ancient Sumer and Egypt, the areas where agriculture was first practiced.

By approximately 4000 B.C. inscriptions that seem to have been associated with meanings began to appear in ancient sites in Mesopotamia and Egypt. Mainly they were crude pictures drawn or scratched on the walls of buildings or other similar surfaces. Within a relatively short time standardization of meanings became a reality. A simply drawn sunrise could mean a day, a bow and arrow a hunt, a human form a man, a wavy line a lake or river. All of these were typical of early graphic symbols from which writing would be developed. Strung together, they could tell a story; for example, one morning a man went hunting beside a river. The key was that rules were invented and *conventionalized* so that such representations were to arouse specific meanings. Such rules permitted information storage. Representations of ideas could be prepared by one person and recovered by another. Even distance and time could be conquered. With standardized pictographs it became possible to decipher the messages of people far away or even those of people who had died! It is little wonder that writing came to be regarded with special awe.

The Egyptians became innovators in the development of elaborate systems of *glyphs*, or symbolic characters. At first these were stone carvings, but in time they were drawn and painted. The Egyptian glyphs were associated with rules for the arousal of complex standard-ized meanings. Their *pictographic* system was like contemporary Chi-nese. Each symbol stood for a particular idea, thing, or concept. To communicate in a sophisticated way, both the person doing the writing and the one who read the message had to command an enormous number of such patterns. In the beginning, therefore, literacy was con-fined to specialists. The ancient scribes studied for years to master the thousands of symbols needed to commit messages to hieroglyphics, or to decipher them for the wealthy and powerful.

Phonetic Writing. Another people, the Sumerians who lived just north of the Persian Gulf, developed another form of writing. They started out using little pictures drawn into a soft clay pad as representations of ideas. Then, because it was difficult to draw the pictures in realistic detail, they increasingly stylized their representations. Before long, they resorted to using the end of a stick, that had been whittled into a wedge shape, to make marks in the clay. It wasn't possible to produce recognizable pictures with such a system, but it was both quick and simple to produce distinctive characters that could be assigned mean-ings. Pictures of the objects were really not necessary. The resulting wedge-pattern representations are called *cuneiform* writing today. Many examples have survived because it was possible to preserve them by baking the clay into a potterylike medium.

What made the Sumerian system so different is that by about 1700 B.C. the Sumerians hit upon the idea of letting each little stylized symbol stand for a particular *sound* rather than an idea. The advantage was enormous. Instead of thousands of separate symbols—one for every thing and idea—a far fewer number were needed to represent the sounds of syllables that made up words. (Our alphabetical writing, in which each vowel and consonant has its own character, is even sim-pler.) Nevertheless, the use of characters to represent syllables was the first step in the development of *phonetic* writing and was a great breakthrough in human communication. In particular it made literacy immensely easier to acquire. One had to remember only a hundred or so symbols for the various syllables in the language.

Alphabetical writing came within less than a thousand years and caught on relatively quickly. It spread throughout the ancient world, and after a number of centuries it reached Greece. By this time, the idea of using letter symbols for consonants and eventually vowels, rather than for syllables, was fully developed. It was a great advance because fewer than one hundred characters were needed. Today, for example, we get by nicely in English with only twenty-six.

Some societies lost out by making the wrong choices during this period. For example, the Egyptians loved their beautiful glyphs and were reluctant to use an alphabet. In time they used characters for consonants only, but one had to know the words to recover the sounds without letters for vowels. For example, we write "bldg" and say "building." If we did this to all words it would become difficult. It was for this reason that Egyptian writing remained cumbersome and could not compete with more efficient forms. Eventually, the Egyptians did develop a phonetic script, but by that time it was too late.

After many variations among many people it was the Greeks who most effectively standardized and simplified the system. By about 500 B.C. they had a widely used alphabet. Eventually the Greek alphabet was passed on to Rome, where it was modified and improved even further. Today we use the Roman *majuscule* (capital) and *minuscule* (small) letters. Centuries later we came to call these "upper" and "lower" case letters, from their positions in the typesetters' trays.

Along with tools, fire, and language itself, alphabetical writing was one of the all-time most significant accomplishments of human beings. Without it the great majority of the populations of the world would still be illiterate. Great movements in science, the arts, government, and religion were made possible because people could read. History itself began with written records, but that was only about 250 generations ago! In the perspective of 70 million years that is a very short time.

The Significance of Portable Media. The great problem with hieroglyphics, and to a certain extent the clay tablets of cuneiform, was that of portability. In particular, stone as a medium had the capacity to endure through time but could not be transported readily across space. As ancient societies became more sophisticated, they sought media by which writing could be transported more easily.

About 2,500 years before Christ, the Egyptians discovered a method of making a kind of durable paper from papyrus. Compared with stone, papyrus was extremely light. Moreover, it was much easier to write on papyrus with brush and ink than it was to chisel glyphs laboriously on stone. Papyrus originally was found only in the Nile Delta. Fresh green stems of the reed were cut and stripped, sliced into thin strips, laid criss-cross on one another, and pounded until they melded into a single mass, which was then pressed out and dried. Long rolls of considerable length could be prepared by joining one sheet to another. The scribe used two types of ink (black and red) and a brush made from another kind of plant. The glyphs began to be simplified as scribes required smoother, easier forms for faster writing.

Among the Maya, a similar transformation of media took place. They had discovered that long strips of light-colored bark could be pulled from the ficus tree. Long, clean strips of this inner bark, six to eight inches wide and as long as twenty feet, were removed from the trees. The strip was soaked in water and beaten to make it both uniform in thickness and pliable. The bark was then folded into a long, pleated, and very neatly trimmed book with wooden end pages to enclose it like an accordion. Hieroglyphic writing was painted on both sides and often beautifully decorated. The conquistadors were astonished to find people in the New World who lived in elaborate stone dwellings complete with libraries and books. During the conquest, unfortunately, thousands of these books were burned by the Spanish military in an effort to reduce the power of the priests and leaders over their people. Only a few examples remain.

The most important point in this change from heavy stone to light and portable media is that it opened the possibility for a significant change in the social organization and culture of society. The acquisition of a communication technology based upon a light and portable medium, plus a system of written symbols that could be produced quickly and read by scribes, provided necessary conditions for great social and cultural changes.[6] The whole institutional structure was influenced. For example, in Egypt by 2000 B.C. papyrus was widely used to transmit written orders and record information of various kinds. The central administration employed an army of scribes. Literacy was a valuable skill, providing a door-opener to prosperity and social rank. Scribes became a privileged class under the control of the elite. Great changes in political and religious institutions took place as a result of the ability to write and record. Libraries opened. Religious doctrines and scriptures were recorded. Schools were established to teach scribes. Even the arts and sciences began to develop. Successful treatments for diseases could be written down. Observations of numerous features of nature and their interpretations could be recorded. The human mind was freed from the burdensome task of having to remember entire cultures and reproduce them in the minds and memories of every new generation. Ideas could be stored, accumulated, and drawn upon by subsequent generations. This was the great step forward as human beings proceeded through the Age of Writing.

The Age of Print

Aside from writing, one of the greatest human accomplishments of all time was the development of printing. Prior to the fifteenth century, people reproduced books in Europe by preparing *manu scripti*, copies of existing books laboriously printed by hand. While it is true that many were beautiful works of art, the process often introduced errors. More important, the number of books available was severely restricted and they could be purchased only by persons of considerable means. Printing brought a fantastic change. Hundreds or even thousands of copies of a particular book could be reproduced with great precision. It was a fabulous invention that astounded the literate world of the time.

A critical point in the eventual emergence of print in the Western world was when paper began to replace parchment in the Islamic world during the eighth century. (Paper originated much earlier, in China.) From there it slowly diffused to Christian Europe, particularly when the Moors occupied Spain. Not until the invention of the printing press in the fifteenth century, however, did priests, political elites, scholars, and scribes begin to lose their monopoly on reading and writing. As literacy spread, few could foresee that it would profoundly affect the directions of human history.

The Press and Movable Type. The concept of making an impression with a seal, or using a rolling-pin-like device with carved symbols to impress an image in soft clay, was an old one. Even the process of printing a whole page of letters, by painstakingly carving them into a smooth wooden block in reverse image and then inking and pressing them onto a smooth paper or other surface, was understood long ago. The Chinese had done it and had printed the *Diamond Sutra*, the world's first book, by about 800 A.D., centuries before printing began in Western society. However, it was far from the system of using individual letters cast in metal.

Printing as we know it was not possible until an obscure goldsmith in Mainz, Germany, one Johann Gutenberg, figured out a unique way to make type. After much experimentation, he developed the idea of making a steel punch for each letter, painstakingly carved in a precise way. Then he could punch the image into a small square of softer metal, such as brass. He made a little clay mold around the impression so that hot lead could be poured into it to make a casting of the letter. This mold could be used over and over, to cast as many individual letters as the printer needed. Once that was done, the letters could be lined up in a tray to form words and sentences. Tightly secured, they could be inked and a piece of parchment or paper oculd be pressed down on them. A very sharp image would result. Lead turned out to be too soft, but Gutenberg eventually discovered a way to mix lead with other metals into a kind of alloy that worked very well indeed.

The only remaining problem was the press. The principle of a screw-type press was an old one. Presses had been used for centuries to press olives for oil, and grapes for wine. Gutenberg obtained a big wine press and modified it considerably, arranging a platform for the tray of type and a flat surface to press down the parchment or paper. Since everything had to be lined up to within a tiny fraction of an inch, a great deal of experimentation was required. Finally, after inking the type and placing a sheet of parchment on top, and with suitable screens on the sides to keep the page neat, he carefully screwed down the press and the page was printed. It was beautiful! The print was sharp and clean; there were no errors such as were commonly made in hand copying.

Gutenberg worried. He was not at all certain that his invention (which took him more than twenty years to perfect) would catch on. He was concerned that those who could afford books would prefer the hand-copied version and would regard his as a cheap imitation. That was one of the reasons that he had chosen an elaborately printed and decorated Bible as his first project. He felt that he would be able to sell it to the wealthy. Time has shown that his experiment was an incredible success. His 42-line Bible was one of the finest examples of the printer's art ever produced.

Sadly, Gutenberg never got to enjoy the fruits of his imagination and creativity. He had borrowed heavily from his lawyer while perfecting his system. Just as he was completing his first project—the famous Bible—his lawyer demanded repayment of the loans, took him to court, and was able to strip him of his shop, the press, his entire invention, the 200 printed copies of the Bible, and virtually everything else that he owned. Ten years later Gutenberg died in poverty, a broken man. He never learned what a truly important service he had performed for all of us.

The Spread of Literacy. As the sixteenth century began, presses with movable type were turning out thousands of copies of books printed on paper. They were being published in all the European languages and thus could be read by anyone who was literate in his or her own language. The availability of these books spurred broader interest in learning to read.

For the first time, the Scriptures were available in a language other than Latin. No longer could the Roman Church carefully guard the holy writings through the use of an ancient language. The availabilty of the Scriptures to ordinary people in their own languages eventually led to challenges of the authority and interpretations of Rome. A new medium of communication, then, opened the way for protesting the existing religious and social structure. The rise of Protestantism led to further profound changes that have had their impact on Western society right up to the present day.

The basic idea of a newspaper developed quite early on the European continent, in England, and in the New World. The American colonial press was established for some years before the United States was formed as a new nation. The colonial press distributed small papers and pamphlets to the educated elite. Their content was, as we shall see in more detail in Chapter 2, at a level of sophistication and taste beyond the capacities of the common citizen.[7] Nevertheless, they provided the basic form around which to develop a new kind of newspaper aimed at the broad base of artisans, mechanics, and merchants who constituted the growing middle and working classes of the emerging urban-industrial society. When a means was found to finance a cheap paper for wide distribution, and the techniques were devised for rapid printing and distribution, the first true *mass* medium was born in the form of the penny press. These events occurred in the mid-1830s in New York City. The mass newspaper was a great success, and within a very few years it spread to many parts of the world. The third decade of the nineteenth century, then, saw the technology of rapid printing and the basic idea of a newspaper combined into the first true mass medium of communication.

Two points are important in these events. First, the mass newspaper, like the other media that followed it, was an invention that occurred only after a complex set of cultural elements had appeared and accumulated within the society. Second, like almost all inventions, it represented a combination of these elements in a social setting that permitted the acceptance and widespread adoption of the newspaper as a culture complex. As a technical device, it was consistent with, and perhaps even required by, other cultural institutions of the day. The relevant institutional structure of the society in terms of economic, political, and educational processes, as well as demographic and ecological patterns, provided a setting within which the particular combination of elements represented by the penny press could emerge and flourish.

Print and the Human Condition. By the end of the nineteenth century it was becoming clear to the pioneer social scientists of the time that the new mass media—newspapers, books, and magazines, all of which were widely used in society—were bringing important changes in the human condition. These media represented a new form of communication that influenced not only patterns of interaction in communities and societies but the psychological outlooks of individuals as well. For example, the American sociologist Charles Horton Cooley stated in 1909 that there were four factors that made the new media far more efficient than the communication processes of any earlier society. The new media were more effective, he said, in terms of

Expressiveness, in that they carry a broad range of ideas and feel-
ings
Permanence of record, or the overcoming of time
Swiftness, or the overcoming of space
Diffusion, or access to all classes of men[8]

Cooley pointed out that these features of the (print) news media, which
had come into existence in the nineteenth century, had forever changed
the mental outlooks of those who used them:

> The general character of this change is well expressed by the two
> words *enlargement and animation.* Social contacts are extended in
> space and quickened in time, and in the same degree the mental unity
> they imply becomes wider and more alert. The individual is broad-
> ened by coming into relation with a larger and more various life, and
> he is kept stirred up, sometimes to excess, by the multitude of chang-
> ing suggestions which this life brings to him.[9]

Thus, even before the establishment of still newer media, it was becoming clear that the Age of Mass Communication would erode the barriers
of isolation among people in the world and produce significant changes
in the organization and functioning of society. Or, as Cooley put it, "the
new mass communication represented a revolution in every phase of
life; in commerce, in politics, in education, even in mere sociability and
gossip. . . ."[10]

The Age of Mass Communication

With the appearance and acceptance of the mass press, the pace of
human communicative activity began to increase sharply. By midcen-
tury the telegraph became a reality. Although not a mass medium of
communication, this device was an important element in a technological accumulation that would eventually lead to mass electronic
media.[11] A few decades later, experiments were being carried out successfully that were prerequisite to motion pictures and wireless telegraphy. With the dawn of the twentieth century, Western society was about
to experience the development of techniques of communication that
had been beyond the wildest flights of imagination a century earlier.
During the first decade of the new century motion pictures became a
form of family entertainment. This was followed in the 1920s by the
development of household radio and in the 1940s by the beginnings of
home television. By the early 1950s radio had reached saturation pen-

etration in American homes, with additional sets widely dispersed in automobiles. There was multiple penetration in the form of bedroom and kitchen radios, and a growing number of transistorized miniature sets. The late 1950s and early 1960s saw television beginning to approach such saturation. By the 1970s it was virtually complete in the United States and progressing elsewhere. New media were added— cable, VCRs, and even interactive Videotex. Mass communication had become one of the most significant and inescapable facts of modern life.

This brief sketch of main transitions in the ability of people to communicate shows two major facts. First, communication "revolutions" have been occurring throughout human existence. Each provided a means by which significant changes could be brought about in human thought, the organization of society, and the accumulation of culture. Second, the rise of mass media has occurred very recently indeed. Many of its major events have taken place within the lifetimes of substantial segments of contemporary populations. Many people alive today can recall a society without household radio. For our oldest generation there were no motion pictures to see on Saturday nights during their youth. Each of these media added to the total daily availability of language-using opportunities for the average person. Thus, the accumulation of these devices within recent history has implied still another dramatic increase in the pace of communicative behavior for the majority of people in society. The impact of the new age remains to be fully assessed.

We live in a constantly changing society. Sometimes it is difficult to determine which changes are important. One of the goals of this book is to show that the entrance of the newspaper, the radio receiver, and the television set into the ordinary citizen's home represents a technological change that has greater significance for ordinary people than our largest accomplishments at the frontiers of science. With satellites and shuttles streaking through space, we may lose sight of the fact that these achievements are remote from the routine daily activities of the majority of us. The television set, however, is a technological device that has an immediate and direct impact. The children of our society spend more time, on the average, viewing its offerings than they spend in school! Thus, the television set and the other media are innovations around which human beings organize their lives in different patterns than has ever been the case in the course of our evolution.

ASSESSING THE NATURE
AND INFLUENCE OF MASS COMMUNICATION

Although communication research scholars have not reached a full understanding of the impact that mass media are having upon the psychological, moral, economic, political, creative, cultural, and educational aspects of the ordinary individual's life, they have begun to accumulate a base of research findings that will increasingly aid in understanding these issues. The growth of the social sciences as disciplines employing quantitative procedures and the logic of science, like the development of the mass media themselves, has occurred principally in the present century. Within that brief span, a limited number of sociologists, psychologists, journalists, speech communication scholars, and others have specialized in the dispassionate study of the role of the mass media within our society. As larger numbers of research specialists turn their attention to this field, we may expect the generalizations growing out of such research to yield a more complete understanding of the relationship between the mass media and the societies within which they operate. In large part, discussions as to that relationship have been carried on in the past within something other than a dispassionate and objective framework. As each of the major media of communication emerged in our society, it became the object of considerable controversy and debate. These debates began when the first issue of the penny press hit the streets of New York in 1834. They continue today with respect to the role of radio, paperback books, television, comic books, magazines, and films in relation to a variety of issues.

One of the major tasks of students of mass communication in assessing this Age of Mass Communication, and the controversies it has caused, is to accumulate scientific findings concerning the impact of the media on their audiences. We must replace emotional speculation with valid evidence as a basis for public discussion about mass communication. The different media have variously been charged with responsibility for (1) lowering the public's cultural tastes, (2) increasing rates of delinquency, (3) contributing to general moral deterioration, (4) lulling the masses into political superficiality, and (5) suppressing creativity. This is a damning list, and if the apparently innocent devices in our living rooms are actually guilty of such monstrous influences, they should, of course, be viewed with alarm. The problem is that advocates of opposite points of view tell us that our newspapers, radios, television sets, and the like, are not insidious devices for evil but are in fact our faithful servants or even saviors in that they are (1) exposing sin and corruption, (2) acting as guardians of precious free speech, (3) bringing at least some culture to millions, (4) providing harmless daily entertainment for the tired masses of the labor force, (5) informing us of the world's events, and (6) making more bountiful our standard of living by their unrelenting insistence that we purchase and consume products to stimulate our economic institution. If such claims are true, to reject such benefactors or even to suggest that their content is uninspiring seems an act of flagrant ingratitude. Until reliable research findings can present a convincing case that the media either are or are not causally related to the claims of their critics (or champions), these controversies will continue to rage.

A second important task confronting communication scholars is to explain the basic nature of the human communication process. Many promising leads are available from such fields as semantics, cultural anthropology, sociology, and social psychology. These need to be brought together into an adequate description of human communication in general. The place of mass communication, using complex media, can then be worked out. Extensive discussions of human communication are presented in this book. They point out that human communication is a biosocial process that is dependent not only upon human memory but upon such factors as perception, symbolic interaction, and the cultural conventions of specific languages. The way in which mass communication is dependent upon these basic processes is also discussed.

Another major task for those who specialize in the scientific study of the media is to provide adequate data with which to evaluate the consequences of operating mass communication systems under varying conditions of ownership or control. That is, within differing political structures, economic systems, and historical-cultural settings, the structure of the mass media themselves can be expected to take different forms. The production, distribution, and consumption of mass media content is sharply influenced by questions such as whether the society is a free-enterprise democracy, an outright totalitarian dictatorship, or something in between. Societies where mass communication systems operate under conditions of ownership and control quite different from those of the United States can provide a basis for comparative research. Similarly, studies of the historical development of each advance in technology provide ways of inducing generalizations about the way in which the various forms of the mass media have developed under sociocultural conditions.

The Central Questions

The task of assessing the nature and influence of mass communication is obviously one with a host of important dimensions. It clearly includes more than simply trying to discover the ways in which message content disseminated by print, film, or broadcast media influences the beliefs, attitudes, or behaviors of audiences. The task includes systematic inquiries into the nature of the historical events and the value systems that have shaped the media in a given society and have led them to produce their particular pattern of content. It includes a systematic probing into the very nature of human communication at the interpersonal level to see if the introduction of media alters the process in some critical way. Finally, that task includes the study of the ways in which mass communication can reshape social and cultural arrangements—the rules and codes of society, its language, and the role expectations that its people have of one another.

Stated more succinctly, the assessment of the nature and influence of mass communication focuses on three critical questions:

1. *What is the impact of a society on its mass media?* What have been the political, economic, and cultural conditions that have led the mass media to operate in their present form?
2. *How does mass communication take place?* Does it differ in principle or only in detail from more direct interpersonal communication?
3. *What does exposure to mass communication do to people?* How does it influence them psychologically, socially, and culturally?

For several reasons, it is to the third question that the majority of mass communication research has in the past been addressed. The first question, although of central significance, has not captured much of the attention of research specialists and scholars. To some degree, the same is true of the second question. It appears likely, since the storm of criticism and controversy surrounding the media has been phrased largely in terms of the third of these fundamental questions, that communication researchers have been guided in their investigations less by theoretical significance than by the dictates of popular interest. Whatever the reasons for this lack of balance among these three issues, the first and second questions have received considerably less scholarly attention than the third. In several of the chapters that follow, special attention is given to discussions of ways in which the social and cultural conditions in the United States have had a role in shaping our mass media. In addition, considerable attention is given to the third question.

Social Paradigms: The Organization of Society

Relationships between media, society, and individuals, as posed in the three central questions above, cannot be studied in a theoretical vacuum. Research on the processes and effects of mass communication must be guided by some set of basic assumptions about the nature of society, of the human individual, and of the relationship between the two. The term *paradigm* is sometimes used to label a set of such basic assumptions. It is an old term that comes to us from the Latin word *paradigma*. In early times, before the development of modern science, it referred to any sort of "model" that could be copied, or against which something could be compared. For example, an account of the life of a virtuous man was a kind of paradigm; it could serve as a model or example of good behavior against which one's own life might be compared.

In communication science today the term paradigm combines the idea of a model for comparison with the more complex idea of a set of fundamental assumptions of the nature of some aspect of social or psychological reality. For example, the Freudian account of the human psyche can be thought of as a paradigm. Freud's basic assumptions about our psychological realities describe conditions and relationships that supposedly underlie the psychological functioning of the human being. While it is not widely used in communication research, at least some investigators have used this paradigm as a broad theoretical framework to guide investigations into consumer decisions related to advertising and the like.

The assumptions that make up a paradigm are actually *postulates*. That is, they are assumptions that provide a beginning point for deriving theoretical explanations of more specific aspects of the social or psychological phenomena whose nature is set forth in the paradigm. Such postulates are themselves not open to testing; one cannot gather empirical data that can be used to accept or reject postulated assumptions. Instead, they are taken as "givens," not in the sense that they are regarded as eternal verities, but only in the sense of *suppositions*. In other words, postulates are statements that specify relationships and conditions that one may choose to regard as true "for the sake of argument"—for the sake of seeing where they logically lead. Postulating a given relationship or condition is like saying "suppose it were true that" (the relationship or condition set forth does indeed accurately describe reality). What then would be the implications for some specific process or effect under study? Those implications are called by various names—corollaries, theorems, or simply derived propositions. It is these implications that serve as *hypotheses* to be tested against data gathered in research projects. Generally, then, paradigms are broad theoretical formulations. They set forth sets of postulates—assumptions that one can choose to regard as descriptions of reality for the purpose of obtaining derived hypotheses. Such hypotheses can then guide research on specific processes and effects.

The most important paradigms available to the communication scientist include sets of assumptions drawn mainly from psychology, social psychology, and sociology. Within these fields many sets of postulates have been formulated concerning the nature of society and human nature. From *sociology*, the four that are of the greatest significance to the study of relationships between the media, society, and the process of mass communications are those that give a central role to (1) the processes by which a society maintains social *stability*, (2) the processes by which it *changes* over time, (3) the nature and significance of social *conflict*, or (4) the forms of interpersonal interaction by which human beings share *meanings*. The more technical terms associated with these distinctive paradigms are *structural functionalism, social evolution*, the *social conflict model*, and *symbolic interactionism*. If the focus of communication research is at the level of individual behavior, such as selecting, perceiving, and being influenced by media messages, then one of the *psychological* paradigms is generally used. There are many to choose from. They range from *behavioristic* learning theories to *psychoanalytic* formulations. For the most part, however, the psychological formulation that has been most widely used in communication research is the *cognitive paradigm*, which stresses such concepts as attitudes, beliefs, perceptions, needs, and gratifications. In the sections that follow, the main postulates of these sociological and psychological paradigms are summarized very briefly.[12] Their significance to the study of mass communication will be made abundantly clear in remaining chapters of the book.

Structural Functionalism. The idea that the organization or structure of a society provides the source of its stability is as old as social philosophy. In his *Republic*, Plato posed the analogy between society and an organism, a system of related parts in dynamic equilibrium. In the ideal society he described, each category of participants in the social structure performed activities that contributed to the overall attainment of social harmony.[13] This general idea was passed on in Western thought and became the central framework for the analysis of societies by the early sociologists. Auguste Comte made the organic analogy central to his conceptions of society. Herbert Spencer organized his entire social philosophy around the idea.[14] The early modern sociologists, such as Emile Durkheim, developed the orientation further at the end of the nineteenth century. The idea of a society as a dynamic system of repetitive activities also became important in the analyses of primitive societies by such anthropologists as Bronislaw Malinowski and (later) A. R. Radcliffe-Brown.[15] In recent times the set of assumptions involved in structural functionalism continues to play a significant role in the development and debates of modern sociology through the writings of Robert Merton, Talcott Parsons, and many others.

The term *structure*, of course, refers to the manner in which the repetitive activities of a society are organized. Family behavior, economic activity, political activities, religion and magic, and many other forms of societal activities are highly organized from a behavioral point of view. The term *function* refers to the contribution a particular form of repetitive activity makes in terms of maintaining the stability or equilibrium of the society. Many versions of this general theoretical orientation for studying social processes have been advanced. Each version lists somewhat different sets of assumptions and includes many debates over which is most useful. Contemporary anthropologists and sociologists are still thrashing out which is the best version and what are the advantages and disadvantages of structural functionalism in all its forms.

Perhaps the clearest statement of the assumptions of classic structural functionalism remains that set forth by Robert Merton in 1957.[16] He reviewed the many existing versions and consolidated them into a brief but succinct statement. While Merton himself had serious criticisms of this classic orientation, he summarized the postulates of structural functionalism concerning the nature of society as follows:

1. A society can best be thought of as a system of interrelated parts; it is an organization of interconnected, repetitive, and patterned activities.
2. Such a society naturally tends toward a state of dynamic equilibrium; if disharmony occurs, forces will arise tending to restore stability.
3. All of the repetitive activities in a society make some contribution toward its state of equilibrium; in other words, all persisting forms of patterned action play a part in maintaining the stability of the system.
4. At least some of the patterned and repetitive actions in a society are indispensable to its continued existence; that is, there are functional prerequisites that fill critical needs of the system without which it would not survive.

But what does such a set of assumptions have to do with the study of mass communication? The media and the process of mass communication are patterned and repetitive actions in the social system of the society in which they operate. The structural dependencies that exist between the media and other social systems not only affect the everyday workings of our society, but also, as will be discussed in Chapter

11, influence the way in which individuals use the media in everyday life. They make some contribution to the social equilibrium of that society. In other words, they have consequences for the society as a whole. Indeed, a good case could be made that mass communication could be listed among those indispensable components of the social structure without which contemporary society, as we know it, could not continue. On the other hand, mass communication may be *dysfunctional,* contributing to disharmony rather than stability, if it has the effect of stirring people to various forms of deviant behavior. A number of such issues are addressed in later chapters.

The Evolutionary Perspective. One of the difficulties with the structural functional paradigm is that it stresses stability and equilibrium in society when it is obvious to even the most casual observer that urban industrial societies undergo constant change. One of the oldest sets of assumptions about the basic nature of society is one that focuses centrally on change. The *evolutionary* paradigm was formulated during the founding years of sociology. This use of the term "evolution" focuses on *social* change rather than on the *biological* changes discussed in earlier sections of the chapter.

This paradigm rests heavily on the so-called organic analogy, at least in its classic form. The idea here is that society is both organized like and develops like a biological organism. This is not to imply that either classical or contemporary evolutionists maintain that society *is* a biological organism; rather, the idea is that it *resembles* such an organism in its structure and processes of change. Depending upon which version of the evolutionary paradigm one refers to, other assumptions are also made. In its classical form (as advanced by Herbert Spencer) this paradigm was the basis for advocating a *laissez-faire* political policy that maintained it was foolish to try to change a society through legislation, welfare programs, and the like, because the immutable laws of social evolution would inevitably lead the society to a more perfect condition.[17] Most of the ideas of the evolutionary paradigm were formulated before Darwin advanced his famous hypothesis about the origins of species. Nevertheless, because of the similarity between the two sets of ideas, it is often referred to as "social Darwinism."

Today there are many variations of the earlier paradigm.[18] Essentially they represent an attempt to account for societal change within some set of natural laws (as opposed to attributing such change to divine intervention, random happenstance, and so forth). The social mechanisms of change that appear most often in evolutionary paradigms are natural selection, survival of the fittest, and the inheritance of acquired characteristics. These sound very biological and do appear in strictly biological accounts of evolution. Nevertheless, they have social counterparts in that they can be used to think about incorporating new standardized forms of behavior into a society and the disappearance of earlier forms from the culture that were passed on from one generation to the next. As is perfectly obvious, modern societies constantly incorporate new social forms, ranging from domestic practices (e.g., live-in lovers) to new kinds of business organizations (e.g., multinational corporations). Such innovations are adopted and become accepted because they permit at least some people to achieve goals that they value more effectively than the behavior forms that were previously available. Therefore, some process of natural selection, survival of the fittest, and passing on of the new social form underlies the constant unfolding of society into increasingly differentiated and specialized behavioral patterns. At the risk of considerable oversimplification, we can summarize the evolutionary paradigm as including such assumptions as the following:

1. Society can best be thought of as a set of interrelated parts; it is an organization of interconnected, repetitive, and patterned activities.
2. Such a society constantly undergoes change, with its social forms becoming increasingly differentiated and more specialized.
3. New social forms are invented or borrowed from other societies by individuals seeking more effective ways to reach goals that they regard as important.
4. Those social forms that do in fact help people achieve their goals more effectively, and that do not clash with existing values, are adopted, are retained, and become stable parts of the developing society; conversely, less effective forms are abandoned.

Specifically, how are such assumptions about societal development significant in the study of mass communication? Their importance becomes clear when one examines the history of the media. During that history, many people saw the need for communication systems that were swifter and that could reach larger audiences. To reach these goals, many new social forms were tried as means for making use of developing technologies. Some of these were abandoned. Others were selected, survived, and were passed on to later generations. In other words, the development of mass communication has been an evolutionary process, both in terms of its mechanical and scientific technology and in terms of the social forms necessary for making effective societal use of that technology to meet goals regarded as important by those in decision-making roles.

The Social Conflict Model. A third paradigm widely used by social scientists assumes that conflict rather than stability or evolution is the most important social process. The idea that a society consists of social elements in conflict is at least as old as the belief that social arrangements are the basis of social stability. The notion that social conflict is the master process in society is another attractive alternative to a commitment to the position that equilibrium is basic. Like the evolutionary paradigm, it is attractive because of the obvious fact of social change, which is very difficult to deal with within a structural functional orientation.

To ancient philosophers it was apparent that many kinds of change were brought about as a result of opposing forces. Much of their thinking was in terms of such concepts as true and false, good and evil; but in the world of ideas they saw new forms emerging from the interplay of antagonistic forces. This conception, of resolving conflict to attain something new, came to be called a *dialectic* process. Plato used a dialectic format in his discussions of various issues in the *Republic.* For centuries the idea continued to be a part of the study of logic, to describe the way in which knowledge could be obtained through a process of debate and examination of opposing views.

Social conflict as a basic human process also has played a key role in social philosophy. Hobbes made it central to his analysis of the origins of sovereign power in his *Leviathan.*[19] It became the central thesis of the social contract theorists. However, it was from the writings of G.W. Hegel, Karl Marx, and Frederich Engels that the ideas of social conflict and the dialectic process were brought together into an analysis of societal change.[20] Marx is generally thought of by contemporary social scientists as the father of the conflict model of society and social change. Indeed, his sociopolitical theories provide well-known analyses of the way that new societal forms supposedly arise from struggles between the "haves" and "have nots." But one does not have to be committed to Marxian ideologies to assume that social conflict can be a significant source of social change.

One of the clearest statements of the social conflict model is that made by Ralf Dahrendorf in 1958.[21] He reviewed the issues and debates and posed a model of society that incorporates conflict and change as the central issues. In more recent times debates have continued as to how such a model can best be formulated and used to derive hypotheses and theories about more specific social processes, including analyses of communication. Essentially, however, the contemporary conflict model can be simplified into the following basic assumptions:

1. A society can best be thought of as consisting of categories and groups of people whose interests differ sharply from one another.
2. All these components of society attempt to pursue their own interests in competition with others or to preserve their interests by resisting the competitive efforts of others.
3. A society so organized constantly experiences conflict as its components try to attain new gains or to preserve their interests; conflict, in other words, is ubiquitous.
4. Out of the dialectic process of competing and conflicting interests comes an ongoing process of change; societies are not in a state of equilibrium but are ever-changing.

Why is such a paradigm important in the study of mass communication? The mass media in America are competitive enterprises devoted to making a profit. They compete with one another and pursue their interests in a complex web of restraints placed on them by the courts, federal regulative agencies, the moral codes of society, their own organizational structures, and the advertisers who support them. In addition, the press and government have a long history as adversaries. There are other arenas of conflict as well. These include controversies concerning the rights of the press versus the rights of citizens to privacy, the rights of government to protect its secrets in times of national emergency, the rights of citizens to a fair trial, the rights of consumers to be protected from false claims in advertising, and so on. Through legal battles over the interpretation of the First Amendment, and other forms of conflict, the process and patterns of mass communication in American society are constantly being reshaped. They are not now and have never been in a total state of stability. In other words, the social conflict model offers a fruitful theoretical paradigm for conceptualizing and studying significant issues concerning our changing system of mass communication.

Symbolic Interactionism. Still another way of viewing the social order is to place an emphasis on the critical role of language in both the development and maintenance of society and in shaping the mental activities of the individual. This is a more social-psychological approach. It emphasizes the relationships between individual mental activities and the social process of communicating. This approach has been developed in modern times by social psychologists whose training has been in sociology. However, the link between reality and the

mind through language was understood by the early Greek philosophers. The role of meanings in human affairs continued to hold the
attention of philosophers for centuries. By the late 1600s, John Locke in
his *Essays on Human Understanding* described the relationship between words, their internal meanings among individuals, and the
bonds between people that form society. Language, he said, is "the great
Instrument, and common Tye of Society."[22] During the eighteenth century such writers as Immanuel Kant developed the theme that human
beings react not to the world as it exists in the sense of objective reality
but to the world they construct in their minds. This distinction between
the world outside and the constructions in our heads was further
refined at the end of the nineteenth and in the early twentieth centuries
in the writings of the American pragmatists, such as John Dewey,
William James, and Charles Pierce.[23] They held the view that people
collectively shape ideas about the environments with which they cope.
One of their basic assumptions was that the significance of objects or
situations resides not in their objective nature but in the behavior of
people toward them.

In the present century, two writers stand out as the founders of
contemporary symbolic interactionism, the sociologist Charles Horton
Cooley and the philosopher George Herbert Mead.[24] Cooley was one of
the most significant scholars in finally resolving the ancient "nature–
nurture" debate. He developed an impressive case for the contemporary
view that people acquire their human nature rather than inherit it in
their genes. His ideas about the subjective nature of social life and the
processes by which people develop beliefs about themselves and others
as guides to social behavior were instrumental in reversing thinking
about the role of instincts in human behavior. George Herbert Mead
developed an elaborate analysis of the central nature of language symbols in individual and collective human life. Today the paradigm continues to be elaborated, debated, and refined. Many of the modern
versions of what should be the proper assumptions of symbolic interactionism can be found in the anthology developed by Jerome G. Manis
and Bernard N. Meltzer.[25] At the risk of vast simplification, however,
the central assumptions of this paradigm can be set forth as follows:

1. Society can best be thought of as a system of meanings. For
   individuals, participation in the shared meanings linked to the
   symbols of a language is the interpersonal activity from which
   emerges stable and commonly understood expectations that
   guide behavior into predictable patterns.
2. From a behavioral point of view, both social and physical realities are labeled constructions of meanings; as a consequence of

people's individually and collectively participating in symbolic interaction, their interpretations of reality are both socially conventionalized and individually internalized.

3. The bonds that unite people, the ideas that they have of others, and their beliefs about themselves are personal constructions of meanings emerging from symbolic interaction; thus, the subjective beliefs people have of one another and themselves are the most significant facts of social life.

4. Individual conduct in a given action situation is guided by the labels and meanings people associate with that situation; thus, behavior is not an automatic response to stimuli of external origin but is a product of subjective constructions about self, others, and the social requirements of the situations.

How are such matters related to the study of mass communication? Clearly, the media are a central part of the communication processes of modern societies. They provide in their portrayals and accounts interpretations of reality that their audiences internalize. People can develop subjective and shared constructions of meaning for the physical and social realities in which they live from what they read, hear, or view. Thus, their personal and social behavior can be shaped in part by media-provided interpretations of social events and issues concerning which people have few alternative sources of information. This is one of the most complex, but most important, paradigms used in communication research, as we will make clear in Chapter 9, it is essential for understanding long-range indirect influences of mass communication on individuals and society.

Psychological Paradigms: The Human Individual

From the complex discipline of psychology come a number of competing paradigms formulated to describe and explain the patterning of individual human behavior. Psychological paradigms are useful primarily with respect to individualistic aspects of central question number 3 that we listed earlier: What does exposure to mass communication do to people? They are important in conceptualizing possible explanations about the relationship between mass media messages and such phenomena as attitudes, patterns of perception, imitating the behavior of models, decision making, and overt behaviors like voting and buying. Psychological paradigms are of less significance in studying such social issues as the historical development of the media, their bureaucratic organization, day-to-day operations, conflicts with other institutions in society, or processes of change. Nevertheless, insofar as mass media messages can stimulate responses in individuals, psychological paradigms offer basic assumptions about the psychological nature of the human being that help in understanding why a given stimulus is likely to elicit a particular form of response. Several of these paradigms are listed below to show the richness of psychology as a field that has developed numerous models for the interpretation of individual behavior patterns.

A continuing focus of some psychologists is on the *neurobiological* approach. This paradigm identifies the brain and other nerve systems as the most significant bases from which to seek explanations of human conduct.[26] This approach is closely related to the *comparative* perspective, a view of human nature that stresses the continuity between *homo sapiens* and other forms of animal life. Psychologists working within the comparative perspective feel that patterns of behavior found in animals are likely to have counterparts in human beings, and vice versa.[27] The implication is that these similarities arise from the principles of biology shared by all living creatures. Such paradigms are not central to the study of mass communication effects.

From Behaviorism to Psychoanalysis. At the heart of much contemporary psychology is the *behavioral* approach. There are several versions.[28] Here the focus is on externally observable phenomena as opposed to "mental" processes. Behaviorists distrust explanations that require assumptions about thought, belief structures, or other unobservable inner activities or processes. Behaviorism is a stimulus—response (S–R) psychology. It studies the stimuli that elicit particular forms of response, in the sense of clearly observable action. It attempts to understand the patterns of rewards and punishments that maintain these responses, and the modifications in behavior that occur when changes take place in reward/punishment sequences. Behaviorism incorporates many of the basic assumptions of the comparative perspective and is generally compatible with the neurobiological approach.

In contrast to behaviorism, stressing overt and observable actions, is the *psychoanalytic* paradigm, which comes in several variations.[29] Generally, these give a central place to individual mental activities, but they stress unconscious processes. The human psychological system is seen as a set of components (e.g., id, ego, superego) in conflict for the control of behavior; in this paradigm, overt conduct and communication behavior are less important in their own right than is their significance as data for making inferences about the unconscious aspects of personality that shape the behavior of the individual. The psychoanalytic paradigms were originally devised as therapeutic aids in treating people with neuroses or other mental problems. While they have been

expanded and advanced as general models of the psychological structure and functioning of human individuals, they remain controversial.
Again, neither classic behaviorism nor psychoanalytic paradigms have
been particularly useful in media studies.

The Cognitive Paradigm. More significant to the study of communication is a paradigm that openly gives a central place to the mental
activities of normal human beings in shaping their conduct. There are
several versions, but collectively they can be called the *cognitive paradigm*.[30] This view of human nature has been developed mainly in the
present century by social psychologists whose training is in psychology
rather than sociology. Many of its concepts have emerged from impressive experimental research. Unlike symbolic interactionism, however, the cognitive approach does not place strong emphasis on
language and meanings. It stresses a variety of concepts and processes
that are said to be part of the personality structure of all human beings.
A major question is how these operate in balance or conflict to shape
behavioral responses. The assumptions of the cognitive approach are
said to be helpful in understanding many aspects of the communication
process. Its basic postulates can be summarized as follows:

1. Individual members of a society can best be thought of as active
   receivers of sensory input, whose behavioral responses to such
   stimuli are shaped by inner mental (cognitive) processes.
2. Cognitive processes enable individuals to transform sensory
   input in various ways; code it, store it, interpret it selectively,
   distort it, and retrieve it for later use in decisions about behavior.
3. The cognitive processes that play key parts in shaping an individual's behavior include perception, imagery, belief systems,
   attitudes, values, tendencies toward balance in such factors,
   plus remembering, thinking, and numerous other mental activities.
4. The cognitive components of a given individual's mental organization are products of his or her prior learning experiences,
   which may have been either deliberate, accidental, social, or
   solitary.

The cognitive approach has wide uses in the study of the effects of
communication on individuals, particularly in attempting to understand how messages are perceived; how patterns of action are learned
from media portrayals; and how attitudes, knowledge, values, and behavioral probabilities can be altered through persuasion. Contemporary
research efforts to understand what needs are met by mass communica-

tion content and the gratifications provided for media audiences also represent the use of this paradigm.

The existence of such a large number of theoretical paradigms from which to choose offers great advantages for the communication scientist. Each provides a set of basic assumptions about the human condition, either at the individual or the social level. They provide broad descriptions of the organization, functioning, or processes of change in society, or about the underlying psychological factors that shape individual human conduct. The fact that there may be several competing paradigms that purport to explain the same thing (e.g., evolution versus conflict theory to explain social change, or behaviorism versus cognitive orientations to explain individual behavior) should not be regarded as a source of confusion. One need not decide which is "really true." In a sense they are all "true"; or any given one can be supposed true to provide a convenient set of theoretical tools from which more specific approaches to understanding and explaining particular communication phenomena can be derived and formulated. For example, in Chapter 5 the functionalist approach is used to derive an explanation of the persistence of low intellectual levels in media content in spite of intense efforts by critics to get the media to raise their standards. In the analysis of the history of the media, Chapters 2, 3, and 4, both the evolutionary and conflict paradigms provide frameworks for understanding. Chapter 11 integrates the structural functional, conflict, symbolic interactionist, and cognitive paradigms around the phenomenon of media effects.

In the past, many communication scholars and researchers have failed to raise the question as to what theoretical paradigm they are assuming in formulating their hypotheses and designing their investigations. As the field has matured, however, it has become increasingly important to clarify the underlying theoretical assumptions that explicitly or implicitly guide one's investigation. There are a number of reasons why this is so critical. Some researchers simply plunge ahead in data gathering, making use of a mixed bag of concepts drawn unsystematically from several theoretical paradigms. Such a naive procedure does little to build an accumulation of well-tested hypotheses that can explain the phenomena under study as special cases of more general propositions. Even worse are the "devotees," the researchers who adopt a given paradigm as the True Faith and naively assume that it provides the only legitimate guide to significant research hypotheses and problems. Often they are unaware that alternative paradigms even exist. Still others make use of theoretical formulations that are themselves derived from underlying paradigms that are not well understood by the researcher. The result is that some specific formulation, such as "cognitive dissonance theory," is dragged into a research problem by the scruff of the neck, often in an arena for which the formulation was never intended. A far better procedure would be to begin designing a research strategy from the base of a particular paradigm or combination of paradigms relevant to the issues that will be studied and then formulate a lower-level theory intended from the outset to describe and explain the issues to be investigated.

This chapter has provided a very broad perspective on major transitions in the behavior forms, techniques, procedures, and technologies used by human beings to communicate. That perspective stretches back millions of years to the time when pre-human beings began to signal each other in order to lead a coordinated social life. As their learning capacities increased over eons, they eventually began to be able to create, use, and pass on techniques for making crude tools. Increasingly, they had a need for more effective communication. They raised children, cooperated in the hunt, coped with a difficult environment, and defended themselves against enemies. If their communication systems had failed, we would not be here now. But locked into an Age of Signs and Signals by the physiology of their skull, tongue, palate, and larynx, the communication systems of early hominids were closer to those of contemporary apes than to the intensely verbal human communication strategies of today. As a result, their ability to conceptualize, analyze, innovate, and communicate complex messages was severely limited.

Somewhere around 40,000 years ago a different kind of human being had developed the ability to talk. The development of speech and language gave our more immediate ancestors an unprecedented advantage in the competition for resources and survival. The great increases in cognitive facility that came with the Age of Speech and Language made it possible for those forebears to think abstractly and to begin inventing a complex human culture that vastly surpassed anything in the animal kingdom. An elaborate technology began to accumulate—agriculture, the wheel, pottery, metallurgy, and so on at an ever-increasing pace to what we have today. Early on, the secret of writing was discovered. It was made more efficient with the development of portable media and alphabets. Human cultural development could then increase and accumulate at a faster and faster pace. These changes in communication greatly altered human existence.

In more modern times, printing became a reality. In a relatively short period, books were available in abundance. There was a flowering of the arts, sciences, and all human knowledge. The mastery of print led eventually to the elite newspaper and then, in the last century, to the mass press. As the twentieth century arrived, the pace of technological development soared and the Age of Mass Communication began. In the flick of an eyelash it seemed, movies arrived, then radio, and now television, plus a host of related technologies. We are in the midst of the new age and may even be making a transition into another—the Age of Computers.

We know precious little concerning what *any* of these recent changes have meant. In particular, research on the effects of mass communication and the media within our midst has barely begun. We can see already, however, that both our individual thinking and our culture are being heavily influenced by our processes of mass communication.

Communication scholars have at their disposal a foundation of theoretical formulations and research methodologies with which they are trying to gain understandings of our dependency on our mass media. The paradigms reviewed in this chapter provide a rich set of alternatives for the development of numerous specific theories about various aspects of both the process and the effects of mass communication. In the remaining chapters, some of the major highlights of what we already know will be reviewed.

NOTES

1. W. W. Howells, "Neanderthal Man: Facts and Figures," in *Proceedings of the Ninth International Congress of Anthropological and Ethnographical Sciences,* Chicago, 1976. See also E. Trinkhaus and W.W. Howells, "The Neanderthals," *Scientific American* 241 (1979): 118–133.
2. Robert Finn, "Origins of Speech," *Science Digest,* August 1985, pp. 52–55.
3. Philip Lieberman, "The Evolution of Human Speech: The Fossil Record," *The Biology and Evolution of Language* (Cambridge, Mass.: Harvard University Press, 1984), pp. 287–329. Many of the inferences set forth in our present chapter have been drawn from this source.
4. The relationship between language and thought has been deeply established in such fields as anthropology, linguistics, philosophy, psychology, and sociology. See, for example: Benjamin L. Whorf, *Language, Thought, and Reality,* ed. J. B. Caroll (Cambridge, Mass.: M.I.T. Press, 1956); George Herbert Mead, *Mind, Self and Society,* ed. Charles Morris (Chicago: University of Chicago Press, 1934); and J. Bronowski, *The Origins of Knowledge and Imagination* (New Haven, Conn.: Yale University Press, 1978).
5. Charles F. Hockett, "The Origin of Speech," *Scientific American* 203 (1960): 89–96.
6. An excellent discussion of media and change in ancient societies is found in Harold A. Innis, *Empire and Communications* (Toronto: University of Toronto Press, 1972). See especially p. 14.

7. Edwin Emery, *The Press and America* (Englewood Cliffs, N.J.: Prentice-Hall, 1972).

8. Charles Horton Cooley, *Social Organization* (Boston: Charles Scribner's Sons, 1909), p. 63.

9. Ibid., p. 64.

10. Ibid., p. 65.

11. For detailed definitions and discussions of the distinctions between *media, mass media, human communication* and *mass communication,* see Melvin L. DeFleur and Everette E. Dennis, *Understanding Mass Communication* (Boston: Houghton Mifflin, 1981), pp. 6–23.

12. These brief summaries do little more than sketch the central ideas of each paradigm in an introductory manner. Each is, in fact, a complex set of propositions that has generated wide controversy. The references cited in connection with each provide entry points for exploring the substantial literature associated with each paradigm.

13. *The Republic of Plato,* trans. Frances M. Cornford (London: Oxford University Press, 1954).

14. Auguste Comte, *The Positive Philosophy,* trans. Harriet Martineau (London: George Bell and Sons, 1915); see vol. 2, Herbert Spencer, *The Principles of Sociology* (New York: D. Appleton, 1898).

15. Bronislaw Malinowski, "Anthropology" *Encyclopedia Britannica,* First Supplementary Volume (London and New York, 1926), pp. 132–33; A.R. Radcliffe-Brown, *Structure and Function in Primitive Society* (Glencoe, Ill.: Free Press, 1956).

16. Robert K. Merton, *Social Theory and Social Structure* (Glencoe, Ill.: Free Press, 1949), Chapter 1, pp. 19–84.

17. Spencer, *The Principles of Sociology.*

18. J.D.Y. Peel, "Spencer and the Neo-Evolutionists," *Sociology,* May 1969, pp. 173–91; reprinted in R. Serge Penisoff et al., *Theories and Paradigms in Contemporary Sociology* (Itasca, Ill.: F.E. Peacock, 1974), pp. 188–209.

19. Thomas Hobbes, *Leviathan* (Oxford: James Thornton, 1881). First printed in 1651.

20. Karl Marx and Friedrich Engels, *The German Ideology* (New York: International Publishers, 1947); Herbert Marcuse, *Reason and Revolution: Hegel and the Rise of Social Theory* (Boston: Beacon Press, 1960).

21. Ralf Dahrendorf "Toward a Theory of Social Conflict," *Journal of Conflict-Resolution* 2, no. 2 (June 1958): 170–83.

22. John Locke, *An Essay Concerning Human Understanding,* ed. Peter Nidditch (Oxford: Clarendon Press, 1975), p. 402. First published in 1690.

23. "Intellectual Antecedents and Basic Propositions of Symbolic Interactionism" in Jerome G. Manis and Bernard N. Meltzer, *Symbolic Interactions: A Reader in Social Psychology* (Boston: Allyn and Bacon, 1978), pp. 1–9.

24. Cooley, *Social Organization,* George Herbert Mead, *Mind, Self,* and *Society,* ed. and with an Introduction by Charles W. Morris (Chicago: University of Chicago Press, 1934).

25. Manis and Meltzer, *Symbolic Interaction.*

26. For example, see H. J. Eysenck, *The Biological Basis of Personality* (Spring-

field, Ill.: Charles C. Thomas, 1967); and M.D. Schwartz, *Physiological Psychology* (Englewood Cliffs, N.J.: Prentice-Hall, 1973).

27. One of the classics is Wolfgang Köhler, *The Mentality of Apes* (New York: Harcourt Brace Jovanovich, 1925). A provocative treatment is R. Audrey, *The Territorial Imperative* (New York: Atheneum, 1966); more typical of contemporary works is D. N. Daniels, M. F. Gilula, and F. M. Ochberg, *Violence and the Struggle for Existence* (Boston: Little, Brown, 1970).

28. The classics include John B. Watson, *Psychology from the Standpoint of a Behaviorist*, 2nd ed. (Philadelphia: Lippincott, 1919); Ivan P. Pavlov, *Conditioned Reflexes* (New York: Oxford University Press, 1927); and B. F. Skinner, *Behavior of Organisms* (New York: Appleton-Century-Crofts, 1938). More contemporary are H. Rachlin, *Introduction to Modern Behaviorism* (San Francisco: Freedman, 1970); Albert Bandura, *Principles of Behavior Modification* (New York: Holt, Rinehart and Winston, 1969); and a work more significant for students of communication: Albert Bandura, *Social Learning Theory* (Englewood Cliffs, N.J.: Prentice-Hall, 1977).

29. The classic source is Sigmund Freud, *Outline of Psychoanalysis*, standard ed. (London: Hogarth Press, 1970). More contemporary are G. S. Blum, *Psychodynamics: The Science of Unconscious Mental Forces* (Belmont, Calif.: Wadsworth, 1966); and K. Menninger and P. S. Holzman, *Theory of Psychoanalytic Technique*, 2nd ed. (New York: Basic Books, 1973).

30. The cognitive paradigm is an outgrowth of the gestalt psychology of the 1920s, field theories advanced during the 1930s, and a large contemporary literature in experimental social psychology. Among the more significant works of later decades are Leon Festinger, *A Theory of Cognitive Dissonance* (Stanford, Calif.: Stanford University Press, 1957); J. W. Brehm and A. R. Cohen, *Explorations in Cognitive Dissonance* (New York: Wiley, 1962); R. P. Abelson et al., eds., *Theories of Cognitive Consistency: A Sourcebook* (Chicago: Rand McNally, 1968); D. J. Bern, *Beliefs, Attitudes, and Human Affairs* (Belmont, Calif.: Brookes-Cole, 1970); and L. Berkowitz, ed., *Advances in Experimental Social Psychology* (New York: Academic Press, 1974).

CHAPTER 2

The Emergence
of the Mass Press

The first of the central questions posed in the last chapter, concerning the nature and influence of mass communication in contemporary society, asks *what is the impact of society on its mass media?* That is, what have been the political, economic, and cultural conditions that led those media to operate in their present form? Quite obviously, that is a very complicated question. First, the sociocultural forces that have shaped the world's media have differed greatly from one society to the next. Second, they have not been the same for every medium within a particular society. And third, they have varied greatly during different historical periods. For that reason, there is no simple or overall answer to the question. Instead, one must trace the growth of the press, film, and broadcasting separately within each society during its relevant time frame. This is precisely the task of Part 1 of this book. It focuses on the American media and their development within the American society.

More specifically, in this chapter and the two that follow we will trace the emergence of newspapers, motion pictures, and the broadcast media within the sociocultural context of the United States. It will be obvious that many events that influenced the American media either occurred before there was an American society or took place outside its borders. Nevertheless, we will leave to others the important task of discussing the media within a comparative or international perspective.

There are two general social paradigms that are useful as theoretical frameworks for tracing the development of the media. These are the *evolutionary perspective* (in its social form) and the *social conflict model*. As a general paradigm, the evolutionary perspective seeks to explain increases in the complexity of society, or some specific part of society (such as mass communication), in terms of adaptation to changing conditions of organized social life. *Social evolution* is a process of change—in this context, change in repetitive, patterned, and interconnected forms of interaction between people. Perhaps more important, the process of social evolution is one in which small changes accumulate as innovations are made so that goals can be reached more effectively. Gradually and inevitably these changes substantially modify the manner in which some social process is organized.

Evolutionary social change is not a mysterious process. Creative people propose, develop, and implement new ways of solving problems. These can be distinctive forms of conduct, solutions to mechanical problems, or more efficient social arrangements that get the job done better. Some are proposed, tried, and retained to become institutionalized parts of the accumulating culture. Others are rejected immediately, or tried but quickly abandoned, or even adopted for a period, only to be replaced eventually by something more effective. Thus, human beings, like other animals, continuously try to improve their chances of survival through a constant process of experimentation and selection. Out of that process comes increasingly effective modes of behavioral, mechanical, and social adaptation—an evolution of human culture.

The *conflict model* is also helpful in understanding the development of our contemporary media. This social paradigm accounts for change in social processes and arrangements according to different principles. It sees a society as consisting of categories and groups of people whose interests differ from one another and who are pursuing goals that are often mutually exclusive. In such a social system, conflict is inevitable and ubiquitous. Change occurs as one side prevails, or as compromises accommodating both sides are worked out. In either case, change takes place. This is an important framework for understanding certain features of our contemporary mass media. Because various groups were in conflict and resolutions had to be found, our media now have a number of significant features that had their origins in this process. These include freedom of the press, support through advertising, protection of sources, and private ownership, all of which were subjects at one time or another of controversy and dispute.

Generally, then, as a result of both a slow evolutionary process and the existence and resolution of numerous conflicts along the way, the mass media as they exist today in our particular society have a somewhat unique structure of *controls,* a particular set of institutionalized *norms* relating them to their audiences and readers, and characteristic forms of *content.* They have worked out specific types of *financial support* and clearly defined *relationships* to each other as well as to important social institutions such as government. Finally, they have all experienced, in greater or lesser degree, a somewhat repetitive set of conflicts between their goals and the preferences, aspirations, and hopes of those whose cultural tastes and educational attainment are substantially higher than those of the common citizen.

RECURRENT PATTERNS IN MEDIA DEVELOPMENT

Each of the media was, from the point of view of the ordinary family, a new device that could be adopted or rejected as a form of technology within the home or at least as an innovation requiring the family to adopt new modes of behavior. The evolutionary principles governing the adoption of innovation by individuals and families are becoming increasingly understood. While the mass media today are intimately involved in the stimulation of innovative behavior, they can also be viewed as innovations themselves. A study of their adoption patterns as well as the social and cultural variables related to their spread can reveal some of the ways in which a society can significantly influence and shape its mass media.

We need not go far back in American history to talk about a society without mass media. For more than half a century after the original thirteen colonies had declared their independence from England, there was no true mass press to bring news to the average person. There were limited-circulation newspapers, to be sure, but these tended to differ sharply in their content, cost, audience, method of distribution, and size of circulation from the later mass readership papers. Motion pictures and broadcasting (both radio and television) have long technical histories, but as devices playing a part in the communication behavior of the average family, they are innovations of the present century.

A full understanding of how our various media came into being at the particular times they did requires considerably more than a mere listing of inventions of technical apparatus along with a few dates and names. The historical study of the mass media within any societal context, for the purpose of establishing recurrent patterns that have appeared during their growth, requires that attention be focused upon three important questions:

1. What technological elements or other cultural traits accumulated in what pattern to be combined into new culture complexes such as the mass newspaper, film, radio, or television industry?
2. What were the social and cultural conditions of the society within which this accumulation took place and how did these conditions create a climate favorable for the emergence and widespread adoption of the innovation?
3. What have been the patterns of diffusion of the innovations through the society, and what sociocultural conditions have been related to their rates and patterns of growth?

Obviously, all complex questions of this kind cannot adequately be answered within three chapters of one small book. Such issues require the extended attention of investigators with different perspectives, using various paradigms from the several social sciences, and scholars devoted to the study of each particular communication medium as well. Our task, then, is to sketch briefly the highlights of these historical developments in an attempt to illustrate, within the context of the American society, the impact a society can have in shaping its mass media. We will summarize very briefly some of the major events and social forces that have been associated with the development of each of the larger media of communication within the United States.

THE MASS PRESS

The basic culture traits later to be combined into a mass newspaper extend far back into history. The modern newspaper is a combination of elements from many societies and many periods of time. Even before the birth of Christ the Romans posted newssheets called *acta diurna* in public places. The Chinese and Koreans were using wood-carved type and paper for printing several centuries before these appeared in Europe. In the sixteenth century, well after printing had come to Europe, the Venetian government printed a small newssheet which could be purchased for a *gazeta* (a small coin). The use of the word "gazette" to refer to newspapers has survived to this day. Something closer to our modern idea of a newspaper appeared in the early 1600s in Germany. Scholars of the history of journalism suggest that many features of the modern newspaper, such as the editorial, sports articles, illustrations, political columns, and even comics, were used in one place or another long before the true mass press came into being.

Forerunners of the Newspaper

Although printing was introduced to England in the late 1400s, it was not until 1621, nearly a century and a half later, that early forerunners of the newspaper began to appear. These were called *corantos*. Their content focused on foreign intelligence, and they were not published regularly (as were the actual newspapers that came later). From the beginning, the publication of corantos was strongly regulated by the government. The seventeenth century in general was one of at least attempted close regulation of all forms of printing. One of the interesting patterns discernible in the history of the press is that in societies with strong central governments, an unregulated press tended to grow very slowly. Where centralized authority was weak, the press tended to develop under less control and to advance more rapidly. In a general way the greater the extent to which a form of government is actually dependent upon favorable public opinion, the more likely it is to support a free press. When the common people play significant roles in the determination of their own political destiny, the distribution of news and political opinions is an important process. Strong monarchies, or societies with other forms of highly centralized power, do not require active public discussion of issues about which every citizen must reach an informed decision.

The long struggle to establish the important principle of freedom of the press was fought during a period when the older feudal monarchies were beginning to decline and new concepts of political democracy were on the rise. Such considerations immediately suggest that one of the most significant changes in Western society, favoring the development of some form of mass communication was the changing political institution that eventually vested voting power in the majority of citizens. This long and complex change established traditions of journalism which from the beginning made the newspaper an arena of public debate, partisan protest, and political comment. By the time the other major media emerged, this political transformation had been substantialy achieved, and neither motion pictures nor the broadcast media, in the United States at least, developed the deep interest in politics during their formative years that characterized the developing press. These variables and factors have obviously been related in different patterns in other countries.

During the period before the seeds of the American and French revolutions began germinating, the whole fabric of Western society was undergoing change. The Dark Ages had given way to the Renaissance, and the ancient feudal society with its rigid stratification pattern was slowly being replaced by a new social structure within which a strong middle class would be a key element. These changes were inseparable from the growth of commercialism that eventually culminated in the industrial revolution. This commercialism was to be dependent upon improvement in the availability of various kinds of communication media. Techniques were sorely needed to coordinate manufacturing, shipping, production of raw materials, financial transactions, and the exploitation of markets.

Newspapers in the American Colonies

Rapid, long-distance media would be slow in coming. Meanwhile, the rising middle class itself began to constitute an *audience*, not only for the latest information about commercial transactions, but also for political expression, essays, and popular literary fare. In England these needs were met by such skilled writers and journalists as Addison, Steele, Samuel Johnson, and Daniel Defoe. In the American colonies a middle class with commercial interests developed rapidly. New England was a land of ships, seaports, and trade of all kinds. During the first part of the eighteenth century a number of small newspapers were published. Many were financial failures, but some survived over a period of years. Their circulations were never large, usually well under a thousand. By the time the Declaration of Independence was written, there were about thirty-five of these small and crudely printed newspapers in the thirteen colonies. For the most part, their publishers eked out a precarious existence by selling their newspapers on a subscription basis (they were relatively expensive) and by carrying a few commercial announcements. If the publisher happened to be a postmaster, or could land a government printing contract to help out, the financial risk was not so great.

The colonial press, as these papers are collectively called, was edited and published by people who were not great literary figures, with the exception of notable American colonial journalists such as the remarkable Benjamin Franklin. They were still using basically the same printing technology used by Gutenberg three centuries earlier. They did not have a huge audience with widespread reading skills. There were no large concentrated urban centers that could serve as markets, and they lacked an adequate basis upon which to finance a mass press. However, a complex array of culture traits had accumulated in the society, including elementary printing technology, private ownership of newspapers, and, as was mentioned, the principle of freedom of the press.

Newspapers for Everyone

Before a true mass press could develop, a series of sweeping social changes was necessary in Western society. The changing political roles of the common citizen have already been mentioned. Also noted was the growth of commercialism, which led to changing patterns of social stratification and the rise of the middle class. To these can be added the necessary development of printing and paper technology, which increased its tempo with the mechanical advances of the early industrial revolution. Finally, when mass public education became a reality with the establishment of the first statewide public school system (in Massachusetts) during the 1830s, the stage was set for a combination of these many elements into a newspaper for the common people.

A number of printers and publishers had experimented with the idea of a cheap newspaper that could be sold not by yearly subscription but by the single copy to urban populations. Various approaches to this problem were tried both in England and in the United States, but without success. It remained for an obscure New York printer, Benjamin H. Day, to find a successful formula. His little paper, the *New York Sun*, began modestly enough on September 3, 1833, with the motto "It shines for ALL." As subsequent events proved, it did indeed shine for all. Day had begun a new era in journalism that within a few years would revolutionize newspaper publishing.

The *Sun* emphasized local news, human interest stories, and even sensational reports of shocking events. For example, to add spice to the content, Day hired a reporter who wrote articles in a humorous style concerning the cases brought daily before the local police court. This titillating content found a ready audience among the newly literate working classes. It also found many critics among more traditional people in the city. The paper was sold in single copies for a penny in the streets by enterprising newsboys. These boys soon established regular routes of customers, and daily circulation rose to 2,000 in only two months. The breezy style and vigorous promotion of the paper shot this figure up to 5,000 in four months and to 8,000 in six months. The astonishing success of this controversial paper had the rest of the newspaper publishers in an uproar. By this time the steam engine had been coupled to the new rotary press. The famous Hoe cylinder press was available in the United States, along with abundant supplies of cheap wood-pulp newsprint. The technical problems of producing and distributing huge numbers of newspapers on a daily basis had largely been solved, and the emergence of the mass press was an accomplished fact.

Additional evolutionary changes took place. The *Sun* attracted its impressive circulation primarily by appealing to new readers who had not previously been reached by a newspaper. One of the most important features of Day's penny paper, and of those that followed it, was the redefinition of "news" to fit the tastes, interests, and reading skills of this less-educated level of society. Up to that time, "news" generally meant reports on social, commercial, or political events of genuine importance, or of other happenings of widespread significance. Benjamin Day, however, filled his paper with news of another sort—accounts of crimes, stories of sin, catastrophe, and disaster—news the people in the street found exciting, entertaining, or amusing. His staff even invented an elaborate hoax, concerning new "scientific discoveries" of life on the moon. When the hoax was exposed by another paper, his readers took it in good humor because it had been fun to read about. The paper was vulgar, cheap, and sensational; it was aimed directly at the newly literate masses who were beginning to participate in the spreading industrial revolution. There was some serious material in the paper, to be sure, but its editorials and reports of political and economic complexities were much more superficial than in the earlier partisan papers written for more politically sophisticated readers. By 1837 the Sun was distributing 30,000 copies daily, more than the combined total of all New York daily papers when the penny paper was first brought out.

Imitators of Day had started rival papers almost immediately. The penny press was a financial success because it had great appeal for advertisers. In fact, advertising revenue was its only real support; the penny for which it was sold could scarcely pay for the raw newsprint, but goods and services for mass consumption could be successfully advertised through the penny press. These advertisements reached huge numbers of potential customers much more successfully than those appearing in the preceding, limited-circulation newspapers. Patent medicines, "for man and beast," were one such mass-use product that played a prominent part in supporting the new penny papers. Early department stores also took readily to the newspaper as a means for publicizing their wares.

For such advertisers, size of circulation was thought to be a good index of the amount of profit one could anticipate. The newspaper that could place an advertising message before tens of thousands attracted the advertising dollar. This simple "law of large numbers" set into motion rugged competition among rival papers for new readers. This form of conflict had important implications for the development of the popular press during the latter half of the nineteenth century, and indeed had implications for mass media that would not even be invented until a full century later! The foundations of an important

institutionalized pattern of social relationships, which linked adver-
tiser, media operators, and audience into a functional system for the
production of particular types of mass communicated content, were
worked out in the early years of the development of the mass press.

Meanwhile, Benjamin Day's most colorful and successful competitor was James Gordon Bennett, who founded a newspaper empire
on only $500 in a barren office in a cellar. Bennett, a shrewd and tough
Scot, started the *Herald* in New York. He flouted the conservative moral
norms of the time and published flaming news accounts of murder
trials, rape, sin, and depravity. At the same time, he reported effectively
on politics, financial matters, and even the social affairs of high society.
This variety of content gave his *Herald* a wide appeal and made it a
strong financial success. Bennett himself made many enemies with his
forceful and often scandalous newspaper articles. For example, in 1836
he wrote:

> Books have had their day—the theatres have had their day—the tem-
> ple of religion has had its day. A newspaper can be made to take the
> lead in all of these in the great movements of human thought and of
> human civilization. A newspaper can send more souls to Heaven, and
> save more from Hell, than all the churches or chapels in New York—
> besides making money at the same time.[1]

Although Bennett's startling prediction did not come true, the newspaper was about to begin its spread through the American society and
to start playing an increasingly important part in its daily affairs.

THE PERIOD OF RAPID DIFFUSION

Although the mass newspaper arrived in the 1830s, it was still limited
in terms of news gathering, printing technology, and distribution. Before it could diffuse widely into the homes of every American city, a
number of important problems remained to be solved. The decades just
preceding the Civil War were filled with important mechanical, scientific, and technical developments that were to make it possible for the
infant mass newspaper to grow into a giant. Railroads were built between the principal cities in the eastern part of the nation. The steamboat arrived as a major transportation link after about 1840. The
telegraph grew increasingly useful as a means for rapid transmission of
news from the scenes of important events to editorial offices. These
developments substantially increased the newspaper's appeal to its
readers and increased the number of people to whom newspapers
could be distributed.

The Evolution of Social and Mechanical Technology

More and more, newspapers began to seek out the news. The role of *reporter* grew more complex and specialized as papers added foreign correspondents and special news gatherers of various kinds. Reporters were sent to the scenes of battles; others were permanently stationed in Washington, D.C., to cover political events. The "surveillance" function of the press became well established.[2]

The rising demand for fresh news was met by newly formed cooperative news-gathering agencies, which made use of the telegraph wires. These agencies sent stories to papers in many parts of the country with which they had contractual arrangements. Through such agreements, the staff of a paper near an event could cover the story for many papers elsewhere, thereby greatly reducing the cost of news gathering. These advances brought the newspaper to the smaller cities and towns and even to the newly established cities in the West.

Printing technology was making rapid strides, moving toward ever-increasing automation. Revolving presses, with print cast in a solid metal stereotype, became capable of rolling out 10,000 and even 20,000 sheets an hour.

The Civil War brought maturity of a sort to the newspaper as it reinforced the concept that the paper's principal function is to gather, edit, and report the news. The older concept of the paper as primarily an organ of partisan political opinion had faded considerably. The post–Civil War papers increasingly clarified their roles as locators, assemblers, and purveyors of the news. This is not to suggest that newspapers become either uninterested or nonpartisan with respect to politics—quite the opposite. Individual editors and publishers often used their newspapers to champion causes of one kind or another and to wage "crusades" against political opponents. But at the same time, they were all heavily involved in straightforward reporting of the news.

The Peak of Newspaper Popularity

Papers continued to gain in popularity. In 1850 there were about two copies of a daily newspaper purchased in the United States for every ten families. The rate of growth of newspaper circulations increased steadily, but not spectacularly, until the 1880s. During the two decades 1890–1910, however, the rate of newspaper circulation per household rose sharply. This rapid growth actually continued until about the time of World War I and then leveled off during the 1920s. The last decade of the nineteenth century, however, is one of special significance in the growth of the press because it was the beginning of a new kind of journalism. Although this new journalism did not become permanently established, it left its mark on the American newspaper. Let us look in greater detail at this development, because it is of importance for understanding patterns in the development of later mass media as well.

CONFLICT AND THE CHANGING NEWSPAPER

While the newspaper was growing up, the second half of the nineteenth century was for American society a period of rapid change, conflict, and transition. It was an era characterized simultaneously by an expanding frontier, a devastating Civil War and its aftermath, the arrival of wave after wave of immigrants, a pronounced rural to urban movement, and an increasingly rapid transition to an industrial society. Any one of these changes could have fundamentally altered the basic social organization of the society. Their combined effect was even more deeply felt. New norms replaced old; firmly established mores were cast aside; a traditional way of life gave way to a new social order. If ever a society was in a state of cultural upheaval and transition, it was American society during the last five decades of the nineteenth century.

Yellow Journalism

The social context within which the mass press spread and matured was one characterized by cultural conflict and consequent *anomie*. The new medium had to devise and institutionalize the basic codes that would regulate its responsibilities to the public it served and would place limits upon the kind of content it contained. With the normative structure of the society itself in a state of turmoil, it is not surprising that the mass press was able to work out its "canons of journalism" only after a rather stormy period of adolescence.

One of the most dramatic episodes in the development of the press was the period of "yellow journalism." By the 1880s the newspaper had achieved wide adoption by American households, and further astronomical increases in circulation were increasingly difficult to stimulate. At the same time, the press was firmly established financially as long as the number of newspapers could be kept at a maximum. Within this competitive context, brutal struggles for additional readers developed between the leaders of giant rival papers. In New York, in particular, William Randolph Hearst and Joseph Pulitzer fought by any means available to expand their circulation figures, which were, of course, the key to increased advertising revenue and profits. Various features, devices, gimmicks, styles, and experiments were tried by each side to make its paper more appealing to the mass of readers. Newspapers today contain many of the devices that were actually products of the rivalries of the 1890s. (One of these was color comics. An early comic character was called the "Yellow Kidd," from which "yellow journalism" is said to derive its name.)

As the competition intensified into open conflict, the papers turned more and more to any sensationalistic device that would attract additional readers, no matter how shallow and blatant. In the early 1890s yellow journalism burst full blown upon the American public:

> . . . the yellow journalists . . . choked up the news channels upon which the common man depended, with a callous disregard for journalistic ethics and responsibility. Theirs was a shrieking, gaudy, sensation-loving, devil-may-care kind of journalism which lured the reader by any possible means. It seized upon the techniques of writing, illustrating and printing which were the prides of the new journalism and turned them to perverted uses. It made the high drama of life a cheap melodrama, and it twisted the facts of each day into whatever form seemed best suited to produce sales for the howling newsboy. Worst of all, instead of giving its readers effective leadership, it offerred a palliative of sin, sex and violence.[3]

Yellow journalism offended a sufficient number of groups and individuals so that a storm of criticism gradually made clear to the operators of the mass press that they had exceeded the limits which the society, and particularly representatives of the norm-bearing institutions, would tolerate. Intellectuals in general and the *literati* in particular were deeply wounded. The great new means of communication, which held forth the tantalizing potential of mass cultural and moral uplift, had in their eyes turned out to be a monstrous influence for societal degeneration.

Emerging Systems of Social Control

Leaders in religion, education, law, and government increasingly voiced strong protests. The press lords were faced with the threat of losing public confidence, and with the even more chilling possibility of regulation imposed from without. These considerations led a number of major publishers to begin to put their own houses in order. Resolution of the conflicts brought new social arrangements and accommodations. Gradually, the press became less sensational and more responsible. A set of codes and norms defining its limits and responsibilities gradually became increasingly clear. Professional associations of editors and publishers established canons of journalism intended to guide their members. While the mass press today varies substantially in its degree of adherence to such codes, the excesses of yellow journalism appear to be a thing of the past. More generally, out of these experiences of the newspaper came a number of institutionalized principles which in one way or another have helped clarify the roles, responsibilities, and policies of media that followed.

THE FUTURE OF THE MASS PRESS

Data on newspaper circulations are given in Table 2.1. These figures report both circulations of newspapers and the growth of the number of households for the period 1850–1986. Rates of newspaper circulation *per household* are given in the last column of the table. The pattern these rates form over time is shown in Figure 2.1. Rates of daily newspaper circulation per household follow an S-shaped "curve of adoption" that is typical of growth patterns followed by a variety of cultural innovations as these are incorporated into their culture by a given population.[4] This particular innovation had been accepted by only a small proportion of the population up to about 1870. A number of factors (e.g., limited education, transportation, and printing facilities) played a part in keeping the number of "early adopters" small. Between 1880 and 1890, however, the newspaper swept rapidly through the American population to a point of new saturation by the end of the century. Improved press technology, better transportation, and spreading literacy were significant factors in this sudden change. By 1910, at the eve of World War I, there was more than one newspaper circulated for every household. Thus, during the first decade of the century, newspapers approached their peak as the major source of news in the American society.

Increases in circulation slowed after 1910. The apparent high point in the American newspaper occurred in about 1920, just following World War I. Since that time, the medium has suffered a steady and very noticeable decline. Even further improvements in the technology of news gathering, printing, distribution, and literacy have not slowed this downward trend. Even though more newspapers are sold today in an absolute sense, and newspaper profits remain high, they have not kept pace with increases in the number of American households.

What has been the basis of this decline? We saw earlier that two paradigms—the evolutionary perspective and the conflict model—provided insight into the *development* of this medium. However, an adequate theory of the relationship between a society and its mass media should be able to account for a decrease in usage as well as for media growth. In other words, an analysis of the invention, adoption, and

TABLE 2.1. DAILY NEWSPAPER CIRCULATION IN THE UNITED STATES (1850–1986)

Year	Total Circulation of Daily Newspapers Excluding Sunday (in thousands)	Total Number of Households (in thousands)	Circulation per Household
1850	758	3,598	.21
1860	1,478	5,211	.28
1870	2,602	7,579	.34
1880	3,566	9,946	.36
1890	8,387	12,690	.66
1900	15,102	15,992	.94
1910	24,212	17,806	1.36
1920	27,791	20,697	1.34
1930	39,589	29,905	1.32
1940	41,132	34,855	1.18
1950	53,829	43,468	1.24
1955	56,147	47,788	1.17
1960	58,882	52,610	1.12
1965	60,358	57,251	1.05
1970	62,108	62,875	.99
1975	60,655	71,120	.85
1976	60,976	72,867	.84
1977	61,495	74,142	.83
1978	61,989	76,000	.81
1979	62,223	77,300	.80
1980	62,201	80,776	.77
1981	61,430	82,400	.74
1982	62,487	83,527	.74
1983	62,644	83,918	.74
1984	63,081	85,407	.73
1985	62,766	86,789	.72
1986	62,489	88,458	.70

SOURCES: U.S. Bureau of Census, *Historical Statistics of the United States, Colonial Times to 1957* (Washington, D.C., 1960), Series R 176, p. 500; Series R 169, p. 500; Series 255, p. 16; Series A 242–44.

U.S. Bureau of Census, *Historical Statistics of the United States, Continuation to 1962 and Revisions* (Washington, D.C., 1965), Series R 170, p. 69.

U.S. Bureau of Census, *Statistical Abstract of the United States* (Washington, D.C., 1973), pp. 53, 503.

U.S. Bureau of Census, *Current Population Reports: Population Characteristics,* Series P 20, no. 166 (4 August 1967), p. 4.

1978–1986 figures from the American Newspaper Publishers Association, Washington, D.C.

NOTE: All figures after 1960 include Alaska and Hawaii.

institutionalization of a cultural item such as the newspaper, and the organizational complex that produces it, would be incomplete without consideration of variables that can lead to its *obsolescence*. As far as the newspaper is concerned, the factors that have led to its decline thus far are not difficult to suggest. Other media forms, meeting needs in the

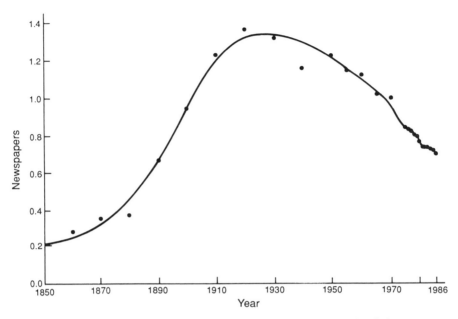

Figure 2.1. The cumulative diffusion curve for daily newspapers; subscriptions per household in the United States (1850–1986).

population similar to those met by newspapers, began to appear in the society during the 1920s. Shortly afterward (during the 1930s) weekly news magazines began to gain widespread acceptance. Even the film played a part. In the late 1940s and the 1950s, of course, television swept through the American society. To a greater or lesser extent, each of these *functional alternatives* to the newspaper has eaten into the circulation of the daily press. Each, in some sense, provides news, information, or entertainment in a way that once was the exclusive province of the newspaper.

What of the newspaper's future? It will undoubtedly survive with some further reduction of market share. Few changes in literacy or other factors related to potential increases in readership are probably in the immediate future. By the same token, research on the kinds of usages, satisfactions, and gratifications provided for readers by the daily newspaper indicates that it is deeply woven into the daily lives of ordinary people. It provides certain unique services and gratifications. When the newspaper does not come, it is sorely missed. It apparently plays a role in our communication system that alternatives are unlikely to displace, at least for the present.[5] Thus, while newer media, and possibly others to come, pose a challenge to the newspaper, it remains as an institutionalized culture complex as one of our fundamental modes of mass communication.

Our brief look at the newspaper has indicated the pattern of its evolution from the crude beginnings, through the penny press of the

1830s, up to the sophisticated chain papers of today. That evolution took place as various innovators proposed new technological and social solutions to handle old problems in the production and distribution of the news. Newspapers became increasingly more differentiated and more specialized, with departments, columns, and features for every taste in every walk of life. At the same time, the influence of social conflict is clear in the unfolding history of the press. Conflict between authorities and printers began early and shaped the historical background that brought the founding fathers to include a First Amendment in the Constitution. Conflict between press and government continues to shape the nature and destiny of the newspaper as the First Amendment and the courts resolve the dialectical process that takes place between those in power and the Fourth Estate. Similarly, intense competition between newspapers produced such forms as yellow journalism and, eventually, codes of good practice governing publishing in the United States. Finally, conflict and competition between the newspapers and newer media have altered the public's use of the newspaper, and consequently its place in the American system of mass communication.

NOTES

1. Eric Barnouw, *Mass Communication* (New York: Holt, Rinehart, and Winston, 1956), p. 7.
2. For an excellent summary of functions of mass communication today, including "surveillance," see Charles R. Wright, *Mass Communication: A Sociological Perspective* (New York: Random House, 1959), pp. 17–23.
3. Edwin Emery and H. L. Smith, *The Press and America* (Englewood Cliffs, N.J.: Prentice-Hall, 1954), pp. 415–16.
4. See, for example, H. Earl Pemberton, "The Curve of Culture Diffusion Rate," *American Sociological Review* 1, no. 4 (August 1936): 547–56; Stuart C. Dodd, "Diffusion Is Predictable: Testing Probability Models for Laws of Interaction," *American Sociological Review* 20, no. 4 (August 1955): 392–401; Everett M. Rogers, *Diffusion of Innovations* (New York: Free Press of Glencoe, 1962), pp. 152–59.
5. The following two research studies bear directly on this point: Bernard Berelson, "What Missing the Newspaper Means," in *Communication Research, 1948–1949*, ed. P. F. Lazarsfeld and F. N. Stanton (New York: Harper & Brothers, 1949), pp. 111–29; Penn Kimball, "People Without Papers," *Public Opinion Quarterly* 23, no. 3 (Fall 1959): 389–98.

CHAPTER 3

The Development
of Motion Pictures

As was the case with the newspaper, the development of the motion picture can be understood within both the evolutionary and conflict paradigms. The process of cultural accumulation that provided the technology of the film took place mainly as a gradual accumulation of scientific achievements in several seemingly unrelated fields. That technology was finally brought together in the form of devices capable of creating the illusion of continuous motion from a series of shadows projected on a screen. There was also a process of social evolution. The motion picture industry developed from crude beginnings in somewhat unsavory saloons and peep shows to become a huge, respectable, and complex economic system for the production, distribution, and exhibition of movies as a form of popular entertainment.

Conflict was a part of the evolutionary process throughout. Significant conflicts occurred, not only between various interests attempting to own and control the emerging medium, but between the moral majority in the society and those who sought to increase profits by appealing to less noble gratifications in preparing motion picture content. Such conflicts have played a central role in shaping the nature of the motion picture in America.

The historical antecedents of the motion picture extend backward in time to the beginnings of science. The major contributors to the fundamental technology upon which motion pictures depend were for the most part individuals who made their discoveries or developed their apparatus while searching for solutions to specific but unrelated problems. There were exceptions, of course, but generally the people who were to become the founders of the motion picture had little interest in the development of a medium by which people could be entertained. They were far more interested in discovering such things as the physical principles of light refraction, the neurological basis of human vision, or the way in which the illusion of motion was perceived. However, throughout the long history of invention and development there were indications of great potential popular interest in a medium of entertainment based upon the projection of shadow images. At least the nonscientific friends of many of the inventors were continuously fascinated by the strange devices and effects these people produced.

We may contrast sharply the development of the motion picture, as it occurred within the institutional framework of science, with that of the newspaper, which was traced out in rough outline in the previous chapter. We saw that the history of the mass press was closely related to important developments within the *economic* and *political* institutions of Western society. Commercialism and political partisanship were characteristics clearly associated with early forms of newspapers as well as the more mature press. When a viable financial structure was found for a mass press in the democratic capitalistic societies, this structure was based firmly upon commercial advertising. And, even though the newspaper redefined its relationship to political affairs more than once, the press continued to regard political activities as one of its major areas of responsibility, at least in reporting and analyzing if not in actual proselytizing.

The motion picture, on the other hand, has never been more than marginally related to the presentation of commercial advertising content in a direct sense. And, although movies occasionally deal with politically or socially significant themes, they have not often been used (in American society, at least) for the open advocacy of political ideologies. A complete understanding of the impact of society upon its communication media requires that we understand why, in the United States, motion pictures became a major communication medium devoted principally to entertainment rather than edification or persuasion, and why paid admissions as opposed to advertising or government subsidy provided their most important means of financial support. The present discussion cannot fully provide answers to these questions. It can show, however, within the American context, how political, social, and economic forces played a role in the formation of the motion picture as a system of mass communication. Comparative analyses of other societies, where the structure of the political institution and the functioning of the economic system have followed different patterns, would indicate why the form and content of the system of motion pictures varies from country to country.

THE EVOLUTION OF TECHNOLOGY

The early history of the motion picture is more accurately the story of developments related to three scientific–technical problems that required solution before an apparatus for the projection of motion pictures could even be envisioned. The first was mastering principles of the *projection* of shadow images; the second was *perceiving* continuous motion from rapidly presented still drawings or pictures; and the third was *photography* itself. We need to consider these three problems and some of the technical devices that eventually led to their solution. The story of these devices and solutions is inseparable from that of the human beings who achieved them, and the accomplishments of these people are intimately related to the social and cultural context within which they achieved their success.

Projection and the Camera Obscura

The first of the major problems was the development of a means for showing shadow images with the use of an *illuminated projector* that passed light through a transparency to cast an image on a reflecting screen in a darkened room. The list of elements making up this complex is obviously extensive. Basic to such projection is some understanding of the principles of optics. The use of mirrors and lenses is involved, including concave mirrors for the focusing of light from an artificial source so as to pass through a lens in suitable intensity. Of these various traits, the lens is probably the oldest. Adequate records exist showing that by the time of the Greeks, the "burning glass" was known by scientists.[1] Archimedes (born 287 B.C.), for example, attempted to construct a large lens, which was purported to have the power to set a ship on fire some distance away by focusing the rays of the sun. Whether this was actually accomplished or not is debatable, but the principle was understood. The field of optics was advanced further by the work of the Arab philosopher and scientist Alhazen (born A.D. 965), who worked out some of the first explanations of refraction and reflection with mirrors and lenses. The pace in invention and cultural accumulation was agonizingly slow in this beginning period. By the time of Roger Bacon (born 1214), scientists and philosophers had done little more than discover various ways to use mirrors in periscopelike devices to reflect images in such ways that the ordinary folk of the time were mystified.

One of the more important elements from this early period of invention and discovery was the *camera obscura* (literally "dark room"). The basic idea is that of the pinhole camera, within which a weak, upside-down, and reversed image of an external scene can be observed on a wall opposite a small hole in a lightproof rectangular chamber.[2] This phenomenon had undoubtedly been observed very early in human experience, but the principles of its operation were not systematically investigated until the time of Leonardo da Vinci (born 1452).[3] Leonardo worked in a small room that was sealed from light and into which light rays coming from a scene outside were allowed to enter through a hole about the size of a pencil. The image formed on the opposite wall could be clearly recognized as the outside scene in full color, although weak and sometimes blurred. With a larger hole and the suitable addition of a lens for focusing, plus a mirror to reverse the image, the camera obscura became a useful device for artists concerned with the problems of perspective and color in the painting of land-scapes. The camera obscura caught the attention of a number of scientists as well as artists, and it was used to observe eclipses of the sun. This device prevented the damage to the eyes that resulted from direct observation, even through darkened glass.

The camera obscura fell into the hands of magicians, charlatans, and others who preyed upon the ignorance of people of the period and who claimed magical powers for themselves on the basis of the effects they were able to produce. Scientists and experimenters were constantly harassed with the problem of magic and witchcraft being associated with their work. Attempts were made from time to time to publicize the "secrets" of these wonders to dispel such charges. This was true not only in the area of optics but in all branches of science. One of the most interesting of the early attempts to popularize science was a book by Giambattista della Porta or Giovanni Battista della Porta (born about 1535). In the seventeenth "book" (chapter") of his famous work, *Natural Magick*, translated and published in English in 1658, della Porta discoursed on the matter "Of Strange Glasses" (lenses and mirrors).[4] After discussing the mechanics of the camera obscura, he went on to describe how the device could be used to present plays and other amusements:

> *How in a Chamber you may see Hunting, Battles of Enemies, and other delusions.*
>
> . . . nothing can be more pleasant for great men, and Scholars, and ingenious persons to behold; That in a dark Chamber by white sheets objected, one may see as clearly and perspicuously, as if they were before his eyes, Huntings, Banquets, Armies of Enemies, Plays and all

things else that one desireth. Let there be over against that chamber, where you desire to represent these things, some spacious Plain, where the Sun can freely shine: Upon that you shall set Trees in Order, also Woods, Mountains, Rivers, and Animals that are really so, or are made by Art, of Wood, or some other matter. You must frame little children in them, as we use to bring them in when Comedies are Acted: and you must counterfeit Stags, Bores, Rhinocerets, Elephants, Lions, and what other creatures you please: Then by degrees they must appear, as coming out of their dens, upon the Plain: The Hunter he must come with his hunting Pole, Nets, Arrows, and other necessaries, that may represent hunting: Let there be Horns, Cornets, Trumpets sounded: those that are in the Chamber shall see Trees, Animals, Hunters Faces, and all the rest so plainly that they cannot tell whether they be true or delusions: Swords drawn will glitter at the hole, that they will make people almost afraid. I have often shewed this kind of Spectacle to my friends, who much admired it, and took pleasure to see such a deceit.[5]

Although della Porta was a scientist, it is clear he also had considerable interest in using various devices and effects to astonish his friends. The moving images of the camera obscura were to be a source of delight and amusement for the wealthy and prominent of Europe for some time to come. All through the historical development of the technological devices that were prerequisites to the modern motion picture, we see the continuous fascination and awe with which the projected image was regarded by the nonscientist.

The camera obscura, of course, produced its image from light reflected from objects in bright sunlight. A step of some importance lay in substituting artificial light for the sun and in passing this light through a transparency instead of depending upon reflected light. The illuminated projector that could throw images on a screen, using precisely the principles involved in the modern slide projector, became a reality through the work of Athanasius Kircher (born 1601).[6] Kircher was a German Jesuit whose learning and scientific discoveries earned him a place at the Collegio Romano, where with the encouragement of Pope Urban VIII and other ecclesiastical authorities he pursued mathematical and scientific investigations. Kircher was able to demonstrate in a dramatic showing before a distinguished audience the crude projector he developed and the dim images it produced with the use of hand-painted transparent slides. Kircher became the object of ugly accusations and gossip as a result of his work. He was accused of being in league with the devil and of practicing the black art of necromancy (conjuring up the spirits of the dead for nefarious purposes). The principles upon which his ghostlike projected images were called forth were

not well understood, or were deliberately misunderstood by his enemies, even among the most highly educated people of the time.

Kircher went on to refine his apparatus. He, too, had a flair for the
dramatic, and he arranged ways in which stories could be told, illustrated with projected slide images. A number of later inventors added
refinements to the "magic lantern" and still others exploited its use as a
means for entertainment. The solution to the first basic technical problem of the motion picture was thus complete by about 1645.

The Illusion of Continuous Motion

The second of the major problems requiring solution was to discover
the way in which the human being perceived the *illusion of continuous
motion*. Unlike the problem of the projector, this involved a relatively
large number of elements. Complex discoveries in the theory of human
vision and perception had to be worked out. Essentially, the problem
was to discover how a series of drawings or other figures could be
presented rapidly to the human eye in such a way that the afterimages
and the visual lag occurring within the neural-perceptual processes
would cause the figures to be consciously experienced as a single figure
in smooth motion.

In the early 1800s children in London and Paris were playing with
a device called the Thaumatrope. It was a small disk, about the diameter
of a teacup mounted on a shaft, and it had a figure on the front and
another on the reverse side. By twirling the device with the aid of short
strings or threads, one could create various illusions. Several forms of
the toy were prepared with amusing figures of one kind or another.
There has been some controversy about the origin of this device, but it
is generally attributed to a London physician, John Paris (born 1785). It
was described and discussed in a scientific work by David Brewster, the
student of the polarization of light and the inventor of the kaleidoscope.
The toy is not of particular significance in itself except insofar as it
depended upon the phenomenon of visual lag and suggested that an
illusion of motion might be produced by rapid presentation of slightly
changed figures in sequence.

One of the great students of the so-called persistence of vision or
visual lag was the Belgian scientist Joseph Plateau (born 1801).[7] Early in
his career he became interested in various aspects of vision and particularly the way in which the human being perceives motion and
color. He probably should be regarded as the father of the motion
picture.

Plateau's doctoral thesis from the University of Liège outlined the problems of vision that had to be considered in producing the illusion of motion in the human perceiver. First, each individual figure, drawing, or picture in a rapidly presented series had to remain stationary for a brief but sufficient amount of time for the neural-perceptual process to apprehend it clearly. The eye does not operate absolutely instantaneously. It takes a certain amount of exposure time for a given scene to register an impression. The rapidly whirling blade of a fan seems to "disappear" because of this feature of the human eye. The second point is also a time factor. An impression once registered within the neural-perceptive mechanisms of vision does not stop registering at the instantaneous moment the stimulus itself is withdrawn. There is a substantial lag as the impression lingers briefly. The simplest demonstration of this principle can be made with a common "sparkler" such as children use on the Fourth of July. If this bright light is moved quickly in a figure-eight pattern in the dark, the individual "sees" a complete figure eight and not simply a rapidly moving dot of light. This is what is meant by visual lag.

With these principles in mind, Plateau worked out a rather cumbersome apparatus of belts, cranks, pulleys, disks, and shutters that enabled him to create a simple illusion of movement, based upon the rapid successive presentation of a drawing. He refined this to a large disk, around whose circumference was arranged a series of drawings, each of which was slightly varied so that the same basic figure advanced to a slightly different position from one drawing to the next. When suitably shown to a subject, a moving figure was perceived. This machine which was called the Phenakistiscope or Fantascope, was the first true motion picture device. A system had thus been invented, based upon known principles of vision, that permitted a human observer to perceive an illusion of smooth and continuous motion from serially presented still figures. Professor Plateau pursued his quest for the principles of vision to the point where he experimented on himself by testing the effect of prolonged staring at the most powerful light he could think of—the sun. As a result of such experimentation, he became permanently and tragically blind, and much of his important work had to be done after his sight had gone completely. The irony of a blind scientist establishing the visual principles of the motion picture is paralleled only by the tragedy of the deaf Beethoven, who wrote some of the world's great symphonic music after his hearing totally failed, and Edison's invention of the phonograph when he himself was deaf. Joseph Plateau moved the accumulation of technology a giant step closer to the day when the motion picture would be used as a form of mass entertainment.

Capturing the Image of the Camera Obscura

Only the last of the three important technical problems needed to be solved before the culture complex of the motion picture as a form of mass communication could be synthesized out of these elements. The technology of *photography* in general, and of taking rapid sequence photographs of objects in motion in particular, remained as prerequisites to the motion picture.

The scientific struggle to achieve a workable photographic process is in itself a story of tremendous difficulties, great complexity, and deep fascination. It depended upon developments within the growing science of chemistry and in particular upon that part concerned with chemical changes in substances produced by the action of light. The development of photography also involved the already familiar camera obscura. When sufficiently reduced in size, provided with a lens and a removable reflecting surface coated with a light-sensitive chemical, it became the camera with which we today capture the inverted images of scenes reflected within. In so doing we are still utilizing principles known in the time of da Vinci.

The problem, then, was not the camera itself, but the film. What chemical processes and techniques could be used in order to fix the image of the camera obscura? Even here knowledge was well advanced by the beginning of the nineteenth century. In the early 1700s it had been shown experimentally that there were particular chemical compounds, such as various salts of silver, that were rapidly altered by exposure to light. This realization permitted speculation about the possibility of capturing the image of the camera obscura. It was not until the third decade of the nineteenth century, however, that the mechanical and chemical techniques for preparing, exposing, developing, and fixing an actual picture from the camera obscura were worked out.

The Daguerreotype. Solutions to this problem were in fact reached by at least three separate individuals. Each worked without knowledge of the others, each employed a somewhat different approach, and each announced his discoveries at almost the same time (between January and March of 1839). Louis Daguerre in France, William Talbot in England, and John Herschel, also of England, all succeeded in producing photographs based upon the same general chemical principles but upon rather different specific mechanical techniques.[8] The Daguerre process produced a sharp image of exquisite detail on a polished plate of copper that had been coated with silver metal and exposed to iodine fumes (to form silver iodide). Light striking this plate, when correctly exposed in the camera, caused the silver iodide to be drastically altered where bright light struck but to remain relatively unaffected where light of less intensity fell on the plate. The resulting *daguerreotype* produced an excellent picture with sharpness and clarity. There were no negatives; only one picture could be obtained at a time. The processes of Talbot and Herschel employed paper treated with similar light-sensitive chemicals and produced negatives, from which it was necessary to make a second (positive) print. Although the latter procedure proved in time to be by far the most useful, it was in its early form very crude, cumbersome, and unreliable. Furthermore, the pictures produced on the paper of the time lacked the precision of the daguerreotype. For this reason, the daguerreotype was an instant success, and the name of Louis Daguerre became well-known. In a world that had never seen a photograph, the daguerreotype seemed an almost incredible accomplishment. Such pictures were, in fact, when carefully produced, the equal of the finest and most carefully made photographs of today. The use of a polished metal plate gave them a great brilliance and sharpness. They were less "grainy" and showed more detail than even a very good modern paper print. Some indication of the world's astonishment and delight with this new product of science can be gained from the following account, written in 1839 by the editor of a popular American magazine, who had just seen a display of the new daguerreotypes:

> We have seen the views taken in Paris by the "Daguerreotype" and have no hesitation in avowing that they are the most remarkable objects of curiosity and admiration, in the arts, that we ever beheld. Their exquisite perfection almost transcends the bounds of sober belief. Let us endeavor to convey to the reader an impression of their character. Let him suppose himself standing in the middle of Broadway, with a looking glass held perpendicularly in his hand, in which is reflected the street, with all that therein is, for two or three miles, taking in the haziest distance. Then let him take the glass into the house, and find the impression of the entire view, in the softest light and shade, vividly retained upon its surface. This is the "Daguerreotype!"[9]

The acceptance of the Daguerre photographic process was immediate and enthusiastic. Improvements in technique were quickly made so that portraits were possible in indoor "salons." Rigid iron head clamps were used to keep subjects from moving, and light was reflected from overhead skylights. The first daguerreotypes were made in the United States in 1839, the same year that the process was announced in Paris. Among the earliest enthusiasts was Samuel F. B. Morse, who, though best remembered for his work with the telegraph, was actually a portrait painter of some distinction. He was also a professor in the arts of design at the University of the City of New York. The daguerreotype was closely related to both these interests. Morse actually visited Daguerre in France in 1839. He became an active daguerreotypist in New York and is said to have supported himself by making portraits, and by training students in the process, while awaiting recognition and financial support from the U.S. government for his telegraph.

The Demand for Portraits. Photography caught on immediately and the demand for portraits was almost insatiable. Here was a new kind of profession, requiring a relatively brief period of technical training and a small outlay for equipment, that had the potential of financial success. The 1840s in the United States was a period of economic depression. A number of enterprising young men were looking about for an opportunity to enter into some venture whereby they could make a living without investing large capital and without having to undergo extensive university professional training. The occupational role of daguerreotypist was almost made to order. There were villages, towns, and cities all over the settled part of the United States that had not yet seen the new process. The cost of having one's portrait made, especially in the smaller sizes, was not prohibitively expensive. A family of average means could easily afford it. Daguerreotype equipment was loaded on wagons, flatboats, oxcarts, and mules. The photographer's art spread out over the country. In all the major cities, daguerreotype salons were established, and business was exceedingly brisk. Quality of work varied greatly. The roving daguerreotypist with poor training and little skill turned out a dreadful product, paying attention neither to graceful poses nor to technical precision in the production of the plates. Some combined the photographic art with other occupational pursuits. A given individual might be a combination blacksmith, cobbler, watch repairer, dentist, and daguerreotypist. It was possible to have one's boots resoled, watch oiled, teeth pulled, horse shod, and portrait made all at one stop—all in a "package deal," so to speak.[10]

At the other extreme were the beautiful and luxurious salons that developed in the principal population centers. Mathew Brady gained an international reputation as a fine portrait artist in Washington, D.C., long before the beginning of the Civil War.[11] Between these two extremes were establishments large and small that were producing over 3 *million portraits a year* in the 1850s![12]

The demand for portraits was undoubtedly related to a number of characteristics of the times. The United States was a society on the move. People were no sooner settled on one frontier than another opened up farther on. The males often left their families in more settled areas until they could be brought out to reasonably favorable accommodations. The population movements associated with the various gold rushes, land rushes, oil booms, and other events separated men from their wives and children from their parents. Along the Atlantic seaboard the Yankees were a maritime people, with menfolk often "gone awhaling" or engaged in world commerce and shipping. The vast upheaval and movement of persons during the Civil War gave portrait photographers a decisive boost. Portraits were a way of reducing the pain of the separations in some small measure. In some degree, they even bridged the great gulf between the living and the dead.

The product of the portrait artist also had a deep tradition as a status symbol. To be able to display portrait paintings of assorted ancestors testified to a family's place in time. It was a society where aristocratic birth or family background was decreasingly related to power and wealth, but still there was a pronounced cultural lag that permitted such symbols to suggest high social position. Achieved status criteria were becoming objectively more and more important, but as-cribed criteria had not lost their significance. In the early period of the industrial revolution, some members of the newly rich are even said to have hired portrait painters to manufacture for them a set of dis-tinguished ancestors. For the less wealthy, and for the growing middle and working classes, the silver iodide plate of the daguerreotypist provided a mass-consumption substitute for the more distinguished canvas of the portrait artist.

Some indication of the rapid adoption of this innovation can be gained by a study of the growth of the occupational classification of "photographer." Table 3.1 indicates the number of photographers in the United States per 100,000 population for the years 1840 to 1930. These data show the rapid diffusion of photography as a cultural innovation in the four decades 1850–1890. By the last decade of the nineteenth century, there is little doubt that the average American was widely familiar with photographs. The transition between a still photograph and one that gave the illusion of motion was not an impossible step for the imagination of the ordinary citizen.

Improvements in Photography. The technology of photography con-tinued to evolve, becoming increasingly sophisticated; it also became more and more important as part of the growing industrial complexes of society. Factories for the manufacture of photographic chemicals, pho-tographic equipment, and photographic plates were developed. Among these, the name of George Eastman is perhaps the most widely known. The first daguerreotype photography had given way to other techniques.

TABLE 3.1. THE GROWTH OF THE OCCUPATION OF PHOTOGRAPHER IN THE UNITED STATES (1840–1930)

Year	Size of Population (in thousands)	Number of Photographers	Photographers per 100,000
1840	17,000	0	0
1850	23,000	938	4
1860	31,000	3,154	10
1870	39,000	7,558	19
1880	50,000	9,990	20
1890	63,000	20,040	32
1900	76,000	27,029	36
1910	92,000	31,775	35
1920	106,000	34,259	32
1930	123,000	39,529	32

SOURCE: U.S. Bureau of Census, *Population Census of the United States* (for the decennial years 1840, 50, . . . 1930, Washington, D.C.).

The ambrotype grew in popularity and then quickly declined. The tintype was widely used during the Civil War but was discontinued with the perfection of newer technology. Wet-plate processes, with light-sensitive chemicals suspended in a thin collodion film on glass, were widely used for many years. It was the dry plate, however, that permitted preparation in advance of glass photographic plates. This led to their commercial manufacture, distribution, and sale. The miniature camera and the amateur camera were popularized when this technology became available. George Eastman went into the business of manufacturing such photographic plates in the year 1880. From a modest enterprise started on a capital of $3,000, he built a business that thirty-four years later could pay $5 million for exclusive rights to the patented process of making flexible photographic plates on nitro-cellulose film.

The development of flexible film actually occurred in several places at the same time.[13] One type of film was developed in France in the early 1880s. One of Eastman's chemists applied for a patent in the United States at about the same time. Still another patent was applied for in 1889, by the Reverend Hannibal Goodwin, an obscure clergyman. These films were all based upon more or less the same process, with minor variations from one to the other. However, several years of extremely complex litigation ensued, during which the patent office reviewed and re-reviewed the various claims. The patent was finally awarded to Goodwin, but in the meantime, Eastman had been manufacturing flexible film for almost a decade. This roll film was designed for his "foolproof" box camera that could be used by the novice (the famous Kodak). With the availability of this flexible film, the development of the motion picture was a step nearer. Edison had produced the light bulb, and the technology of electricity was widely understood. The study of objects in motion had progressed with the use of instantaneous still photography. As we have seen, the principle of projection had long been common knowledge. The neurophysiology of visual lag had been worked out to an adequate extent. It remained only for these various elements to be combined into a workable projected motion picture. The camera obscura and the magic lantern were about to be combined in ways that would have astonished Kircher, della Porta, and da Vinci.

Motion Pictures Become a Reality

It was Thomas Alva Edison who achieved the basic technological combination that made motion pictures possible, but hundreds of others in various parts of the world also contributed.[14] From Edison's laboratory came the motion picture camera and a motion picture projector. It was early in the last decade of the nineteenth century.

Edison lacked confidence in the financial feasibility of the commercial projection of motion pictures on the ground that they would be a novelty and the public would soon lose interest. His conception of the way to exploit his device commercially was to develop a machine that could be used by only one person at a time, paying a fee to view a few moments of photographed motion. His peep show Kinetoscope became available for paid public viewing in 1894 when an enterprising exhibitor opened up a "Kinetoscope Parlor" with ten of the machines right on Broadway in New York. However, the limitations of the Kinetoscope were severe, and the possibilities for a more complete exploitation of the magic lantern of movement were seen by a number of people both in the United States and in Europe. Although Edison made the most significant contribution to the actual emergence of the motion picture by achieving the basic technological combination, it remained for more adventurous souls to try to perfect the technique and to turn it into a process for the mass entertainment of the multitude.

In the final years of the century literally dozens of people were clamoring for patents in as many countries. They were looking for financial backing and for recognition of a variety of motion picture cameras or projectors. From England, France, Germany, and the United States came conflicting claims and reports that these devices had been invented, improved, modified, or perfected. It was in fact a period of high excitement, intense activity, and inventive ferment. Showmen

such as Emile Reynaud in Paris were exhibiting projected motion picture stories, based upon the principle of animated drawings, with great
success. It took no vast stretch of imagination to see that the commercial
exhibiting of projected motion pictures could be a considerable financial success.

SOCIAL EVOLUTION: THE MOVIES
AS A MASS MEDIUM

In 1895 an establishment called the Cinematographe was opened in
Paris. For a single franc, patrons were admitted to a "salon" where they
could view a few very brief films. The exhibition became so popular
within a few days that it attracted thousands of viewers and was operated on a standing-room-only basis.

The Cinematographe was soon exhibited in New York, and the
system was widely imitated. In the meantime, in England the motion
picture camera was focused on such events as the Derby of 1896, and
the exhibition of these projected films caused a stir. These and other
attempts at public showings stimulated further interest in the idea of
projected motion pictures for the public's entertainment. It was clear
that there were fortunes to be made in the motion picture business.

By this time, Edison had become convinced. He combined efforts
with a young American inventor named Thomas Armat, who had obtained certain patents involved in the improvement of the projector.
Together they manufactured the Vitascope, or Armat-Edison projector,
which was used in the most successful of the early efforts to exhibit
motion pictures to the public.

With the dawn of the twentieth century, then, all the technological
problems had been solved. The motion picture had been more than two
thousand years in the making, but it was now ready to take its place as
the second of the major mass media of communication and to play its
role in a major communication transition.

The Content and Audiences of the First Films

From the outset, motion pictures were concerned with content of low
cultural taste and intellectual level. Even the very first moving pictures
in the Edison Kinetoscope parlors exhibited such inspiring works as
Fatima and Her Danse du Ventre. She was the sensation in an exhibition of the device at the Chicago World's Fair in 1893. For early patrons,
naive and slapstick comics were popular. A view of a mischievous boy
squirting a hose on a dignified dowager or even pornography (within

the limits of the era), such as the brief *How Bridget Served the Salad Undressed*, were received with enthusiasm in the arcades in which the Kinetoscopes were installed.[15]

These first films, with their boxing matches, low comedy, and shimmy dancers, can be contrasted with the efforts of the first printers. Gutenberg's first product represented the most significant and important ideas of his time. Books in the early period were works of philosophy, science, art, or politics. The motion picture on the other hand, concerned itself in its early period with the trivial and inconsequential. The content mattered little to anyone; it was the novelty of movement that was the important factor. The film's first audiences stared with open mouths at any picture that moved. But even among the habitués of the arcades, an important principle quickly began to manifest itself. Such films as *Beavers at Play* or *The Surf at Dover* brought in fewer coins than the brief but exciting *Danse du Ventre* or the titillating *What the Bootblack Saw*. Efforts toward the filming of more serious or artistic subjects were not received with enthusiasm. Film content aimed at more elementary gratifications brought in the money. From the first, then, systematic relationships between audience tastes and the financial structure of the infant "industry" governed the production of film content. Audiences were selective in what they would pay to see, and because of this, producers were selective in what they produced.

It would be tempting to analyze the characteristics of the clientele of the arcades, which were, to say the least, not located in the more discriminating sections of the urban centers. One might be tempted to draw the inference that it was their low level of cultural taste that left a permanent stamp of mediocrity upon the film. The problem was that the film moved out of the arcade environment very quickly, but it did not noticeably rise in the seriousness or the artistic taste of its content. The film went from the arcade to the vaudeville house, where it was exhibited as a scientific novelty following the major acts. Again, the tastes of the burlesque theater governed the content of the films.

The Nickelodeon Era

In about the year 1900 a number of enterprising arcade owners, former circus operators, medicine showmen, ex-pitchmen, barkers, and the like, began to rent unused stores, equip them cheaply with benches or chairs, and project films with second-hand equipment. Their working capital was meager, their repertoire atrocious, their establishment dismal, but above all it was cheap. For only a nickel the audience member could watch an assortment of exciting short pictures, ranging from *Life of an American Fireman* to *Dream of a Rarebit Fiend*. These were either trick movies of brief length or exciting little sequences of dramatic events such as the firemen responding to a call. Various names were used, but the term "nickelodeon" caught on as a popular way of referring to these enterprises. The most important things about them were that they were popular with people at the bottom of the social structure, and they made money. Then nickelodeons began to clean up their interiors and dress up outside. Many opened up in principal cities in the country. The first decade of the twentieth century, then, saw a new form of communication begin to spread. The film was about to become a true mass medium.[16]

The content of the films soon changed markedly. They became longer and more sophisticated technically. At first they did not rise far in taste or seriousness. Such fare as *The Great Train Robbery* was just about what the nickelodeon audience wanted to see in 1903. Films with stories became the norm in a very short time. These places of entertainment thrived in their most prosperous form in the same areas of the metropolis where the amusement arcades were located. As the motion picture was establishing itself, its audience tended to be heavily weighted with poor immigrants, drifters, and the anonymous residents of the city's zones of transition. The most significant groups in numbers were by far the immigrants. The first ten years of the 1900s were a period of unprecedented immigration, unequaled in more contemporary times. People from many cultures were pouring into the United States, particularly from eastern and southern Europe. By the millions they established ethnic neighborhoods within the ecological and social structure of the city. Immigration laws were not strict by today's standards, and many of these new citizens were illiterate even in their own language. A large proportion had no knowledge of English whatsoever. Substantial numbers were agricultural peasants in their own land. For these humble people, surrounded by a bewildering and complex industrial society that they had not yet begun to understand, the primitive movie was a source of solace and entertainment. The plots were simple; the stylized acting needed no knowledge of the language in order to understand the idea. Today's viewer is amused at the stereotyped facial expressions and the gross body movements of the actors in early films. Such techniques become more understandable when it is realized that the audience had only occasional subtitles with which to follow the plot in a verbal sense. Many of the English-speaking members of the audience could read only with difficulty, if at all, and a great many of the foreign-born knew not a word.

The immigrants, then, along with rustic Americans newly arrived in the big city, were the most important audience types toward whom the early nickelodeon movies were aimed. With slapstick and burlesque they even poked fun at such people themselves and made them laugh at their own plight. The country bumpkin and the immigrant were often seen in films. The cop, the crook, the pretty girl, and jealous husband, the boss—this was about the total range of personalities that appeared in the movies. It was enough. Their antics were easily understood. In intensified form, this stereotyping and slapstick led to such content as the Keystone Kops and the pie-throwing scenes.

The Movies Mature

Within a short time the nickelodeon had spread far beyond urban centers. The movies began to be a form of family entertainment. People wanted longer films with more interesting content. The novelty of merely seeing motion had worn off. Movie producing companies sprang up to fill the demand for films, and operators worried about how they could shake the sordid image of the medium. A number of changes were made, and this booming entertainment medium was well on its way. The "star" system came; movies discovered the classics; more flexible techniques of photography were developed. The films grew longer to the feature length we are now accustomed to. This increase in technical competence was due in part to the growing enthusiasm of motion picture audiences. The dreary nickelodeons had given way by the beginning of the 1920s to much larger and more elaborate picture palaces. Some were so luxuriously decorated that they almost appeared to be temples of worship for the new gods and goddesses of the screen. Such stars were receiving the adoration of millions of shop girls and factory hands. They were also receiving astronomical salaries, which made Hollywood synonymous with ostentatious consumption of wealth.

The Influence of World War I. The Great War had given the American film industry an unprecedented boost. The production of motion pictures in the studios of Europe had ceased after 1914, but the demand for films had become tremendous and worldwide. This placed U.S. films in the export market with an advantage, which was retained for years. The silent film, with written subtitles easily changed to any language, was made by directors and producers who were themselves immigrants. It was a particularly flexible product for export to foreign countries. Almost inexhaustible markets were opened up when the more remote regions of the world began showing films with subtitles in Urdu, Hindi, Chinese, Arabic, or whatever local language was required. If the local audience was not literate in its own language, a "storyteller" was employed to explain to the native audience what was transpiring in the film as it progressed. Any relationship between these versions and the original intent of the film's designers was purely coincidental. The political position of the United States in World War I, then, had the most significant impact upon the American motion picture as a mass medium. It made the medium one of world significance.

The events of the Great War also point up other ways in which a society can have an impact upon its media. When the war broke out in Europe, the American public increasingly began to focus its public opinions in two opposite directions. The pacifists wanted to stay out of the European war and avoid engaging in any military expansion that might eventually lead the country into participation in the war. Those in favor of preparedness felt that the United States would more than likely have to enter the war at some point, and it might as well make military preparations to make the task easier if the need arose. These were issues of great importance during the years just before the United States declared war on Germany. When war came, a large bloc of the American public still retained attitudes, opinions, and sentiments unsuitable for total commitment and participation in the war effort. To reduce these "unhealthy" pacifist feelings, George Creel, chief of the Committee on Public Information (the official U.S. agency for domestic propaganda), mobilized motion pictures as part of an all-out effort to "sell the war to the American public." This thrust upon motion pictures a propaganda role they had not played before, at least in the United States.[17] Motion pictures had been a form of entertainment. They had not seriously engaged in persuasion for political partisanship, moral uplift, social responsibility, or cultural betterment. In general, they had *followed* public tastes and attitudes rather than *led* them. In the minds of some, experiences of the war opened up new possibilities and objectives for the film as a medium of persuasion. Actually, the motion picture as a medium of entertainment has never become a consistent vehicle for effective political or social comment. While Hollywood has cooperated during wartime and has occasionally produced a film with a social "message," these are considered departures from the norm. The position of the film in this respect is distinct from that of the newspaper, which has consistently assumed that it has the responsibility to play a part in the political process.

Talking Pictures. During the last part of the 1920s the sound track came to the film. By this time the motion picture theater was a deeply established and respectable place of entertainment for American families. As a business the production, distribution, and exhibition of motion pictures was firmly entrenched in the American economy, and as a cultural innovation it had become institutionalized into our weekly routines. Accurate records of motion picture attendance are available on a national basis beginning with 1922. By that time, the film was so popular that the number of paid admissions in an average week in the United States already exceeded 40 million! About the time of World War II, movies were produced in color and this became the norm. The peak was reached in the 1940s, when admissions soared to 90 million a week.

QUANTITATIVE PATTERNS

The adoption of the motion picture as a cultural innovation for mass use was both swift and extensive. The United States was literally transformed into a nation of moviegoers between 1900 and 1930. Table 3.2 shows both average weekly attendance from 1922 to 1986 and the number of households during the same period. Although attendance data are not available from 1900 to 1921, it appears most likely that this early period of movies followed the estimated trend as shown in Figure 3.1.

Perhaps the most significant aspect of the adoption pattern for the film is its *variability*. This is particularly apparent in the middle section of the curve, when attendance figures fluctuated wildly. These were the Great Depression years; hard times in the early 1930s had a sharp impact on moviegoing. Admissions dropped by more than 30 percent between 1930 and 1932. However, the late 1930s and the decade of the 1940s were Golden Years for the film. Even so, functional alternatives were becoming increasingly available, and as these grew in number and popularity, their impact on motion picture attendance was to be little short of disastrous. Clearly, the rapid rise of television, beginning at the end of the 1940s and continuing through the next decade, had the deepest possible impact on the mass use of the motion picture. Even though the society as a whole was moving toward unprecedented economic affluence, average weekly attendance per household dropped from 2.37 in 1946 to only .53 in 1960. This drop continued to the remarkably low rate of .23 in 1986.

The movie industry struggled mightily to slow the rate of decline. As competition with television increased, numerous experiments were tried. At one point, moviegoers were issued special glasses so that they could see the picture in three dimensions. Screens widened—to almost unbelievable proportions in some cases. Special sound effects, with speakers in various parts of the theater, were tried. These gimmicks did not help much; the decline continued. Perhaps more significantly, the older moral standards governing film content collapsed. At an earlier

TABLE 3.2. MOTION PICTURE ATTENDANCE IN THE UNITED STATES (1922–1986)

Year	Average Weekly Movie Attendance (in thousands)	Total Number of Households (in thousands)	Weekly Attendance per Household
1922	40,000	25,687	1.56
1924	46,000	26,941	1.71
1926	50,000	28,101	1.78
1928	65,000	29,124	2.23
1930	90,000	30,000	3.00
1932	60,000	30,439	1.97
1934	70,000	31,306	2.24
1936	88,000	32,454	2.71
1938	85,000	33,683	2.52
1940	80,000	35,000	2.29
1942	85,000	36,445	2.33
1944	85,000	37,115	2.29
1946	90,000	37,900	2.37
1948	90,000	40,523	2.22
1950	60,000	43,468	1.38
1954	49,000	46,893	1.04
1958	40,000	50,402	.79
1960	28,000	52,610	.53
1965	21,000	57,251	.37
1970	15,000	62,875	.24
1975	20,000	71,120	.28
1980	19,600	80,776	.24
1981	20,500	82,400	.24
1982	22,600	83,527	.27
1983	23,000	83,918	.27
1984	23,100	85,407	.27
1985	20,300	86,789	.23
1986	19,600	88,458	.23

SOURCES: U.S. Bureau of Census, *Historical Statistics of the United States, Colonial Times to 1957* (Washington, D.C., 1960), Series H 522, p. 225; Series A 242–44, p. 15.

U.S. Bureau of Census, *Historical Statistics of the United States, Continuation to 1962 and Revisions* (Washington, D.C., 1965), Series H 522, p. 35.

U.S. Bureau of Census, *Statistical Abstract of the United States* (Washington, D.C., 1968), tables 11 and 302, pp. 12, 208 (1973); tables 53, 347, 349, pp. 41, 211, 212.

U.S. Bureau of Census, *Current Population Reports: Population Characteristics,* Series P-20, No. 166 (24 August 1967), pp. 1, 4.

U.S. Bureau of Economic Analysis; U.S. Bureau of Labor Statistics, Industry and Trade Administration, *U.S. Industrial Outlook,* 1979, p. 503.

1980–1986 figures from the Motion Picture Association of America, New York.

NOTE: Figures do not include Alaska and Hawaii.

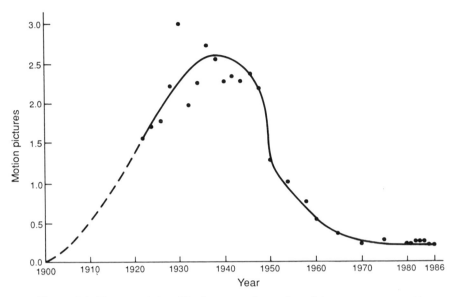

Figure 3.1. The cumulative diffusion curve for motion pictures; average weekly attendance per household in the United States (1900–1986).

time, motion pictures shown to American audiences were about as racy as a Sunday school picnic. Solid, middle-class America didn't need to be titillated with taboo themes to get them to pay at the box office. Today, unless a movie promises a blood-bath shock or frank sex it may not be a big money-maker. Much legal maneuvering and litigation have accompanied this change, and the issues of "freedom of speech" versus "obscenity" have been widely discussed in connection with motion picture portrayals. Currently, public officials and others are sharply criticizing film violence as well as explicit sex. In other words, conflict continues to shape the further development of the industry.

Whatever the eventual significance of these issues within the context of the motion picture, it seems reasonably clear that the real pressure for change has been an economic one. The most logical projection for the future would be that the movie theater as it existed in the 1930s will never regain its popularity. This does not mean that films will no longer be made. Television provides an insatiable demand for even the dullest films, as any viewer of the "Late Late Show" will testify. Furthermore, as we will see in the next chapter, the growing home use of VCRs and rented cassettes promises even harder times for the movie house. Thus, while the industry may survive, or even prosper, the behavioral forms of its consumers appear likely to continue their present trend. The strong shift of interest of the American public after about 1960 from the movie screen downtown to the television screen at home is likely to continue as cable TV and VCRs achieve saturation, and as TV moves toward codes concerning content which will probably eventually resemble those of contemporary movies.

The conditions and factors related to the decline of a given behavioral form within a social system have largely been neglected in the recent surge of interest in the innovation process. Obsolescence is a natural counterpart of innovation, and a necessary feature of an adequate theory of social change. There are undoubtedly systematic principles that govern the way in which a given item, trait, or culture complex is abandoned by a population. We no longer make much use of quill pens, detachable collars, automobile cranks, and the chaperoned party for young adults. These forms undoubtedly followed some reverse pattern of declining usage, symmetrical in form to the usual S-curve of adoption. In spite of the obvious significance of such obsolescence patterns for understanding social and cultural change, no systematic theory is available concerning the conditions under which they are generated.

In the case of the motion picture theater, the causes of obsolescence are not particularly obscure. The depression, the population shift to the suburbs, and, of course, the continued growth of the electronic media have cut deeply into paid attendance. To these fairly obvious factors could be added the increasing congestion of central business districts, where most of the older large movie theaters were located and the burden of mounting labor costs, which has resulted in continuous box-office price increases and a correspondingly smaller number of consumers. Even the newer trend of smaller multiple-screen theaters in malls has not reversed this long-term pattern.

Overall, our analysis has shown the long and complex evolution of the motion picture. That evolution has been characterized by an accumulation of culture traits and technological innovations that were necessary for the emergence of the film as a medium of mass communication. It has indicated the many social and cultural conditions, such as wars, population shifts, and conflicts in the economic institution, that were significantly related to the eventual widespread adoption and possible impending obsolescence of motion picture theaters as a behavioral innovation on the part of the American population.

The impact of a society on a communication medium could not be clearer than in the case of the motion picture. As a technology, and as an industry, it will undoubtedly continue to occupy a place in our social system. However, there are considerable doubts concerning its survival in the form in which it was originally adopted by our population.

NOTES

1. Martin Quigley, Jr., *Magic Shadows: The Story of the Origin of Motion Pictures* (Washington, D.C.: Georgetown University Press, 1948), pp. 18–20.

2. Helmut Gernsheim and Alison Gernsheim, *The History of Photography from the Earliest Use of the Camera Obscura in the Eleventh Century Up to 1914* (London: Oxford University Press, 1955). See especially Chapter 1, "The History of the Camera Obscura," pp. 1–19.
3. Quigley, *Magic Shadows*, pp. 29–35.
4. A reproduction of this famous work has recently been made available. See John Baptista Porta, *Natural Magick*, ed. Derek J. Price (New York: Smithsonian Institute for Basic Books, 1957).
5. Ibid., pp. 364–65.
6. Quigley, *Magic Shadows*, pp. 48–61.
7. Ibid., pp. 85–97.
8. Josef M. Eder, *History of Photography* (New York: Columbia University Press, 1945), pp. 209–45, 263–64, 316–21.
9. Robert Taft, *Photography and the American Scene* (New York: Macmillan, 1938), p. 3.
10. Ibid., p. 48.
11. Ibid., pp. 55–62.
12. Ibid., p. 76.
13. Ibid., pp. 384–404.
14. Quigley, *Magic Shadows*, see especially Chapters 15 and 16.
15. Richard Griffith and Arthur Mayer, *The Movies* (New York: Simon and Schuster, 1957), pp. 1–8.
16. Ibid., p. 19.
17. Ibid., pp. 113–19.

CHAPTER 4

The Establishment of the Broadcast Media

Broadcasting today represents the contemporary outcome of a long and continuous evolutionary process that includes an almost staggering number of technological innovations, scientific advances, and new economic and social forms. As was the case with the other media, the development of broadcasting as a mass medium has been influenced by numerous conflicts, and its characteristics today have been shaped by the resolution of those conflicts. Huge corporations fought over patent rights; rival transmitters competed on the same frequencies to a point where the federal government finally had to intervene with emerging forms of control unique to this medium; radio fought newspapers for the right to broadcast the news; advertisers have fought regulatory agencies over false claims and puffery; and in recent times, battles have been waged over the portrayal of violence on television. Both the evolutionary and the conflict paradigms, therefore, provide essential frameworks for interpreting the way in which broadcasting has been shaped into the media we know today.

THE EVOLUTION OF TELECOMMUNICATION

In tracing the principal ways in which society has influenced the broadcast media, three somewhat distinct issues require clarification. First, there are the numerous and complex social factors that established the need and consequent search for an *instantaneous* medium of communication that could leap across oceans and span continents. Second, there is a chain of scientific and technical *innovations* that accumulated as one invention led to another when various means of fulfilling the need were sought. Finally, there are the events that resulted in the translation of commercial wireless-telegraphy and radio-telephone technology into a *mass medium* with which to broadcast programs to the home receivers of entire nations. We might add, of course, the growth of television out of radio as still another issue; as will be made clear, however, the newer medium not only shared a common history with radio but inherited its financial basis, traditions, structure of control, and even much of its talent.

Expanding Communication Needs

People's need for a reliable means of communicating rapidly over long distances increased relentlessly as societies grew in complexity. As long as social activities were confined to a small band, which moved about together or stayed close to a fixed village, the range of the human voice, or at most the distance a strong runner could cover without rest, proved sufficient as a means for handling communication problems. But as complex social organizations were invented for military, commercial, and governmental purposes, such groups were continuously faced with the problem of coordinating their activities without a really reliable method of transmitting information quickly over long distances.

Human ingenuity is vast, and people of every age have shown a remarkable ability to take the technology of their time and apply it in some fresh way to the solution of practical problems. So it was with long-distance communication. Our earliest records tell of military commanders who signaled information at night from the tops of hills with the use of torches arranged in previously agreed upon patterns or crude codes.

The word *telegraph* itself comes from the Greeks, hundreds of years before Christ. Its two component words imply "at a distance" and "to write." In the Greek, Persian, and Roman civilizations, social organization in military affairs, government, and commerce had far outstripped communication technology, and the inability to coordinate complex activities was a frequent source of great difficulty. Armies were defeated, navies were sunk, governments collapsed, and fortunes were lost, all for the want of a word.

The Search for Solutions. An impressive array of technical gadgets was invented and pressed into service over the intervening centuries to find a solution to this cultural lag. Even primitive people, needing to communicate but sorely handicapped by their crude technology, were able to burn out the inside of a log and stretch the skin of an animal over one end to form a drum, with which they could conquer surprising distances using coded sounds. Smoke signals are another familiar example. Carrier pigeons are still another (used right up into the twentieth century). Flashing mirrors, lantern signals, cannon shots, and fire beacons were all used in the struggle to surmount distance and time. However, these early communication techniques were severely limited. Most were terribly cumbersome and distressingly unreliable. Many depended upon good weather, and the others could handle only very simple messages.

In more recent times, many interesting communication systems were invented. All were in some way dependent upon line-of-sight vision between communicator and receiver. By relaying a message along a series of stations, however, one could send complex messages over surprisingly long distances. During the height of Napoleon's power in France, that country actually had a total of 224 semaphore stations that spanned over a thousand miles.[1] This type of system was the most elaborate and widely used of all the line-of-sight communication devices. An outgrowth of a simple idea developed by three French schoolchildren for sending messages to each other, it depended upon positioning a pair of large wooden arms on top of a tower in such a way that given configurations represented the letters of the alphabet in agreed-upon patterns. The signals could be read and interpreted by a receiving operator in another tower several miles away. This operator in turn sent the message along to the next station, and so on. It was expensive and cumbersome, but the system was in use in a number of European countries right up to the time that the electrical telegraph replaced it. Semaphore communication still has some limited applications, especially aboard naval vessels maintaining radio silence.

As Western society came into the nineteenth century, the need for a means of communication that would quickly transverse even the oceans began to become critical. The tempo of commercial intercourse between nations had increased greatly with the advent of the industrial revolution. Great Britain was developing a colonial empire so vast and far-flung that it would be able to boast with impunity that it was one upon which the sun never set. Britannia ruled not only the waves but also a substantial portion of the world's land surface and a sizable segment of the world's population. Other nations, too, were building mighty navies and great merchant fleets. They were consolidating new political systems, developing colonial markets, and exploiting new sources of raw materials. Along with all of this came fundamental changes in the organizational nature of Western society. These changes have been discussed by social scientists in various terms such as complex organic evolution analogies, the movement from Gemeinschaft to Gesellschaft, the change from mechanical to organic solidarity, and the trend from a sacred to a secular society, to mention only a few. There can be little doubt that in the face of growing societal complexity, a communication medium such as the electrical telegraph was sorely needed and could have been put to immediate, practical, and important use long before it was finally available.

The Dream of Instantaneous Communication. The idea of an instantaneous telegraph based upon magnetic principles had been around in one form or another for a long time. Giovanni della Porta, the author of *Natural Magick*, had discussed a very special kind of lodestone (a type of iron ore with magnetic properties).[2] If two similar compasses were to be fashioned with this mineral used to magnetize their needles, it was said they would be locked together by some mysterious force so that if the needle of one were forced to point in a given direction, the other would then instantly and automatically move to the same orientation, regardless of intervening distance. With the alphabet fixed around the circumference of the compass, the telegraphic possibilities which such a system might provide were obvious. But sadly, search as they might, scientists, philosophers, and learned people were never able to find quite the right variety of lodestone needed to construct such a marvelous *sympathetic telegraph*. Like the philosopher's stone, the Golden Fleece, and the fountain of youth, it remained forever beyond their grasp.

Scientific Progress in Understanding Electricity

Although the legendary lodestone failed to provide the means for a telegraph, the scientific laboratory eventually would yield devices that would transcend the hopes and dreams of all the ancient wise ones. The development of an adequate understanding of electricity came during the nineteenth century as part of the great surge of accomplishment in the physical sciences. Radio itself was a by-product of a long, continuous, and basic inquiry into the nature of electrical energy.

The theorizing and research that led to this communication medium occupied the lifetimes of large numbers of scientific workers, only a few of whom ever achieved popular recognition, financial success, or even lasting scientific honors. The list of problems these people solved is simply staggering. Today's teenagers who tune in to their favorite music program while lying on the beach, and the factory workers who prop up their feet at night and view their favorite wrestling exhibition are using the end products of centuries of brilliant scientific advances, the solution of which absorbed some of the most creative imaginations and most tireless workers of the last two centuries. These pioneers grappled with an endless list of conceptual, theoretical, and mechanical-technical problems whose solutions permit today's systems of broadcasting.

The problems needing solution before radio could become a reality included the basic theory of electricity and elementary circuitry, including generating, conducting, and measuring electric currents. Also included were the theories of electromagnetic fields, coils, and the electromagnetic radiation and detection of high-frequency oscillations. Another series of problems centered around the alteration of currents, such as rectification and amplification. The diode and triode electron tubes were required to couple voice transmission to the dot-and-dash wireless telegraph. Finally, for television, an offspring of radio, the problems associated with broadcasting patterns of light and shadow and receiving these on a viewing screen had to be solved. The light-sensitive photoelectron tube in the heart of the television camera was a substantial advance, as was the kinescope-receiving picture tube. The latter two opened the way for commercial television.

The Elements of Electrical Theory. The principles by which sound or light are converted to electromagnetic waves that can be broadcast through space, to be received and converted back into sound or light, involve the most basic of the physical sciences. Some of these principles govern the nature of matter itself.

The key to radio transmission and reception and to television is the *electron*. In oversimplified terms, the electron is conceptualized by physicists as an infinitesimally small *particle* that has the electrical characteristic of being negatively charged. Electrons, of course, are one major type of particle that make up *atoms*. There are other kinds such as protons and related types that constitute the *nucleus* of a given atom. These tiny nuclear particles have positive electric charges that exactly match the negative electrical charges of the atom's electrons. It is this balance of electrical forces that holds the particles together in a given atom.

Each atom of the elements has a different number of electrons and other particles making up its overall structure. The heavier a given element is, the more electrons it has in its atoms. An atom of a given element is a tightly organized structure of particles that are electrically balanced against each other in a tiny system. Some elements, however, have atoms whose outer electrons for various reasons are less solidly attached to their structures.

For some elements (like copper and many other metals), electrons can be picked off or added to the outer parts of these systems by chemical or electromagnetic processes, thus throwing the atom into a temporary electrical imbalance. When this happens, the atom attracts an electron from its neighbor to replace the one lost. Or if it has too many it passes one on to its neighbor. Then the neighbor reacts similarly with *its* neighbor, and so on. If the element is a good "conductor" of electricity and is arranged in a long thin wire, the result will be a "flow of electrical current" along that wire. Nothing really "flows," of course, but the successive electrical imbalances in the atoms of the wires making up an electrical circuit can be thought of in this way. Storage batteries, generators, solar cells, and many other devices are capable of producing these electrical imbalances at the end of a wire, and this disequilibrium creates an energy source in the form of an electrical charge at the other end. From this phenomenon comes our familiar host of applications of the resulting energy. It is used to create magnetic fields, heat, light, and other effects such as radio and television. If the foregoing seems complex, it is an indication to the reader of the difficulties that were overcome as part of the accumulation of ideas and technology prior to the invention of radio.

Electrical Technology: Applications of Theory. All during the period from the early Greek philosophers up to the latter part of the eighteenth century, experimenters had marveled at the phenomenon of electricity. Static electricity was easily produced by friction, and with that principle in mind, experimenters built larger and larger devices for generating charges. The early Greeks rubbed an amber rod on a piece of cloth and generated weak electrostatic induction currents capable of attracting a light pith ball suspended on the end of a thread. Centuries later, European scientists of the 1700s had elaborated the mechanics of this process to a point where they could generate awesome charges of static electricity with ponderous friction machines. They constructed huge rotating disks with cloth pads to pick up the electrical charges, and they astounded their friends by letting those charges smash between two metal points in lightninglike fashion up to a distance of several feet. Such machines were capable of attracting bits of thread or other objects from as much as thirty feet away. Actually, however, they were still using the same principle that had fascinated the Greeks, and they really did not understand why it worked! While they must have been having a great deal of fun with their dramatic devices, they had not been able to solve the critical problem of *storing* electricity so that it could be used when and where it was needed.

Several people seem to have found a crude solution to this problem at about the same time. A jar half filled with water and corked with a wire down through the middle of the cork can "store" a charge of electricity. One end of the wire must dip into the water and the other end must be temporarily attached to the business end of a friction machine that is generating static electricity. An unsuspecting soul who later grasps the wire coming out of the jar will receive a bone-jarring shock if a large enough static charge has been fed into the storage jar. Called a Leyden jar (after the place where it seems most likely to have been invented), this device was used by Benjamin Franklin in his well-known experiment with the kite. He succeeded in charging up a Leyden jar with a kite flown into an electrical storm. One end of the (wire) kite string is said to have been attached to a key dipped into the water. The experiment demonstrated that the electricity of lightning and the electricity of the laboratory are the same. Why Mr. Franklin was not instantly electrocuted remains a mystery; it definitely is not advisable to attempt to repeat this interesting experiment. The storage battery of Alessandro Volta eventually replaced the Leyden jar, and more adequate devices for generating electrical currents were under development by Michael Faraday and others.

The Telegraph

A key element in the inexorable movement of technology toward the electrical telegraph was the development of the electromagnet. By the 1830s the various technical traits prerequisite to an electrical telegraph were available within the scientific culture. It remained only to put them together in the required pattern. The idea of the sympathetic telegraph had tantalized people for centuries. The need for such a communication device was critical, and the technological base had accumulated to a point where no fundamental problem remained to be solved.

Several people at about the same time seem to have hit upon one scheme or another that would constitute a workable telegraph, but it was the American Samuel F. B. Morse whose patents and system prevailed. Morse, the portrait painter, was not a scientist, and in his naiveté he seems to have blundered onto solutions for making a workable telegraph that scientists had overlooked as unlikely possibilities. He had set up a workshop in one of the buildings of the University of the City of New York, where he served as professor of literature and the arts of design. He tinkered with numerous gadgets, frequently seeking the advice of several of his somewhat skeptical scientific friends, and he eventually worked out a telegraph system that permitted him to transmit messages through ten miles of wire strung around and around in his workshop.

Morse immediately applied for a government grant to enable him to perfect the device (which he had promptly patented). After a great deal of fumbling, hesitation, and delay, the federal government eventually financed a telegraph line between Washington, D.C., and Baltimore. The historical message "What hath God wrought?" flashed between the two cities on May 24, 1844, and the world entered into the era of instantaneous electric communication. Giovanni della Porta's dream was slowly being realized. All that was needed was to get rid of the wires.

The Principle of Private Ownership. After an initial period of hardship, hesitation, and financial loss, the electric telegraph was gradually accepted by business, the military, and other groups, and the thin wires soon led to most major centers of population. The federal government, which had financed the original long-distance line, threw away its opportunity to control the patents and relinquished all its rights. They became the property of private corporations, with Morse as a major stockholder, and the development of this medium was left to private enterprise. It is clear now that the failure of the government to maintain itself in the telegraph business *set a precedent* that would be followed in the United States, whereby private ownership of the public communication media constitutes a central condition in determining the type of content the audiences of the broadcast media now enjoy. It was this obscure turn of events that forged an important link in the chain of development of the mass media in this country. As the telephone came, then the wireless telegraph, the wireless telephone, and eventually home broadcasting, the federal government was never again a serious contender for controlling rights to these media (although on one occasion it obtained and relinquished control of radio). This was certainly not the case in other countries.

Spanning the Oceans. After conquering tremendous financial and technical problems, cables were laid across the Atlantic Ocean by Cyrus W. Field, and on July 27, 1866, a message crossed the great sea with incredible speed. Within a very short time, networks of cables were laid under the oceans to the principal population areas of the world. By 1876 Alexander Bell and his brilliant assistant had succeeded in transmitting the human voice over electrical wires, and the pace of cultural accumulation in the area of communication technology was increasing swiftly. Soon the huge cultural lag between communication technology and complexity of social organization would begin to close. From the telegraph and the telephone it was only a short and very natural step to elimination of the wires to achieve a wireless telegraph and eventually a wireless telephone.

The Wireless Telegraph

While the development of the telegraph and telephone had been occurring, scientists like Volta, Ampère, Henry, Faraday, Maxwell, and Hertz were continuously working to understand the basic nature of electricity. The growth of increasingly sophisticated theory permitted an ever more elaborate technology for generating, storing, measuring, transmitting, modifying, and variously harnessing electrical power. Along about the time of the American Civil War, James Maxwell in Scotland had worked out a mathematical theory of mysterious electromagnetic waves which were supposed to travel at the speed of light. By 1888 a young German, Heinrich Hertz, had demonstrated the actual existence of these waves and built a laboratory apparatus for generating them and detecting them. The scientific world became intensely interested in this phenomenon, and experiments with the Hertzian waves were being carried on in laboratories in many countries.

Marconi's Gadget. In the early 1890s in Italy, Guglielmo Marconi, who was then only twenty years old, became acquainted with the experimental studies of Hertzian waves and the apparatus used to generate and detect them. He reasoned logically that if their distance could be extended beyond the few hundred feet of the laboratory devices, signals in code might be transmitted with them in a kind of telegraph without wires. He promptly purchased an apparatus and began experimenting with it, sending its signals across the garden on his parents' estate. Although not a scientist, Marconi was an imaginative tinkerer, and he succeeded in modifying the laboratory device and strengthening it to a point where he could send dot-and-dash messages up to about a mile. His apparatus had become the first wireless telegraph.

Marconi's work was never intended to advance basic science. His experiments had immediate practical and commercial goals rather than theoretical or scientific ones. He hurried to England in 1897 to patent his wireless telegraph. It was essentially a system of fairly common laboratory devices built on a very large scale for sending and receiving the Hertzian waves in the dots and dashes of Morse's telegraph code.

> There was a well-defined raising of eyebrows among the scientists when they learned that their laboratory gear had found its way into

the patent office. Only a few, notably Crookes, Sir Oliver Lodge, and Ernest Rutherford, had given any thought at all to its practical use.[3]

Achievement of the Ancient Dream. Marconi soon built larger and larger devices that reached out over longer distances. Eventually even the Atlantic was spanned. Although Marconi's work may not have advanced basic science noticeably, it did represent a most significant step in the development of radio as an instantaneous medium of long-range communication. The dream of della Porta had become a reality. Marconi brought the end product of more than a century of scientific research out of the labaoratory and into the hands of groups who desperately needed a device with which to communicate rapidly over long distances.

"Marconi had come to England from Italy because he believed that England with her large mercantile marine, would prove the more profitable market for the discoveries he had made."[4] The wireless was by no means a mass medium at this time. By the end of the first decade of the new century it was in the hands of commercial, military, and governmental groups for the transmission of confidential information. It was especially suitable for use on ships, which would carry its heavy and bulky apparatus. The general public knew of the wireless telegraph only through what they occasionally read in the newspaper. The thought that they would ever have one in their homes or that it would begin to alter their family's daily routines surely never entered their heads.

FROM WIRELESS TELEGRAPH TO RADIOTELEPHONE

When radio had proved itself capable of performing the task Marconi and others had envisioned, powerful economic resources were brought to bear upon its development. The British and American Marconi companies soon had strong rivals. The naval establishments of powerful countries lost little time in adopting the wireless. Shipping firms found at last a practical means of keeping in contact with vessels at sea. When ships with wireless apparatus found themselves colliding with icebergs or otherwise in difficulties, dramatic messages of distress brought other ships similarly equipped to the rescue. These events attracted great popular attention. Meanwhile, radio technology continued to develop. Involved legal battles were fought over invention after invention during the time that radio's pioneers were improving the reliability, power, distance, and clarity of wireless messages. International conferences attempted to work out rules governing the transmission and receiving of messages. Hundreds of shore stations were built along coastlines by commercial, marine, and official naval interests. In the years just before World War I, wireless telegraphy was a widely used, commercially sound technique that had substantially begun to close the great cultural gap between communication technology and the development of complex and far-flung social organization. But no one had yet thought of the device as a medium of communication for the ordinary member of society.

Transmitting the Human Voice

The transmission of the human voice by wireless was the next step, and a number of inventors and scientists were working on the idea. It was not really such a tremendously difficult problem. The existing dot-and-dash wireless system had been developed in such a way that it was technically capable of receiving such broadcasts if they could be properly incorporated into the radiated signal. It was on Christmas Eve 1906 that wireless operators on ships up and down the Atlantic sea lanes off the coast of the United States first heard a human being speak to them through their earphones. They could scarcely believe their ears!

Reginald A. Fessenden had prepared an apparatus that permitted the broadcasting of infinitely more complex signals than those of the simple tone of the dot and dash. He had also constructed a very powerful transmitter to use in his experiments. Several persons spoke over the wireless on that eventful evening; one made a speech, one read a poem, and one even played the violin. The radiotelephone had become a reality.

In spite of Fessenden's early success with radiotelephony, it was to be many years before Americans had regularly scheduled radio programs to listen to in their own homes. Yet there was a growing popular interest in radio. In that same year of 1906 it was discovered that several mineral substances were capable of detecting radio transmissions when used in an extremely simple circuit. A very inexpensive "crystal set" radio receiver could be built by almost anyone with elementary mechanical skills. The cost of the parts was insignificant. This meant that people all over the country, even youngsters, could listen in on the code signals in the air. Once the code was learned, the sport had great appeal, and they never knew when they might eavesdrop upon an agonized signal of distress from some vessel sinking in mid-ocean.

> Thus at the very period when it was important that the general public
> be educated to the possibilities of radio the efficient crystal detector

came along to boost the industry. The Morse code had great appeal to boys and young men, but when music and spoken words might occasionally be picked up out of the ether there arose a veritable army of enthusiasts for the new science. Boys love to tinker, to experiment with chemistry or mechanics, and here was the opportunity of the ages.[5]

The first decade of the new century brought many refinements, improvements, and significant new ideas. One of these was to revolutionize radio broadcasting and was even to provide the basis of an entire electronics industry that would follow. Its inventor, Lee De Forest, called it an *audion:* in the technical jargon of early radio it was called a *valve:* today we would call it a *vacuum tube.* It has since been displaced by solid state devices which perform approximately the same task. De Forest's audion was the key element in electronic amplifiers that could enlarge both broadcast and received radio signals. After refinement, it permitted the human voice to be transmitted to all parts of the globe. Radio receivers became far more reliable and the clarity of reception improved. Refinement followed refinement. The heterodyne circuit and superheterodyne circuit significantly improved reception. Radio equipment, which was once so huge and heavy that only ships could easily transport it, now became increasingly light and portable. In fact, during World War I, radiotelephones were successfully mounted in airplanes for the purpose of informing gun batteries on the ground of the accuracy of their fire.

Private Ownership and the Profit Motive

In some ways, the most perplexing of the social conditions surrounding the early development of radio were private ownership and the profit motive. They both facilitated and held back the development of the emerging medium. Every minor and major invention was immediately patented in the United States, in Britain, and in other countries as well. It became nearly impossible to make needed improvements in radio components or to market equipment thus improved without falling into bitter court entanglements over patent claims. In fact, all the major pioneers in radio, from Marconi on, frequently found themselves battling each other in court. Lee De Forest, one of the principal inventors of major radio components, was actually arrested and charged with fraud. The problem was, of course, that there were fortunes to be made in wireless, and the competition to tie up important inventions for exploitation was intense.

At the same time, it is also true that millions of dollars were expended by private individuals and syndicates to aid inventors in improving their ideas to the point where they could be turned into marketable devices. In the final analysis, this financial support for research may have compensated for the many conflicts that the concepts of private ownership, corporate profit, and commercial exploitation generated for radio.

World War I brought urgent military needs for the improvement of radio systems. Not only did it result in new organization, manpower, and funds to bear upon unsolved technical problems but it had another important effect. All patent litigation and restrictions were temporarily suspended for the duration of the war. The federal government was in complete control of the infant industry, and this central control brought new cooperative efforts to the task of technical advancement which would have taken much longer in peacetime.

THE RADIO MUSIC BOX

A young radio engineer by the name of David Sarnoff had advanced rapidly in the ranks of the American Marconi Company. He had achieved considerable public attention during the sinking of the ill-famed *Titanic* when it was ripped by an iceberg in mid-Atlantic. Sarnoff remained at his telegraph key in a radio station in New York City decoding messages from the disaster scene. For three days and three nights he kept a horrified public abreast of developments concerning the tragic incident. He later moved up from his post to more important positions in the company. In 1916 Sarnoff sent a memorandum to his superiors, and this now-famous memo in a sense did for radio what Benjamin Day did for the press almost a century earlier: it showed an economically profitable way by which radio could be used as a medium of mass communication for ordinary families. Although the company did not immediately follow Sarnoff's advice, he successfully predicted the major outlines of radio as a mass medium. He wrote:

> I have in mind a plan of development which would make radio a "household utility" in the same sense as the piano or phonograph. The idea is to bring music into the houses by wireless.
>
> While this has been tried in the past by wires, it has been a failure because wires do not lend themselves to this scheme. With radio, however, it would be entirely feasible. For example—a radio telephone transmitter having a range of say 25 to 50 miles can be installed at a fixed point where instrumental or vocal music or both are produced. . . . The receiver can be designed in the form of a simple "Radio Music Box" and arranged for several different wave lengths,

which should be changeable with the throwing of a single switch or pressing of a single button.

The "Radio Music Box" can be supplied with amplifying tubes and a loudspeaking telephone, all of which can be neatly mounted in one box. The box can be placed on a table in the parlor or living room, the switch set accordingly and the transmitted music received. . . .

The same principle can be extended to numerous other fields as, for example, receiving lectures at home which can be made perfectly audible; also events of national importance can be simultaneously announced and received. Baseball scores can be transmitted in the air by the use of one set installed at the Polo Grounds. The same would be true of other cities. This proposition would be especially interesting to farmers and others living in outlying districts removed from the cities. By the purchase of a "Radio Music Box" they could enjoy concerts, lectures, music, recitals, etc. While I have indicated a few of the most probable fields of usefulness for such a device yet there are numerous other fields to which the principle can be extended.[6]

If Sarnoff had added the singing commercial and the soap opera, his description of radio as it would develop into a system of mass communication would have been almost perfect. Within ten years he was to see radio grow into a medium for household use, following almost to the letter the outline that he had dictated. David Sarnoff's suggested application of existing radio technology to this imaginative, new, and practical usage ranks as an insight with that of Marconi's idea of taking existing laboratory devices and using them as a wireless telegraph. Sarnoff himself played a major role in bringing about this transformation; in a short time he became the manager of a new corporation in the radio field and was able to help make his dream a reality.

The Issue of Control

Feeble attempts to perpetuate governmental control over radio at the close of the Great War were crushed by the outcries of private interests. Just as the federal government had allowed control of the telegraph to fall into the hands of private persons, it similarly handed over this important new medium of public communication to commercial interests. Radio was defined by this act as an *arena of business competition* as opposed to a public medium of communication to be operated by organizations of government. This decision was to have far-reaching effects and ramifications with which we live today. Other societies formulated different definitions concerning the control of broadcasting, and the systems of broadcasting that have developed in countries such as Great Britain, the Soviet Union, and others offer interesting contrasts with our own. That is not to say that they are better, only that they are very different largely because of historical decisions and events.

Once direct governmental control was eliminated, British and American commercial interests, which had prospered during the war, fought each other to gain control. The General Electric Company finally bought up the British shares of American Marconi and formed a new corporation with a patriotic name (apparently designed to dispel fears of foreign control). The new Radio Corporation of America (RCA) was able to consolidate a number of conflicting patent interests, and it gave control over wireless telegraphy and radio broadcasting in the United States to American stockholders. In 1919 David Sarnoff, who had forecast the "Radio Music Box," was appointed its first commercial manager.

Scheduled Broadcasting Begins

Shortly after World War I the Westinghouse Company, a major American manufacturer of electrical equipment, attempted to move into the international wireless telegraph field. Westinghouse was not particularly successful, largely because its rival RCA owned most of the important patents. However, some of its directors were interested in the newer field of wireless telephony, and the company had done considerable research in this area. Dr. Frank Conrad was in charge of experiments with new and powerful transmitters of this type. In connection with this work, he not only built such a transmitter for experiments at the Westinghouse laboratory, but he constructed one at home over his garage so that he could continue his work in the evening. He licensed his home transmitter nearly a year later, in April 1920, as station 8XK. Conrad started to broadcast signals during the evening hours as he worked with his apparatus in attempts to improve its design. He soon found that people in the area were listening in on their amateur receiving sets. This proved to be a boon at first because their letters, cards, and phone calls gave him some indication of the range and clarity of his transmitter. Before long, however, his circle of amateur radio listeners, began to become a problem. To create a continuous sound, he had started to play the victrola over the air. His listeners began to demand particular songs and would even call him at odd hours to ask him to play a favorite record. Dr. Conrad solved the problem by regularizing his broadcasts, and with the cooperation of a local phonograph dealer, he was able to present continuous music for a two-hour period two evenings a week. The number of listeners grew rapidly, and his family enthusiastically joined in the fun to become the first "disc jockeys."

Stimulating the Sale of Sets. All this activity increased the demand for receiving sets in the area, and it became increasingly clear that there might be money to be made in the manufacture of such sets for home use. The commercial possibilities did not escape the attention of officials of the Westinghouse Company. They decided to build a larger transmitter in East Pittsburgh for the purpose of stimulating the sale of home receivers of their own make and the sale of the components from which amateurs built such sets. It was in this way that Station KDKA, Pittsburgh, came into existence in the year 1920.

Although David Sarnoff had forecast the radio music box several years earlier, it was the decision of Harry P. Davis, vice-president of the Westinghouse Electric and Manufacturing Company, that concretely gave birth to commercial household radio. He decided that a regular transmitting station, operated by the manufacturer of receivers, would create enough interest in the sale of sets to justify the expense of operating the station. Although this financial basis for broadcasting has long been replaced by the sale of air time for advertising, it was sufficiently practical at the time to get radio started as a medium for home use.

To stimulate interest in the new station and, of course, to promote the sale of receiving sets, it was announced that the transmitter would broadcast the results of the 1920 presidential election over the air. Bulletins were phoned to the station from a nearby newspaper, and the returns were broadcast during the evening of November 11 as they came in. An audience of between five hundred and a thousand people heard the word through the air that Warren G. Harding had been elected President of the United States. The event was a great success; the dream of David Sarnoff had become a reality.

Growing Public Interest. The Pittsburgh experiment was so successful that other stations were quickly launched. Transmitters began regular broadcasts in New York in 1921, followed by stations in Newark and other cities. Westinghouse soon had several competitors. The public's interest in radio had been growing, its appetite for the new signals in the air whetted by the glamor and excitement of radio's brief history. The dramatic stories of rescues at sea, of daring flights over wild terrain with radiotelephones, and the struggles of giant corporations to gain control over wireless telegraphy had all contributed to this surging interest. When radio stations actually began to broadcast during regular periods with music and voices people could receive at home in their own cities, this latent interest suddenly burst into a full-blown craze. The public began to clamor for radio. By 1922 the manufacture of home receivers was lagging hopelessly behind the receipt of orders. New stations were being built at a staggering pace. In the last half of 1921, licenses were issued for 32 new stations, but in the first half of 1922 this number had risen to 254! Although there were still many problems to work out concerning its financial base, its content, and its technical functioning, radio as a mass medium was off to a flying start.

The Problems of Interference and Finance

One of the earliest problems that household radio encountered was brought on because of its own popularity. There is a limited spectrum of frequencies available that are suitable for broadcasting. In the beginning, no attempts were made by either government or private groups to regulate the frequencies that transmitters in a given area would use. The Radio Act of 1912 did not specify frequencies for privately operated broadcast stations. The Secretary of Commerce, who licensed all new transmitters, had selected two frequencies, 750 kilocycles and 833 kilocycles and all stations were assigned one or the other.

Conflict on the Airways: Competing Transmissions. As the number of transmitters operating grew quickly, there developed an annoying number of instances where two stations were operating near enough to each other so that the program of one would be imposed upon the sound of the other. This type of interference could not easily be controlled. Many stations worked out informal agreements to divide up available time. There was no legal authority that could assign different positions on the radio band for every station to use and could rigorously enforce such regulations. Obviously, such a problem could be handled only by some form of governmental agency, but there was no adequate provision by Congress or by the states for such a controlling body. The Department of Commerce issued licenses to operate transmitters but did little else. Because of the lack of control over this technical problem, confusion began to mount.

In the meantime, radio was advancing at a tremendous pace. Late in 1922 station WJZ in Newark successfully broadcast the World Series. Stations began to broadcast opera, concerts, news, dance music, lectures, church services, and a great variety of events. To avoid overlap, voluntary experiments were tried, with nearby stations being broadcast on wavelengths at least twenty meters different from each other. In spite of efforts to combat interference, however, the problem continued to grow.

Successful experimentation with networks was tried, and it was found that several stations linked by wires could simultaneously broadcast the same program. The rush to build new transmitters continued, and by 1923, stations were to be found in most major cities across the nation.

Paying for the Broadcasts. Two major problems continued to plague the medium: The technical problem of interference was already badly out of hand, and there was also the problem of paying for the broadcasts. While the larger electrical manufacturers could afford to finance their stations out of their profits on the sale of sets, this was a limited expedient at best, and it was no help at all to the owners of stations who were not electrical manufacturers.

By the end of 1923 some of the initial enthusiasm for constructing radio transmitters began to sag as the hard financial facts had to be faced. There was simply no profit as such, and only those with other financial resources were in a position to continue in operation.

> Now that a full year of nation-wide radio broadcasting had been completed the summer of 1923 afforded an opportunity to cast up the accounts, so to speak. This was indeed a disturbing experience, since the studio ledgers of every station disclosed entries almost entirely in the red ink. Fortunes had been squandered in the mad rush. . . . As early as December, 1922, the Department of Commerce reported the suspension of twenty stations for that month alone. With every succeeding month the casualty list had grown more appalling. Between March 19 and April 30, 1923, forty-two stations gave up their franchises. In the month of May there were 26 failures. June, 1923, saw fifty radio stations become silent. In July twenty-five franchises were surrendered. Thus in the period from March 19th to July 31st of this fateful year 143 radio stations went out of business.[7]

Unless some viable financial basis could be found, radio as a medium of communication to the American home was doomed.

Attempted Solutions. But the public was not to be denied radio. The mid-1920s were years of prosperity for most Americans. The grim remembrances of the Great War were fading, and the nation was entering a period of industrial and financial growth. The new practice of installment buying was part of a great expansion of credit that was taking place in the economic structure. No one had any inkling of the eventual collapse that would begin following October 1929. Installment buying made it easier for families of modest means to purchase consumer goods such as radio receivers. Radio listening was becoming increasingly popular, and pressure was being exerted on Secretary of Commerce Herbert Hoover to do something about the interference problem. He did work out a system for assigning different wavelengths to various broadcasting stations, but the attempt to implement it was not completely successful. People who owned sets capable of picking up only one major frequency did not like the idea. Also, there was no actual way of enforcing the assignments, and some transmitters simply ignored the plan. On the other hand, many of the major stations, which were engaged in regular broadcasting, tried to follow the secretary's assignments and did so with success.

The industry itself was exerting great pressure upon the Department of Commerce not only to regulate frequencies but to limit the number of stations that could be licensed in a given area. The public, too, was becoming disenchanted with the cacophony that came out of their sets night after night. The problem of interference was getting unbearable. Ancient spark transmitters used for marine broadcasts, Morse code amateurs, powerful stations that broadcast regularly, and local fly-by-night operators were all blasting each other over the airwaves.

Four major conferences were held in Washington, D.C., during the years 1922–1925 to discuss the problems of broadcasting. The government's position was that it was up to the industry itself to clean up its own house. The newspapers had gotten along without government control; in fact they had fought it bitterly. The film industry was cleaning up its products. In a political system that stressed private initiative, it was felt by many government officials that federal control over broadcasting would be a dangerous precedent. In fact, Congress had repeatedly refused to consider bills on the subject. The only legislation in existence on radio was the old Radio Act of 1912, which was hopelessly out of date.

The problem was not an easy one to solve, even by government control. Since wireless telegraphy would also need regulation, the matter had international complications. In addition, there were the thousands of amateurs whose rights had to be protected. Not only were there more than 500 major stations operating on a regular basis, but there were approximately 1,400 small stations of very low wattage that operated when their owners had the urge. Yet, to pick up this jumble of signals, Americans spent $136 million for receiving sets in 1923 alone.[8]

Secretary of Commerce Hoover struggled valiantly to find a solution. He tried limiting the power and hours of operation of some stations so that they could share a given frequency. By 1925 every spot on the frequency band was occupied, some by several stations. The broadcast band could not conveniently be extended without severely infringing upon other important kinds of radio and wireless operations. There were 175 additional stations clamoring for licenses that could not be accommodated.

Public Ownership of the Airwaves. In 1926 this arbitrary system collapsed. A federal court decided that the Secretary of Commerce had no legal basis to impose any restrictions on the station's power, hours of operation, or transmitting frequency. In that same year also, the Attorney General issued the opinion that the only existing legislation, the Radio Act of 1912, really did not provide a legal basis for any of the regulations he had been using. Hoover simply had to abandon the entire attempt in disgust, and he issued a public statement that urged radio stations to regulate themselves. They were unable to do so.

In the face of the utter chaos that followed, President Coolidge asked Congress to enact appropriate legislation to regulate broadcasting, including provisions for adequate enforcement. They did so in 1927. They first enunciated the important principle that *the airwaves belong to the people* and that they can be used by private individuals only with the formal permission of government on a short-term license basis. Licenses were to be granted or revoked when it was in the public interest, convenience, or necessity to do so. All licenses of existing stations were automatically revoked, and the industry had to start all over by applying formally for a franchise to operate and by providing adequate statements and explanations as to why it would be in the public interest for them to do so.

The Federal Communications Act of 1934. The Radio Act of 1927 was to be a temporary solution. After a seven-year period of observation, trial, and some readjustments, a new and more permanent set of statutes was written and a Federal Communications Commission (FCC) was established to enforce the provisions. The Federal Communications Act of 1934 has since become, with appropriate amendment from time to time, the principal regulating instrument for the broadcast industry in the United States.

Financial Support. Meanwhile, the boisterous new industry continued to seek an adequate means of financial support. By the mid-1920s, broadcasters were still grappling with this problem. A committee of New York businesspeople tried the experiment of soliciting funds directly from the listening audience for the purpose of hiring high-quality talent to perform over one of the larger stations in the area. While a trickle of funds came in, most listeners decided they would rather listen free to whatever happened to come their way than pay directly out of pocket to be assured of higher-quality programs. This response typifies the feelings of the majority even today. It also explains in part why the public eventually accepted advertising messages as a means of financing broadcasting. They would rather put up with somewhat objectionable commercials than pay directly for their entertainment.

Other schemes were proposed. David Sarnoff felt that wealthy philanthropists should endow radio stations just as they did universities, hospitals, and libraries. Others suggested charging a license fee for operating a home receiver, the proceeds of which were to be divided among broadcasters. Many felt that the industry itself would solve the problem. The larger manufacturers of receiving sets were said to have an obligation to provide something to hear on their products. It was thought that this arrangement would eventually result in a small number of networks, each operated by a different manufacturer or group of manufacturers, and that there would be few if any independent stations.

Radio Goes Commercial

But while these debates were being carried on, advertising was quietly creeping in as a dependable source of revenue for radio broadcasts. In fact, as early as 1922, station WEAF had sold radio time for ten-minute talks on behalf of a Long Island real estate company that was selling lots. Then major companies began to sponsor programs. A department store paid for an hour-long musical program. A tobacco company sponsored a radio variety show. A candy company presented two comedians. The public was much drawn to these shows, and audiences wanted more. At first, these sponsors made no direct advertising appeal for their products. Their name was simply mentioned as sponsor or the program was titled after the name of the product. This form of subtle advertising found little criticism. The general goal of sponsoring such a program was to create goodwill among the audience.

The Secretary of Commerce was dead set against open huckstering on radio. He said, "It is inconceivable that we should allow so great a possibility for service, for news, for entertainment, and for vital commercial purposes to be drowned in advertising chatter."[9] Many other voices were added to this view. Responsible officials in government, leaders of the industry, and many groups of listeners concurred.

In our society, however, such an idealistic position was doomed from the outset. With listeners more interested in "free" entertainment than quality programming; with government playing only a technical role, primarily to keep frequencies unscrambled; with ownership of the media in the hands of profit-seeking companies and corporations, the noble views of the Secretary of Commerce and his supporters were not consistent with the value system, the political structure, and the economic institution of the society within which the new medium was developing. The same socioeconomic forces that led newspapers to turn to selling space to advertisers so they could sell their products to a mass audience were to result in a parallel pattern for radio. The surrender to advertising was strongly resisted for some time, but inevitably it came. It was somewhat artificially held back briefly by the policies of the American Telephone and Telegraph Company, which controlled many patents, transmission lines, and radio equipment used by broadcasters, but even this opposition was relaxed, and the way was open for the flood of commercial messages that are now so much a part of broadcasting in the United States.

At first, advertising was restrained and dignified. Soon, however, it became increasingly direct and to the point. It would be incorrect to say the public welcomed advertising, but it is certainly true that it welcomed what advertising revenue made possible. People were willing to hear the sponsor's pitch in order to be able to listen to their programs. One reason for this attitude was that programs were quickly designed to have great popular appeal. Money from advertising made it possible to hire effective talent. Individual comedians, singers, and bands soon developed large and enthusiastic followings. Weekly drama programs became popular. Programs for children were developed; sports broadcasts drew large audiences. A great variety of content was designed to capture the interest of different large components of the population.

By the end of the 1920s the major problems of radio as a mass medium of communication were solved. Almost everyone could buy a reasonably priced and reliable receiving set on time payments. The broadcasters received generous profits from selling their time to advertisers; sponsors sold products effectively over the air to a mass market; and talent with great popular appeal captured the nightly attention of the public. In the background, the new federal legislation had brought order out of chaos with respect to the interference problem. Only the ominous crash of 1929 threatened to muddy the picture. As it turned out, however, this was to have little negative impact on the growth of radio.

The Golden Age of Radio
Radio flowered during the 1930s and 1940s. These were very trying decades for the American society. The Great Depression and World War II affected the destinies of every citizen, but they had little inhibiting effect on radio.

An overview of radio's growth in the American society can be obtained from Table 4.1, which shows the number of receiving sets in operation for selected years. By the end of the 1930s there was slightly

TABLE 4.1. THE GROWTH OF RADIO SET OWNERSHIP IN THE UNITED STATES (1922–1985)

Year	Households (in thousands)	Average Number of Sets
1922	25,687	.02
1925	27,540	.2
1925	27,540	.2
1930	29,905	.4
1935	31,892	1.0
1940	34,855	1.5
1945	37,503	1.5
1950	43,468	2.1
1955	47,788	2.5
1960	52,610	3.7
1965	57,521	4.1
1970	62,875	5.1
1975	71,120	5.6
1980	80,776	5.5
1981	82,400	5.5
1982	83,527	5.5
1983	83,918	5.5
1984	85,407	5.5
1985	85,789	5.5

SOURCES: U.S. Bureau of Census, Statistical Abstract of the United States, 106th ed. (Washington, D.C., 1986).

U.S. Bureau of Census, *Historical Statistics of the United States, Colonial Times to 1957* (Washington, D.C., 1960), Series A 242–44, p. 15.

U.S. Burea of Census, *Current Population Reports: Population Characteristics,* Series P 20, no. 106 (9 January 1961), p. 11; no. 119 (19 September 1962), p. 4; no. 166 (4 August 1967), p. 4.

National Association of Broadcasters, *Dimensions of Radio* (Washington, D.C., 1974).

Electronic Market Data Book (Washington, D.C.: Electronic Industries Association, 1979).

NOTE: Figures after 1960 include Alaska and Hawaii. Some figures have been revised from previous editions because of revisions in source materials.

more than one set per household in the United States. This remarkable growth in the use of radio receivers had occurred in spite of ten years of economic depression following the stock market collapse of 1929. It should be emphasized for those who did not experience those tragic days that this was a period of great distress for American families. Millions of workers were unable to find employment, and there were few public agencies to turn to for relief. The trauma of such conditions cannot be adequately appreciated without having been personally involved. It was a time when the people of the United States were gravely depressed in spirit as well as in an economic sense.

Quantitative Patterns. In spite of the hardships of the times, radio seemed to thrive on the depression! Advertising revenue, instead of drying up, grew at an ever-increasing pace. The number of radio sets owned by Americans approximately doubled every five years. Families who had reached the limit of their financial resources would scrape together enough money to have their radio receiver repaired if it broke down. They might have to let the furniture go back to the finance company or stall the landlord for the rent, but they hung grimly on to their radio sets.

Radio fit the needs of millions of hard-pressed people during that trying time. It had music to restore their sagging spirits, funny people to cheer them up, and dramatic news to divert their attention from their personal problems. Amateur nights, evening dramas, soap operas, Western adventures, and variety shows were all followed avidly by loyal listeners night after night. On a summer night people could walk down a street on the evening that a particularly popular comedian was on the air and hear the program uninterrupted through the open windows of every house they passed.

By the time the depression eased and World War II was about to begin, radio was reaching every ear. In mid-1940 there were one and a half sets per household in the United States. Radio had also become increasingly sophisticated in every sense. It was technically excellent. It was possible for direct broadcasts to be picked up and relayed to listeners in their homes from almost any point on the globe. News broadcasting had become a sophisticated art, and outstanding journalists had established themselves within this new medium. The press and radio had learned to live with one another after prolonged feuding, and radio had full access to the world's wire services.

During World War II the radio industry made all its resources available to the federal government. War information messages, domestic propaganda, the selling of war bonds, campaigns to reduce the civilian usage of important materials, and many other vital services were performed. It should be noted that the manufacture of home receiving sets was completely curtailed during the war years. Table 4.1 and Figure 4.1, the cumulative diffusion curve for radio sets, show that from 1940 to 1945 few new sets were acquired by American households. Special attention should be called, however, to the continued rise in ownership following the conflict, when the cumulative diffusion curve recovered from the retardation of the war years and resumed its regular pattern of growth.

Competition from Television. Of significance are the postwar years when radio was faced with vigorous competition from television. Here

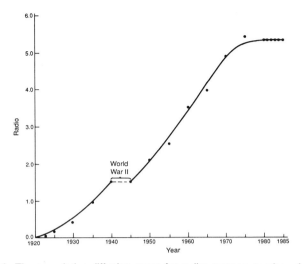

Figure 4.1. The cumulative diffusion curve for radio; average number of receiving sets per household in the United States (1922–1985).

we see how conflict provides social change. If radio had retained its original format and content, it would have remained a direct competitor of the newer medium, which was apparently capable of gratifying the relevant needs of the mass audience in a more effective manner. At first, radio attempted to do this with the somewhat optimistic argument that over the years people had built up a deep loyalty to radio, which had served them so well, and they could not easily be lured away to a flashy new thing like television. The public turned out to be completely fickle, however, and as soon as families could afford television, they gleefully abandoned radio in favor of the tube. Or, to put in it the language of structural functionalism, radio had been satisfying certain needs within the American society as a social system; when a more effective functional alternative became widely available, the earlier medium had to change or become obsolete.

Faced with the prospect of oblivion, radio was forced to find audience needs to satisfy that were not being effectively served by television. It successfully found such needs, and radio remodeled itself along new lines. During the 1930s, 1940s and even the early 1950s radio had successfully captured the attention of the American family during the major evening hours. People turned to their radio to listen to the country's most popular entertainers. As television grew, it took over these entertainers along with the family's evening time. Radio was displaced from the living room and had to be content with the bedroom, the kitchen, the automobile, and the beach. Transistors and later solid state technology, which opened up a huge market for miniature sets, helped keep radio from the type of postwar decline that occurred with motion picture theaters as a result of television (Figure 3.1).

At present, radio seems to have found a workable formula. It caters to its audience during times when television is inappropriate. People listen when they wake up in the morning, while they are working, driving, jogging, playing, and the like. But when evening comes and they settle down in their living rooms, the radio dial is turned off in favor of the television set. Nevertheless, radio remains one of the most massive of our mass media in terms of the ownership of sets. Table 4.1 shows that Americans now own well over five and a half sets per household. Figure 4.1 suggests that the curve of diffusion for radio has finally leveled off. Needless to say, the impressive number of sets owned by American families does not imply that they spend a corresponding amount of time in radio listening.

DEVELOPMENT OF THE TELEVISION INDUSTRY

The newest of the broadcast media inherited many of the traditions of radio. Several factors worked well to make its technological development and its diffusion through the American society a much more rapid and less chaotic process than was the case with its parent medium. The technology of television was really quite sophisticated before mass-manufactured sets were placed on the market for the public. There was no period comparable to the "crystal set" era in any widespread sense. The new medium did not have to work out a structure of control with the government; the FCC and its supporting legislation were simply taken over from radio. The financial basis of television was clear from the start. The public was completely accustomed to "commercials," and television promised to be even more effective as a vehicle for the sales pitch. No great problem was foreseen in attracting advertising money. There was no period of feuding with newspaper and wire-service interests. These arrangements were simply extended from established radio interests. The network idea was already popular from the older medium. An adequate coaxial-cable technology was available, and only the physical facilities needed to be constructed. The public was already completely familiar with the moving picture, and its transmission through broadcasting was not difficult for them to accept. For this reason, little public resistance to adoption of the new device was anticipated.

The TV Set as Status Symbol

Actually, the television set quickly became a status symbol. In its early period of diffusion, families who could ill afford a set would sometimes scrimp on necessities to be able to buy one. The "easy payment plan," by now a deeply institutionalized feature of the American economy, was widely used by families of modest means to acquire their sets. The urge to be identified as a set owner in the initial period of diffusion was so strong that in some cases families are said to have purchased and installed television antennas conspicuously on top of their dwellings long before they actually had sets to hook on. Stories of this type were widely circulated during the late 1940s. The definition of the television set as a luxury and a status symbol led to occasional public outrage when it was discovered that people on public welfare or other forms of relief owned sets. Apparently the experiences of the depression years when radio sets were regarded as extremely comforting to people in trying economic circumstances had been forgotten.

Impediments to Growth

Actually, television might have been a household medium even earlier had it not been for two factors that held back its growth—World War II and a government-imposed freeze. The electronic technology of television was worked out during the 1920s and 1930s. By 1939 television broadcasts were being made in the United States. The World's Fair of that year featured demonstrations of this latest marvel of science, and President Roosevelt gave an address over the new communication medium. This particular broadcast was viewed by only a handful because commercial manufacturers had not yet begun to mass-produce sets. In 1941, on the eve of World War II, the FCC approved home television, and the communication industry began to work out elaborate plans for its development. By this time there were nearly 5,000 television sets (mostly in the New York area) in private hands, and several small stations were broadcasting regularly for two or three hours a day.

World War II. The war interrupted any further development during its duration. In some ways this block to development may have accounted for the very rapid growth of television when the country returned to a peacetime economy. Electronics manufacturing techniques that aided in overcoming problems of television receiver production were developed during the war. Furthermore, the war completely ended the depression of the prewar period. In fact, with minor fluctuations the country entered a period of continuous economic growth, which has been uninterrupted for decades. The purchasing power of the average family rose to and remains at a point where television ownership is within the means of almost everyone.

The Freeze. With the bitter lessons of the interference chaos in the early days of radio before them, the government took a much more active role in controlling the broadcasting frequencies of television. By 1948 there were about seventy stations in operation and several million sets in use. Applications for new permits began to come in rapidly. Since television has only thirteen VHF channels for the whole nation, a rigorous means of control was needed to avoid interference. Fortunately, the television signal does not follow the curvature of the earth as does a radio signal. This means that two stations broadcasting on the same channel would not interfere with each other if there were sufficient distance between them. A master plan for the whole United States had to be worked out so television channels could be fairly allocated. There was also the need to study competing color systems to see what problems lay there. In addition, there were a substantial number of UHF channels on the spectrum, and these had to be allocated among competing interests. With these and other technical problems in mind, the FCC stopped granting new permits for television stations in 1948. Those stations in operation were permitted to continue, but time was needed to work out the details of a master plan so that as many problems as possible would be avoided when television reached its maturity. Actually, the stations already in operation (about seventy) were located in urban centers and were concentrated in the more eastern, and therefore more populated, sections of the country. Thus, the sale of sets could continue, even though no new stations were being built.

The Rapid Adoption of Television

When the freeze was discontinued in 1952, a large number of applications were received for new stations in areas of the United States that had been without a signal. With the new plan in place, these were quickly granted and signals became available in virtually all parts of the country. This greatly stimulated sales of television sets, and the curve of adoption shot upward. Figure 4.2 shows that the period of the early 1950s was one of very rapid diffusion of the new medium. By 1960 some 87 percent of the households in the United States had at least one television set. As is shown in Table 4.2 and Figure 4.2, this surge was followed by a slower rate of increase, but by 1980 the saturation point had been reached. Very few homes in the United States were without a

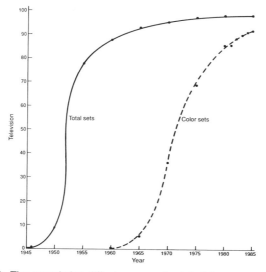

Figure 4.2. The cumulative diffusion curve for television; percent of households with television sets in the United States (1946–1985).

television receiver, and it became a replacement market. Also, as Table 4.2 shows, color sets became increasingly common, with the majority of households owning such a receiver after 1975.

What the above data do not show is the continuous upgrading of technology that took place during the period. The early sets used vacuum tubes and had relatively small screens. The typical home receiver in 1950 had a screen not much larger than half of a page of this book. Such a set cost about three hundred dollars, which represented about a thousand dollars or more in terms of today's purchasing power. The more affluent could buy a "large-screen" model with a viewing surface about the size of this page. Such a set sold for about half the price of a new car. During each succeeding decade, screen size, color reception, and reliability increased greatly. After about 1975 the Japanese took over the U.S. market with sets of good quality at a low price. After about 1950 coaxial cable and other technologies brought still other developments.

The Arrival of Cable TV

Coaxial cables are wires enclosed in plastic that is surrounded with a metal shielding to prevent signal loss or interference. They quickly came into use to transmit television programs over long distances, and they served this purpose quite well. The use of such cables to deliver signals to home sets (for a fee) was an obvious application. With early

TABLE 4.2. THE GROWTH OF TELEVISION SET OWNERSHIP IN THE UNITED STATES (1946–1977)

Year	Total American Households (in millions)	Households with Television Sets (in millions)	Color Sets Households (millions)	(percent)	Percent with TV
1946	37.9	.008	—	—	.02
1950	43.5	3.9	—	—	9.0
1955	47.8	37.4	—	—	78.0
1960	52.6	45.8	.3	.07	87.0
1965	57.5	52.7	2.8	5.0	93.0
1970	62.9	58.5	20.9	36.0	95.0
1975	71.1	68.5	46.9	68.0	97.0
1980	80.8	76.3	63.4	83.0	98.0
1981	82.4	79.9	66.6	83.0	98.0
1982	83.5	81.5	71.4	88.0	98.0
1983	83.9	83.3	73.9	89.0	98.0
1984	85.4	83.8	75.8	90.0	98.0
1985	85.8	84.9	77.7	92.0	98.0

Source: U.S. Census, *Statistical Abstract of the United States, 106th ed.* (Washington, D.C., 1986).

television this was often necessary because of the nature of the broadcast transmissions. In the late 1940s, when people first began to acquire home receivers, many were not able to receive a clear picture. It was very frustrating for those who had just purchased an expensive set. The reasons for the poor reception were well understood. For one thing, the early transmitters were not very powerful. If one lived close to the station there were few limitations, but for those living some distance away, reception could be poor; the picture was often fuzzy, distorted, or faint. Even a passing car could create electrical interference and fill the screen with "snow" or cause the picture to roll. In addition, the fact that the television signal travels in a straight line reduced the quality of reception or even made it impossible behind large buildings, on the back side of hills or mountains, and in similar positions.

There is some debate about where the use of cable for home reception actually started. One likely account maintains that it was in 1950 in Lansford, Pennsylvania. Robert Tarlton, who owned a radio and television repair shop, received many complaints about reception. Owners brought in their sets, claiming that there was something wrong with the receivers. But Tarlton understood the problem. While the community was only 65 miles from Philadelphia, it was behind a mountain that interfered with the signal. Tarlton decided to try a new approach. He put up a big antenna, and for a monthly fee he provided a cable hook-up to each subscriber's home. He called his new business the Panther Valley Television Company, and he was able to supply excellent signals to people who could not otherwise operate a receiver. He did not originate any new programming; all he did was capture network broadcasts with his "community" antenna and relay them to homes on his system.

The idea caught on quickly, and CATV (Community Antenna Television) systems went into business in all parts of the country. The majority were small businesses in remote areas with a few hundred subscribers. Even ten years later, in 1960, fewer than 2 percent of American television households received their signal in this manner, but some 640 cable companies were supplying the service.

As the systems expanded, however, more and more subscribers signed up. The stations that were originating the signals began to object. They saw the CATV systems as parasites, paying nothing for the signal they distributed but reaping profits nevertheless. Furthermore, as technology became more sophisticated, the cables were able to offer their subscribers signals from other cities far more distant. To the local broadcaster this was unwanted and unfair competition. The result was a number of legal suits.

Out of the conflict came the principle that cable television was under the jurisdiction of the FCC, in the same manner as signals broadcast over the air. This ruling brought further development of cable TV to a virtual halt. Complex regulations were imposed concerning what could and could not be transmitted on local CATV or other cable systems. By 1979, however, the FCC began to relax many of these restrictions. Local governments were given the power to grant private cable companies exclusive franchises to operate a system in their area. In exchange, the community retained the right to impose numerous conditions and controls over what went over the wires. Today this situation is constantly changing as court cases arise.

By the 1980s the number of towns, cities, and other areas served by cable television had grown rapidly. Some of the systems became huge corporations. There were more than 4,000 cable systems at the beginning of the decade, and some 20 percent of American homes received their TV signal in this manner. In 1987 about 45 percent were "wired." Some of the largest systems operating in urban areas serve millions of subscribers.

Cable is in many ways little different from off-the-air reception, but there certainly is more variety from which to choose. For a monthly fee, one can receive the "basic" service, which is usually a mixed bag that includes network broadcasts plus special channels that feature weather, sports, religious programs, news, public service announcements, rock music, and various other kinds of content. For additional fees one can add movie channels or other special services.

Some people thought that the cable systems would bring more sophisticated programming. However, that was not to be the case, and the content of the cable systems was a great disappointment to many subscribers. As it turned out, the same programming found on broadcast television appeared on the cable—soap operas, wrestling, situation comedies, old movies, sports, news, rock music, and the like. The reason that the level did not rise is that cable television is dependent upon the same advertising support system, which is aimed mainly at the lower-middle socioeconomic level of society (whose combined purchasing power exceeds that of other levels), as has long been the case with the networks. Thus their content is not at a different taste level; there is just more of it.

The coming of cable hurt, but has not yet severely damaged, network broadcasting. Broadcast television is surviving but the competition of cable is undeniably very real. One fear was that cable would develop specialized audiences in the manner of contemporary magazines. Before television, there were numerous general magazines that appealed to huge segments of the population. Virtually all of them are no longer being published. In their place came special-purpose magazines designed to appeal to segments of the public who shared a common interest or taste. We now have thousands of magazines that have smaller circulations built around such interests as computers, fishing, automobiles, boating, high fashion, dieting, and so on. In other words, magazine readership became highly specialized. But in spite of dire predictions, the multiplicity of channels available on cable has not split the viewing audience hopelessly into a plethora of focused topics or tastes. Large numbers of people continue to watch the usual scheduled programs.

Currently, the networks are locked into an increasing struggle to retain their viewers. Earlier, only three major networks shared a more-or-less captive audience. Today at least some viewers are turning to programming that they can receive only via the cable. Even more ominously, they are using recording devices to view movies or other content that they can rent and play on their home receiver. What will happen to network television in the future is anybody's guess.

The Video Cassette Recorder

Just as television was undergoing its most rapid period of adoption, the Ampex Corporation in New York was developing a device that would eventually have the most profound impact on both the television and movie industries. In 1952 Charles Ginsberg, along with five other Ampex engineers, set out to develop a way of recording television programs on magnetic tape. The use of such tape for recording audio programs was already in wide use, so it was not a revolutionary idea. Furthermore, there was an existing technology—called *kinescope*—that was used to record television programs, but it was cumbersome and it did not provide for high-quality reproduction.

After numerous delays, the recorder was developed and introduced to the television industry in 1956. Called the VTR (Video Tape Recorder), it was a suitcase-sized machine that used four rotating recording heads to record on tape that was two inches wide. The reels were rather large by today's standards—almost twelve inches in diameter.[10]

The practical nature of the new recorder was recognized immediately by the industry. CBS became the first network to use the VTR technology. It broadcast the show "Douglas Edwards and the News" by tape delay on November 30, 1956. Ampex, the company that produced the recorder, received an "Emmy" award the following year in recognition of its new development. If the television networks could have foreseen the trouble that the device would eventually cost them, they might have considered denouncing both the inventor and the machine instead.

The VTR spread quickly throughout the industry, although it remained virtually unknown to the public. It was a godsend to television studios. Mistake-free shows could be prepared ahead of time and aired when schedules were convenient. Furthermore, the tape could easily be edited, reduced in length, and made to fit into allocated time slots. Its use soon spread beyond the television studio. A number of people began to recognize the practical value of recording video material for later replaying. It also began to find wide use as a training device.

Schools adopted the new technology, and many people thought that it would revolutionize education. Professors could be taped for later presentation on television sets. In a number of colleges and universities classrooms were set up with TV sets located so that they could be seen from all parts of the room. No longer would lectures be a matter of a professor, a blackboard, and a piece of chalk. Televised lectures could be presented that were better, more permanent, based on more interesting visuals, such as charts, photos, film clips, and the like. Above all, college administrators believed, they would be cheaper; fewer professors would be needed and tapes could be purchased from national distributors for a number of standard courses. Needless to say, it did not work out that way. Students continued to want a live body in the front of the room. Even a boring one was better than a TV set.

Many other applications became commonplace. The VTR was used to train workers, as an advertising medium, to record the speech and behavior of people who were arrested for drunk driving, and even for recording court testimony. Before the end of the 1960s, however, VTR was still based on tape reels and was not particularly portable.

The Cassette Version. As the 1970s began, the size of the VTR was reduced and various versions using smaller tapes were under development. More important, a number of developers were able to place the tape inside a cassette so that the user had merely to push it into a slot and press a button or two to have it record or play back. When it was linked to a home television set, one could record the programs of one's choice and play them back at any time. Cable television was still unavailable for most people at the time, and the VCR (Video Cassette Recorder), as it came to be called, appeared to have a bright future.[11]

A great scramble ensued to get as many topics on cassettes as possible. In anticipation of an unleashed consumer demand, everything was recorded—cooking lessons, Shakespeare's plays, boxing matches, and untold numbers of older movies. However, the great stampede failed to materialize. For one thing, the price was too high. In the early 1970s, a recorder cost almost $800, which was too much money at the time. Some affluent people bought them, but the masses of consumers did not.

A more significant deterrent to adoption was the confusion over technology. The various companies producing the devices could not agree on standards. By the mid-1970s five different types of VCRs were on the market, each with a technology incompatible with those of the others. Manufacturers were trying to use everything from 8mm film to small disks as a recording medium. The situation was reminiscent of the technological chaos experienced early in the century by radio. In this case, however, the federal government had no authority to impose standards.[12]

Eventually, and after various manufacturers lost millions, standardization was achieved. However, by the mid-1970s the Japanese stepped in, taking over the technology developed by Ampex and other American firms. They made a few improvements and began producing a lightweight and relatively inexpensive system called *Betamax*. By 1977 over 200,000 of the machines had been sold. Americans were about to begin to buy the VCR for home use. Unfortunately, most of the profits from the manufacture of the machines would go to Japan.

Legal Conflict. The Japanese intrusion into the U.S. market did not go unnoticed by American businesses. They went to court. Numerous legal battles broke out over the sale, and even possession of video recorders and cassettes. Two movie producers brought suits against Sony, charging them with copyright infringement, interference with the sale of recorded programs to broadcasters, unjust enrichment, and anything else that their teams of lawyers could invent. At the center of the controversy was the idea that the VCR could be used to reproduce copyrighted material illegally and that doing this would create harm to legitimate producers of television programming.

The Americans lost. The courts initially ruled that people in their homes had a right to record and view whatever they wanted, as long as it was only for their personal use.[13] The case was appealed and eventually found its way to the U.S. Supreme Court. Congress even got into the fray and held various hearings on what laws should prevail. The main issue was that Hollywood movie producers did not want people to have VCRs. They felt that people would show taped movies in their homes and therefore box office receipts would suffer.[14] Even television advertisers agitated to ban the VCRs, or at least make them expensive to purchase and use via surcharges and other hurdles. They were especially concerned about the "zap" button that could speed the tape through the commercial message and thereby make it ineffective.[15]

After seven years of legal wrangling, the case was finally resolved. In 1984 the Supreme Court ruled that using the VCR to tape programs at home was legal and that it did not violate the copyright laws.[16] This was an important principle which opened the way for a whole new industry.

Ironically, while the Sony Corporation won the legal battles in the American courts, it lost the war for domination of the VCR market to a Japanese competitor. The giant Matsushita Corporation introduced so-called Video Home System (VHS) permitting the recording of up to six hours (as opposed to three) on a single cassette. Matsushita also licensed other firms, including American companies, to produce their own brands of the VHS. The resulting flood of VHS recorders overwhelmed the Sony product and by 1987 Betamax was all but obsolete.

The Growth of Ownership. With the legal situation clarified, the technology standardized, and great reductions made in the price of machines, Americans began to buy VCRs at an increasing pace. Table 4.3 shows that by 1986 some 40 percent of American homes were equipped with VCRs. The rate of acquisition was growing sharply, paralleling the rapid rise of television during the 1950s.

A major incentive for set ownership was the mushrooming growth of video rental stores. A clause in the Copyright Act of 1976 is the "first sale doctrine," which states that once a purchaser has bought a

TABLE 4.3. THE GROWTH OF VIDEO CASSETTE RECORDER OWNERSHIP IN THE UNITED STATES (1977–1987)

Year	Total Number of VCRs Sold (in thousands)	Total Number of Households (in thousands)	VCRs Purchased per Household	Cumulative Percent of Households with VCRs
1977	200	74,100	.002	—
1978	459	76,000	.006	0.8
1979	507	77,300	.006	1.4
1980	763	80,776	.009	2.3
1981	1,361	82,400	.01	3.3
1982	2,300	83,527	.02	5.3
1983	4,091	83,918	.04	9.3
1984	7,016	85,407	.08	17.3
1985	11,853	86,789	.13	30.3
1986	13,174	88,458	.14	44.3

Source: compiled from the U. S. Bureau of Census, Statistical Abstract of the United States, 106th Ed., and the Electronic Market Data Book (Electronic Industries Associates, 1987).
Note: The cumulative percents may overestimate the number of households with VCRs if older machines have been abandoned. On the other hand, some households may have more than one VCR.

copyrighted work, that individual can do what he or she wishes with it. This includes renting it out. Thus, retailers can buy movies on tape from motion picture studios or their distributors and rent them to VCR owners at low cost.[17] Today one can rent video cassettes for a very nominal fee. They are available not only in establishments that specialize in video rentals, but in supermarkets, drug stores, and even neighborhood convenience stores. As a result, movies are becoming very popular again, but millions see them on their home TV screen rather than in a movie theater.

The VCR is one of the most popular inventions in history. Machines are being eagerly purchased in every country. In parts of the world where movie theaters, night clubs, and bars are banned (as in many Moslem countries) the VCR and the video movie are used extensively for entertainment at home by those who can afford them. Huge black markets and pirating operations have sprung up that copy and sell illegally imported (and often banned) American films. In the Soviet Union, for example, demand for American video cassettes, such as Jane Fonda's workout tape and recent movies, far exceeds the available supply.

AN OVERVIEW

Overall, the foregoing chapters on the newspaper, the film, radio, and television have given some of the details concerning the impact of a society on its mass media. The study of the media within this perspective emphasizes the evolutionary process of social change. That is, it focuses on the accumulation of technological culture traits. It notes the invention of media as new configurations of such traits. It follows their transformation from technical devices known only to a few to forms that can be used by the multitude. It traces their diffusion patterns as they spread through the society and it studies their curves of obsolescence as they are replaced by functional alternatives. This type of analysis says little about the psychological processes of individuals as they decided to adopt the various media or as they were influenced by the absorption of media content. Such an analysis also stresses the broad social, economic, and political conflicts that characterize the society during the development of each medium. Such factors as war, depression, affluence, immigration, urbanization, the spread of education, and the presence of given technological elements in the culture of a society produce strains that facilitate, inhibit, or otherwise affect the development and adoption of a given mass medium. Thus, the many events that make up the history of our mass media cannot be interpreted in a theoretical vacuum. Viewing them as part of the complex evolutionary processes that occur when a society becomes more differentiated and achieves greater specialization of functions places them in a context of social change. Showing the media to be a part of the broad evolutionary process of industrialization and urbanization relates them to the two master trends in modern society. The older idea that the media are independent forces shaping and molding the society as they wish is simplistic and outmoded. The media are shaped by events in the society as a whole, and they are deeply influenced by the dialectic process of conflict among opposing forces, ideas, and developments within the media system and between the media and other institutions of society. In other words, there are numerous and pervasive ways in which a society has profound influences upon its media.

NOTES

1. Gleason L. Archer, *History of Radio to 1926* (New York: American Historical Society, 1938).
2. John Baptista Porta, *Natural Magick*, ed. Derek J. Price (New York: Smithsonian Institute for Basic Books, 1957).
3. Monroe Upton, *Electronics for Everyone*, 2nd rev. ed., (New York: American Library Association, 1962), p. 137.
4. S. G. Sturmey, *The Economic Development of Radio* (London: Gerald Duckworth, 1958), p. 17.
5. Archer, *History of Radio*, p. 91.
6. Ibid., pp. 112–13.

7. Ibid., p. 312.

8. Girard Chester, Garnet R. Garrison, and Edgar Willis, *Television and Radio,* 3rd ed., (New York: Appleton-Century-Crofts, 1963), p. 24.

9. Alfred N. Goldsmith and Austin C. Lescarboura, *This Thing Called Broadcasting* (New York: Henry Holt, 1930), p. 279.

10. *Billboard Magazine,* February 22, 1986, p. 32.

11. *Newsweek,* July 10, 1970, p. 42.

12. *Time,* July 10, 1970, p. 40.

13. *Time,* October 15, 1979, p. 86.

14. *Newsweek,* April 26, 1982, p. 72.

15. *Consumer Reports,* May 1982, p. 236.

16. *Newsweek,* January 30, 1984, p. 57.

17. *Forbes,* November 19, 1984, p. 41.

CHAPTER 5

The Mass Media as Social Systems

Our previous chapters have shown the background, technological development, and patterns of adoption of each of the major mass media that now disseminate information to American audiences. As each arrived, it faced a unique set of social, economic, and political circumstances that shaped its particular pattern of adoption in the society. Because of the characteristics of the nation at the time, the newspaper spread relatively slowly over almost a century, reaching its highest point of usage per capita about the time of World War I. The film, in its traditional form, spread more rapidly, over a forty-year period, reaching its peak during the 1930s and 1940s. Radio showed a different pattern, rising at first rapidly and then steadily over half a century to reach a peak of set ownership in recent times. Television, on the other hand, swept through the society in a remarkably short time; set ownership jumped from 10 to 90 percent of households in a single decade. As each new medium arrived, it had to find its niche among the existing media. In some cases the consequences of that arrival were rather drastic. Certainly the broadcast media seriously challenged the newspaper as a source for first learning the latest news. Television brought a dramatic reduction in the traditional form of seeing movies. Radio had to find new needs to serve in the society when television arrived. The history of the media in the United States, therefore, *is more than the sum of its parts*. That is, it would not be possible to understand the mass communication system of the American society as a whole by even the most detailed examination if one looked only at the separate media. While such medium-by-medium analyses are necessary, it is also essential to understand how the media constitute an overall system that is deeply embedded into the American society.

It seems abundantly clear that mass communications today are a central part of our *institutional* structure. That is, while they are industries in their own right, they have penetrated deeply into each of the five basic social institutions of our society: For example, with their emphasis on the services and products of our commercial and industrial establishment, they are a central part of the *economic* institution. With their increasing role in the election process, their use in various hearings, and their focus on government in the news, they have become a significant feature of our *political* institution. With their heavy emphasis on entertainment and popular culture, much of which is consumed as entertainment in the home, they are indisputably an important factor in our *family* institution. For many, the electronic ministry has become a significant part of the *religious* institution. To a limited degree they are also a part of our *educational* institution. The media, in short, have penetrated our society to its institutional core. The American way of life as we know it today would not be possible without mass communications.

This institutional aspect of our media system implies equilibrium rather than transformation. Up to now, we have emphasized *change* as the most conspicuous aspect of the mass media. It is important in this chapter to shift our perspective and show that our present system is made up of components that now may provide for increasing *stability.* This aspect is important in an extended theory of transitions such as has been set forth in earlier chapters. Such a theory implies not continuously ongoing evolution, but a series of stages in which the *basic* form of human communication has undergone relatively rapid modification from one stage to another. During a given stage, the basic technology or process of communication was continuously upgraded, but not radically altered. We may be in just such a situation now as the twentieth century comes to a close.

Therefore, further improvements in our media will undoubtedly be made, but what can be suggested is that we now have a system of mass communications in our society that is more or less here to stay for an extended period. It will operate much as it has for the last half century, regardless of the advances in technology that will undoubtedly come. Our media survive as a system because important *functions* are provided for the society as a whole. That is, the media system has consequences for the population that are regarded as truly important. As long as our media meet those needs of society that are seen as important, the system that satisfies them will remain in place.

What can be concluded from the above is that individual shifts and trends within specific media are relatively unimportant in this system perspective. Whether newspapers become more or less popular, whether network television grows or declines, or whether AM radio disappears in favor of FM, media-related functions will continue to be served in one way or another. Even if some totally new medium were to be invented suddenly and find its place into our homes, our overall media system would survive in a more or less stable manner because the functions that it provides would still be there.

In this chapter the mass media system of the United States will be viewed within just such a perspective. This will require a very different theoretical orientation than that which is most often used for understanding mass communications and their influences. Studies of the effects of mass communication have long been conducted within a psychological framework. For decades the cognitive paradigm provided the basis for media research that sought to understand the influence of the content of mass communications on the "mental" processes of individual members of the audience. The assumption was that once individuals perceived the information provided by the media, it would modify such cognitive factors as opinions, needs, attitudes, and beliefs; those changes, in turn, would bring about alterations in the behavior of members of the audience.

While we will review theories of media effects within that kind of theoretical framework in later chapters, the intention of the present analysis is very different. The focus here is not on the individual but on the media system as a whole and its relationship to the larger society within which it operates. Looking at the mass media as a social system composed of various components, functioning within the larger societal system, requires quite different assumptions and a unique form of analysis. By this means, however, important characteristics of the media as they operate in the American society can be better understood.

Early in this book several paradigms for developing theoretical analyses were set forth. At least three dealt with *systems* rather than individuals: structural functionalism, social evolution, and the conflict model. Each has its own focus and uses. It is to this type of framework that we must turn for understanding such matters as the organization, stability, or change of mass communication industries in our society, rather than to psychological influences achieved on individuals. Specifically, in the analysis that follows, the focus will be on the stability of our media system, and the basic perspective will be the structural functional paradigm.

THE STABILITY OF MEDIA IN AMERICAN SOCIETY

One of the most challenging issues related to systems of mass communication is the ability of the media to survive within a society over extended periods. This phenomenon is not difficult to understand in an authoritarian society, where the government operates the media for purposes of controlling the flow of information, shaping public opinion, and providing approved collective interpretations. Such societies *need* their media to maintain the compliance and support of their populations. In a democratic society, however, where government plays a limited role, the stability and continued survival of media systems are much less easy to explain. This is particularly true in societies such as the United States, where conspicuous elites regularly condemn the media as being in bad taste, or even downright dangerous. Regularly, mass communications are charged with being the factor that stimulates crime, sexual excesses, deteriorating intellectual capacity, and general erosion of the moral standards of the society.

A continuous dialogue has been carried on between the representatives of the mass media and self-appointed guardians of the public's morals, intellectual development, and cultural tastes. This dialogue has ranged across many topics, including pornography, violence, trivial entertainment content, shallow news reporting, preoccupation with sports, political puffery, dreary advertising, mindless music, and almost every other topic that can be characterized as "tacky," "trivial," or "trashy"—that is, in "low taste."

Many who attack the media want them to stop the manufacture and presentation of popular culture (low-taste material) and present to the public more art, literature, insightful political analyses, good music, high drama, and other forms of elite culture. This issue of elite culture versus popular or mass culture has on occasion stirred debate in the highest political, educational, religious, and legal circles of the nation. The fact is, however, that the mass media in America, no matter how often they are criticized, denounced, or attacked, continue to emphasize unsophisticated presentations, popular culture, and content in low taste. The question is *why* is this the case, and how does such an emphasis continue to contribute to the stability of our national systems of mass communication? To place these questions in perspective, we turn to the structural functional paradigm. We will show that the media in American society constitutes a deeply institutionalized system that serves critical needs of the society. For that reason it cannot easily be changed in any significant way.

THE LONG HISTORY OF THE PROBLEM

Long before the mass media were invented, Plato may have provided the opening round in the controversy over the social costs and benefits of mass culture. In his commentary on the training of the children who were to become the leaders of his ideal Republic, he saw the mass culture of his day as posing a threat to the minds of the young:

> Then shall we simply allow our children to listen to any stories that anyone happens to make up, and so receive into their minds ideas often the very opposite of those we shall think they ought to have when they are grown up?
> No, certainly not [replies Glaucon].
> It seems, then, our first business will be to supervise the making of fables and legends, rejecting all which are unsatisfactory; and we shall induce nurses and mothers to tell their children only those which we have approved. . . . Most of the stories now in use must be discarded.[1]

This theme—popular entertainment is harmful to the minds of the young—has been a consistent one from the beginnings of mass communication. It has been claimed from time to time that such charges can be validated by scientific evidence, but repeatedly this evidence has turned out to be difficult to interpret and therefore controversial.[2] Social scientists insist that any important conclusions about the effects of the media be supported by solid evidence. Because of such insistence upon data rather than emotion, they sometimes find themselves in the awkward position of seeming to defend the media when actually they are simply refusing to accept the inadequately supported claims of critics.

Nevertheless, the insistence that conclusions be based on adequate evidence has never deterred the literary critic from charging the media with a deep responsibility for society's problems. Most nineteenth-century American writers at some point in their careers took time to criticize and condemn the newspaper for superficiality and distortion. The following excerpts from the pens of well-known and influential literary figures are samples of the climate of opinion prevailing among the literati during the time when the mass newspaper was diffusing through the American society:

> *Henry David Thoreau* (written just prior to 1850):
> The penny-post is, commonly an institution through which you seriously offer a man that penny for his thoughts which is so safely

offered in jest. And I am sure that I have never read any memorable news in a newspaper. If we read of one man robbed, or murdered, or killed by accident, or one house burned, or one vessel wrecked, or one steamboat blown up, or one cow run over on the Western Railroad, or one mad dog killed, or one lot of grasshoppers in the winter—we never need read of another. If you are acquainted with the principle, what do you care for a myriad instances and applications? To a philosopher all news, as it is called, is gossip, and they who read it and edit it are old women over their tea.[3]

Samuel Clemens (written in 1873):
That awful power, the public opinion of this nation, is formed and molded by a horde of ignorant self-complacent simpletons who failed at ditching and shoemaking and fetched up in journalism on their way to the poorhouse.[4]

Stephen Crane (written about 1895):
A newspaper is a collection of half-injustices
Which, bawled by boys from mile to mile,
Spreads its curious opinion
To a million merciful and sneering men,
While families cuddle the joys of the fireside
When spurred by tale of lone agony.

A newspaper is a court
Where everyone is kindly and unfairly tried
By a squalor of honest men.

A newspaper is a market
Where wisdom sells it freedom
And melons are crowned by the crowd.

A newspaper is a game
Where his error scores the player victory,
While another's skill wins death.

A newspaper is a symbol;
It is a feckless life's chronicle,
A collection of loud tales
Concentrating eternal stupidities,
That in remote ages lived unhaltered,
Roaming through a fenceless world.[5]

One remarkable aspect of these statements is that you could simply substitute the word "television" for "newspapers" and obtain a rather parallel version of the hostility and attacks directed primarily at television by critics today.

THE BASICS OF FUNCTIONAL ANALYSIS

The *tenacity* and *stability* of the mass media generally in the face of such a long history of criticism by powerful voices needs explanation. The problem at first seems deceptively simple: the media appeal to the masses, and the masses want the kind of content they get, and so the media continue to give it to them.

Many social scientists, such as Skornia,[6] have exposed the inadequacy of this explanation by noting the old chicken-and-egg problem. It is difficult at best to know if the public taste determines the media fare or if the media fare determines public taste. The answer probably lies somewhere in between, with public taste being both a cause and effect of media fare. The relationship between public taste and media fare thus becomes a circular one which, in terms of the chicken–egg analogy, is an ongoing process of chickens producing eggs and eggs producing chickens.

A promising approach to understanding the relationship between mass media content and public taste, and for accounting in part for the remarkable continuity of the (low) cultural level of media content, is provided by the *structural functional* paradigm. Such an analysis begins by viewing the media as *social systems* that operate within a specific external system—the set of social and cultural conditions that is the American society itself. In certain respects, this rise of interest in the analysis of social phenomena as occurring within the boundaries of social systems represents a renewal of interest in the theoretical strategies of the past, such as those of Spencer, Tönnies, and Durkheim that will be discussed in Chapter 6.

The structural functional analysis of social systems (or "functional analysis" for short) concerns itself with the *patterns of action* exhibited by individuals or subgroups who relate themselves to one another within such systems. A social system, for this reason, is an *abstraction*—but one not too far removed from the observable and empirically verifiable behaviors of the persons who are doing the acting. The social system, then, is a complex of stable, repetitive, and patterned action that is in part a manifestation of the culture shared by the actors, and in part a manifestation of the psychological orientations of the actors (which in turn derived from that culture). The *cultural system*, the *social system*, and the *personality systems* (of the individual actors), therefore, are different kinds of abstractions made from the same basic data, namely, the overt and symbolic behaviors of individual human beings. They are equally legitimate abstractions, each providing in its own right a basis for various kinds of explanations and predictions.

Generally speaking, it may be difficult or nearly impossible to analyze or understand fully one such abstraction without some reference to the others.

Granted, however, that the term "social system" is a legitimate scientific abstraction, how does this general conceptual strategy help in understanding the mass media of communication? To answer this question, we need to set forth in greater detail exactly what is meant by the term social system, and what type of analysis it provides. To aid in providing such an explanation we turn briefly to several ideas that are important aspects of the study of social systems. One of the most important of these ideas is the concept of the "function" of some particular *repetitive phenomenon* (set of actions) within such a system; it was with questions about a particular repetitive phenomenon (the continuous production and distribution of media content in "low" cultural taste) that this chapter began. The fact that such content has long survived the gibes of influential critics was said to require explanation. One form of explanation will be provided by noting the *function* of such a repetitive phenomenon within some stable system of action. The term "function" in this context means little more than "consequence." To illustrate briefly, we might hypothesize that the repetitive practice of wearing wedding rings on the part of a given married couple has the function (consequence) of reminding them as well as others that the two are bound together by the obligations and ties that matrimony implies. This practice thereby contributes indirectly to maintaining the permanence of the marriage—the stability of that particular social system. The practice is in a sense "explained" by noting its contribution to the context within which it occurs. A comparison of a number of such systems with and without this particular item (but in other respects matched) would test the assertion.

In the above example, the social system is a relatively simple one. There are only two "components," and each of these happen to be the behavior pattern of an individual. Their patterns of action are derived both from the individual psychological makeup of the partners and from the cultural norms concerning marriage prevailing in their community, social class, and society. It is a miniature system whose stability is dependent upon satisfaction of its "needs." For example, such a system requires that the partners perform roles that meet the expectations each has of the other and the expectations the community has of married couples. This can be thought of as a "need" for adequate role performance, without which the stability of the system would be endangered. Other "needs," related to economic matters and emotional satisfactions, could also be cited.

More complex illustrations of social systems can easily be pointed to, where the "components" of the system are not the actions of individual persons but subsystems. A department store, for example, is a complex social system consisting of the actions of managerial personnel, buyers, salespersons, the clerical staff, customers, transportation workers, a janitorial team, and security employees. Each of these components is a smaller system of action within the broader system of the store itself, and it in turn is a complex system of action carried out within the context of the external social conditions of the community. In spite of the complexity, any given set of repetitive actions might be analyzed in terms of their contribution to maintaining or undermining the system's stability. Granting to employees the right to buy merchandise at discount could have the function (consequence) of maintaining their morale and loyalty and thus would contribute fairly directly to the maintenance of the system. Rigid insistence on the observance of petty rules, such as docking the pay of an employee who on rare occasions was late for work, might be disruptive of morale and loyalty, and by contributing to labor turnover it could be *dysfunctional*. Instead of contributing to the maintenance of the system, it could cause disruptions and instability. Such inductively derived conclusions would be subject to testing for validity, of course, but the functional analysis would have generated the hypothesis to be tested (an important role of theory).

STRUCTURE AND FUNCTION IN MEDIA SYSTEMS

A "functional analysis," then, focuses on some specific phenomenon occurring within a social system. It then attempts to show how this phenomenon has consequences that contribute to the stability and permanence of the system as a whole. The phenomenon may, of course, have a negative influence, and if so, it would be said to have "dysfunctions" rather than "functions." The analysis is a strategy for inducing or locating hypotheses that can be tested empirically by comparative studies or other appropriate research methods.

The analysis of social systems is extremely difficult. No infallible rules specify precisely how to locate and define the exact boundaries of a given social system, particularly if it is relatively complex. As yet, no completely agreed-upon criteria exist for establishing linkages between the components of a system, and no standard formulas can uncover the precise contribution that a given repetitive form of action makes to the stability of a system. A functional analysis of the contribution of some item to the stability of a system, then, is a procedure that is somewhat less than rigorous. But in spite of this source of potential criticism, this strategy has proved useful in our attempts to understand complex social phenomena, such as the mass media.

Low-Taste Content as a Repetitive Phenomenon

How can this type of analysis be applied to the mass media? First, we can identify that portion of the content of the mass media that is in "low" cultural taste or provides gratifications to the mass audience in such a manner that it is widely held to be potentially debasing as the "relatively persistent trait or disposition"[7] of the mass media we seek to explain. It would be difficult in practice to construct a *set of categories* under which to analyze the content of the media so that material of "low" cultural taste could be identified readily. It would be difficult, but actually it would not be impossible. Excessive violence, the portrayal of criminal techniques, horror and monster themes, open pornography, suggestive music, and dreary formula melodramas are typical categories of content that arouse the ire of critics. Considerable disagreement would probably occur as to the exact content that should be included in any given category. There would also be debates over the number of categories used. Nevertheless, it is theoretically possible to identify the content of any given medium that is *most* objected to by the largest number of critics. We will assume that given sufficient time and resources, and by use of survey techniques, preference scales, attitude-measuring instruments, and other research procedures now available, the content of any given medium could be divided roughly into something like the following three categories:

> *Low-taste content:* This would be media content that has been widely distributed and attended to by the mass audience and that has consistently aroused the ire of critics. Examples would be television crime dramas that emphasize violence; openly pornographic cable TV, videos, or motion pictures; daytime serials; confession magazines; crime comics; suggestive music; or other content that has been widely held to contribute to a lowering of taste, disruption of morals, or stimulation toward socially unacceptable conduct (whether or not such charges are true).

> *Nondebated content:* This would be media content, widely distributed and attended to, about which media critics have said very little. This category is seldom at issue in the debate over the impact of the media on the masses. Examples would be television

weather reports, some news content, music that is neither symphonic nor popular, magazines devoted to specialized interests, motion pictures using "wholesome" themes, and many others. Such content is not believed either to elevate or lower taste, and it is not seen as a threat to moral standards.

High-taste content: This would be media content sometimes widely distributed but not necessarily widely attended to. It is content that media critics feel is in better taste, morally uplifting, educational, or in some way inspiring. Examples would be serious music, sophisticated drama, political discussions, art films, or magazines devoted to political commentary. Such content is championed by critics as the opposite of low-taste material, which they see as distinctly objectionable.

Of course, the *first* of the above categories is the one to which we wish to direct most of our attention. It is the repetitive phenomenon whose contribution to the media (as a social system) needs analysis. It would also be possible to study the other two categories with somewhat parallel perspectives, but they will receive relatively little attention in the present discussion.

The Components and Boundaries of the System

We need now to begin to identify the components and boundaries of the social system within which low-taste content occurs, so that eventually the contribution it makes to the system can be inductively hypothesized.

Rather than develop a purely descriptive scheme that will apply only to a single medium, it will be more fruitful to develop a *general* conceptual scheme into which any or all media could be placed, with minor modifications in details. Such a general scheme will emphasize the similarities between media, particularly in terms of relationships between the components in the system. The general components and their relationships are outlined in Figure 5.1.

Audiences. The first major component of the social system of mass communication is the *audience.* This is an exceedingly complex component. The audience is stratified, differentiated, and interrelated in the many ways that social scientists have studied for years. Some of the major variables that play a part in determining how this component will operate within the system are the major needs and interests of audience members, the various social categories represented in an au-

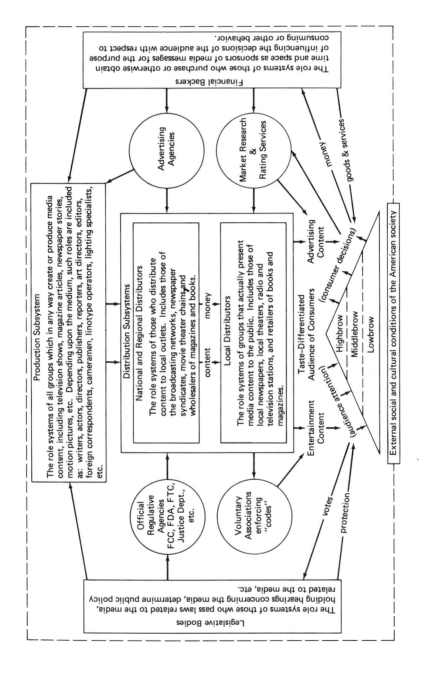

Figure 5.1. Schematic representation of the mass media as a social system.

134

dience, and the nature of the social relationships between audience members. These variables point to behavioral mechanisms that determine the patterns of attention, interpretation, and response of an audience with respect to content of a given type.

Research Organizations. The rough typology of content suggested earlier in this chapter is in some degree related to the characteristics of this audience. Organizations devoted to *research*, to measuring the preferences of media audiences, or to various forms of market research provide information to those responsible for selecting the catagories of content that will be distributed to the audience. There is a link, then, between the audience as a component in the system and the market-research/rating-service organizations as a second component. In purely theoretical terms, both components are role systems themselves and are thus actually subsystems. In a sense the link is one-way. For very minor (or usually no) personal reward, audience members selected for study provide data about themselves to such an agency, but very little flows back. This linkage between components is by comparison relatively simple.

Distributors. The content itself, of whatever type, flows from some *distributor* to the audience. The role system of the distributor component varies in detail from one medium to another. In addition, several somewhat distinct subsystems exist within this general component. First, there are local outlets, which are likely to be in the most immediate contact with the audience. The local newspaper, the local theater, and the local broadcasting station play the most immediate part in placing messages before their respective audiences. Inseparably tied to them, however, are other subsystems of this general component. Newspaper chains, syndicates, broadcasting networks, magazine and book distributors, and movie theater chains pass content on to their local outlets. The link between these two subsystems is a two-way one. The local outlet provides money, and the larger distributor supplies content. Or the linkage may be that the local outlet provides a service, and the distributor (who is paid elsewhere) provides money.

The relationship between audience and distributor seems at first to be mostly a one-way link. The distributor provides entertainment content (and often advertising), but the audience provides little back in a direct sense. However, it does provide its *attention*. In fact, it is precisely the attention of the audience that distributors are attempting to solicit. For media supported by advertising they sell this "commodity" directly to their financial backer or sponsor. In addition, the audience supplies information to the research component and this is indirectly supplied to distributors in the form of feedback so that they may gauge the amount of attention they are eliciting. The linkages between components grow more complex as we seek the boundaries of the system.

Producers and Their Sponsors. To the audience, the research, and the distributing components, we may add the role system of the *producer* of content. This component's primary link is with the *financial backer* (or *sponsor*) component and with the distributor, from whom money is obtained and for whom various forms of entertainment content are manufactured. A host of subsystems are included in this producer component, depending upon the particular medium. Examples are actors, directors, television producers, technicians, foreign correspondents, wire-service editors, film producers, labor union leaders, publishers, copy editors, clerical staff, and many, many more.

Advertising Agencies. Linking the sponsor, distributor, producer, and research organization are the *advertising agencies*. Paid primarily by the sponsor, this component provides (in return) certain ideas and services. For the most part, it provides the distributor with advertising messages. It may have links with the research component as well.

Subsystems of Control. Over this complex set of interrelated components, there are other subsystems that exert *control*. The legislative bodies, at both the state and national level, which enact regulative statutes concerning the media, constitute an important part of such a control component. Another important part of this role subsystem is the official regulative agencies, which implement the policies that have been legislated. The link between the legislative body (control component) and the audience is, of course, one of votes and public opinion, to which the component is presumably sensitive and dependent. Information lines between audience, legislative bodies, and regulatory agencies are more or less open.

To the regulatory components whose role definitions are found in legal statute can be added the private voluntary associations that develop "codes" and to some degree serve as a control over the distributors. Such distributors provide them with money, and they in turn provide surveillance and other services.

The External Conditions

The regulatory subsystems draw definitions of permissible and nonpermissible content from the general set of *external conditions* within which this extremely complicated system operates. Surrounding the entire structure as an external condition are our society's general norms concerning taste and morality, and the expressions that these find in formal law. Similar, although less likely to be incorporated into law, are our general cultural norms and beliefs regarding what will be likely to entertain or otherwise gratify Americans. Thus, we seldom see traditional Chinese opera but frequently see western "horse" opera. We seldom hear the strains of Hindu temple music but frequently hear the "strains" and other noises of the latest rock star whom teenagers admire. If our interests run to more serious fare, we are likely to hear the music of a relatively small list of European or American composers who created their works within a span of about three centuries. Or we are likely to view ballet, opera, drama, and so on, of a fairly limited number of artists whose products are defined by our society as classics or as innovative new approaches.

Each of the several media will fit into this general model of a social system in slightly different ways. A complete description of each of the media separately would be tedious. Indeed, each could well occupy the contents of an entire book. More than two decades ago Opotowsky attempted just such a detailed analysis of the television industry, although he did not use the social system concept.[8]

To add to the complexity of this conceptual scheme, it must be remembered that although each medium constitutes a somewhat separate social system in itself, the media are also related *to one another* in systematic ways. Thus, we may speak of the entire set of communication media, including those that have not been specifically analyzed in this volume, as *the mass communication system of the United States.*

The structure of this mass communication system has been heavily influenced by the general social, political, economic, and cultural conditions that were current during the period when our mass media were developing and that remain important sociocultural forces in the society within which they operate. Because of their importance for understanding our mass media as they are today, these conditions were analyzed in some detail in earlier chapters. Our free enterprise beliefs, our views of the legitimacy of the profit motive, the virtues of controlled capitalism, and our general values concerning freedom of speech constitute further *external conditions* (in addition to those related to moral limits and cultural tastes) within which the American mass communication system operates.

MAINTAINING SYSTEM STABILITY

Within the system itself, the principal *internal condition* is, of course, a financial one. Most of the components in the system are occupational role structures, which motivate their incumbent personnel primarily through money. To obtain money, they are all ultimately dependent upon the most central component of all—the audience. Unless its decisions to give attention, to purchase, to vote, and the like, are made in favorable ways, the system would undergo severe strain and would eventually collapse.

Almost any dramatic change in the behavior of the audience would cause the most severe disruption in the system for any given medium. In an earlier chapter the swift acquisition of television sets by the movie audience was plotted (Figure 4.2). The consequences of attention loss to the motion picture theater as a mass medium was shown to be severe (Figure 3.1).

Such disruptions are infrequent, but they do occur. The key to heading off dramatic changes in audience behavior is, of course, to provide entertainment content that will satisfy and motivate the largest possible number of audience members to carry out their roles in accord with the needs of the system. Such content will, in other words, *maintain the stability of the system.* The ideal, from the standpoint of the system, is content that will *capture audience members' attention, persuade them to purchase goods,* and at the same time *be sufficiently within the bounds of moral norms and standards of taste* so that unfavorable actions by the regulatory components are not provoked.

The entertainment content that seems most capable of eliciting the attention of the largest number of audience members is the more dramatic, low-taste content that makes up so much of our popular culture. Since the most central media system goal is economic profit, sex and violence or any other attention-getting and attention-maintaining content is functional in the sense that even though it may be of low taste, it maximizes the size of the audience exposed to advertisements. In general, the larger the audience, the more the distributor and producer can charge for advertising. For example, ads in prime-time television periods cost substantially more than those aired during relatively low-audience-size periods, such as early in the morning.

Many critics deplore the dependence of the American media on advertising. This view is completely understandable. For the person of refined tastes there is a great deal that is deplorable and even disgusting about advertising. Anyone who has looked up from the dinner table while watching the evening news to see vivid commercials extolling the virtues of preparations for hemorrhoids, constipation, diarrhea, underarm smells, bad breath, and other gross human afflictions is bound to have such a reaction. Those are the costs of having a media system that is funded mainly by advertising. On the other hand, the benefits of such a system need to be weighed in view of the alternatives. How else can a mass communication system be funded? Control by government would be unacceptable. Dependence on philanthropy would provide a very limited system. Pay-as-you go—as in the movie channels on cable TV—would produce an elitist system with content aimed at the more affluent.

The present system of heavy dependence on advertising produces an emphasis on content most attuned to the tastes of the lower middle class.[9] This segment of the population makes up the largest block of purchasing power in the society. It is the lower middle class that purchase most products advertised in the media. The next largest segment in terms of collective purchasing power is the level below—the skilled and semi-skilled blue-collar workers. Individually, their incomes are limited; collectively they are impressive. Together, these two levels of society represent the vast majority of people who buy the products of American manufacturers, importers, and retailers. It is little wonder, then, that the tastes of these segments of society weigh heavily among those who design media content.

A second factor accounting for the importance of these two categories of the population is that it is the lower and lower-middle segments that attend most to the media as a whole. There is a great deal of evidence to show that the relatively uneducated spend more time than the educated being exposed to the mass media.[10] It may be misleading to conclude that they do so only because they relish low-taste content. The relatively uneducated majority also have relatively low personal incomes, which probably means they have less choice than their more educated and wealthier counterparts in how they spend their nonworking hours. The mass media may be more appealing to them in large part because the media are relatively inexpensive forms of leisure. Moreover, as Baker and Ball point out, it is probably superficial to think that the only reason people in general spend time with the media is because of the inherent appeal of their content.[11] Many need fulfillments and gratifications, over and above those related to entertainment or staying informed, are provided by the media. Babysitting and companionship (even when it is electronic companionship) are examples.

When all is said and done, however, it is still true that low-taste content sells—and sells big. This fact establishes it as the key element in the social system of the media. It keeps the entire complex together by maintaining the financial stability of the system. Critics who provoke public attention by denouncing media content or by proclaiming that a causal connection exists between media content and socially undesirable behavior may temporarily receive some recognition. They may also achieve some temporary disturbance in the system, or if they are persistent enough, they may ultimately even displace some specific form of low-taste content from a given medium altogether. Examples from the past are quiz shows that were found to be "rigged," and popular disc jockeys who were receiving "payola" (a fee for repeatedly playing a song to make it popular). In such cases the audience may be temporarily disaffected. However, low-taste content comes in such a variety of forms that the temporary or even permanent absence of one minor form does not alter the major picture. Critics have been complaining about newspaper concentration on crime news for a century, yet there has been no noticeable abatement in the reporting of such stories. Critics of the soap opera may have breathed a sigh of relief years ago when these programs at last disappeared from radio. Their joy must have been short-lived when such daytime serials turned out to be quite popular with television viewers, so popular in fact that soap operas now appear during prime evening hours. Analyses of the level of violent television content show that it goes down slightly after federal government investigations on the effects of television violence or widespread campaigns by voluntary associations (e.g., the P.T.A.), only to return shortly after the public outcry has subsided.[12]

When a formula is discovered for eliciting attention and influencing purchasing decisions from any large segment of the audience, it will be abandoned by the media only with great reluctance, if at all. The broadcast ballgame, the war movie, the star comedian, the family situation comedy, the western thriller, the detective story, the adventures of the secret agent, the drama of the courtroom—all are beginning to rank with such time-honored formulas as the sob story, the funnies, the sex-murder account, the sports page, and disclosure of corruption in high places as attention-getting devices that can bring the eye or ear of the consumer nearer to the advertising message.

In short, the social system of the mass media in the United States is becoming more and more deeply established. Few future changes can be expected in the kind of content it will produce to maintain its own stability. The function of what we have called low-taste content is to maintain the finanical stability of *a deeply institutionalized social system that is tightly integrated with the whole of American social institutions.* The probability that our system of mass communication in this respect can be drastically altered by the occasional outbursts of critics seems small indeed.

If change does occur, future developments in the nature of the mass media are not likely to be simple. A basic principle of Emile Durkheim (see Chapter 6) is that as organisms or systems grow, they are likely to become more differentiated or complex.[13] Taking this assumption and combining it with the enormous technological advances in electronic communications' technology witnessed in recent years, it may be hypothesized that media systems will become more specialized. Some media organizations, for example, might specialize in low-taste content, others in knowledge and technical information, others in news content, and still others in high-taste content. Such technological developments as satellite and cable television, computer networks, and videotex already are making such specialization possible. In a later chapter we will present a brief examination of such technological developments and consider how they, along with changes in the economic system, may bring about significant alterations of the content and structure of mass media systems.

NOTES

1. *The Republic of Plato*, trans. Frances M. Cornford (London: Oxford University Press, 1954), pp. 68–69.
2. Examples of such claims are Herbert Blumer and Philip Hauser, *Movies, Delinquency and Crime* (New York: Macmillan, 1933), and Frederick C. Wertham, *Seduction of the Innocent* (New York: Rinehart, 1954). The latter is a bitter denunciation of comic books.
3. Henry David Thoreau, *Walden, Or Life in the Woods* (Boston and New York: Houghton Mifflin, 1854), 2:148–49.
4. Samuel Clemens, *Mark Twain's Speeches* (New York: Harper & Brothers, 1923), p. 47.
5. Quoted in Milton Ellis, Louise Pond, and George W. Spohn, *A College Book of American Literature* (New York: American Book, 1939), 1:704.
6. Harry J. Skornia, "Television and the News: A Critical Appraisal," in *Mass Media and Mass Man*, ed. Alan Casty, 2nd ed. (New York: Holt, Rinehart & Winston, 1973), pp. 214–24.
7. Carl G. Hempel, "The Logic of Functional Analysis," in *Symposium on Sociological Theory*, ed. Llewellyn Gross (New York: Harper & Brothers, 1959), p. 280.
8. Stan Opotowsky, *T.V.: The Big Picture* (New York: Collier Books, 1962).
9. Melvin L. DeFleur and Everette E. Dennis, *Understanding Mass Communications*, 3rd ed. (Boston: Houghton Mifflin, 1988), pp. 500–501.
10. See, for example, Bradley S. Greenberg, "The Content and Context of Violence in the Mass Media," in *Violence and the Media*, ed. Robert K. Baker and Sandra J. Ball (Washington, D.C.: Government Printing Office, 1969), pp. 423–49.
11. Baker and Ball, *Violence and the Media*, pp. 330–33.
12. Ibid., pp. 151–59.
13. Emile Durkheim, *The Division of Labor in Society*, trans. George Simpson (New York: Free Press of Glencoe, 1964).

PART II
The Effects of Mass Communication

CHAPTER 6

Mass Society and the Magic Bullet Theory

Our previous chapters have traced the development of human communication from ancient times to the present. We have suggested that human beings passed through several distinctive communication stages in their evolutionary progression. At an ever-increasing pace they moved from the age of signs and signals to successive stages in which speech and language were acquired. Eventually they acquired the ability to write, then print, and finally to conquer both time and distance in our present age of sophisticated mass media.

An important conclusion about those transitions was that each had significant "effects." That is, each brought major alterations in both human thought at the individual level and cultural development at the collective level. Just as the development of speech gave our primitive ancestors an enormous advantage over earlier human beings, the successive emergence of writing, print, and contemporary mass communication gave people of the relevant eras advantages over their predecessors. Thus, as each age merged into the next, human thought became more sophisticated and culture increasingly complex.

The process of technological, social, and cultural evolution is by no means at an end. We continue to develop our technology, and our ability to communicate is extended by those advances. In previous chapters we traced the manner in which each of our principal media has been based on a continuously evolving mastery of scientific principles and practical applications. These made possible an incredible number of devices that altered the way we communicate. They ranged

145

from Gutenberg's printing press to the latest satellite television network. Obviously, from a technological standpoint, the mass media will continue in a process of development.

At the same time, societies themselves undergo continuous modification. They are not completely stable social systems; the ways of the past shape the social patterns of the future. But the grip of tradition is not rigid in modern urban-industrial societies. Innovations are adopted; conflicts emerge and are resolved; fads and fashions rise and fall; social movements bring fresh perspectives; social problems develop and are addressed; and the social order is modified by each of these influences. No generation is just like the one that preceded it, either psychologically or in terms of social characteristics.

Because both the technology of communication and the social order are in constant processes of modification, there is every reason to suspect that the influences of mass media on society will not be the same from one point in time to another. Therefore it is difficult to describe regularities or to develop explanations about the effects of mass communication that will be valid for all citizens at all times. Yet the essence of science is that it seeks lasting verities. Scientific research is aimed at describing orderly relationships among phenomena and developing explanations of how some events influence or cause others to produce patterns and regularities. In other words, science searches for unchanging principles. Obviously, this is not an easy task in the case of the effects of mass communication on people because of the evolving nature of the media on the one hand and the society on the other.

In spite of these difficulties, scholars have from the beginning of the age of mass communication sought to understand the influences of media on their audiences. The result of this search has been a series of formulations that attempt to describe, explain, and predict what will happen when given categories of people are exposed to specific forms of message content via particular media of mass communication.

The remaining chapters of this book will present a brief review of those formulations. It is not an easy task. The development of theory in mass communication did not follow an orderly plan. In fact, what we have today emerged from a chaotic and uncoordinated search for different kinds of principles conducted by scholars from different disciplines who were investigating the effects of mass communication for different purposes.

Perhaps the only unifying link among the various explanations that constitute our intellectual heritage in the study of mass communication is that each of the major theories is grounded, directly or indirectly, in basic conceptions of the human individual or the social order that have been supplied by the several social sciences. Thus, we have theories of media influence based on psychological, sociological, and anthropological paradigms. To those can be added the contributions of the historian, the economist, the political scientist, and the legal scholar—all of whom have made contributions to our contemporary understanding of mass communication.

Even though explanations of the influence of mass communications are grounded in the general paradigms of the social sciences, the lines of influence between the two have by no means been perfectly clear.[1] Often, media scholars reinvent the wheel when they do not realize that a particular form of behavior has been studied for decades in the social sciences. On the other hand, social scientists have often blithely ignored the role of mass communication as they pursue paradigms that relate symbols, communication, the social order, and individual behavior. Nevertheless, the lines of influence are there, even if they are sometimes difficult to trace out. For present purposes it is important to show some of the ways in which students of mass communication have been influenced by more general paradigms concerning the psychological and sociological nature of human beings. Even though this influence has sometimes been unwitting and indirect, tracing out these linkages can clarify in part why media scholars have concentrated on the particular concepts, topics, and issues that make up the body of mass communication theory of both the past and present.

This chapter looks specifically at the earliest formulations that characterized thinking about the influences of mass communication. Even though those formulations are now regarded as obsolete, they have a great importance beyond that of being mere historical curiosities. They help us understand the theories of mass communication that followed and replaced the initial formulations. The second and third generation of mass communication theories—which will be addressed in later chapters—were in many ways reactions against the postulates of the earliest formulations, and to understand today's explanations it is necessary to start at the beginning.

During the first decades of this century the media were in their infancy. Even so, the public was alarmed about what these new forms of communication—daily newspapers, moving pictures, and radio broadcasts—were doing to them, their children, and their neighbors. It was at that time that sociological theories of the nature of society were emphasizing the concept of the *mass* as a form of impersonal human relationships that characterized the emerging urban-industrial social order.

It was from such thinking that we obtained conceptions of the *mass* society and, consequently, *mass* communication. Our first task, therefore, is to understand the origins and nature of this foundation concept.

THE EVOLUTIONARY PARADIGM AND THE CONCEPT OF MASS SOCIETY

Society is large and organized. It also seems to grow more complex. These two elementary observations were the foundations upon which the systems of thought of the founders of sociology were developed. Speculation about the nature of the social order—the manner in which it is changing or how it might be improved—had been the subject of philosophical writing since the beginning of recorded human experience. However, the founding of sociology as a systematic discipline devoted specifically to the study of societal processes did not take place until the first half of the nineteenth century, at about the same time that Benjamin Day started selling his newspaper on the streets of New York for a penny a copy.

Comte's Conception of the Collective Organism

Auguste Comte is usually credited with giving the new field its name, and he also advocated the application of the Positive (Scientific) Method to the study of society. Comte's major contributions to the task of studying social phenomena scientifically were more philosophical than substantive. Nevertheless, he did include in his voluminous writings an *organic conception of society*, which was widely used by pioneer sociologists.

The concept of society as organism was not original with Comte, but he made it a fundamental postulate. The significance of this idea is that important consequences follow from it. In simple terms, society can be thought of as a particular type of organism, namely a *collective organism*. This did not mean for Comte that there is just a rough analogy between the organization of some individual biological organism, such as a particular plant or animal, and a human society. Comte assumed that society was an organism in its own right. He saw that it had structure, that specialized parts functioned together, that the whole was something more than the sum of its parts, and that it underwent evolutionary change. These characteristics were those of organisms in general, and so society could be properly classified as such, with the recognition that it clearly differed from other specific varieties of organisms.

The Role of Specialization. Comte marveled at the great diversity of tasks, goals, and functions that characterized a society and commented on how each individual and group can seem to be pursuing private ends and yet the overall result is that of a harmoniously functioning system. One of the basic principles of the organization of society (as organism) that accounts for this situation interested him greatly. That principle was *specialization*. The division of functions that people voluntarily assume, he felt, was the key not only to the continued stability of society but also to its possible disorganization.

> The main cause of the superiority of the social to the individual organism is, according to an established law, the more marked specialty of the various functions fulfilled by organs more and more distinct, but interconnected; so that the unity of aim is more and more combined with diversity of means. We cannot, of course, fully appreciate a phenomenon which is forever proceeding before our eyes, and in which we bear a part; but if we withdraw ourselves in thought from the social system, and contemplate it as from afar, can we conceive of a more marvellous spectacle, in the whole range of natural phenomena, than the regular and constant convergence of an innumerable multitude of human beings, each possessing a distinct and, in a certain degree, independent existence, and yet incessantly disposed, amidst all their discordance of talent and character, to concur in many ways in the same general development, without concert, and even consciousness on the part of most of them, who believe that they are merely following their personal impulses? . . . This reconciliation of the individuality of labour with cooperation of endeavors, which becomes more remarkable as society grows more complex and extended, constitutes the radical character of human operations [at the societal level].[2]

Comte saw great harmony and stability, then, arising from the assumption of specialized functions by individuals. He felt that inevitably these specialized activities would all contribute to the general equilibrium of society in that "all individual organizations, even the most vicious and imperfect (short of monstrosity), may finally be made use of for the general good."[3]

The Consequences of Overspecialization. Comte also saw danger in too much specialization. It should be added that this point is of considerable significance for the student of mass communication, because the same idea was used by later theorists to develop the concept of the *mass society*, a concept that was of central importance for early thinking about the media. The most important element of this idea was that ineffective social organization failed to provide adequate linkages between individuals to maintain an integrated and stable system of social control. This theme is clearly stated by Comte:

> Some economists have pointed out, but in a very inadequate way, the evils of an exaggerated division of material labour, and I have indicated, in regard to the more important field of scientific labour, the mischievous intellectual consequences of the spirit of specialty which at present prevails. It is necessary to estimate directly the principle of such an influence, in order to understand the object of the spontaneous system of requisites for the continuous preservation of society. In decomposing, we always disperse; and the distribution of human labours must occasion individual divergencies, both intellectual and moral, which require a permanent discipline to keep them within bounds. If the separation of the social functions develops a useful spirit of detail, on the one hand, it tends, on the other, to extinguish or restrict what we call the aggregate or general spirit.[4]

Comte went on to discuss extensively and critically the possible consequences of an overexpansion of the division of labor. He felt that the more that individuals were unlike one another in their position in the social system, the greater would be their reduction of understanding of other people. He saw that people with the same specialty would develop ties with each other but would become alienated from other such groupings. "Thus it is that the principle by which alone general society could be developed and extended, threatens, in another view, to decompose it into a multitude of unconnected corporations, which almost seem not to belong to the same species."[5]

As the societal organism evolves (according to this paradigm), it develops harmony and stability through its division of labor. At the same time, there is the possibility that overdevelopment can lead to disorganization and decline by disrupting the basis for effective communication between individual parts of the organism. Given the postulate of the organic nature of society, the concept of specialization of function follows by definition. But an increasing degree of such specialization leads to increased social differentiation. If such differentiation reaches the point where effective linkages between parts of the system are threatened, then the equilibrium and harmony of the organism are also threatened. This theme recurs in the writings of later theorists and is one of the *basic beginning points for discussing "mass" society*. The relationship between this idea and "mass" communication will be made clear.

It should be recalled that Comte worked out his views of the nature of society during the 1830s, before the industrial revolution had achieved a wide impact on Europe. Comte felt somewhat threatened by the possibility of an increasing level of specialization in the society he saw before him. But social theorists who came later were confronted with the *reality* of a great increase in the division of labor as a result of the new industrialization. It is little wonder they were deeply impressed with its implications.

Spencer's Organic Analogy

Speculation about the organic nature of society and its consequences constituted only a minor part of the work of Comte. The second founder of modern sociology, Herbert Spencer, pursued the organic concept with great vigor and in great depth. Spencer, like Comte, was primarily a philosopher and was concerned about science as a means for obtaining valid knowledge. This concern led him to formulate what he thought were the most important principles that seemed to him to pervade all the sciences. His famous *laws of evolution* (from which Darwin drew inspiration) were given complete development in his work *First Principles,* published in 1863, more than twenty years after Comte had completed his *Positive Philosophy.*

Spencer applied his evolutionary concepts to the study of society and wrote *The Principles of Sociology* in four volumes between 1876 and 1896. There are many parallels between the two writers, but Spencer claims that his own ideas were worked out independently of those of Comte. In any case, the theory of society that Spencer elaborated in great detail was a purely organic one. After defining society as a functioning system, he discussed the social order at length in terms of its growth, structures, functions, systems of organs, and so on, developing an extremely elaborate analogy between society and an individual organism.

The division of labor was a very important part of this analysis and was regarded as the basic unifying factor which held the organism together:

> The division of labour, first dwelt upon by political economists as a social phenomenon, and thereupon recognized by biologists as a phenomenon of living bodies, which they called the "physiological division of labour," is that which in the society, as in the animal, makes it a living whole. Scarcely can I emphasize enough the truth that in respect of this fundamental trait, a social organism and an individual organism are entirely alike. . . .
>
> [Society] undergoes continuous growth. As it grows, its parts become unlike: it exhibits increase of structure. The unlike parts simultaneously assume activities of unlike kinds. These activities are not simply different, but their differences are so related as to make one

another possible. The reciprocal aid thus given causes mutual dependence on the parts. And the mutually dependent parts, living by and
for one another, form an aggregate constituted on the same general
principle as an individual organism.[6]

But Spencer did not go to the next step and contemplate the possible
difficulties for society that might occur if specialization went too far. He
was convinced that the most fundamental process of nature was evolution and that evolution was natural and therefore good. The great
changes he observed in English society, as the industrial order came, he
regarded as an unfolding of society according to natural evolutionary
laws. To suggest that social changes brought by natural evolution might
be undesirable was unthinkable. So deeply did he hold these views that
he became convinced that any interference in the natural development
of society was completely unwarranted and was bound to have disastrous consequences. He bitterly opposed legislation aimed at any form
of social improvement on the grounds that nature meant the fittest to
survive and that in the long run society would benefit. While Comte
advocated planned social change, Spencer argued vigorously for a
policy of almost complete *laissez-faire*.

Even so, it can be seen that the two major founders of sociology
developed similar organic evolutionary models of the social order and
that both postulated a process leading to increasing social differentiation. The one had grave reservations as to the possible consequences of
overspecialization, and the other had grave reservations over any attempt to interfere in what he regarded as the natural evolution of the
society. Neither had any full appreciation of the fundamental changes
in the structure of the social order that were to come with the twentieth
century. Comte, writing on the eve of the industrial revolution, and
Spencer, writing during its early phases, could not foresee that the very
fabric of society would be changed by the upheaval in the economic
institution that the factory system and the new economic order would
bring. The same acceleration in science that brought the mass media of
communication, and indeed that prompted these two philosophers to
found a science of society, also fashioned the forces of society's new
industrial organization. The impact of this new order was to be felt in
every corner of the world.

Tönnies' Theory of Social Bonds

Another important theoretical formulation came from the province of
Schleswig-Holstein in Germany. In 1887 a young man of that region by
the name of Ferdinand Tönnies produced a theoretical sociological

analysis entitled *Gemeinschaft und Gesellschaft*. In this work he posed two contrasting types of societal organization—one preindustrial and the other largely a product of industrialization. In his analysis of the nature of society, Tönnies concentrated less on organic analogies, or the possible consequences of specialization, and focused his attention on the kinds of social bonds that exist between the members of societies and groups in two very distinct types of social organization.

Gemeinschaft versus Gesellschaft. The term *Gemeinschaft* does not translate easily into English. The word "community" is often offered as its equivalent, but the complexity of Tönnies' meaning is not well captured by such a simple translation. The idea of Gemeinschaft is best illustrated by suggesting some of the kinds of interpersonal ties that are included within it. The bonds and feelings that exist between the members of a normal family offer one example, but the idea goes beyond the bounds of family. The members of a particular village or even of a given small society can be said to be characterized by Gemeinschaft. This type of relationship can develop because people are related to each other by blood and hold each other in mutual respect; it can be produced because people are tied by tradition to a particular place where they lead a deeply integrated life; there can even be a Gemeinschaft of the mind, as when members of a religious order share a deep commitment to a given set of beliefs that become a basis for a strong social organization. The Gemeinschaft organization, in short, is one in which people are strongly bound to one another through tradition, through kinship, through friendship, or because of some other socially cohesive factor. Such a social organization places the individual within the nexus of exceedingly strong systems of informal social control. In short, Gemeinschaft refers to a "reciprocal, binding sentiment .... which keeps human beings together as members of a totality."[7] That totality may be a family, a clan, a village, a religious order, or even an entire society, but it has as a basis for its common unity this particular kind of social relationship among its members.

It is clear that there probably have been few societies whose social bonds were based completely on such intense feelings of "community" in the sense of Gemeinschaft. However, even as an abstract construction, this "ideal type" can serve as a framework for discussing changes in social organization and new kinds of linkages between members that take place if the society evolves into some other form. For example, under the impact of industrialization, when the division of labor becomes vastly more complex through increasing specialization, is there a decline in Gemeinschaft? Tönnies saw his own homeland undergo a transition from a basically agrarian society to one that was increasingly urban and industrial. While he did not suggest that societal evolution was simply a movement from Gemeinschaft in social relations to some other form, it was clear to him that another constructed polar type was going to be increasingly important to describe adequately an entirely different system of social relationships betwen the members of the newer society.

The second of his theoretical constructs was *Gesellschaft*. The essential condition of the social relationship in the Gesellschaft is the contract. The contract in its broadest sense is a rationally agreed upon voluntary social relationship in which the two parties promise to fulfill specific obligations to each other or to forfeit specific commodities if the contract is breached. Whereas the contract is a formal relationship (often written, and always backed by impersonal mechanisms of social control), the social relationship of the Gemeinschaft is informal. In the new society of complex credit, world markets, large formal associations, and a vast division of labor, the contractual relationship is widely found between members. The buyer and seller relate themselves in this way, as do the employer and employee. In fact, throughout all the major social institutions, the economic order, the political structure, the educational system, religion, and even in some instances the family, the older Gemeinschaft bond, based upon "reciprocal, binding sentiment," is being replaced by relationships of the contractual type. In certain spheres of social exchange, it is almost the exclusive kind of relationship that can exist between two parties (e.g., buying or renting a dwelling). In some spheres it may seldom be found (e.g., within the family).

While no society has been or probably ever will be exclusively Gesellschaft, it is clear that this type of social bond has become ubiquitous and pervasive. It is also clear that Gesellschaft implies a very different outlook for individuals as they contemplate societal members than is the case in the Gemeinschaft.

> In the Gesellschaft . . . everybody is by himself and isolated, and there exists a condition of tension against all others. Their spheres of activity are sharply separated, so that everybody refuses to everyone else contact with and admittance to his sphere; i.e., intrusions are regarded as hostile acts. Such a negative attitude toward one another becomes the normal and always underlying relation of those power-endowed individuals, and it characterizes the Gesellschaft in the condition of the rest; nobody wants to grant and produce anything for another individual, nor will he be inclined to give ungrudgingly to another individual, if it be not in exchange for a gift or labor equivalent that he considers at least equal to what he has given.[8]

The Impersonal and Anonymous Society. The Gesellschaft, then, places the individual within a social system that is impersonal and anonymous. It is a situation where individuals are not treated or valued for their personal qualities, but where they are appreciated to the degree that they can uphold their end of contracted obligations. The Gesellschaft is a system of competitive relationships where individuals seek to maximize what they get from exchanges and minimize what they give, at the same time learning to be wary of others.

The reader will recognize that these two pictures of societal organization have been deliberately overdrawn for theoretical purposes. Nevertheless, the Gemeinschaft and Gesellschaft polarity does provide a very useful framework for interpreting the impact of changing social conditions upon the citizen of the emerging industrial order. The Gemeinschaft could easily be idealized as psychologically comforting and supporting, while the Gesellschaft could easily be condemned as psychologically distressing and tension producing. Such interpretations abound in literature, in popular thought, and even in social science, where the simpler Gemeinschaft life of an earlier or more rural society is identified as "good" while the impersonal Gesellschaft of the urban area is defined as "evil." But while many have speculated in these directions, our present task is to extract from such nineteenth-century writers as Tönnies ideas that were to influence those who turned their attentions to assessing the impact of the new media of communication on society. Just as an accumulation of theories and inventions in the natural sciences led to the physical basis upon which the media themselves were developed, the accumulation of sociological thought concerning the nature of the contemporary social order provided the basis of ideas upon which interpretations of the media were first attempted when they became realities.

Durkheim's Analysis of the Division of Labor

Before pulling together the various concepts we have examined into some kind of composite theoretical image of society as it was viewed by the end of the nineteenth century, there is one additional writer whose ideas were of particular significance. Near the end of the period (1893) Emile Durkheim published *The Division of Labor in Society*. In this important work he brought together the several related themes we have noted above from the writings of Comte, Spencer, and Tönnies.[9]

Mechanical versus Organic Solidarity. The overall purpose of Durkheim's extended analysis was to show how the division of labor of a society was the principal source of *social solidarity* in that society, and that as the division of labor was altered (as, for example, through social evolution), the unifying forces of the society underwent corresponding change. Solidarity refers to the kinds of social psychological bonds that unite the members, and although Durkheim used a very different terminology, he was addressing himself roughly to the same general problem as did Tönnies. By division of labor Durkheim meant more than simply the degree of specialization in the economic institution:

> (We must ask) if the division of labor . . . in contemporary societies where it has developed as we know . . . would not have as its function the integration of the social body to assure unity. It is quite legitimate to suppose . . . that great political societies can maintain themselves in equilibrium only thanks to the specialization of tasks, that the division of labor is the source, if not unique, at least principal, of social solidarity. Comte took this point of view. Of all sociologists, to our knowledge, he is the first to have recognized in the division of labor something other than a purely economic phenomenon. He saw in it "the most essential condition of social life," provided that one conceives it "in all its rational extent; that is to say, that one applies it to the totality of all our diverse operations of whatever kind, instead of attributing it, as is ordinarily done, to simple material usages."[10]

To show the social implications of the division of labor, Durkheim contrasted *mechanical* and *organic* solidarity. Mechanical solidarity is that which unites a people who are essentially alike. Through their common life, and in the presence of only a rudimentary division of labor, the members of a given population work out a set of beliefs, values, and other orientations to which they are deeply, commonly, and uniformly committed. To the extent that these orientations are truly characteristic of every member, there is little basis for the development of extensive individuality. Where there is little or no division of labor, people not only act in like ways, Durkheim suggested, but also think and feel in like ways. In this kind of society, "solidarity can grow only in inverse ratio to personality," because personality is what distinguishes one person from another. "If we have a strong and lively desire to think and act for ourselves, we cannot be strongly inclined to think and act as others do."[11] In the extreme case, *all* individuality would be submerged, and the members of the society would be completely *homogeneous* in their personal psychic organization. In such an admittedly theoretical case, the members of the society would be completely uniform in their action.

> The social molecules which can be coherent in this way can act together only in the measure that they have no actions of their own, as

the molecules of inorganic bodies. That is why we propose to call this type of solidarity mechanical. The term does not signify that it is produced by mechanical and artificial means. We call it that only by analogy to the cohesion which unites the elements of an inanimate body, as opposed to that which makes a unity out of the elements of a living body.[12]

It is perfectly obvious that no society was ever characterized completely by this kind of social organization. The idea of mechanical solidarity as a basis for binding members of a collectivity to the whole is posed in this way as an abstract construct rather than a description that is supposed to portray reality with complete accuracy. The same can be said of Durkheim's second major concept, organic solidarity. The two taken together, however, offer a third useful interpretive framework in understanding the emergence of modern society.

If mechanical solidarity is based upon *homogeneity*, then organic solidarity is based on *heterogeneity*. In a society with a well-developed division of labor, all persons performing specialized tasks are dependent on others whose activities are coordinated with theirs. Spencer had elaborated in extraordinary detail the parallels between organisms and society as unified systems of reciprocally functioning parts. Durkheim saw the mutual dependency that specialization produced, and he recognized this as a kind of social force that bound the members of a society together to form a more or less harmonious functioning whole. But the important factor is that the division of labor, which produces organic solidarity, also greatly increases the degree of individuality and *social differentiation* within the society:

> Whereas the previous type (of solidarity) implies that individuals resemble each other, this type presumes their difference. The first is possible only insofar as the individual personality is absorbed into the collective personality; the second is possible only if each one has a sphere of action which is peculiar to him; that is a personality. It is necessary, then, that the collective conscience leave open a part of the individual conscience in order that special functions may be established there, functions which it cannot regulate. The more this region is extended, the stronger is the cohesion which results from this solidarity.[13]

Psychological Isolation. Durkheim went on to show how the growth of the division of labor increases the dependence of each specialized person on the rest, but this does not mean that such increasing heterogeneity leads to consensus of thought. On the contrary: "Each individual is more and more acquiring his own way of thinking and acting, and submits less completely to the common corporate union."[14] Thus, while in one sense highly specialized persons are locked into a web of functional dependency upon others, they are at the same time isolated in a psychological sense as specializations lead them to develop greater and greater individuality.

Durkheim also noted that the evolution of society to a more complex form leads to an increase in social relationships of much the same type that Tönnies called Gesellschaft: "It is quite true that contractual relations, which were originally rare or completely absent, multiply as social labor becomes divided."[15] Thus, an increase in the division of labor has the result not only of increasing individual heterogeneity, but of introducing an increasing number of more formal and segmental relationships between people.

Anomie. Finally, Durkheim saw that under some circumstances the division of labor could result in what he called "pathological forms." "Though normally," he said, "the division of labor produces social solidarity, it sometimes happens that it has different, and even contrary results."[16] If social functions, that is, parts of the organic structure, are not well articulated with each other, organic solidarity can break down. Commercial crises, depressions, strife between labor and management, civil upheavals, riots, demonstrations, and protests by subgroups offer various examples.

Thus, the very division of labor that produces harmony up to a point contains the seeds of social disharmony if pushed beyond a certain point. This, of course, was (as Durkheim noted) the thesis of Auguste Comte. Such a state of disharmony Durkheim called *anomie*. This is a pathology of the social organism that results when the division of labor becomes elaborated to a point where individuals are not capable of effectively relating themselves to others.

> Functional diversity induces a moral diversity that nothing can prevent, and it is inevitable that one should grow as the other does. We know, moreover, why these two phenomena develop in parallel fashion. Collective sentiments become more and more important in holding together the centrifugal tendencies that the division of labor is said to engender, for these tendencies increase as labor is more divided, and, at the same time, collective sentiments are weakened.[17]

In short, as society becomes more and more complex—as the members of the society become more and more preoccupied with their own individual pursuits and development—they lose ability to identify with and feel themselves in community with others. Eventually they become a collectivity of psychologically isolated individuals, interacting with one another but oriented inward, and bound together primarily through contractual ties.

THE EMERGENCE OF THE THEORY OF MASS SOCIETY

As the nineteenth century came to a close, the image of society that had emerged was that it was changing from a traditional and stable social system in which people were closely tied to each other into one of greater complexity in which individuals were socially isolated. The developing and accumulating body of sociological theory, uncoordinated and even conflicting though it was, seemed in one way or another to stress those themes. Society was a large and complex system and it was growing even more complex. To some this complexity represented Progress via natural laws of evolution to a more desirable and ultimately more harmonious system than before. To others it represented an insidious movement to a bleak and isolated existence for the individual, narrowly concerned with special pursuits, and incapable of intense identification with others. Great debates arose concerning the advisability of interfering with the evolution of society through legislation. Other arguments arose concerning the best possible strategy for proceeding with the further development of theories about these vast changes. In spite of these divergent points of view over strategies and consequences, however, it seemed clear to most students of the social order that the Western world was experiencing an increase in heterogeneity and individuality, a reduction in the degree to which society could effectively control its members through informal means, an increasing alienation of the individual from strong identification with the community as a whole, a growth of segmental, contractual social relationships, and a great increase in the psychological isolation of the human being.

These general social trends were said to be leading to the *mass society*. The idea of mass society is not equivalent to *massive society*, that is, to large numbers. There are many societies in the world, such as India, that have astronomical numbers of people but are still more or less traditional in their organization. Mass society refers to the relationship that exists between individuals and the social order around them. In mass society, as has been emphasized in the theories we have examined: (1) individuals are presumed to be in a situation of psychological isolation from others, (2) impersonality is said to prevail in their interactions with others, and (3) they are said to be relatively free from the demands of binding informal social obligations. These ideas have been carried by some sociologists well into the twentieth century and are still important considerations, along with a number of modifications and countertrends.[18] In discussing the organization of the urban industrial social order of the contemporary Western world, Broom and Selznick have summarized the principal outlines of the idea of mass society very succinctly in the following terms:

> Modern society is made up of masses in the sense that "there has emerged a vast mass of segregated, isolated individuals, interdependent in all sorts of specialized ways yet lacking in any central unifying value or purpose." The weakening of traditional bonds, the growth of rationality, and the division of labor, have created societies made up of individuals who are only loosely bound together. In this sense the word "mass" suggests something closer to an aggregate than to a tightly knit social group.[19]

This view of the *social* nature of human beings was coupled with equally developed general paradigms of their *psychological* nature. Briefly, human conduct was, according to neurobiological and comparative approaches, largely a product of genetic endowment. That is, the causes of behavior were sought within biological structure. This line of thought was to have important implications for the early interpretation of the new mass media. The nature of these general psychological paradigms and their importance in interpreting the mass media will be made clear in later sections.

MASS SOCIETY AND THE MAGIC BULLET THEORY

It was against this intellectual backdrop that the mass media of communication diffused through the major Western societies during their early years. To assess the influence that such general interpretations of the "nature of human nature" had upon some of the early thinking about the media, we need to look briefly at the period when mass communication was still a relatively new social phenomenon with which the world had to contend.

Wartime Propaganda and Beliefs of Media Power

The first decade of the twentieth century had barely passed before Europe and later the United States were plunged into the Great War. The very division of labor and the resulting heterogeneity and individuality that had made the new industrial societies possible now became a problem. World War I was really the first of the global struggles in which entire populations played active and coordinated roles in the effort against their enemies. In most previous wars, the opposing military forces carried on their struggles somewhat independently of civilian populations. Unless combat happened to take place in their immediate area, the people left at home were not deeply and personally involved. This had been particularly true of England, which had not been occupied by an enemy since the Norman invasion. It was also true of the United States, which had last known foreign soldiers on its shores during Revolutionary times, although the Civil War had brought great hardships in some areas.

This new kind of war was, in effect, a pitting of the manufacturing capacity of one nation against that of the other, and the armies in the field were backed by and totally dependent upon vast industrial complexes at home. These huge industrial efforts required the whole-hearted cooperation and enthusiasm of the civilian populations who served in them. Total war required total commitment of the entire resources of the nation. Material amenities had to be sacrificed; morale had to be maintained; people had to be persuaded to leave their families and join the ranks; the work in the factories had to be done with unflagging vigor; and not the least important, money had to be obtained to finance the war.

Propaganda and the Need for Gemeinschaft. The diverse, heterogeneous, and differentiated populations of the industrial societies, however, were not bound together by that "reciprocal, binding sentiment . . . which keeps human beings together as members of a totality."[20] They were not Gemeinschaft societies but were in fact more like mass societies, which lacked such effective bonds. Yet it was just such bonds of sentiment that were needed to unite these people into effective solidarity behind their respective war efforts. As each country became politically committed to the war, there arose a most critical and urgent need to forge stronger links between the individual and society. It became *essential* to mobilize sentiments and loyalties, to instill in citizens a hatred and fear of the enemy, to maintain their morale in the face of privation, and to capture their energies into an effective contribution to their nation.

The means for achieving these urgent goals was *propaganda*. Carefully designed propaganda messages engulfed the nation in news stories, pictures, films, phonograph records, speeches, books, sermons, posters, wireless signals, rumors, billboard advertisements, and handbills. Top-level policy makers decided the stakes were so high and the ends so important that they justified almost any means. Citizens had to hate the enemy, love their country, and maximize commitment to the war effort. They could not be depended upon to do so on their own. The mass media of communication available at the time became the principal tools of persuading them to do so.

Following the war, a number of persons who had been importantly involved in the manufacturing of propaganda were ridden with guilt about the gross deceptions they had practiced. Outrageous lies were told by one side about the other and, when placed before the populations of the time via the mass media, they were often believed. Such large-scale persuasion of entire populations with the use of mass media had never been seen before, and it was conducted in a skillful and highly coordinated manner. Also, those were apparently more innocent times; even the word "propaganda" was not understood by the ordinary citizen. After the war, when former propagandists published a rash of sensational exposés about their wartime deceptions, the general public became more sophisticated.

To illustrate briefly the material the propagandists found effective and the responses they were seeking to their stimuli, the following is quoted from one widely read postwar exposé:

> The Atrocity Story was one big factor in English propaganda. Most . . . were greedily swallowed by an unsuspecting public. They would have been less ready to accept the stories of German frightfulness if they had witnessed the birth of the most lugubrious atrocity story at the headquarters of the British Intelligence Department in the Spring of 1917.
>
> Brigadier General J. V. Charteris . . . was comparing two pictures captured from the Germans. The first was a vivid reproduction of a harrowing scene, showing the dead bodies of German soldiers being hauled away for burial behind the lines. The second picture depicted dead horses on their way to the factory where German ingenuity extracted soap and oil from the carcasses. The inspiration to change the captions of the two pictures came to General Charteris like a flash . . . the General dexterously used the shears and pasted the inscription "German Cadavers on Their Way to the Soap Factory" under the dead German soldiers. Within twenty-four hours the picture was in the mail-pouch for Shanghai.
>
> General Charteris dispatched the picture to China to revolt public opinion against the Germans. The reverence of the Chinese for the dead amounts to worship. The profanation of the dead ascribed to the Germans was one of the factors responsible for the Chinese declaration of war against the central powers.[21]

Whether this particular propagandist was correct in his assessment of the impact of this falsified newspaper picture need not concern us. The example and the claimed effect give a classic illustration of the kind of theory of mass communication upon which such propaganda efforts were premised. It was a relatively simple theory and it was consistent with the image of mass society that was the intellectual heritage from the nineteenth century. It assumed that cleverly designed stimuli would reach every individual member of the mass society via the media, that each person would perceive them in the same general manner, and that they would provoke a more or less uniform response from all.

Media Messages as Magic Bullets. In the aftermath of the war there emerged a general belief in the great power of mass communication. The media were thought to be able to shape public opinion and to sway the masses toward almost any point of view desired by the communicator. An American political scientist who tried to analyze objectively the impact of wartime propaganda and the role of the media in the mass society came to these conclusions:

> But when all allowances have been made, and all extravagant estimates pared to the bone, the fact remains that propaganda is one of the most powerful instrumentalities in the modern world. It has arisen to its present eminence in response to a complex of changed circumstances which have altered the nature of society. Small primitive tribes can weld their heterogeneous members into a fighting whole by the beat of the tom-tom and the tempestuous rhythm of the dance. It is in orgies of physical exuberance that young men are brought to the boiling point of war, and that old and young, men and women, are caught in the suction of tribal purpose.
>
> In the Great Society it is no longer possible to fuse the waywardness of individuals in the furnace of the war dance; a newer and subtler instrument must weld thousands and even millions of human beings into one amalgamated mass of hate and will and hope. A new flame must burn out the canker of dissent and temper the steel of bellicose enthusiasm. The name of this new hammer and anvil of social solidarity is propaganda.[22]

The basic theory of mass communication that is implied by such conclusions is not quite as simple as it might appear. To be sure, it is relatively straightforward stimulus-response theory, but it is also one that presumes a particular set of unspoken assumptions concerning not only the social organization of society but the psychological structure of the human beings who are being stimulated and who are responding to the mass communicated message. It is important to understand the full range of these implicit assumptions because *it has been through their systematic replacement or modification* that more modern theories of the mass communication process have been developed. As new concepts concerning the nature of the individual human being and the nature of society became available, these were used to modify the basic theory of mass communication by introducing different sets of *intervening variables* between the stimulus side of the stimulus-response equation and the response side.

This first set of beliefs about the nature and power of mass communications was never actually formulated at the time into a systematic statement by any communication scholar, but in retrospect it has come to be called the "magic bullet theory." (It has also been called by other colorful names, such as the "hypodermic needle theory" and the "transmission belt theory.") The basic idea is that media messages are received in a uniform way by every member of the audience and that immediate and direct responses are triggered by such stimuli.

In view of today's more elaborate perspectives on the mass communication process (which we will discuss later), the magic bullet theory may seem naive and simple. Yet there was more to its assumptions than what such writers as Katz and Lazarsfeld have suggested: "the omnipotent media, on the one hand, sending forth the message, and the atomized masses, on the other, waiting to receive it—*and nothing in between* [italics added]"[23] There were very definite assumptions about what was going on in between in terms of individual psychology. These assumptions may not have been explicitly formulated at the time, but they were drawn from fairly elaborate theories of human nature, as well as the nature of the social order (which we have already examined). It was these theories that guided the thinking of those who saw the media as powerful.

Magic Bullet Theory as a Corollary of Underlying Postulates

What were the psychological assumptions from which the magic bullet theory was derived? Actually, those assumptions were drawn from a combination of the psychological paradigms mentioned in Chapter 1. Even so, these were in a less sophisticated form than they are today. For example, during World War I, and under the influence of Darwin, *instinct* psychology was in its peak. It was not until the end of the 1920s that the facts of human individual modifiability and variability began to be demonstrable with the use of new mental tests and other research techniques. As a consequence, the image of *homo sapiens* represented by the writings of William McDougall and his contemporaries was called into serious question. Prior to that time it was assumed that a given individual's behavior was governed to a considerable extent by inherited biological mechanisms of some complexity that intervened between the stimuli and the responses. Consequently, basic human nature was thought to be fairly *uniform* from one human being to another. People inherited (according to the theories) more or less the same elaborate set of built-in biological mechanisms, which supplied them with motivations and energies to respond to given stimuli in given ways. Much was made of the nonrational or emotional nature of such mechanisms, particularly among theorists of psychoanalytic bent. But even these were, in the final analysis, inherited forces (e.g., libido), which each person received at birth in more or less uniform degrees. The psychology of individual differences had not progressed to the point where a consuming interest in learning would develop among academic psychologists as a means of accounting for such differences.

Given a view of a uniform basic human nature, with a stress upon nonrational processes, plus a view of the social order as mass society, the magic bullet theory, based on instinctive S–R mechanisms and the belief that the media were powerful devices, seemed entirely valid: It stated that powerful stimuli were uniformly brought to the attention of the individual members of the mass. These stimuli tapped inner urges, emotions, or other processes over which the individual had little voluntary control. Because of the inherited nature of these mechanisms, each person responded more or less uniformly. Furthermore, there were few strong social ties to disrupt the influence of these mechanisms because the individual was psychologically isolated from strong social ties and informal social control. The result was that the members of the mass could be swayed and influenced by those in possession of the media, especially with the use of emotional appeals.

Thus, the magic bullet view was completely consistent with general theory in both sociology and psychology as it had been developed up to that time. In addition, there was the example of the tremendous impact of wartime propaganda. This *seemed* to offer valid proof that the media *were* powerful in precisely the manner so dramatically described by Lasswell when he concluded that they were the "new hammer and anvil of social solidarity."[24] There were also the seemingly indisputable facts from the mass advertising of the time that the media were capable of persuading people to buy goods in degrees and variety hitherto undreamed of. This belief added to the conviction of great power and it reinforced the seeming validity of the magic bullet theory.[25]

There is no doubt that World War I propaganda was effective. However, this does not mean that only one theory is capable of accounting for those effects. If scholars of the day had been in possession of the results of research and thought on mass communication that have accumulated since that time, they might have chosen very different explanations to account for the fact that the population of the United States entered the war with enthusiasm, entertained a series of unrealistic beliefs about the enemy, and so forth, and that the media played a part in shaping their behavior and beliefs.

Theories of human nature, in terms of both social order and personal organization, did not remain static. In the United States both psychology and sociology had become more firmly established and were increasingly escaping the domination of the thoughtways of their European origins. Both fields became heavily concerned with empirical research. As a result, their theories were forced to be more closely checked against reality. In consequence, many earlier ideas were abandoned and many new ideas were advanced. Inevitably, these new theoretical directions had their impact on those who were attempting to understand the effects of mass communication. The magic bullet theory had been built upon assumptions that were no longer regarded as tenable by general theorists, and consequently the theory had to be rather reluctantly abandoned by students of the mass media. In the meantime, there was very little to take its place. However, even as newer general paradigms were being devised to describe human nature and the nature of the social order more adequately, the field of mass communication itself was acquiring an *empirical* base. During the late 1920s and early 1930s scholars developed an interest in the media as objects of research. They were beginning to turn from mere speculation about their effects to systematic studies of the impact of particular communication content upon particular kinds of people. As an increasing variety of research tools became available, their ideas about mass communication could be more adequately checked against findings. Thus the field of mass communication began to accumulate a body of data from which concepts and propositions could be inductively formulated. As the following chapter indicates, more contemporary views of the media place greater stress on social and cultural factors that limit their operation and power.

NOTES

1. Shearon A. Lowery and Melvin L. DeFleur, *Milestones in Mass Communication Research*, 2nd ed. (White Plains, N.Y.: Longman, 1988). See Chapter 1.
2. Auguste Comte, *The Positive Philosophy*, trans. Harriet Martineau (London: George Bell and Sons, 1915), 2:289. First published in France between 1830 and 1842.
3. Ibid., p. 292.
4. Ibid., p. 293.
5. Ibid.

6. Herbert Spencer, *The Principles of Sociology* (New York: D. Appleton, 1898), pp. 452–62. First published in England in 1876.
7. Ferdinand Tönnies, *Community and Society (Gemeinschaft und Gesellschaft)*, trans. and ed. Charles P. Loomis (East Lansing: Michigan State University Press, 1957), p. 47. First published in German in 1887.
8. Ibid., p. 65.
9. Emile Durkheim, *The Division of Labor in Society*, trans. George Simpson (New York: Free Press of Glencoe, 1964). First published in France in 1893.
10. Ibid., pp. 62–63.
11. Ibid., p. 129.
12. Ibid., p. 130.
13. Ibid., p. 131.
14. Ibid., p. 137.
15. Ibid., p. 206.
16. Ibid., p. 353.
17. Ibid., p. 361.
18. See, for example, the well-known treatment of the "mass" by Herbert Blumer, which is still regarded as the classic modern statement of the concept: Herbert Blumer, "Elementary Collective Behavior," in *New Outine of the principles of Sociology*, ed. Alfred McClung Lee (New York: Barnes and Noble, 1939), pp. 185–89.
19. Leonard Broom and Philip Selznick, *Sociology*, 2nd ed. (Evanston, Ill.: Row, Peterson, 1959), p. 38. The quotation within the passage is from Kimball Young, *Sociology* (New York: American Book, 1949), p. 24.
20. Tönnies, *Community and Society*, p. 47.
21. George Sylvester Viereck, *Spreading Germs of Hate* (New York: Horace Liveright, 1930), pp. 153–54.
22. Harold D. Lasswell, *Propaganda Technique in the World War* (New York: Alfred A. Knopf, 1927), pp. 220–21.
23. Elihu Katz and Paul Lazarsfeld, *Personal Influence* (Glencoe, Ill.: Free Press, 1954), p. 20.
24. Lasswell, *Propaganda Technique*, p. 221.
25. Katz and Lazarsfeld point out that those who feared the media as potentially insidious devices if controlled by evil men and those who hailed them as beneficial means to improve democracy were assuming a similar great degree of media power. See Katz and Lazarsfeld, *Personal Influence*, pp. 15–17.

CHAPTER 7

Theories of Selective Influence

We suggested in the previous chapter that two events occurred early in the twentieth century that would eventually make it necessary to abandon the idea that exposure to mass communications had immediate, uniform, and direct effects on their audiences. First, large-scale empirical research on the process and effects of mass communication was started. The findings from such research slowly revealed a picture inconsistent with the magic bullet theory. The second event was that significant new conclusions were developed by psychologists and sociologists concerning the personal and social attributes of human beings. Those conclusions resulted from a radical revision of basic theory concerning both the sources and the characteristics of human nature. The new paradigms had clear implications for understanding the influences of mass communication, and they were completely inconsistent with the basic theories from which the magic bullet theory had been drawn. Both sets of circumstances made it necessary, therefore, to reformulate thinking about the personal and social influences of the media. In this chapter we will review these changes in research and theory in order to show how they led to new formulations concerning the influences of mass communications.

Empirical studies of the effects of mass communications started during the 1920s with the Payne Fund studies, a large-scale program investigating the influence of motion pictures on children. The movies were a new medium that had arrived with the new century to become increasingly popular, especially after World War I. During an almost incredibly short period—less than twenty years—the movies evolved from a mere novelty to a major form of family entertainment. They moved out of the salons and crude nickelodeons where they were first shown to ornate and elegant movie palaces, where they became the favorite entertainment of the majority of society. By the mid-1920s millions of families attended every week; some 45 million children under fourteen were among those audiences. Understandably, parents were deeply concerned about the potentially harmful influences of these movies.

The Payne Fund studies investigated the impact of exposure to the movies on the ideas and behavior of thousands of children. They were impressive studies done with great care by the top research experts of the time. Their findings received great public attention and, inevitably, they caused considerable alarm. They seemed to support the idea that the movies influenced their audiences strongly.[1] At first movies did seem to have direct, immediate, and widespread influences on the children who saw them. However, those conclusions did not hold up as other media and other audiences came under investigation. Generally, as more sophisticated research was completed and a larger body of findings accumulated, it became increasingly clear that the magic bullet conception was not consistent with the facts.

As the limitations of the magic bullet formulation became better understood, it was obvious that new theories of mass communication were needed to guide research in a more realistic manner. Like the earlier theories, the new approaches would be derived from the basic paradigms that were being developed in both psychology and sociology. Those two fields actively sought to understand human nature—from a personal perspective on the one hand, and from a collective or interactive point of view on the other. Their goal was to explain individual and collective action in *all* of its aspects, including behavior stimulated by mass communications.

It would be from those emerging basic psychological and sociological paradigms, then, that new explanations of the influence of the mass media would be derived. For that reason, a brief review of theoretical developments in the two social sciences will be necessary foundations for understanding why thinking about the nature and consequences of mass communication was reformulated and why it took certain directions.

Certain cautions in interpreting this intellectual history are in order: While the above sequences of basic theory development and derivation of thinking about the mass media now seem obvious and logical enough, the linkages at the time were by no means as orderly as we will make them seem. In the early years of mass communication research (e.g., before World War II), there was no academically consolidated field called "mass communication" in the same sense that there were disciplines called "history," "sociology," "psychology," "anthropology," and so forth. Researchers who studied the media were usually investigators from the basic social sciences, or from other academic backgrounds, who used the behavior of media audiences as a convenient arena within which to study and test concepts, hypotheses, and theories that were actually from their own disciplines. For example, in the context of mass communications, the educator could study how children received lessons from the movies; the political scientist could investigate the role of the newspaper in influencing voting; the psychologist could study attitude change brought about by exposure to radio; and the sociologist could analyze juvenile delinquency as it was influenced by the media. Once the research was done, such specialists returned to their own fields to continue their research without trying to unravel the implications of their findings for explaining mass communication behavior as such.

In spite of the varied backgrounds of the early investigators and the uncoordinated nature of their inquiries, knowledge *did* accumulate. Numerous concepts, hypotheses, and generalizations about the process and effects of mass communication were yielded by an increasing number of studies. At the same time the structure—or, more precisely, the *lack* of structure—of the emerging field was such that there was no real basis for bringing together, consolidating, and synthesizing formulations that could be called "theories of mass communication."

Theoretical development in the early years, then, was uncoordinated and even chaotic. It did not follow the neat and orderly model of an unfolding science, where later investigators systematically test the leads of those who went before. Thus, a number of the theories referred to in this text—"magic bullet," "selective influence," "individual differences," "social differentiation," plus others to be presented later—are in many cases *retrospective creations*. At least some of those names will not be found in the literature of the early period because they did not exist at the time. They have been brought together, synthesized, systematized, and labeled *post hoc*, mainly by the present authors but sometimes by others, so as to make it easier to understand what the early researchers were doing. It is not at all unusual for later scholars to try to systematize and classify the contributions of earlier ones in new ways and under new labels. In philosophy, for example, various scholars are now classified as "rationalists," "empiricists," "pragmatists," and so on. At the time they set forth their ideas, those classifications did not exist, but using the labels today makes it easier to look back at the way in which philosophy developed and to understand the contributions of various individuals. So it is with the development of communication theory.

In spite of the unorganized nature of mass communication research in the early years, there gradually accrued a body of knowledge about the media and their effects as well as an increasing consensus about how they should be studied. Out of that accumulation a discipline called *mass communication* eventually emerged—decades later, when schools and graduate departments of communication offered systematic degree programs in mass communication studies. The discipline came into being when such institutions began to train doctorate-level specialists in scientific research on the media. Those are relatively recent events (post–World War II). Indeed, the argument as to whether the study of mass communication can be considered as a discipline, or only as a loosely organized field of interdisciplinary interests, still rages. The issue is not critical. In fact, there are grounds for concluding that it is both: There is a central corps of researchers who devote themselves exclusively to the study of mass communications, and that group, along with their academic units, professional societies, and technical journals, forms something very like a discipline that is systematically advancing knowledge about the process and effects of mass communications; however, there is also a large body of social scientists, journalism educators, speech communication specialists, and others who contribute to that accumulation from time to time, while their central interests remain in their parent disciplines.

Generally, then, we can review the development of theories of mass communication within the cautions set forth above, recognizing that many of the names we apply to the conceptualizations of the past were not current at the time and that they were not as neatly formulated during the period as we now make them seem. We will review a body of explanations of the mass communication process that, taken together, can be called "selective influence theories." They consist of three distinct but related formulations that emerged from social scientists' increasing recognitions of patterning in the behavior of individuals and groups. When these patterns are used to help us understand how people attend to and are influenced by mass communications, they are called the *individual differences theory,* the *social differentiation theory,* and the *social relationships theory.* As will be evident, each rests upon fundamental assumptions about human behavior developed in this century by the basic social sciences.

THE INDIVIDUAL DIFFERENCES THEORY

Psychology underwent a rather drastic transformation after the turn of the century.[2] Early psychology had its roots in philosophy,[3] but as the nineteenth century advanced, the field began to be characterized by two basic characteristics that were to influence strongly its later development. These were a concern with the *physiological basis of behavior* and a commitment to the use of the *experimental method* as the legitimate means for gathering valid knowledge. These became deep-seated articles of faith within the mainstream of the discipline.

Early in the twentieth century a great "nature versus nurture" debate broke out, centering on the question of the sources of variability or uniqueness in human personality. As psychologists undertook studies in human learning and motivation, it increasingly became clear that people were all different in their psychological makeup. Like fingerprints, the personality of every human being was found to be unlike that of any other. While they all shared the behavior patterns of their culture, each individual had a different *cognitive structure* of needs, habits of perception, beliefs, values, attitudes, skills, and so on. Therefore, the study of *individual differences* in such factors—and their distributions in the population—eventually became an important focus of psychological research.

Learning versus Inheritance as a Source of Individual Differences

A critical question concerning the source of our human nature was whether we inherit our individualistic cognitive structure as part of our genetic endowment, or whether we somehow acquire it as a result of living in a social environment. It was around this issue in particular that the nature/nurture debate swirled.

A number of early psychologists were actually physiologists who were investigating ways in which behavior was influenced by bodily structure. After 1860 the new field came to be heavily influenced by Charles Darwin's remarkable evolutionary perspectives on the relationship between biological factors and adaptation to environment. Psychologists quickly adopted the idea that human beings are not totally unique creatures, as religious thinkers had long claimed, but an animal species located at the end of a continuum of evolutionary development. To understand human beings, therefore, it was necessary to study animal behavior in general. Thus psychologists turned enthusiastically to the study of animals in an effort to formulate principles of behavior that would apply to *all* organisms, including humankind.

They saw the behavior of living creatures as largely a product of *inherited* capacities, tendencies, and patterns of coping that had come down to modern people through a long process of evolution. This "comparative" psychology implied strongly that behavior was rooted in physiology. People, it was assumed, were neurologically "pre-wired" to act in certain ways because of millennia of adaptations that had shaped their nature through natural selection.

It was for these reasons that one of the most popular concepts of the time was "instinct," which was used to explain all kinds of human as well as animal behavior. The generalization that behavior was biologically determined and governed by instincts seemed to fit observations of behavior across the whole range of species in the animal kingdom, and, since the human being was very clearly an animal, it was presumed to be a valid interpretation of the patterning of human conduct as well. In other words, it seemed to follow logically that the keys to explaining human actions and choices were to be found within the inherited biological structure. This was the "nature" side of the nature/nurture debate.

On the other side of the controversy were those who insisted that human beings *acquired* their individualistic characteristics and abilities from their experiences in their environment. They pointed to the patterned nature of human social organization and the complexity of human culture that anthropologists were describing. They saw that human beings were socialized and enculturated in a complex milieu in which the young learned their habits, predispositions, skills, and individuality. This was the "nurture" side of the debate.

In some ways that debate has never been completely resolved. Fields like sociobiology still attempt to link human behavior to inherited tendencies that have supposedly survived from ancient sources in human history. Such matters as the differences in male and female temperament and their traditional roles are said to be derived from the ways in which human beings evolved in hunting-gathering cultures from prehistoric times to relatively recent centuries. Thus, males are said to have an inherited propensity to assume roles as providers and dominant members of households, whereas females are said to be biologically inclined toward child-rearing, domestic tasks, and subordinate positions in the family. Those on the opposite side of the debate today continue to maintain that such roles and temperaments are products of differential socialization of males and females in institutionalized social and cultural environments.

Following the turn of the century, the field of psychology grew rapidly in both numbers and prestige. The fascinating theories of Sigmund Freud electrified the intellectual world and gave the field high visibility. The studies of "scientific management" conducted by early industrial psychologists appealed to practical-minded Americans. The intelligence testing movement, starting on a large scale with hundreds of thousands of Army recruits who had been drafted during World War I, seemed to reaffirm that psychology was an important field of study that could solve many practical problems.

However, psychologists were not to remain committed to the idea that "nature" was the source of all human characteristics. A new branch of psychology had its beginnings at the turn of the century. It was to retain its focus on animals and its commitment to the experimental strategy, but its central goal was to understand how the human individual was shaped by his or her environment through a process of *learning*. Those in this branch of psychology were trying to find out how learning experiences in a social environment left lasting influences on the individual. In particular they were interested in the way that an individual's acquired inner psychological organization—cognitive structure—would shape the kinds of responses the person made to the external environment.

This "psychology of learning" would ultimately become of central importance to the student of the effects of mass communications. The media were a means by which ideas were transmitted to huge numbers of people who made up their audiences. It seemed obvious that those ideas would produce changes in the psychological organization (cognitive structure) of those who received the messages. Such learning would in turn alter their behavior.

The Development of Learning Theory. Speculation about the mental aspects of human beings goes back to the Greek philosophers. A more specific interest in learning (by "association") was well established by the 1600s, when it found expression in the writings of John Locke, David Hume, and other British philosophers. Actual experiments on human memory, however, did not start until the 1880s. The German psychologist Hermann Ebbinghaus conducted elaborate experiments on himself as a subject who learned and tried to recall "nonsense syllables."[4] He showed the effects on learning of such independent variables as length of the material and the number of repetitions in presenting it to a subject. In studying how memory lapsed, he formulated his famous "curve of forgetting," showing the relationship between time and accuracy of recall. Such early studies were innovative and thorough, but the use of human beings in experiments had many limitations. Willing subjects were hard to obtain, control over extraneous conditions was difficult, and human beings could be subjected to only a limited range of experimental conditions.

Focusing on animals offered a way to study learning that avoided these dangers. We noted that a conviction had increased in comparative psychology that processes characterizing animals would also be found in human beings, and vice versa. During the first decade of the 1900s this phylogenetic perspective focused the attention of psychologists on the study of learning among animals as a way to uncover basic and universal principles of the process. Just as animal subjects could be used for medical experiments that would yield conclusions applicable to human beings, it seemed to the comparative psychologists that studies of animal learning could provide the key to how human beings acquired new forms of behavior. Animals were readily available, they introduced far fewer extraneous conditions (such as language) that could confound research, and they could be used in experiments under conditions that would be impossible for human beings.

Even before the end of the century Edward L. Thorndike (a graduate student at the time) conducted clever experiments with cats to see how they learned to escape from a puzzle box to obtain food as a reward.[5] He found that the cats learned more quickly when rewards were swift and certain. In now famous "trial and error" experiments he studied the behavior of chicks in mazes crudely constructed of books set on end. He was able to plot learning curves and to reach important conclusions about the relationship of learning to what would later be called "reinforcement" (providing rewards for correct responses).

These various experiments led him to formulate his "Law of Effect," a variation of the ancient pleasure/pain principle. His conclusions provided the foundation for B. F. Skinner's later and more elaborate theories of operant conditioning, extinction of responses, and the shaping of behavior by periodic reinforcement.[6]

At roughly the same time, just after the turn of the century, a Russian physiologist named Ivan Pavlov accomplished something with animal subjects that seemed almost incredible at the time. He was able to link a behavior pattern that was part of a dog's natural activity (salivating) with a completely extraneous stimulus (a buzzer).[7] It seems likely that no dog in its natural environment had ever salivated upon hearing a buzzer, but Pavlov's experiment linked the two into a stable habit pattern. It was one of the rare advances in science that led to a total reformulation of thinking—in this case about the importance of inheritance versus learning in the lives of complex animals. Pavlov's remarkable experiment laid the foundation for the development of numerous variations of theories of "classical conditioning."

The importance of all of this early experimentation was that it showed how animals could, through a process of learning, acquire from their environment patterns of behavior that were *not* simply produced by their inherited or genetic endowment. Although in retrospect this might seem like a pretty obvious idea, it did not seem so at the time. Psychologists of the period had been convinced that all animals, including human beings, *inherited* whatever it was that guided their behavior. Suddenly, various forms of conditioning and learning were thrust to prominence, causing wrenching revisions in thinking, not only about animals but about human beings. In the United States, in particular, the study of animal learning experiments jumped to the forefront of the concerns of the discipline. Belief increased that the study of how animals learned under a variety of conditions would ultimately provide the keys to understanding human learning.

Over succeeding decades a number of competing theories of learning were developed. These included not only classical, instrumental, and operant conditioning, but such alternatives as verbal, cognitive, and social learning through modeling.[8] All were aimed at showing how "organisms" (including human beings) were psychologically modified by experiences in their environments in such a way that stable patterns of action and behavior were established under specific circumstances.

Today the task of understanding human learning remains unfinished. There is lively debate as to whether the learning theories developed from laboratory studies of animals such as rats, cats, and monkeys apply to language-using human beings at all! Nevertheless, it now seems inescapable that human beings have an extraordinary capacity to learn and that they do so in a variety of ways.

Whatever principles of learning turn out to be correct for human beings, this focus developed by psychologists showed why people in a society are all so different in their psychological makeup. Although all individuals inherit a biological endowment that provides them with different potentials for development, their patterns of behavior are modified in uncounted ways because of what they learn from their society and culture. Thus, to understand people is to understand that each is psychologically distinct. No two people have identical learning experiences. Therefore, no two wind up having the same inner patterns of learned modes of adaptation to the world around them. Individual differences (in cognitive structure), then, have their origins in the learning process.

Learning to Be Motivated. Along with the recognition of the importance of learning came an associated interest in *motivation*. The study of incentives in laboratory settings gained a prominence in animal experiments along with a focus on learning. Indeed, the two concepts were closely linked. Animals were offered various kinds of pleasures or rewards, or were caused to suffer different types of deprivations or pains, to see if they learned faster or more slowly under such conditions. A long list of motivational factors was studied in animal experiments. The use of human subjects in many of the investigations would have been unthinkable. Rats, dogs, monkeys, and other kinds of creatures were variously starved, shocked, burned, brain-damaged, overfed, deprived of water, sleep, sex, or space, and treated in innumerable ways that might provide clues to what did or did not motivate them to make specific responses to stimuli. The end result was a realization that biological needs in animals as well as human beings can be powerful motivators. Perhaps a more important conclusion was that many of the motivations that impel human conduct are themselves acquired. That is, we *learn* to need certain substances, situations, and experiences that prompt or urge us to engage in particular kinds of behavior. While our inherited, biological motivations (hunger, thirst, sexual appetites) may be relatively similar from one person to another, the acquired or learned motivators are products of our social experiences. Since everyone has a distinctive set of learning experiences in his or her own unique environment, the motivations that an individual acquires provide for great individual differences. In time, this realization brought new ways of thinking to the study of the influences of mass communications.

From Instincts to Attitudes. The classic formulation of a motivational force based in biology was *instinct*. This concept was deeply established in physiological psychology early in this century. The best-known formulation was that of William McDougall, who set forth more than a dozen basic instincts that propelled and patterned human conduct in complex ways.[9] The concept also became popular in psychoanalytic theories. Freud made much of such ideas as life and death instincts, and an innate drive for sexual gratification that brought about complex behavior. However, during the 1920s social psychologists took an increasingly hard look at the idea that human beings had universal and complex motivational systems that were inherited. The increasing evidence of human variability and the growing appreciation of the importance of socialization, enculturation, and learning as shapers of personality were totally inconsistent with the instinct idea. The end result was that by the end of the 1920s the instinct concept was simply abandoned and discredited by social psychologists. The evidence was overwhelming. In many societies the patterns both McDougall and Freud described were absent, or even reversed, because of the nature of the culture. Today, while the concept remains important for understanding animal behavior, theories of human instincts are mainly a historical curiosity.

   With the demise of the instinct concept, social psychology was left with something of a vacuum. What was needed was a theoretical concept that could be thought of as motivational and that was broad enough to be a prime mover of a range of behaviors. Above all, however, it had to be a product of learning!

The concept that came along to occupy the central place that had been held by instinct was *attitude*. It was ideal for the times. It stressed differences between human beings acquired through learning rather than similarities due to biological makeup. By the end of the 1920s it had grown in importance as a means of explaining differing directions and intensities of human preferences, likes, dislikes, acceptances, and rejections. It was a cognitive concept around which many diverse disciplines could integrate their research and conceptualization.

The attitude concept was introduced as a systematic tool of analysis in the writings of sociologists W. I. Thomas and Florian Znaniecki at the end of World War I. They defined it as "a process of individual consciousness which determines real or possible activity of the individual in a social world."[10] Hundreds of similar definitions were soon offered. Most retained the idea that attitudes were some sort of "predisposition" that was learned, and that they played a strong part in shaping behavior.[11] Attitude quickly became the most basic and central theoretical concept of psychology—and in many respects it remains so today.

The significance of the attitude concept to social psychology was given additional emphasis during the 1920s with the invention of several elaborate and mathematically sophisticated techniques for attitude measurement. With these available, the search for the correlates and consequences of people's attitudes assumed almost massive proportions. Within a decade, hundreds, even thousands, of articles, dissertations, and monographs were available with attitude as their central focus.

There were at least three reasons for the great popularity of the concept. As we noted, several kinds of scales were available and they were relatively easy to construct (although they became and still are one of the most frequently misused tools of social science). They were ideal as instruments of measurement in surveys where subjects could fill out forms. Equally important, they yielded numerical data that readily lent themselves to statistical analysis, which was rapidly becoming the accepted mode of scientific description and the basis of decision making for testing hypotheses. Finally, the concept was easy to use in "before/after" experiments to see if some intervening experience changed people's attitudes. As a result, the number of attitude experiments and surveys soared during the 1930s in all fields devoted to the study of human behavior. The study of mass communication was no exception.

There were two additional aspects of the attitude concept that quickly brought it to center stage in the study of the effects of mass communication: The first was that by the time of World War II it was firmly believed that *communications in the form of persuasive messages could alter attitudes.* Indeed, massive research projects and programs of the time were predicated on this psychodynamic conception (that such cognitive factors shape behavior). Specifically, studies of the use of films to train soldiers during the war, and the Yale Program of Research on Communication and Attitude Change, were directly focused on the appeals, message structures, and other stimulus conditions that could be used to achieve such changes.[12] The second aspect of the concept was that it was assumed, without question, that *attitudes and behavior were highly correlated.* Indeed, the idea that attitudes shaped behavior had been part of its definition from the beginning. Thus, if one could change the attitudes of audience members through the use of persuasive messages, correlated modifications of their overt behavior would surely follow.

It was this kind of conceptualization that made the attitude concept seem so important to the fledgling field of mass communication research. In perfect hindsight, we now see that the assumptions made during the period from the 1930s to the 1960s were unwarranted. Attitudes and overt behavior are seldom uniformly consistent with each other. Indeed, a substantial body of research shows without question that they are usually uncorrelated.[13] In spite of this contrary research, however, many communication researchers continue doggedly to assume that attitude change achieved by exposure to persuasive messages will correspondingly alter behavior.

In any case, the role of individual differences in shaping responses to mass communications was the major guiding formulation for media-related research from just before World War II until well into the 1960s. The basic idea was that individual differences in the psychological or cognitive structure of audience members were key factors in shaping their attention to the media and their behavior toward the issues and objects discussed there. As we will see, there is nothing particularly wrong with that idea; its major limitation is that it presents an incomplete picture of the relationship between human beings and mass communications.

Psychographics and Market Segmentation

As the significance of individual differences for understanding the behavior of audiences unfolded, it did not go unnoticed by people who made practical use of the media. Large, powerful groups in society were responsible for showing results connected with advertising, public relations, charity drives, election of politicians, and public persuasion campaigns.

Whether the goal was to sell more soup, to get a candidate elected, or to keep the forests from being set on fire, all such efforts shared a common problem: When using the mass media for persuasive purposes, how does one get the message across in such a way that the likelihood of compliance on the part of the audience is increased? One strategy is to obtain space or time in the media and set forth advertisements, commercials, or appeals on a "one message fits all" basis; that is, aim a general message at the entire audience and hope for the best. The increasing understanding of the great range of individual differences in cognitive structure among human beings that was yielded by basic research in psychology, however, suggested that a different strategy was likely to be more effective. The logical implication was that persuasive messages should be tailored to those with specific interests, needs, values, beliefs, and the like. This segmented approach was more likely to achieve the desired goals than the "one message fits all" approach. Before a persuasive campaign was designed, then, the specific cognitive characteristics of various types of people to whom messages were to be directed had to be identified. To make the message more effective, appeals, arguments, slogans, and other features could be built into the content to attract the attention of that specific segment of the audience and, hopefully, trigger the desired action.

Thus the groundwork was laid for the concept of *market segmentation* as a principle for understanding and developing strategies to sell goods, politicians, and prosocial behavior among large media audiences. This approach, in turn, emphasized the need for *market research* aimed at identifying what kinds of people bought, voted, gave, or otherwise acted on the basis of what motivations, interests, attitudes, or other psychological conditions. Such research into the "psychodynamics" of persuasion used in advertising, public information campaigns, and marketing brought the methodology of psychological experimentation and measurement to market research. The measurement of psychological variables, such as preferences, attitudes, needs, and values, gave insight into consumer and voter motivations. In this way, the experimental format that psychologists had used so widely in animal learning studies and the psychometric procedures that had proved so useful in measuring cognitive variables were adopted to test such factors as consumer brand identification, candidate recognition, preferences for appeals, and the like.

This is not to imply that no one in the practical world had ever thought of such ideas before 1930. A few had, but they did not represent their industries as a whole. Those advertisers or campaign managers that understood the principle of market segmentation, and the attendant need to conduct psychodynamic market research, tended to do so intuitively and without relating their insights systematically to underlying theories in psychology. In summary, then, the great advances in basic learning and motivational theory in psychology gave a firm foundation to the market segmentation principle. This, in turn, led to the widespread use of market research to study the relationship between individual psychological structure and the behavior changes desired by those using the media for persuasive purposes.

As important as it turned out to be, the individual differences theory of mass communication behavior was not the only game in town. A line of thinking had emerged from sociology that would also have a profound impact on conceptualization in both basic and applied media-related research. That line of thinking, based on empirical studies of communities and other large-scale groups, would look not at the psychological structure of individuals, but at the *social* structure of the emerging urban-industrial society.

THE SOCIAL DIFFERENTIATION THEORY

Gradually, the assumptions made earlier by sociologists of the last century—that people in modern societies were undifferentiated, anonymous, and lacking social ties—had to be replaced. Armed with the technique of the quantitative social survey, supplemented by sensitive, qualitative field studies, research slowly revealed a different picture. It became clear that the members of contemporary urban-industrial societies were not all similar. They could be conceptually arranged into well-defined social *categories* insofar as they shared some common characteristic, such as social class, religion, ethnic identity, rural-urban residence, and so on. But study of such categories revealed that people in any particular grouping, such as the middle class, farmers, Catholics, or Italian-Americans, had many *similarities* that had a significant impact on their behavior. Those similarities would have important implications for the emerging field of mass communication research.

Sociology had entered the twentieth century with a rich heritage of broad theoretical formulations concerning the nature of modern society but with little in the way of empirical research. As we saw in Chapter 6, a major theoretical conclusion reached by such writers as Comte, Spencer, Tönnies, and Durkheim was that the onset of industrialization had brought a new kind of impersonal relationship between people in the emerging social order. In agricultural societies, they noted, strong bonds between people were based on such foundations as family ties, time-honored friendships, traditional loyalties, and long-term residence in a local area. These linkages bound people together firmly. In the emerging industrial societies, in contrast, those traditional ties were giving way to far less intimate and personal relationships. Nevertheless, the new ties effectively held the society together. Examples were contractual relationships backed by the authority of the state, or anonymous functional interdependencies (such as the interdependent link between farmers who produced food and city factory workers who consumed their products, in turn supplying the farmers with profit so that they could purchase the goods produced by the factory worker). Thus the organization of society was undergoing fundamental alterations.

The Significance of Social Change

These new relationships were products of specific social changes that were taking place as the pace of industrialization increased. It was difficult to sort out, but the picture that emerged focused on several significant forms of change that were adding to the complexity of society: urbanization, modernization, migration, expansion of the division of labor, increased stratification, and increased social mobility.

Urbanization, that is the growth of towns and cities, was an inevitable consequence of industrialization. It was a constant trend which began to increase toward the end of the seventeenth century and which has continued right up to the present. It concentrated unlike people in urban centers as they came to take jobs in the new factories and the service industries that supported them. Gradually, this trend made urban living the dominant lifestyle of the industrial societies.

Modernization came about as industrialization and urbanization proceeded. The products of the industrial order and the concentration of people in towns and cities brought not only new technology but alterations in basic aspects of human life. More and more people were living by the clock, abandoning their traditional ways, and using efficient machines for everything from transportation to operating a household. Families were transformed from units of production (on the farm) to units of consumption (as city dwellers). Basic values shifted as the pursuit of a happy life was redefined to include the enjoyment of urban amenities and the aquisition and consumption of the products of the industrial order.

Migration has accompanied the rise of industrialization. Vast population movements mixed people from many backgrounds and concentrated them into new areas. Europe had long been in turmoil, but in the nineteenth century the New World waited to receive the disen-franchised, the displaced, and the discontented. People were urgently needed to establish farms, dig canals, cut the forests, work in the factories, lay the tracks, mine the coal, labor in the steel mills, and do the other hard work of a dynamic society. They came in the millions from every part of the globe, not only to the United States and Canada, but to Argentina, Brazil, and dozens of other countries in the western hemisphere that were industrializing to one degree or another. Within the United States people moved in a steady stream from east to west, from south to north, and from farm to city, searching for a better life. These movements further mixed people of unlike characteristics and effectively delayed the development of new forms of traditionalism.

The *division of labor* increased greatly as industrialization pro-ceeded. The new factories and greatly expanded commercial enter-prises brought an increasingly specialized work force. New kinds of experts, entrepreneurs, skilled industrial workers, service personnel, and armies of managers at various levels were required within the industries and bureaucracies of the industrializing societies. This type of work force increased the need for education and specialized training, which became the principal ladder used by people to move up in the emerging class systems.

Stratification, that is, societal systems of social ranking, underwent an important transition. The stratification systems of urban industrial societies became more open and complex. The lines between tradi-tional social classes that had been distinct entities—lower, middle, and upper—were becoming blurred and indistinct. People who would have remained in one of those fixed positions in older social systems were now moving up or down. Even the criteria for defining social class had changed. The meaning of inherited family position declined after the aristocracy were displaced in European societies. In other words, the new stratification systems were based less on ascribed criteria and more on achieved criteria, such as income, educational attainment, and oc-cupational prestige.

Upward mobility became a common goal. The Horatio Alger myth provided an increasingly important vision to enormous numbers of people. They were determined to "work their way up"—something that had not been possible in the more fixed systems of the traditional societies. Not everyone "got ahead," but the dream of doing so was widely shared, and indeed advancement in status became a necessity to avoid being labeled a "failure." The emerging urban-industrial culture emphasized success as a central principle in the lifestyles and thinking of millions.

Social Differentiation in Modern Society

Because of the great social changes noted above, the urban industrial societies, and particularly those in the western hemisphere, developed greatly *differentiated* social structures. In plain language, "social differentiation" means societal complexity. The people in such societies make up numerous and unlike social categories when classified on the basis of specific shared characteristics. Not only can they be differentiated into male and female, old and young, rural and urban, but into an almost endless number of distinctive divisions based on ethnic origin, religious affiliation, race, political orientation, income, occupation, and education, to name only a few.

The fact of social differentiation weighed heavily on the thinking of sociologists trying to understand and describe the society of the turn of the century. To some it seemed an ominous condition. The new era was, said Gustav Le Bon, an *age of crowds*, in which emotion rather than reason ruled collective action. Influenced by the interpretations of the psychoanalytic movement, he saw it as the time when the unbridled, even irrational, psychic traits of the individual rather than the stable bonds of a social order were the determining factors of civilization.[14] History proved Le Bon wrong, however. The pessimistic conclusion— that the society was composed of individuals who lacked meaningful social bonds to others and were therefore driven by the nonrational side of their human nature—was about to give way to another view revealed by sociological research. While the society had become very complex, many informal ties between people remained.

The Rise of Empirical Research in Sociology

Although quantitative studies of populations have been conducted throughout history, basic or theory-driven empirical research began in sociology with Durkheim's classic study of suicide.[15] At the heart of the study was the influence of social categories on the propensity of individuals to commit this final act. Those who were married had lower rates than the unmarried. Catholics had lower rates than Protestants. The rates among military differed from those of civilians, and so on. His theory of the relationship between category membership and the likelihood of suicide remains a significant one today. In any case, the study was a turning point in the transformation of sociology from a field of broad theoretical formulations concerning the overall structure of society to one in which quantitative empirical research on specific forms of social behavior was the basis for obtaining new knowledge.

Early in the century sociologists began to develop the *sample survey* as their major research methodology. It was based on a combination of ancient and modern ideas. In the 5th century B.C. Herodotus reported that as far back as 3050 B.C. officials conducted a systematic accounting, a complete census survey, of the population and wealth of Egypt. They needed the information and the funds to build pyramids. Other leaders, including various Roman emperors and William the Conqueror, had taken surveys of taxable wealth and populations (e.g., the *Domesday Book*). In fact, the census idea had become well established by the time of the rise of modern nation-states.[16]

Above all, the new methodology was possible because of the availability of appropriate statistical techniques for analyzing the results of surveys. By the end of the nineteenth century an increasingly sophisticated body of statistical theories and procedures was available. Over a span of three centuries they had been developed by a combination of astronomers, gamblers, agronomers, mathematicians, and biologists.[17] The sampling designs and techniques of statistical analysis used in survey research today differ little from those available during the 1920s. Computers permit computations to be completed faster, but the underlying conceptions have changed relatively little.

Two features make the modern survey technique different from the older idea of the complete census. First, it is based on a *sample* of the population to be studied, rather than the whole. Second, it makes use of objectively organized interview schedules for measurement. Thus, it brings together the census concept, probability sample designs, statistical theories of population parameter estimations, and techniques of careful quantitative measurement of social and psychological variables. In this form it is usually thought of as beginning in 1855 with Frederic Le Play's study of French coal-mining families.[18] After the turn of the century the use of the sample survey became increasingly well established in sociology. It then was widely adopted and ultimately became the major tool of quantitative analysis in social research.

As the survey research tradition grew, statistical comparisons of people's behavior on the basis of social categories became a common strategy. The end result was that over and over it was found that *social differentiation produced distinctive patterning in behavior.* In other words, people who shared a common identity in terms of social category membership often behaved in similar ways. This principle would have great importance for later theoretical developments in the study of mass communication.

Subcultures

As knowledge accumulated concerning the complex structure of contemporary societies and their great range of social differentiation, a second important concept emerged from sociological research. The concept was *subculture*. Using a method they called "participant observation," adapted from the field study methods of anthropology, sensitive observers lived among people in every imaginable walk of life and social setting—slum dwellers, convicts, medical students, drug addicts, hoboes, ethnic groups, combat soldiers, homosexuals, suburbanites, farmers, doctors, auto workers, and a host of others. These researchers constantly encountered the fact that within such categories people shared a somewhat distinctive way of life that made up a kind of "microculture" distinct from that of the larger society.[19] For example, their members used *argots* that were not part of the mainstream language; they shared distinctive attitudes, values, beliefs, and skills related to their position and activities in the social structure. Furthermore, each category confronted a somewhat unique set of problems that were not identical with those of the society at large.

An illustration of subcultural beliefs and techniques for handling unique problems would be those of industrial workers early in the century. They developed strong negative beliefs about management and formed unions as a means of coping with their lack of power, limited status, and low incomes. Their subculture included shared orientations toward their work, each other, their employers, their unions, the legitimacy of the strike, and a host of associated beliefs. It was a relatively successful strategy, and within a limited time many of their earlier problems had been ameliorated.

It soon became apparent that virtually every other significant category of people in society had a distinctive pattern of skills, beliefs, concerns, language, and values. Some were successful in achieving change; others were not. In any case, microcultures that were distinct from the general or mainstream culture existed in virtually every corner of society. Generally these subcultures were and remain products of social differentiation, and they play a significant role in shaping the kinds of behavior engaged in by members of each category.

It was not a difficult step to apply this generalization to the behavior associated with mass communications. Almost without realizing it, investigators studying the influence of the mass media on people began to do so within a framework of social differentiation. Even before World War II, comparisons of different kinds of people's media behavior revealed that audience members within distinctive social categories were likely to select different content from the media, interpret the same message in ways unlike those of other social categories, remember the messages selectively, and act quite differently as a result of being exposed.

The Uses and Gratifications Perspective

During the 1940s the realization of the consequences of individual differences and social differentiation for behavior related to mass communications led to a new perspective on the relationship between audiences and the media. It was a shift from a view of the audience as *passive* to the realization that its members are *active* in their selection of preferred content and messages from the media. Earlier theories (e.g., the magic bullet formulation) considered the audience as relatively inert, passively waiting for the media to transmit information which was then perceived, remembered, and (presumably) acted upon more or less uniformly. Once the powerful role of cognitive variables and subcultures became clear, it was no longer possible to conceptualize audiences in this manner.

The search for the kinds of needs that were fulfilled and the gratifications provided by media content began early. During the 1930s numerous studies were conducted within this perspective on book reading, radio soap operas, the daily newspaper, popular music, and the movies to probe why people attended to the products of the media and the rewards such exposure provided. A substantial body of findings on needs and gratifications was available by the time of World War II.[20] Today the study of the reasons for which people say they attend to the media, and the rewards that they feel such attention provides, is an established, if somewhat controversial, strategy for understanding the active role of audience members.[21]

Some critics feel that the uses and gratifications approach is less an independent theory in its own right than it is a rather limited restatement of certain aspects of selective influence theories. They point to the fact that its main proposition is that individual needs and the rewards that they obtain influence people's patterns of attention to media content and the uses to which they put the information obtained there. This is essentially a simple version of the individual differences theory based on considerations of cognitive structure.

Another limitation is that, thus far, research using the uses and gratifications perspective has generated little more than lists of "reasons" (various kinds of self-identified "needs") for which people claim that they select and attend to different categories of media content (e.g., news, books, television plays, etc.) or lists of "satisfactions" (e.g., self-identified "gratifications") that people say they obtain from attending to the media. The perspective does not provide much in the way of systematic explanation beyond that. Whether such self-identified factors are the actual reasons and satisfactions underlying media attention

remains an open question. Thus, while this formulation and its attendant research strategy may in the future lead to a more systematic
approach, the needs and gratifications perspective currently remains
limited and unsystematic.

"Demographics" as a Basis of Market Segmentation

The accumulation of knowledge about the distinctive characteristics
and correlated behaviors of people within specific social categories
provided a second foundation on which the principle of market segmentation was developed within business, government, and industry.
That knowledge pointed to the need to use the survey method to study
the clusters of predispositions, preferences, and other aspects of consumer or voter behavior as these differed among different kinds of
people. For example, it soon became commonplace that there were
significant differences between the purchasing habits and consuming
behavior of people of different incomes, ages, levels of education, ethnic backgrounds, and so on. Indeed, the use of survey techniques to
study the demographics of markets has now become routine.

The Link Between Basic and Applied Research

These developments in psychology, sociology, and the emerging discipline of mass communication have an important implication that
should be pointed out. We have noted how the concepts of individual
differences and social differentiation, generated in the experimental
laboratory and in survey research studies, provided a foundation for
theories of selective influence concerning the effects of mass communications on audiences. We also noted how these ideas were picked up
and used in the practical world of the media-related industries for a
better understanding of market segmentation and market research.

What these developments confirm is that there is a *link of dependency* between academic social science and the concerns of industry in
developing new basic knowledge, explanations, and research methodologies pertaining to human behavior. Such a link of dependency is
well recognized by industry regarding the theories produced by the
physical and biological sciences, because basic understandings produced in numerous disciplines have made it possible to develop many
consumer products. But in the social sciences generally, and in communication specifically, that dependency is only reluctantly recognized, indeed if it is recognized at all.

Those in profit-driven industries have been manifestly impatient
with research on social behavior, on the grounds that it often seems

impractical. They either fail to understand, care little about, or choose to ignore the fact that the foremost responsibility of every scientific discipline is to conduct *basic* research aimed at the development of cause-effect explanations—that is, theory. To many, such a pursuit of knowledge for its own sake seems exotic, ephemeral, or pointless. At times, much of it is. Yet those who dismiss *all* such research as pointless are often happily making large profits by using theoretical explanations and research methodologies that were originally developed by the very disciplines that they criticize. That gap of understanding is especially clear in the case of academic communication researchers and the mass media industries.

Selective Influences in the Mass Communication Process

There was, of course, much more to the study of the media than the effects of content on audiences and the factors that caused them to attend in a selective manner. It had become clear by the 1940s that among the factors that had to be studied were the characteristics of the *communicator*, the *content* of the messages themselves, and the *channels* over which people received information. By 1948 Harold D. Lasswell summed up these factors in his well-known dictum when he stated:

> A convenient way to describe an act of communication is to answer the following questions:
>
> > Who
> > Says What
> > In What Channel
> > To Whom
> > With What Effect?[22]

Quite clearly, the individual differences theory and the social differentiation theory pertain specifically to the "to whom" factor in Lasswell's convenient summary. In this sense, they are not sweeping or all-encompassing theories of the mass communication process as a whole. Nevertheless, they add critical elements to our understanding of how research on mass communication can proceed—that is, what factors have to be taken into account. And this, after all, is one of the most important functions of theory. Thus the development of the individual differences and social differentiation theories gave researchers in both academe and the media-related industries clear guidelines as to at least *some* of the factors that had to be considered in developing more inclusive basic theories or in planning effective strategies for practical uses of mass communications for manipulating the behavior of audiences.

The two formulations already reviewed did not, however, provide a complete picture of the basis of selective behavior among the audiences of the mass media. Each theory became and remains important in its own right, but a third consideration came to light almost as an afterthought. That third factor was social relationships between members of the audience. The discovery that people's ties to family, friends, coworkers, and others could have strong influences on behavior related to mass communication led to the formulation of still a third theory of selective influence.

THE SOCIAL RELATIONSHIPS THEORY

Like many other significant discoveries in science, the role of group relationships in the mass communication process seems to have been discovered almost by accident. Also like many other important ideas, it appears to have been independently discovered at about the same time by more than one researcher. From the standpoint of mass communication research on how people encounter and respond to the media, one study stands out as the context within which the importance of group ties, as a complex of intervening variables between media and audience influence, was discovered. Early in 1940, before television was available as a mass medium, Lazarsfeld, Berelson, and Gaudet developed an elaborate research design to study the impact on voters of that year's mass-communicated presidential election campaign. At first they were interested in how the members of given social categories selected media material related to the election and how this content played a part in influencing their voting intentions.[23]

The study took place in Erie County, Ohio, a rather typical mid-American area, which for decades had voted as the nation voted in presidential elections. The media content under study was the campaign speeches and other political messages presented in newspapers, magazines, and radio during the contest between Wendell Willkie (the Republican candidate) and President Franklin D. Roosevelt (the Democratic candidate). The subjects were several representative samples of residents of the county.

An imaginative *panel design* was used in the study for the first time in large-scale survey research. A main sample of 600 was interviewed at monthly intervals between June and November. Additional

fresh samples of 600 each were interviewed during several of the intervening months. The results from the fresh samples were compared with
results from those being repeatedly interviewed, in order to see if
differences were introduced because of the repeated interviewing of the
main panel. No such differences were found to have been produced.

Some of the effects under study were *participating in the campaign,* by seeking information about the candidates and the issues;
formulating voting decisions as a result of exposure to the campaign;
and actually going to the polls to *vote.* As it turned out, other kinds of
effects were discovered: Some respondents were *activated* by the media
campaign. That is, they had "latent predispositions" to vote in a given
direction (because of social category memberships) and the campaign
messages crystallized those predispositions to a point where they became manifest. Others had pretty much made up their minds early in
the campaign, and these voting decisions were *reinforced* by a continuous and partisan selection of additional content from the media. Early
vote intentions were reversed by the mass communicated messages in
only a small proportion of the cases. Thus, *conversion* was not a widespread effect.

Social differentiation theory explained many of the results very
well. The influence of various social categories on vote intentions and
media behavior was pronounced in many cases. Age, party affiliation,
sex, rural versus urban residence, economic status, and education were
key variables. These social category memberships determined "interest" and led to early or late decisions. Acting in concert, this complex of
variables influenced not only people's degree and direction of exposure
to the mass-communicated campaign material, but also the kinds of
influences such content would have on them.

Little attention was given in the study to a possible role of informal
social relationships, such as would be implied by the concept of *primary group* (small numbers of people who have close and affective ties,
such as families and close friends). It was, after all, firmly believed at
the time that this type of social relationship was on the decline in the
emerging urban-industrial society. Elihu Katz has set forth this position
cogently in the following terms:

> Until very recently, the image of society in the minds of most students
> of communication was of atomized individuals, connected with the
> mass media, but not with one another. Society—the "audience"—was
> conceived of as aggregates of age, sex, social class, and the like, but
> little thought was given to the relationships implied thereby to more
> informal relationships. The point is not that the student of mass
> communication was unaware that members of the audience have

families and friends but that he did not believe that they might affect the outcome of a campaign; informal interpersonal relations, thus, were considered irrelevant to the institutions of modern society.[24]

But when the interviewers talked with the people of Erie County, they kept getting somewhat unanticipated answers to one of their major lines of questioning:

> Whenever the respondents were asked to report on their recent exposures to campaign communications of all kinds, *political discussions* [italics added] were mentioned more frequently than exposure to radio or print.[25]

As a matter of fact, on the average day during the election campaign, about 10 percent more people engaged in some sort of informal exchange of ideas *with other persons* than were exposed to campaign materials directly from the media. About midway through the project, the researchers revised their strategy in the interviews. They began to probe more systematically into these informal contacts as a source of "personal influence." They wanted to understand what part this form of person-to-person communication played in modifying the influences of mass communications.

The Two-Step Flow of Communication and Influence

The end result of the serendipitous discovery of the role of informal social relationships in the Erie County setting was the formulation of a new perspective on the mass communication process. After the research had been completed, it seemed clear that informal social relationships had played a part in modifying the manner in which individuals selected content from the media campaign and were influenced by that content. Family members, friends, and others brought ideas from the media to the attention of voters who were themselves not exposed directly. Thus there was an indirect but important flow of ideas and influences from the media to those who *were* directly exposed, and from them to additional people who had *not* read or heard the original messages.

Thus, the research suggested a movement of information through two basic stages: first, from the media to relatively well-informed individuals who frequently attended to mass communications; second, from those persons through interpersonal channels to individuals who had less direct exposure to the media and who depended upon others for their information. This communication process was called the "two-step flow of communication."[26]

Those individuals who were more in contact with the media were called "opinion leaders" because it was soon discovered that they were not merely neutral transmitters of information; they were playing an important role in providing *interpretations* of the campaign that helped shape the vote intentions of those to whom they were passing on information. This form of "personal influence" became immediately recognized as an important intervening process that for many people operated between the mass communicated message and the responses made to that message.

This finding set off an intense effort to investigate the nature of opinion leaders and the process of personal influence. A large literature accumulated indicating that informal social relationships were indeed important intervening factors that shaped the way people selected media content, interpreted it, and acted upon it. Thus, the *social relationships* theory was added to a growing understanding of the basis of the selectivity exercised by audiences as they respond to mass communications.

The Adoption of Innovation

It was suggested earlier that the role of informal social relationships in the mass communications process was independently discovered by more than one research team at about the same time. While the Erie County study was in process, students of rural sociology were investigating how farmers adopted new techniques and products to make their farms more productive. Unlike the students of mass communication, they had long recognized that informal social relationships among those that they studied played an important role in shaping decisions. In particular, they felt that farmer-to-farmer influence would be an important factor in decisions to adopt a given agricultural innovation. The rural society was one in which the farm family retained strong social ties with its neighbors. When new ideas came from the outside, interpretations made by neighbors could be of critical importance in determining the likelihood of adoption.

The acceptance of new farm technology may seem a very different topic from influence by a mass communicated election campaign. Yet, conceptually speaking, the two have many features in common. New ideas are first presented to farmers via some communication medium, perhaps a radio program designed for a farm audience, a pamphlet distributed by a county agent, an agricultural experiment station bulletin, or even an advertising brochure from a company specializing in farm products. The question is whether the individual farmer will respond to these communications in ways hoped for by the communicator, that is, by adopting the recommended item. In this sense, the process is like persuasion in other areas. A farmer adopting a new weed spray or a new kind of seed as a result of a campaign of persuasion is not that different from a householder switching to a new detergent or breakfast cereal as a result of advertising. Both may adopt the innovation or resist it, and the underlying causes of doing so may be quite similar in each case.

Empirical research soon established that the adoption of innovation was a general social process similar to that which occurred during election campaigns. Intensive studies were undertaken to identify opinion leaders and the nature of their personal influence in a variety of occupational and community settings. It was found that a two-step flow of information and influence exists in almost every situation where people have to make decisions about purchases, candidates, causes, or other issues and where they lack firsthand information. They turn to others, whose opinions they trust, for advice that ultimately influences their decisions and actions.

In general, it has been found that opinion leaders who are influential in the adoption process are very much like those whom they influence. They tend to conform more closely to the norms of their groups, and they tend to be regarded as particularly knowledgeable in one area but not necessarily in others.[27] Opinion leadership is not necessarily exercised by people who are higher in the ranking system than those they influence. Influence appears to take place between persons of somewhat similar status, although this is not always true.

In the definitive study on the matter, Katz and Lazarsfeld found that "position in the life cycle" was a critical variable determining who would influence whom and in what area. For example, young working women, in closer contact through media sources with the world of fashions, hairstyles, and cosmetics, were sought as leaders by full-time housewives who were less aware of these matters. Married women with large families, on the other hand, were turned to for advice about household products, marketing, bargains at the supermarket, and so on. Thus such social category considerations as age, marital status, family size, and employment predisposed some to monitor the mass media selectively so as to be knowledgeable about specific topics and, as a result, they appeared as good sources for advice on those issues to those who lacked such media exposure.

Overall, then, the patterns of a person's social relationships proved to be a significant factor that influenced how information from media sources reached them and what they did about it afterward. Some were directly exposed and selected information consistent with their psychological makeup. Others attended to the media and were influenced by them in ways typical of others in their social categories. Still others received their information filtered through the interpretations of others and were thereby influenced as much by their opinion leaders as by the media information itself. In all, the three selective influence theories presented a far different picture from that posed by earlier assumptions about the nature of mass communications and their influences on people.

THE CONTEMPORARY SIGNIFICANCE OF THE SELECTIVE INFLUENCE THEORIES

The shift from the magic bullet theory to the perspectives of the selective influence theories was one from a relatively simple to very complex conceptualizations. Suddenly, all of the factors—both psychological and sociological—that distinguished people from one another were potential intervening variables. They operated between the *stimulus* (S) on the one hand—the content presented by the mass media—and the *response* (R)—changes in feeling, thinking, or action produced among audience members who were exposed to that content. Instead of the simple S–R situation of the magic bullet formulation, with no factors operating between media and mass, there were now several sets of *intervening* variables modifying the relationship (see figure 7.1).

As these formulations began to be used as guides to conducting research, it became clear that each set of factors was contributing in some way to the selectivity with which audiences attended to the media, interpreted what they were exposed to, remembered that content, and were thereby influenced in their actions. In other words, these were distinct sets of intervening variables characterizing audiences, but their influences were somewhat similar in the process of mass communication. That idea can be best understood if we look at four basic principles that govern the actions of audiences who are influenced by these three sets of intervening variables. These principles are concerned with selective attention, perception, recall, and action, and they lie at the heart of the selective influence theories.

1. *The principle of selective attention.* First, individual differences in cognitive structure result in distinctive patterns of attention to media content. Our media societies are so saturated with competing messages that people cannot possibly attend to everything that is directed toward them. If they even tried they would suffer almost instant overload. To avoid this, people develop "mental filters" that screen out vast amounts of information. Their attention is confined to only a limited segment of what is available daily. Just as many throw out junk mail without even

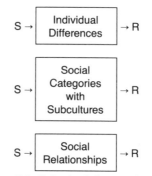

Figure 7.1. Selective influence theories.

opening it, keeping only the first-class letters, people screen out other media content in which they have little or no interest and attend to what they like. For example, those motivated to keep up with current events pay more attention to the news than do those with little interest and understanding. Similarly, those with deep concerns about their health pay closer attention to content dealing with medical issues than do those who are more complacent.

In a similar manner, membership in social categories influences attention. For example, religious broadcasts hold little interest for secular audiences but are enthusiastically received by the devout. Those with limited education and income may avidly follow wrestling on television, while those with more schooling and money often avoid such programs. Similarly, the rural, the urban, males and females, and those of other social categories with distinctive subcultures show clearly defined differences in attention to different forms of media content.

Third, people who have deeply established social ties are more likely to attend to issues and topics that they know are of interest to their friends or families than to unrelated themes. Furthermore, patterns of friendship can be powerful influences on people in directing or even redirecting their reading, viewing, and listening habits. Social relationships can even lead to attention to media content that the individual does not like! Many a wife has suffered through "Monday Night Football" to please a husband, and many a male has viewed episodes of "Dallas" just to keep peace in the family.

Thus, the principle of selective attention is that cognitive structure, category membership, and meaningful social linkages result in patterns of attention to media content linked to those factors.

2. *The principle of selective perception.* A second underlying principle operates in much the same manner. Because of differences in such

cognitive factors as interests, beliefs, prior knowledge, attitudes, needs, and values, individuals will perceive—that is, attribute meaning to—virtually any complex stimulus differently than will people with different cognitive structures. For example, a given newspaper article, movie, radio program, or television presentation can be viewed by a number of individuals and each will come away with a somewhat different interpretation of what he or she has been exposed to. Perception refers to the psychological activity by which individuals organize meaningful interpretations of sensory stimuli that they receive from their environment. Variations in cognitive structure cause individuals to put together different patterns of meaning and interpretation for any given pattern of stimuli such as a media presentation.

In like manner, members of specific social categories who support subcultures will attribute distinctive patterns of meaning to particular media content. Blacks, for example, often interpret news stories about capital punishment, busing, school dropouts, and other social issues that have an impact on black people in ways that are not the same as the interpretations of whites. Veterans of World War II read different meanings into media messages about Germans and the Japanese than do young people who did not participate in that conflict.

Selective perception and attribution of meaning are also influenced by social relationships. Parents with young children may interpret a particularly violent or sexually explicit television program with a different set of sensitivities than do childless people. Lovers may read deep shared meanings into songs or movie scenes that leave others yawning.

Thus the principle of selective perception is that people of distinct psychological characteristics, subcultural orientations, and social network memberships will interpret the same media content in very different ways. Selective perception has been linked to these sets of variables in literally thousands of studies conducted by social scientists, and it is one of the most significant of all the factors for understanding the selective influence theories.

3. *The principle of selective recall.* A parallel situation exists with remembering. Some kinds of content for some kinds of people will be actively remembered for a long time. For others, with different cognitive structures, category memberships, and social linkages, the same material may be forgotten quickly. Thus the principle of selective recall parallels those of attention and perception. That principle too has been deeply established by research over decades.

4. *The principle of selective action.* Finally, not everyone will act in the same way as a result of being exposed to a given media message. Action is the final link in the chain. Before it can take place, a member

of an audience has to attend to the media presentation, perceive its meaning, and remember its content. All of these responses will be dependent upon the intervening influences of cognitive variables, categories and their subcultures, and social linkages with other people.

The above summary shows that the selective influence theories can be summed up in two ways. The first is in terms of the nature of the intervening conditions that they pose between media content and the responses people make. The second is in terms of the four principles of selectivity that lead individuals to attend to, interpret, recall, and act upon media messages in distinctive ways. At the risk of oversimplification, we can combine these ideas and sum up the basic propositions of the selective influence theories in terms of the following propositions:

1. Variations in the cognitive structures of individuals result from learning experiences in social and cultural environments.
2. Social categories in complex societies develop distinctive subcultures as their members invent and share beliefs, attitudes, and patterns of action that meet their needs and assist in coping with their special problems.
3. People in urban-industrial societies retain significant social ties to family, friends, neighbors, work associates, and so on.
4. Individual differences in cognitive structures, category subcultures, and social relationships among members of audiences lead them to selective patterns of attention, perception, recall, and action regarding specific forms of media content.

Given the complexity of the picture of media influences that is presented by the selective influence theories, it is little wonder that predicting the responses of audiences to various forms of media content came to be seen as a very difficult and even discouraging task. It is also little wonder that effective keys as to how to persuade people to engage in specific forms of behavior through media-presented appeals eluded the early investigators, and indeed in many ways continue to do so.

However, in spite of their complexity, the selective influence theories still provide very sound guides as to the kinds of factors that must be researched thoroughly before we will be able to understand and predict the effects of mass communication on audiences. They are as relevant to the study of media influences today as they were during the decades when they were being developed. It is true that they pose a long list of variables intervening between media and mass. Fortunately, hundreds of experiments and surveys have probed these variables in the past, and at least some of the influences are understood. It is hoped that investigators will continue to pursue this theoretical strategy so that these theories can be more effectively formalized.

Even though the selective influence theories remain very promising, however, there also exist entirely different theoretical strategies, focusing on equally important variables. As we will see in the next two chapters, both the process of socialization and the role of meanings in the mass communication process provide very different perspectives on how the media influence their audiences.

NOTES

1. W. W. Charters, *Motion Pictures and Youth* (New York: The Macmillan Company, 1934). This is a summary and overview of the Payne Fund studies, a large-scale research program conducted during the late 1920s.
2. R. J. Hernstein and E. G. Boring, *A Source Book in the History of Psychology* (Cambridge, Mass.: Harvard University Press, 1965).
3. Edwin G. Boring, *A History of Experimental Psychology* (New York: The Century Company, 1929). This is the most thorough work of its kind that sets forth the philosophical foundations of the discipline.
4. Hermann Ebbinghaus, *Memory*, trans. H. A. Ruger and C. E. Bussenius (New York: Teacher's College, 1913). First published in German in 1885. The learning and forgetting curves uncovered in this work are still regarded as valid guides to the functioning of human memory.
5. Edward L. Thorndike, "Animal Intelligence: An Experimental Study of the Associative Processes in Animals," *Psychological Monographs* 2, no. 8 (1898).
6. B. F. Skinner, *The Behavior of Organisms* (New York: D. Appleton Century, 1938). The title of this work reveals the comparative framework within which much of the early research on learning was conducted. The goal was to uncover laws of learning that applied to all living organisms, including human beings.
7. R. M. Yerkes and S. Margolis, "The Method of Pavlov in Animal Psychology," *Psychological Bulletin* 6 (1909), 257–73; See also Ivan R. Pavlov, *Conditioned Reflexes*, trans. G. V. Aurep (London: Oxford University Press, 1927). First published in Russian.
8. For a good summary of this area of psychology, see J. W. Donahoe and M. G. Wessells, *Learning, Language, and Memory* (New York: Harper & Row, 1980).
9. William McDougall, *Introduction to Social Psychology* (London: Methuen, 1908).
10. William I. Thomas and Florian Znaniecki, *The Polish Peasant in Europe and America*, 2nd ed., Vol. I (New York: Knopf, 1927), p. 22.
11. Melvin L. DeFleur and Frank R. Westie, "Attitude as a Scientific Concept," *Social Forces* 42 (October 1963), 17–31.
12. The World War II film experiments are presented in Carl Hovland, Arthur

A. Lumsdaine, and Fred D. Sheffield, *Experiments on Mass Communication* (Princeton, N.J.: Princeton University Press, 1949); the Yale program of research is fully reported in Carl Hovland, Irving Janis, and Harold H. Kelly, *Communication and Persuasion* (New Haven, Conn.: Yale University Press, 1953).

13. See Allen E. Liska, *The Consistency Controversy: Readings on the Impact of Attitudes on Behavior* (New York: John Wiley and Sons, 1975).

14. Gustave Le Bon, *The Crowd: A Study of the Popular Mind* (New York: The Viking Press, 1960). Originally published in French in 1895, translated in 1896, the work had undergone twenty-nine editions by 1922.

15. Emile Durkheim, *Suicide* (New York: The Free Press, 1951). First published in French in 1897. This work represented an important turning point in sociology. It was the first large-scale quantitative study of a specific form of action.

16. George A. Lundberg, "Statistics in Modern Social Thought," in *Contemporary Social Theory*, ed. H. E. Barnes and F. Becker (New York: Appleton-Century, 1940), Chapter 6.

17. For a readable account of the development of major statistical techniques and theories during the nineteenth century, see James W. Tankard, *The Statistical Pioneers* (Cambridge, Mass.: Shenkman Publishing Company, 1984).

18. Frederic Le Play, *Les Ouvriers Europeens* (Paris: 1879) An English version appears in C. Zimmerman and M. Frampton, eds., *Family and Society* (New York: Van Nostrand, 1935).

19. For a more detailed explanation of the nature and importance of subcultures in modern societies, see Melvin L. DeFleur et al., *Sociology: Human Society*, 4th ed. (New York: Random House, 1984), pp. 164–72.

20. Examples of the early studies are: Douglas Waples, Bernard Berelson, and Franklin R. Bradshaw, "Why They Read," in *What Reading Does to People* (Chicago: University of Chicago Press, 1940); Bernard Berelson, "What Missing the Newspaper Means," in Paul Lazarsfeld and Frank Stanton, eds., *Communications Research, 1948–49* (New York: Harper and Brothers, 1949); Herta Herzog, "Motivations and Gratifications of Daily Serial Listeners," in Paul Lazarsfeld and Frank Stanton, *Radio Research, 1942–1943* (New York: Duell, Sloan, and Pearce, 1944). These studies and a number of other works from the 1940s based on selective influence factors and important in the uses and gratifications perspective are reprinted in Wilbur Schramm, *The Process and Effects of Mass Communication* (Urbana, Ill.: University of Illinois Press, 1954).

21. A good summary of this perspective, its literature, and its limitations is presented in Werner J. Severin and James W. Tankard, Jr., *Communication Theories*, 2nd. ed. (New York: Longman, 1988), pp. 300–310.

22. Harold D. Lasswell, "The Structure and Function of Communication in Society," in *The Communication of Ideas*, ed. Lymon Bryson (New York: Harper and Brothers, 1948), pp. 37–51.

23. Paul F. Lazarsfeld, Bernard Berelson, and Hazel Gaudet, *The People's Choice* (New York: Duell, Sloan, and Pearce, 1944).

24. Elihu Katz, "Communications Research and the Image of Society: Convergence of Two Research Traditions," *American Journal of Sociology* 65, no. 5 (1960), 436.
25. Lazarsfeld, Berelson, and Gaudet, *The People's Choice,* p. 150.
26. A excellent summary of this process is contained in Elihu Katz, "The Two-Step Flow of Communication: An Up-to-Date Report," *Public Opinion Quarterly* 21, no. 1 (Spring 1957), 61–78.
27. A definitive work on opinion leadership and related issues is Everett M. Rogers and F. Floyd Shoemaker, *Communication of Innovations: A Cross-Cultural Approach* (New York: The Free Press, 1971).

CHAPTER 8

Socialization and Theories of Indirect Influence

A major feature of the theories of selective influence examined in the previous chapter is that they are focused on the *here* and *now.* That is, they attempt to account for what happens to individuals, in a more or less immediate time frame when mass media present specific kinds of content to audiences with particular characteristics. They are not designed to explain long-term influences on individuals or to deal with indirect effects of mass communication on society or culture.

There are reasons to suspect that the true significance of mass communications in society lies not in their immediate effects on specific audiences, but on the indirect, subtle, and long-term influences that they have on human culture and the organization of social life. Because of the unfolding events of history, such as wars, depressions, and the advance of technology, society and culture are in a constant process of change. This is reflected, and in some instances influenced, by changes in the beliefs and behavior of their individual members. At the social and cultural level, the establishment of new rules for social interaction, or the modification of old ones, brings new guides to behavior.

It is unlikely that the theoretical formulations we described in the previous chapter will be of much value in developing subtle understandings of the long-term influences of mass communications. We noted that those theories focus on immediate results, and they were developed with the use of methodologies borrowed from physical science—epistemologies that assume causal systems of independent and dependent variables. That framework is well suited for the study of immediate and direct connections between causes and effects, but it is clearly a short-term perspective. Unfortunately, we have yet to develop equally sophisticated procedures for the identification, assessment, and interpretation of long-range and indirect consequences of participating in different systems of human communication such as exist in oral versus media societies.

Before we look at some of the potential consequences of long-term exposure to mass communications, it will be useful to understand in some detail *why* the research methodologies currently in use to study the effects of the mass media became so firmly entrenched. That understanding will provide a basis from which to try to peer ahead. It can be understood at the outset that it is very difficult to imagine the kinds of methodologies that are needed for the future study of long-range, indirect, and subtle influences of mass-mediated communications. At best, all such a review can tell us is what research designs and methodologies will *not* be particularly useful as theory and research move forward.

SHORT-TERM VERSUS LONG-TERM PERSPECTIVES

There are two major reasons why the selective influence theories were tied to a short-term rather than a more extended time frame. One was that they originated in the basic cognitive paradigm of psychology, which is little concerned with changes in human social activities over an extended period of time. The other is that they were discovered through the use of methodological strategies that were ideally suited to uncover immediate influences of independent variables on dependent factors at a specific point in time, rather than a long accumulation of delayed effects.

The Constraints of Paradigm

We discussed in Chapter 7 the origins of the individual differences theory of selective influences of the mass media on their audiences. Essentially, it was derived from the basic cognitive paradigm that developed within psychology. That paradigm itself is a variant of the fundamental S–R view of human behavior that is the conceptual foundation of both historical and contemporary psychology: The central task of psychology has for more than a century been to understand why individuals who apprehend stimuli from their physical or social environment respond, behave, or adjust in patterned ways.

As psychology shifted its theoretical interpretations over the decades, various kinds of influences have been assumed to operate *between* the stimulus and response sides of the expression. During the history of psychology three very different sets of factors have been assumed to intervene between the perception of stimuli by the senses and the individual's choice of appropriate responses. The first set was a structure of mental faculties in the consciousness of the individual. This gave way to an extended list of inherited instincts that were presumed to be more or less similar for all individuals. In more recent times that set of factors has been replaced by organizations of learned cognitive factors. That is, intervening between the S and R is some set of attributes of the individual "organism" that influences the manner in which it makes its adjustments to perceived stimuli. Thus psychology came to assume an S–O–R framework, with the O representing characteristics of the organism that can be used to explain different types of responses toward particular categories of stimuli.

We have seen that the selective influence theories are variants of this conceptual form. They postulate that cognitive, subcultural, and social characteristics of individuals are all somewhat distinct sets of O-factors operating as intervening influences. These are said to shape selective patterns of attention, perception, recall, and overt action of individuals responding to mass communications. The majority of early studies of the media tried to use such individual attributes to explain the immediate responses of people who were stimulated by a particular film, printed message, or radio program.

The Constraints of Method

A second reason why the selective influence theories are concerned mainly with short-term influences is that they were developed with the use of methodological procedures that are suitable for the study of immediate and direct effects rather than long-term and indirect relationships between variables. Specifically, the *experiment* has from the beginning been the methodological strategy of choice for psychology, and the *sample survey* served in the same capacity for sociology.

Preference for the experiment in psychology comes from the early days of the discipline. The established sciences looked at psychology with great suspicion, because its subject matter was "mental" phenomena, such as "thoughts," "emotions," and "memories." At the time, such topics seemed esoteric and ephemeral. They were not defined as legitimate objects of study by serious scientists. In fact, claiming that they could be subjected to scientific analysis was regarded in some circles as perilously close to quackery, not much different from dealing in ghosts, spirits, and magic, the mumbo-jumbo of charlatans and mountebanks.

Determined to overcome this stigma, psychologists did two things: First, they turned with a vengeance to the experiment because they believed it to be virtually the only valid means of gathering trustworthy conclusions about their subject matter. It was the accepted method of the established physical and biological sciences. Therefore, it became an important means by which psychologists hoped to establish legitimacy of their field as a scientific discipline. To a considerable extent, that belief continues to prevail in psychology, even today.

Second, early in the century, and for much the same reasons, John Watson proposed a strict *behaviorism*. Its central article of faith was that the only legitimate data on which to develop theories explaining human behavior were direct observations of overt actions of individuals. Any explanations that postulated "mental" concepts (which are not directly observable) to account for human conduct were taboo. Such views achieved wide acceptance in psychology.

Rigid behaviorism has long since given way to a modified or neo-behaviorism, which does accept inferences to concepts that can be tied closely to direct observation (such as cognitive factors). Even so, many psychologists remain skeptical concerning conclusions that are not products of direct empirical observation. For example, verbal reports from subjects about their inner psychological states were called "introspection" in earlier times and were dismissed as having little scientific value. Even today such reports are awarded less than full scientific status by some psychologists. For example, there remains controversy within the discipline about the merits of "clinical" observations that are not conducted within an experimental format. Even "mental tests," such as personality inventories and IQ measures that require subjects to examine their own beliefs and give personal reports, are still open to question in some circles. Thus the direct observation of human behavior and the experimental approach to its study are regarded as the most legitimate methods for the development of valid knowledge.

In many ways, scientifically oriented sociologists hold similar views, although at first glance the parallels are not obvious. The problem in sociology is that it is difficult (or simply impossible) to design experiments to study the characteristics and behaviors of large groups, communities, and societies, which are often the most meaningful units of observation for sociologists. What sociologists did to get around this problem was not to abandon the strategy of the experiment, but to develop alternative methodologies that incorporate its logic! By that means they felt that they could retain their claim to scientific status.

The problem was handled in the following way: A substitute for the experiment was needed that retained its advantages. The advantage of the experiment is that the influence of extraneous variables can be controlled while empirical observations can be made of the relationship between independent and dependent variables. A high degree of control is possible because the investigator can directly manipulate the conditions experienced by subjects and either eliminate or minimize factors that can potentially influence the results and lead to false conclusions.

To gain these same advantages, sociologists developed the sample survey as an empirical observational procedure. Then they adapted complex statistical strategies—such as regression analysis, multiple and partial correlation, analyses of variance, and many others—to the problem of control. Such statistical procedures made it possible to sort out quantitative relationships between independent and dependent variables while assessing and accounting for the influence of other factors.

Today, empirical, quantitative, and statistical strategies remain the methodology of choice in sociology. Other more "qualitative" approaches to the study of sociological variables, such as "participant observation" and "field studies," are used by some, but they remain controversial. They lack the respect of hard-core quantitative survey research and are not truly mainstream methodologies. However, in their enthusiasm to be "scientific," sociologists, and others who use polls and surveys, have all but forgotten the older questions about the "introspective" nature of their observations. The complex, multivariate, statistical analyses that are performed today with the aid of large-capacity computers are impressive and seem most "scientific," but the data that are fed into these statistical programs are still based on "introspection"—on asking people in interviews what they feel or believe, what they did earlier, or what they anticipate in the future.

Our purpose in noting the substantial preference of psychology for the experiment, and of sociology for its complex statistical counterpart, is that *both* of these methodological strategies are useful mainly for the study of behavior in a short-term perspective. An experiment can reveal what people do within the specific conditions imposed by the experimental design. Similarly, a survey provides a one-time description of human behavior under the conditions that prevailed when the interviews were conducted. It is difficult to use either for studying changes in behavior over long periods of time, however. Thus both the *the-*

oretical paradigms underlying the selective influence theories and the *methodologies* used in their development locked them into a short-term perspective and a search for immediate effects of exposure to mass communications.

When research based on these paradigms and methods failed to turn up significant and immediate effects of exposure to media content, few scholars attributed the results to the nature of the underlying theories that were guiding their research or the methodologies that they were using. Instead, they came to the conclusion that mass communications had little power to modify human behavior! Only in more recent times has it been realized that the selective influence theories had little to say about long-term effects for individuals, about continuous and accumulative exposure to media content, or about indirect influences on culture and society. Also, only in relatively recent times has it been realized that those are precisely the kinds of influences that may prove to be the most powerful in the long run.

In the sections that follow we will review the background and nature of theories that are concerned with long-term perspectives and with indirect influences on both individuals and society. One broad perspective that provides an organizing framework within which to study the long-term and indirect influences of mass communications is *socialization*. It is an umbrella term, encompassing several aspects of that process by which the beliefs, attitudes, and behavior of members of societies are shaped by the sociocultural systems in which they participate. One aspect of socialization focuses directly on the individual's personal response systems—how that person acquires new forms of action, or new ideas, that modify his or her habitual modes of responding to the physical or social environment. Another aspect of socialization looks at individuals in a framework of social interaction in order to understand how they are prepared to enter and take part in organized groups and to make personal transitions through their life cycle.

THE MEDIA AS AGENTS OF SOCIALIZATION

Plato was the first to provide us with a detailed explanation of the socialization process. In his *Republic* he set forth a plan for ensuring that through systematic training the leaders of his ideal society would develop the best possible personal attributes.[1] In more modern times the long-term development of the human from infancy to old age has been a focus of study in all of the basic social sciences from their beginnings in the nineteenth century.

The Nature of Socialization

We noted earlier that human development has been viewed from both a biological and a behavioral perspective. Today both sources of human nature are seen as interdependent. As individuals change biologically from infancy to adulthood and then continue into older years, they also change psychologically and socially. As they move through the life cycle, they are called upon to assume new roles, accept different statuses, alter their responsibilities, and modify the ways in which they think about themselves.

In traditional societies the stages of the life cycle are clearly marked by various rites of passage. The definitions of what each includes is controlled by the family, the tribe, or the society as a whole. This system provides for orderly transitions and the proper preparation of the individual to move from one stage to another. In contemporary urban-industrial societies the process is by no means as clear. Competing and often contradictory sources of information, ranging from peers to corporations, vie for the attention of the individual to provide definitions and directions as to what behavior to imitate, what rules of action are important, and what meanings to attribute to events. Conspicuous among those competing sources of information are the mass media. In modern societies they have become an inescapable, omnipresent, and compelling source of definitions as to how people should behave. For that reason, it is essential that their long-term influences on the socialization process be studied.

Exactly what is socialization? We can begin to answer that question by recalling our earlier discussion of the classic nature/nurture debate. The question at issue was from what sources the individual obtained those characteristics that set people apart from other animals. Specifically, it asked whether we learn or inherit the human "personality"—that unique internal psychological organization that constitutes each individual's "human nature." While the debate has moderated, and the critical role of learning has been recognized, the question is still vital. How is the individual prepared over a period of years so as to become and remain a fully participating member of society? That is, from what sources and as a result of what experiences does each of us acquire all of the internal orientations, controls, and understandings that make it possible to interpret the world around us in meaningful ways, to cope with our physical environment, and to relate to others in a manner that is acceptable to our fellow human beings? The answer is through socialization.

The term "socialization," then, is a very broad one. It is a label for a complex, long-term, and multidimensional set of communicative exchanges between individuals and various agents of society that result in the individual's preparation for life in a sociocultural environment.[2] From an *individual* perspective, socialization equips us to communicate, to think, to solve problems using techniques acceptable to society, and generally to make our own unique adaptations to our personal environment. From the point of view of *society*, socialization brings its members into sufficient conformity so that social order, predictability, and continuity can be maintained.

Socialization and the Individual

Socialization has been viewed from several rather different but complementary perspectives by each of the major social sciences.[3] Each of these perspectives is important for an understanding of how the mass media may contribute to the process:

Anthropologists use the term *enculturation* to refer to the process of acquisition whereby new members of a society internalize all aspects of their culture. This includes not only the customs and traditions of their people, but the language, the use of the material artifacts, and the entire body of legends, myths, shared beliefs, and common folklore. If people shift from one society to another and resocialization takes place, the process is called *assimilation*. The mass media can play a part in showing either the child the nature of his or her social order, or the immigrant the ways of the host society.

Psychologists tend to see socialization as *learning to control inborn drives* which if allowed to develop unchecked, would lead to socially unacceptable and disruptive behavior. An informative example of a psychological view of socialization is contained in the psychoanalytic theories of Sigmund Freud, who analyzed the organization of human personality in terms of three elements or components—the *id, ego,* and *superego*. He believed that these three aspects of human nature were constantly competing for control of the individual's behavior.[4] According to the theory, the id is the pleasure-seeking part of (what he called) the psyche; it is made up of inborn drives, including those for sexual gratification. The superego is that part of the human personality that has internalized society's moral rules; it is what is commonly referred to as "conscience." The ego is the part of the personality that provides conscious awareness of, and gives direction to, ongoing behavior. In directing that behavior, it is the aspect of the psyche that mediates between the unconscious demands of the id and the restrictions of the superego's learned codes for socially acceptable behavior. It is said that the ego resolves conflicts between the two—for example, by channeling the energy of the id into forms of behavior that will not cause social disapproval. In this perspective, socialization provides the individual with knowledge of the rules of acceptable social conduct and definitions of deviant behavior. Thus the task of civilization in training the child, said Freud, is to "cage the beast within." Socialization, in other words, encourages the individual to accept society's standards of right and wrong and to hold in check inborn drives for gratification that would cause social disruption and disapproval.

Not all psychologists accept Freud's interpretations, or indeed any other form of psychoanalytic theory. Nevertheless, the essential principles of psychological definitions of socialization are illustrated: Socially unacceptable drives have to be controlled; the moral dictates of society must be learned; and daily behavior involves sorting out conflicts between the two.

For present purposes the question is, what is the role of the mass media as agents of socialization in achieving these critical goals? Does exposure to their content help individuals control fundamental urges and drives, or encourage them to seek gratification in unacceptable ways? Do the media teach the moral standards that are widely accepted in society, or do they present distorted versions that may bring individuals into conflicts with the conforming majority? Media research focusing on the portrayal of excessive violence, deviant sexual behavior, criminal activities, illegal drugs, and other socially negative issues, particularly as these influence children, is a standard way to try to develop insights as to the long-term socializing influences of mass communications.

Sociologists stress that socialization prepares individuals for *participation in group life*. Here the focus is specifically concerned with two issues. One is the way in which people acquire the knowledge they need actually to become *members* of particular groups like the family, a school, the Navy, a club, a work group, and so on. The other is to provide individuals with a broader understanding of many kinds of groups that make up their society. They may never become members of such groups, but they have to relate to them on various occasions. Examples are hospitals, banks, government agencies, insurance firms, football teams, police departments, and many, many more.

These are complex lessons. What it means is that to get along in a group, or even in society as a whole, each of us must carry around in our heads detailed sets of *expectations* concerning the workings of many different kinds of groups. Only if we have internalized such expectations can we walk into a bank, a supermarket, a church, our place of work, or even our family, anticipating what people will do, and participate smoothly in its pattern of social activities.

People also need to gain insights into themselves. They change from children to adolescents, from young adults to middle age, and from active senior citizens to those nearing the final years, and each stage requires a new *conception of self*. What does it mean in a particular society to be young, middle-aged, or elderly? Such definitions and self-conceptions are acquired through the process of socialization. They already exist as part of the general culture, and each new stage is internalized as an individual approaches and moves into it.

Mass communications in modern societies present numerous lessons daily on all these topics. The images of the young, of the elderly, of men and women—whether factual or false, distorted or realistic, right or wrong—are presented repeatedly in media content to which people are exposed over and over, day after day. The long-range implications of such experiences for the individual obviously need to be understood.

Socialization and Society

Socialization is basic to the survival of a society as a continuous and stable system. Despite the constant change of its membership through birth and death, the system continues. This is possible because the foundations of social organization and the general culture are transmitted to succeeding generations via the socialization process.

Training new members into the language definitions of the society enables them to participate in the shared or conventional interpretations of the external world of reality. Through this ability to communicate, new members take on the common folkways, approved values, accepted wisdom, and widespread beliefs that enable people to relate to each other in routine social situations. In other words, as a result of socialization, members come to take many of the same things for granted, make the same assumptions about numerous aspects of their social system, and use acceptable techniques in relating to each other. If this does not happen, and if those features of social living become blurred or unclear, predictable and efficient social interaction becomes less and less possible. It is important, therefore, to discover ways in which the mass media develop or modify the shared basis of stable patterns of social interaction.

The above discussion of socialization, its personal and social significance, and the potential roles played by the media presents a complex picture. Yet certain common features are present in the way each of the social sciences looks at socialization. No matter whether the focus is on control of inner psychological drives, training to understand groups, or internalizing the entire way of life of a society, some five essential elements stand out: All of these versions of the socialization process are concerned with the way in which various forms of *culture*—such as shared beliefs, traditional lifestyles, language, rules for moral living, or various kinds of skills—that are *external* to the individual become *internal* parts of that person's psychological organization. Each of the social sciences assumes that this takes place through a process of *learning*, either deliberate or unplanned, and that it is a product of social influences. That is, there are various kinds of formal or informal *agents* that function as teachers of which the subject may or may not be aware. Those agents may be unplanned, as is the case in casual family influences on children, or they may be deliberately designed by the society, as would be the case of schools. Still other kinds of agents may perform their function accidentally, unwittingly, and inadvertently.

The important point is that among those unintentional agents in contemporary societies, the mass media appear to be playing an increasingly significant role. As yet, that role is poorly understood and it is probably seriously underestimated. The research of the past, based on the cause–effect methodologies and on short-range assumptions, has done little to clarify the situation. For this reason, research in the years ahead is likely to focus increasingly on questions of long-range and indirect influences on individuals and society. A strong beginning has already been made. In the remainder of this chapter some of those beginnings will be reviewed.

MODELING THEORY

A major contribution to understanding the manner in which mass communications can play a part in the socialization process is *modeling theory*. Although he did not call it by that name, it was originally formulated by psychologist Albert Bandura and his associates in the 1960s as part of a broader *social learning theory*.[5] In order for us to understand its application to the study of mass communications, it is essential to have a basic grasp of social learning theory itself.

Social or Observational Learning Theory

Social (or observational) learning theory is not specifically an account of learning from exposure to mass communication, but rather is a general explanation of how people acquire new forms of behavior. It is called "social" because it attempts to explain how individuals observe other people's actions and how they come to adopt those patterns of action as personal modes of response to problems, conditions, or events in their own lives.

In spite of its general nature, social learning theory is particularly relevant to the study of mass communication because the portrayal or description of social life is a frequent subject in media content. The actors who portray real people in visual or auditory media, or whose actions are described in print, can serve as models for others to imitate. Under specific circumstances, which we will review, members of audiences who observe such portrayals may try out and ultimately adopt the modeled behavior on a more or less permanent basis. After we consider social learning theory in a more general sense, we will look closely at the way in which, in the form of modeling theory, it provides useful explanations of how the media can serve as agents of socialization.

As a general explanation of the acquisition of new forms of behavior, social learning theory shares many features with other accounts of learning. However, it also has aspects that make it very different from alternative explanations. It is those distinctive factors that have made it particularly applicable to the study of how people learn and adopt new patterns of behavior as a result of exposure to mass communications.

Like other psychological explanations, social learning theory assumes that people acquire new *linkages* between particular stimulus conditions in their environment and stable patterns of action (that they become capable of performing) as responses to those conditions. Such linkages, referred to by psychologists as "habits," tend to become relatively stable or recurrent when they are *reinforced* in some manner. Reinforcement is usually a consequence of reward, that is, some pleasurable experience, for performing the behavior as a response to the stimuli. The removal of some irritating or punishing situation can also result in reinforcement. If a pattern of action used as a response to a stimulus is reinforced, the probability of that particular behavior's becoming the individual's usual (habitual) way of responding to those stimulus conditions is increased. In fact, psychologists often define learning itself as just such an increase in probability.

In short, reinforcement or strengthening of the connection between S and R usually takes place when the adoption of the relevant pattern of action by the individual results in some gratification, including relief from some stressing situation. Contemporary learning theories postulate that this process of reinforcement can take place in many ways, even accidentally. It need not be in the form of a reward deliberately provided by an agent of socialization, such as a parent or teacher.

Another important concept in learning theory is "operant" conditioning. It refers to the acquisition of a response pattern through sequences of reinforcement of a given S–R linkage that occur in an *unplanned* way. This means that some reward or relief from stress results when the particular response occurs, at least with some more or less regular frequency, and the individual need not be aware of the events. Such reinforcement sequences occur in many ways in every person's environment, raising the probability that the reinforced S–R pairing will become habitual. While social learning theory is much more than an explanation of behavior acquisition resulting from operant conditioning, it does recognize that reinforcement and consequent learning can occur quite incidentally.

At the heart of social learning theory is a process that is very close to the old-fashioned idea of behavioral *imitation*, but coupled with reinforcement as explained above. For example, if a person sees another using a particular technique for coping successfully with a problem that the observer also faces from time to time, he or she may try out that behavior pattern as a potential personal solution. If it works well, the experience of being able to cope with the problem more effectively when it recurs is rewarding. Thus, the connection between the problem and the behavior that solves it is reinforced.

An illustration of how such sequences can result in a person's adopting a socially significant form of behavior is the case of learning to use alcohol: Young males eager to begin thinking of themselves as "men" look to adult models to identify what constitutes "manly" behavior. A rich arena for social learning often exists in the home, where just such definitions are provided by fathers, older brothers, and their male friends. If alcohol is freely consumed by adult males in such a setting, and if the ability to engage in heavy drinking brings admiration and status within such a group, the probability is high that a youngster will start consuming alcohol as soon as doing so is permitted. If a particular schedule of reinforcement follows, with the new drinker being rewarded for having made the transition to "manhood" in this manner, it is unlikely that he will grow up to be a teetotaler. In fact, the probability is higher that he will become a problem drinker.

In other words, if a particular pattern of behavior is performed by a model, and if that pattern is identified as problem-solving, rewarding, or in some other way desirable in its consequences, the probability that it will be adopted by an observer is increased. If its adoption does indeed result in positive consequences, that particular pattern (habit) is likely to persist as a more or less permament part of the individual's repertoire.

Most operant response theories, and especially those derived from animal studies, make no assumptions that lessons posed by the environment are deliberately presented, or consciously acquired. This could also be the case with social learning theory. The model who displays the behavior may be totally unaware of the observer/adopter. In turn, that person may have no conscious recognition or recollection of linking the performance of the model with the acquisition of the coping technique. This learning can take place in an unwitting fashion, without awareness, planning, or manipulation. There is abundant evidence that such effects do occur.

Although social learning theory can include such incidental acquisitions, it takes the position that human response acquisition is usually different. People often have very clear recognitions, understandings, and recollections of modeled behavior and they are likely to be completely aware that they are adopting behavior patterns they have previously observed. That is not to say that they fully grasp all that is motivating them to do so, but they usually know what they have seen modeled and they realize that they are imitating the pattern.

One of the principal reasons why social learning theorists take the position that the adoption of modeled behavior is often by deliberate choice is that they recognize clearly that people use *language*. The theory postulates that symbolic behavior is a significant factor in people's overall behavior and that it is very important in understanding how they acquire new habits. As Bandura puts it:

> The capacity to use symbols provides humans with a powerful means of coping with their environment. Through verbal and imagined symbols people process and preserve experiences in representational forms that serve as guides for future behavior. The capability for intentional action is rooted in symbolic activity. . . . Without symbolizing powers, humans would be incapable of reflective thought. A theory of human behavior therefore cannot afford to neglect symbolic activities.[6]

In other words, people use language and doing so enables them to think, remember, and plan ahead. That is scarcely a new insight into the human condition, but it is a marked shift in position for learning theorists.

It may seem surprising that psychologists, led by theorists such as Bandura, have only in recent years readmitted such "mental" processes as language into their explanations of human behavior. We discussed the psychological retreat into strict behaviorism that started early in this century. We also noted the preference for animal experiments. Both were a part of the general strategy for developing "laws of learning" that would transcend species and apply to all "organisms." Since only human beings use language and have inner subjective lives dependent on symbolic behavior, that had to be left out. With the emergence of social learning theory and related formulations, however, the older taboos on admitting that human beings have a subjective mental life are beginning to fade.

Another important feature that social learning theory shares with other psychological explanations is a long-term perspective. Most learning theories are based on the notion that organisms learn not through a single experience, but over a number of "trials" in which the link between the stimuli and the response to be learned is reinforced according to some schedule. Social learning theory places some emphasis on single-exposure acquisition of new behavior but does not preclude learning as a result of stimulus repetition. Adoption can be a result of seeing the behavior modeled repeatedly. Thus social learning theory provides for both an immediate and a long-term perspective on the acquisition of new responses.

The Modeling Process

The term *modeling theory* is useful for describing the application of the general social learning theory to the acquisition of new behavior from media portrayals. The media are a readily available and attractive source of models. They provide symbolic modeling of almost every conceivable form of behavior. A rich literature has shown that both children and adults acquire attitudes, emotional responses, and new styles of conduct from all the media, and especially from films and television.[7]

When the theory is applied to explaining the acquisition of new forms of behavior from exposure to mass communications, the heart of the matter is the *modeling process.* In brief, it consists of several stages that can be summed up in the following terms:

1. An individual member of an audience *observes* or reads about a person (model) engaging in a particular pattern of action in media content.
2. The observer *identifies* with the model, that is, believes that he or she is like the model, wants to be like the model, or sees the model as attractive and worthy of imitation.
3. The observer consciously *realizes*—or unconsciously reaches the conclusion—that the observed or described behavior will be functional. That is, the person comes to believe that the behavior will bring about some desired result if it is imitated in a particular situation.
4. The individual *remembers* the actions of the model when confronted with the relevant circumstances (stimulus situation) and

> *reproduces* the behavior as a means of responding to that situation.
> 5. Performing the reproduced activity in the relevant stimulus situation brings the individual some relief, reward, or satisfaction, thereby causing the link between those stimuli and the modeled response to be *reinforced*.
> 6. Positive reinforcement increases the probability that the individual will use the reproduced activity *repeatedly* as a means of responding to similar situations.

This is not a simple formulation. It is based on complex concepts like "identification" and "realization," which are clearly subjective and internal to the observer. These continue to trouble many psychologists who prefer to develop theoretical explanations that do not depend on such "mental" ideas. However, their (somewhat belated) recognition of the role of language in human affairs has led to an increasing acceptance among learning theorists that people do have a subjective life and that it is a powerful influence on their conduct.

One thing modeling theory has done is to raise interest in the procedures of *content analysis* to a very high level. Content analysis of media presentations can reveal almost limitless varieties of behavior patterns that are there as models for potential adoption. Thus, the stimulus side of the S–R expression has been the subject of hundreds, perhaps thousands, of descriptive investigations. Careful counts and measures of almost every form of media content have been completed. They include detailed descriptions of sexual activity of pornographic videotapes, the kind and amount of violence shown on network TV, how sex roles are portrayed, what foods are advertised, how minorities are depicted, how specific occupational roles are portrayed, and so on almost endlessly.

The proliferation of content analysis studies of media content triggered by modeling theory appears to parallel what happened when the first attitude measurement instruments became available in the late 1920s and early 1930s: It quickly became apparent that everyone's attitudes needed to be measured, and thousands of studies were published. It did not matter that attitudes had not been shown to be good predictors of behavior. (In fact they were later shown to be very *poor* predictors.) It was simply assumed that if people had particular attitudes, they would behave in a corresponding manner. We know now that they do not and that there is little consistency between measured attitudes and overt conduct.[8]

A somewhat similar situation seems to have arisen in connection with the numerous content analysis studies that are now in vogue.

Because various forms of behavior are widely portrayed in media content, *it cannot be assumed that they will be widely adopted.* Any such assumption is without foundation and, in fact, is uncomfortably close to the assumptions underlying the magic bullet theory. Therefore, while there is nothing wrong with the systematic descritpion of media content, it is not a short-cut to predicting how the S and the R factors will actually be linked. Content analysis says nothing about the acquisition of stable habit patterns among people exposed to specific actions portrayed or described in mass communications.

Social learning theory provides a good account of the conditions under which individuals may observe and adopt specific coping techniques and various other kinds of stable behavior patterns in group settings. Its application to mass communications in the form of modeling theory shows clearly that the media can serve as agents in the socialization process. Those who design, produce, and disseminate media content may not *intend* their portrayals of human behavior to serve as models for others. (If they think about it at all, they may even wish that they would not.) Those who adopt behavior forms that are shown or described in the media may not have deliberately sought exposure to behavior patterns that they could copy from the models, but they do so anyway, either consciously or otherwise.

In spite of the fact that psychologists are generally enamored with the experiment as a basis for testing and developing theory, there are some forms of behavior that simply cannot be duplicated, simulated, or demonstrated with short-term laboratory-type studies. Some modeling influences can and have been demonstrated in experiments, but long-term adoption of modeled behavior resulting from repeated exposures to mass communications cannot easily be studied in this way. That is not a shortcoming of modeling theory; it is a limitation of the experimental method.

An individual's realization of the functional nature of such modeled behavior may occur on the basis of a single exposure in the media or only after a number of repeated exposures to similar content. The particular pattern of action may be adopted after a single trial or only after a number of reinforcing experiences. The theory does not provide clear guides to such issues, and they remain at the forefront of research.

What is clear is that modeling theory is a very promising formulation for the study of mass communications. As long as no assumption is made that, because behavior is modeled in the media, audiences will surely adopt it as their own, it is a powerful theory capable of accounting for at least some direct and immediate, as well as *indirect* and *long-term,* influences on individuals who are exposed to media content.

At the same time, there are many influences of mass communication for which modeling theory is not a suitable guide to research. Like the more general social learning theory, it is aimed at *individual* action and not shared behavior. That is, it is capable of explaining why a specific person adopted a particualr form of behavior that was portrayed or described in a given instance of media content, but it has little or nothing to say about either the shaping of the social organization of any group or society, or the contributions of mass communications to culture—two very powerful influences on the behavior choices of individuals who interact with other people. Therefore, different approaches are needed to account for long-term and indirect effects of mass communications in shaping people's shared conceptions of the rules of conduct and conceptions of the patterning of group activities.

SOCIAL EXPECTATIONS THEORY

Psychologists see human behavior in terms of inner processes that shape the actions and behavioral choices of individuals. The research task is to uncover what forces or factors operating in their minds explain what people choose to do when responding to the patterns of stimuli that they experience through their sensory functions. Depending upon the theoretical persuasion of the particular psychologist, those inner processes may be thought of as conscious, unconscious, learned, or inherited. All of these variations are the independent or causal variables, while the dependent or effect variable is the overt behavior of the person to be explained by the psychological theory.

Sociologists (and some anthropologists as well) approach the study of human behavior from a different perspective. They recognize without question the need for a psychological/individualistic level of analysis, but they believe that it presents a very incomplete picture of the human condition. Perhaps the most obvious fact about human beings is their intensely *social* nature: They are conceived in a social act; they are reared in a group characterized by intimate interpersonal bonds; they live out their lives in webs of complex social interaction; and finally, they are sent to their graves in a social ceremony. In other words, they are far more than individualistic organisms responding to stimuli. For that reason, sociologists focus mainly on social interaction—observable events that take place *between* people rather than inside their nervous systems or cognitive structures.

Social Organization Theory

Sociological analysis of human behavior begins with an understanding of the nature of human groups. The fundamental postulate of sociological explanations is that stable patterning of human social interaction is what gives direction to human conduct. In most circumstances of life, when people choose what course of action to follow, their primary considerations are the expectations of others and their probable responses. Simply put, people worry about "what other people will think"—about the approvals, disapprovals, rewards, punishments, recognitions, or disgrace that their actions might provoke. As the pioneer sociologist Charles Horton Cooley put it:

> The imaginations which people have of one another are the solid facts of society.[9]

Cooley was referring to the fact that people in groups organize their exchanges with each other within mutually understood rules. Those rules provide definitions of acceptable behavior, predictability in what each member of a group is expected to do, and understanding of what each can anticipate from the others. Without such stability, life as we know it would be impossible; every human encounter would have to be worked out anew on a trial-and-error basis. There could be no organized group life, no society, and in fact, no civilization; human existence would be a Hobbesian nightmare—continuously chaotic, unpredictable, inefficient, stressful, dangerous, and probably short!

The patterns that arise out of stabilization of rules for interpersonal interaction are collectively called *social organization*. This is an umbrella term that refers to several categories of conventionalized arrangements for ensuring stability and predictability of interpersonal behavior in every kind of human group. Human beings who either are members of groups or have to have transactions with groups must have understandings of each group's pattern of social organization. It is such expectations of probable social behavior that provide them with guidelines as to what patterns of action and reaction can be expected in such behavioral settings.

Social organization within groups ranges from relatively simple to exceedingly complex. Groups can range in size from two members (e.g., husband and wife) to hundreds of thousands, or in some cases even millions. Social organization increases in complexity as group size increases. In large groups, such as corporations, government agencies, or military services, patterns of social organization are complex indeed. Even entire societies can be thought of as huge groups characterized by extremely complex patterns of social organization. Their economic, political, educational, religious, and other types of activities are carried on within shared rules, traditions, and laws that define how people are supposed to behave. In the case of societies as a whole, the term *social structure* is often used to indicate major divisions of their social organization into social institutions (such as the family, the economy, government, and so on) or into socioeconomic classes, castes, or other broad divisions.

Whatever the size of a group and whatever its level of complexity, its major components of social organization can be understood in terms of four fundamental concepts: *norms, roles, ranking,* and *sanctions.* These are the essential subdivisions of social organization that provide predictability in human interpersonal activities, and it is to these concepts that we must look to understand the idea of social maps.

In 1970 DeFleur set forth a relatively simple *cultural norms theory* that provided the foundation for the more comprehensive social expectations theory. In brief, the earlier formulation included the following idea:

> . . . the mass media, through selective presentations and emphasis of certain themes, create impressions among their audiences that common cultural norms concerning the emphasized topics are structured or defined in some specific way. Since individual behavior is usually guided by cultural norms (or the actor's impressions of what the norms are) with respect to a given topic or consideration, the media would then serve indirectly to influence conduct.[10]

While the theory was developed at some length, it was at best only a first step toward a more comprehensive understanding of some of the indirect influences of mass communmications on behavior. In other words, it simply did not go far enough. For that reason, it has been expanded in this edition to include *all* of the components of social organization: roles, ranking, and sanctions in addition to norms. After these components have been discussed briefly, the manner in which mass communications can influence socialization will be made clear.

Norms are general rules that are understood and followed by all members of a group. They cover an enormous range of activities, from simple rituals (such as what to do when answering the phone) to emotionally significant prescriptions on who is permitted to have sexual access to whom. Some are of little consequence if people deviate from them (e.g., belching in public). Others are of such a serious nature that people expect them to be rigidly followed (e.g., "thou shalt not kill"). Some are informal, arising spontaneously out of people's exchanges on a day-to-day basis (e.g., borrowed tools should be returned). Others become legislated into formal written codes that are backed by the power of the state (e.g., laws pertaining to contracts). Thus, whether they pertain to trivial or serious forms of action, and whether they are informal or formal, norms are general rules that presumably apply to all members of a given group, community, or society. Behavior within group settings requires that people have internal, that is acquired, "maps" of these norms—which can be very subtle and complex—if they are to interact smoothly with others within the bounds of accepted conduct.

Roles are also rules, but they apply to specific positions in the organization of a group's activities. They define specialized parts people play in group activities, rather than general guides to action for all members. An obvious example is that husbands, wives, and children play distinctive parts in the family. Larger groups, such as business companies, colleges, or military units, often have many distinctive roles. In communities and societies the role structure becomes very elaborate.

Roles permit people acting collectively in a coordinated manner to accomplish goals that could not be achieved if each member acted independently. The key factors here are *specialization* of activities, and their *interdependence*. People acting within a set of specialized and interdependent roles are like the parts of a machine or an organic system. Each specialized function in the division of activities makes its contribution, and the end result is an emergent consequence (goal achievement) that is more than the sum of its parts.

For the above reasons, a group is sometimes referred to as a *social system*, with interlocking components that contribute to the overall stability and continuance of the group as a whole. An example often used to illustrate the point is a baseball team, with each member playing a particular part that is coordinated with the activities of the others. If each player simply decided what he or she wanted to do and acted independently, few games would be won.

While each role is a pattern of specialized activities, the whole interlocking set in a group needs to be understood by all of its members. Or, if the group is large and complex, each member needs, at least, to understand the roles that link up in some manner with his or her own. This means that the system of role definitions within a group must be learned reasonably well by every member in order that the individual's assigned role can be coordinated with those of others linked to it. Again, the point can be illustrated with the baseball example. Imagine, if you can, a team where each member knew his or her own role quite well but had no idea of what other players would do if the batter struck the ball. It would truly be a comedy of errors! Thus, effective group activity requires that each member have a kind of "role map" in mind, so that the reactions of others can be predicted under a wide variety of circumstances.

A third component of social organization is *ranking*. Some members of groups have more power, authority, and prestige than others.

Often these lead to significant differentials in privilege, rewards, and perquisites. Differential power means that some are able to get others to follow their orders. Authority implies that such individuals have the backing of the group as a whole in the exercise of that power. Prestige or "social honor" means that some members are shown deference for one reason or another. In fact, every member of a group earns, or is assigned, a position or *status* in a hierarchy of ranking based on some combination of the above factors.

It is essential for the smooth functioning of a group that social ranks be recognized by every member and that behavior toward others takes these into account. Whether one likes ranking or not, it is an inescapable and probably necessary component of social organization, even in seemingly egalitarian groups.

Finally, *sanctions* are administered within groups for the purpose of maintaining social control. Human nature being what it is, there are always tendencies toward deviant behavior. People transgress norms; they fail to play roles according to expectations; they defy the wishes or orders of the powerful; or they fail to recognize the status of those who enjoy social honor. Such deviance disrupts the functioning of the group as a system of predictable social behavior and thereby limits efficiency in the attainment of goals and makes life stressful for the majority. For those reasons negative sanctions are applied to punish deviants and to try to deter those who might contemplate such transgressions. Positive sanctions are used to reward those who conform conspicuously, assisting the group in its goal attainment. Obviously, it is critically important to have reliable expectations of the social control practices of groups if one wants to avoid negative sanctions.

Generally, then, social organization theory places an emphasis on events that occur between people rather than only in their heads. Obviously, people have to *learn* norms, roles, and all the rest, but those internal modifications of the psyche are not the whole story. Social behavior is more than the sum of its parts. Groups take on their own existence that is at least conceptually independent of their current members. As people form groups and collectively seek goals through patterned social interaction, their shared expectations become stable social systems in their own right. Cooley was correct in identifying the "imaginations we have of one another" as the "solid facts" of society. Thus, social organization theory shows how the stable expectations characterizing a social system can be powerful influences on behavior.

Media Portrayals as Sources of Social Expectations

The mass media are a major source of patterned social expectations about the social organization of specific groups in modern society. That is, in their content they describe or portray the norms, roles, ranking, and sanctions of virtually every kind of group known in contemporary social life.

By reading books, watching television, going to the movies, and the like, youngsters who have yet to leave home can see the norms of dozens of groups—criminal gangs, fashionable restaurants, surgical teams, the police, rich families, rock bands—the list is almost endless. From the same sources they can learn what role behavior would be expected of them if they became a private investigator, professor, ballet dancer, professional scuba diver, or tennis coach. Similarly, they can see the patterns of social honor or dishonor, the acts of deference or disdain, that are awarded people in various positions within groups. Finally, they can vicariously experience the rewards and punishments that accompany social disapproval of deviance or recognition of conspicuous accomplishment.

These are powerful and complex lessons. Obviously not all youngsters will enter and participate in all of the groups whose patterns of social organization are portrayed by the media. However, they will probably enter at least *some* groups for which media portrayals have provided their only form of socialization. Even the earliest studies of the influence of mass communications on children (the Payne Fund studies completed during the 1920s) revealed that youngsters internalized norms, role definitions, and other understandings of social organization from what they saw on the screen.

Social expectations theory, therefore, pertains to socialization influences of mass communications that result from their portrayals of stable patterns of group life. Such stable patterns define what people are expected to do when they relate to each other in families, interact with fellow workers, worship, study, purchase consumer goods, and in many other ways take part in community life. Specifically, portrayals of everything from child–mother relationships to the social observances of death help define the expectations that potential members of groups have prior to participation in organized social activities. They are also a source of anticipations about how people will behave in other kinds of groups that make up the society. The basic ideas can be summarized in the following propositions:

1. Patterns of social organization in the form of norms, roles, ranking, and sanctions pertaining to specific types of groups are frequently *portrayed* in media content.
2. Those portrayals for any particular type of group may or may not have *authenticity*. That is, they may be trustworthy or misleading, accurate or distorted.

3. Whatever their relationship to reality, members of audiences assimilate such definitions and they become their learned *sets of social expectations* of how the members of such groups are expected to behave.
4. Such expectations are an important part of people's prior understandings of behavior that will be required of participants within groups *of which they will become members.*
5. People's sets of expectations of behavior of members of the many other groups that make up their community and society are an important part of their *general knowledge of the social order.*
6. The definitions provided by these expectations serve as *guides to action,* that is, definitions as to how individuals should personally behave toward others playing roles in specific groups, and how others will act toward them in a variety of social circumstances.

Such assertions bring together two sophisticated areas of study of the modern behavioral sciences: learning in the form of socialization, and the patterning of human activity in the form of social organization. Learning and social organization are the two central concepts of psychology and sociology. It would be difficult to imagine a viable theory of the long-term influences of mass communication that ignored them. In addition, social expectations theory provides for an accounting of social action that is not dependent upon cognitive forces and factors that shape and control human behavior. The older idea that mass communications (1) convey *information* (2) that the individual remembers in such a way that it shapes inner forces, such as *attitudes,* which (3) are closely correlated with and (4) both motivate and give direction to overt *behavior,* becomes unnecessary. Social expectations theory is a conceptually simpler formulation: It is based on the idea that (1) the media convey information regarding the rules of social conduct that the individual remembers and (2) that directly shapes overt behavior. The complex apparatus of attitude formation or change, assumptions of attitude–behavior correspondence, and all of the other difficult assumptions of the cognitive explanations are simply unnecessary. That being the case, the theory is more *parsimonious*—an important consideration in the development of explanations.

In summary, social expectations theory is an explanation or account of long-range and indirect influences of the media. Like many theories, it is a derivation from more basic considerations. We have shown that it is an application of more general theories of socialization and social organization. It portrays the media as an agent of (unwitting and unplanned) instruction that links the two.

In this sense social expectations theory is much like modeling theory, which is also an explanation of long-range influences. It is also derived from the more general sources—both socialization and broader social learning theory. Both attempt to show that people can use the mass media as sources, either deliberately or without conscious awareness, from which to acquire guides to appropriate behavior that will help them adapt to the complex world in which they live.

Neither modeling theory nor social expectations theory is particularly useful as a guide to research if the strategies are limited to the experiment or the sample survey. They both help in explaining how certain kinds of media presentations and content can play a part in the long-term socialization of people in a society where mass communications are abundantly available. However, it would be difficult to design a controlled experiment in which all of the actions modeled in media content over any long-term period could be carefully tabulated for any individual. Similarly, it is difficult to imagine a social survey that could show in a single assessment, or even repeated assessments, the kind of norms, roles, ranking, and sanctions that a sample of persons encountered in the media during a relatively lengthy period.

What this seems to imply is that both modeling theory and social expectations theory are explanations *of a different order* from those derived from the cognitive paradigm. They are not tightly articulated sets of propositions that set forth systematic relationships between a few independent and dependent variables, following the model of the physical sciences. They are relatively broad *conceptual frameworks* that help organize and interpret relationships between various categories of media content and long-term influences on individuals and society. Each offers, in miniature, a *synthesizing principle*. Each does so in the same sense that Darwin's conceptual framework of evolution made it possible to see relationships between adaptation to environment and the emergence of species. It would be absurd to suggest that either modeling theory or social expectations theory will ever have, or should have, the elevated status of Darwin's renowned formulation. But that is not the point. The important point is that, on a very small scale, their conceptual structure is the same.

No one has ever performed an experiment, or a sample survey of biological phenomena, that "proves" or "disproves" Darwin's famous synthesizing principle. It is not likely, or even necessary, that they ever will. In the same sense, it is highly unlikely that such final proof will be forthcoming regarding the two theories of indirect influence discussed here. However, they can stimulate a great deal of systematic observation of the content of the media in terms of both modeled actions and the portrayal of social expectations. They also encourage long-term observation of populations to seek the traces of their workings in the daily behavior of citizens in our emerging media society.

NOTES

1. *The Republic of Plato*, trans. Frances MacDonald Cornfield (London: Oxford University Press, 1941), pp. 66–92.
2. For a classic statement of the significance of the process, see John A. Clausen, ed., *Socialization and Society* (Boston: Little, Brown, 1968).
3. Robert A. Levine, *Culture, Behavior, and Personality* (Chicago: Aldine Publishing Company, 1973). See especially pp. 61–68.
4. Sigmund Freud, *An Outline of Psychoanalysis* (New York: W. W. Norton and Company, 1949).
5. Albert Bandura, *Social Learning Theory* (Englewood Cliffs, N.J.: Prentice-Hall, 1977).
6. *Ibid.* p. 13.
7. The earliest accounts of extensive modeling of behavior shown in films were part of the Payne Fund studies. In particular, the large-scale qualitative studies of Herbert Blumer showed the enormous extent to which youngsters of the time took on the mannerisms, speech styles, overt behaviors, and even clothing fads of the stars. See Herbert Blumer, *The Movies and Conduct* (New York: The Macmillan Company, 1933). For other well-known accounts, see: Albert Bandura, *Aggression: A Social Learning Analysis* (Englewood Cliffs, N.J.: Prentice-Hall, 1973); and R. M. Liebert, J. M. Niele, and E. S. Davidson, *The Early Window: The Effects of Television on Children and Youth* (New York: Pergamon Press, 1973).
8. Allen Liska, *The Consistency Controversy: Readings on the Impact of Attitudes on Behavior:* (New York: John Wiley and Sons, 1975).
9. Charles Horton Cooley, *Human Nature and the Social Order* (New York: Schocken Books, 1964), p. 184. First published in 1908.
10. Melvin L. DeFleur, *Theories of Mass Communication*, 2nd ed. (New York: David McKay, 1970), p. 129; see also pp. 129–39.

CHAPTER 9

Mass Communication and the Construction of Meaning

The study of communication, broadly conceived, has an ancient history, but it has never enjoyed the popular prestige or visible accomplishments of many of the traditional scientific disciplines. That is the case undoubtedly for many reasons, including the complexity of the subject matter and the fact that what *has* been learned is largely hidden from the public in esoteric works of philosophers, social scientists, and other scholars.

The study of *mass* communication as a separate discipline has barely begun. While the public is often eager to have answers as to what some specific form of content is doing to them, research on mass communications has yet to develop a favorable image among the community of scholars. The reasons are fairly clear. Attempts to develop media research as a scientific enterprise have been in full force for only a few decades. Those attempts are succeeding, but at the outset the fledgling suffers from the same syndrome as older kinds of communication studies. An additional handicap is the fact that much of the content of the media is at a low intellectual level, ranging from commercials and cartoons to soap operas and spectator sports. This suggests that since much of the content of the media is superficial, its effects are probably unimportant and therefore those who study such things must be intellectually limited people engaging in pursuits of little consequence. As one pair of observers have put it:

The study of the process of communication has a long history, but usually has been treated trivially. In our judgment, various forms of communication often have been the primary concern of second-rate minds and the secondary concern of first-rate minds."[1]

In defense against such claims, one is tempted to quote Mark Twain, who, upon hearing that he had been denounced in public for being a dullard and a bully who often staggered home in a drunken state and viciously beat his wife, simply claimed that "scarcely half of that is true!"

Perhaps more to the point is the fact that it often takes a new discipline a very long time to get started. Before it can become accepted by others, it has to identify its boundaries clearly, establish its credentials in a variety of ways, organize its teachings, agree on its methods, identify its criteria for acceptable knowledge, and certify its practitioners. Finally, a very important step is to identify and appreciate its intellectual roots.

The intellectual foundations of a discipline are often found in the writings of earlier thinkers who grappled with some of the same issues that confront contemporary scholars, although obviously within the limits imposed by their time. When a new discipline is in its founding stages, it is usually not clear that earlier writings had focused on issues that are now seen as contemporary. At some point it is realized that the older scholars did in fact place certain concepts and conclusions into the general intellectual culture and that these inevitably became part of the principles of the new discipline. Those ideas then have to be thoroughly studied and made part of the discipline's intellectual heritage.

Being influenced by the thought of philosophers whose names one scarcely knows, or whose works one has never read, is a subtle process. The influences are embedded in one's heritage of language and self-evident truths, but they are difficult to identify. Even if they are rediscovered, conclusions about their influence will remain controversial. Nevertheless, each discipline must seek and recognize its intellectual ancestors.

Once the foundations of the field are identified, a much-needed maturation takes place. The discipline becomes a contemporary version of a quest for knowledge that began long before, with its current investigators standing on the shoulders of those giants who first sought to discover its principles. For one thing, that maturation helps to establish the discipline's legitimacy among the community of scholars. More important, however, it brings *efficiency* to its search for knowledge. Its investigators are no longer doomed to a recurrent rediscovery of its basic principles. Instead of naively reinventing concepts and interpretations that were known centuries earlier—like the proverbial rediscovery of the wheel—it can go about tracing out their consequences for current concerns.

Other disciplines have undergone this maturation. The earliest were the physical sciences, which found their roots in the writings of ancient scholars who began the study of mathematics, of the heavens, of matter, and of the human body. During the nineteenth century, social scientists traced their roots back to philosophers who discussed theories of virtuous living and structures of government that could provide for a just social order. During the same period psychologists retraced their history back to ancient scholars who tried to understand the distinctions between the human body and the mind.

The same now has to take place in the study of mass communication. Many of the ideas that are being addressed today had their beginnings long ago. There certainly were no newspapers or television sets in previous centuries, any more than there were antibiotics or space vehicles, but that is not the point. It is not the technology of the media themselves that need to be traced back in this manner; what is important is that certain aspects of human communication, and particularly *mediated* communication, need to be examined in the perspective of intellectual history. It is the identification of *principles* of the human condition that can help media scholars understand how mediated communication today is a process that is both similar to and distinct from the interpersonal communication of the earliest human societies. Without their making that effort, the field will continue to engage in rediscoveries of intellectual wheels.

THE SEARCH FOR PRINCIPLES IN AN AGE OF TRANSITION

A search for timeless principles of communication that are relevant today—in an age of cable television, satellite transmissions, and computerized newspaper systems—must be conducted with a full realization of how far human beings have come from their earliest attempts to exchange meanings. A *theory of transitions,* set forth in first pages of this book, is based on the observation that very distinct and critically important changes in communication systems were developed by human beings during various periods in their prehistory and history. The first was the long change from an era of signs and signals to one of speech and language. This was followed by a period in which writing developed. The transition to print came more suddenly, and it eventually led to our present swiftly changing era of mass communication.

The important features of these transitions are not their specific technologies or the dates during which they occurred. What is important is the *principles* of communication and their consequences for human life that they revealed. Each of these changes radically increased the capacity of human societies to store, recover, and transmit information. Each increasingly set human beings further ahead of other species, as significant expansions followed each stage in the uniquely human ability to innovate and accumulate solutions to problems of coping with the physical and social environments. Some of those transitions took a very long time; others occurred more rapidly. Whatever their pace, their consequences were truly impressive elaborations in the social organization of society, increases in the sophistication of culture, and gains in the thinking abilities of individuals.

These developments have profoundly important implications for the development of knowledge in the discipline of mass communication. In spite of the startling accomplishments in the area of moving visual images, and instantaneous transmission, mass communications remain totally and fundamentally dependent upon the use of language—the first of the great accomplishments that was truly and uniquely human. Therefore, understanding the principles of language lies at the heart of the discipline. The ways in which people share or fail to share *meanings* through the use of language are critical to understanding how communication takes place as well as its consequences for audiences. Thus the serious student of mass communications must understand the nature of words and other symbols, language conventions, the nature of meaning, the implications of shared meanings for perception, and the relationship between language-acquired knowledge and behavior.

The second great transition was the invention and spread of writing. The principles of written communication remain as important in our society today as they were when the earliest works of philosophy were being recorded. While other media have grown in popularity, writing remains our most respected system of storing, retrieving, and exchanging information. Even though many citizens in contemporary societies are not fully literate, writing is the means of communication on which contemporary civilization depends. Therefore, it remains critical for the discipline of mass communication to continue to study how its principles influence our personal and social lives.

Only a few centuries ago another transition came with the invention of printing. It greatly extended the use of writing and became the foundation for the modern development of science, the arts, literature, universities, scholarship, and knowledge of the world in general. Within an incredibly brief time, printed books provided the means by which the philosophers, scholars, explorers, poets, and scientists of the period could record, exchange, and disseminate their ideas. As the press spread, print in all its forms was the medium by which great ideas were disseminated through Western society. They altered forever the nature of religion, government, education, art, commerce, theater, literature, and even popular culture. Today the principles governing printed communication in newspapers, magazines, and books tend to take second place to more fashionable concerns with television. However, the continued search for those principles is as important to the developing discipline as it was in earlier times.

It would be shortsighted indeed to assume that our present transition will have influences on society, culture, and each individual that are any less profound than those that occurred earlier. At the same time, it is difficult to understand the changes that are taking place. Even though we are so deeply immersed in them, long-term trends of a subtle and complex nature can be all but impossible to identify, understand, or assess. A good example of this problem is in the conclusion of Thomas Hobbes in 1651 about the significance of printing. A full century after the use of the press swept through Europe, and in spite of astronomical increases in the availability of books, he dismissed the new form of communication as of little consequence. Yet he was very much aware of earlier great transitions on which he had the perspective of intervening centuries:

> The invention of *Printing*, though ingenious, compared to the invention of *Letters* [alphabetical writing], is of no great matter . . . [But writing is] a profitable invention for continuing the memory of time past . . . But the most noble and profitable invention of all was that of SPEECH, consisting of *Names*, or *Apellations*, and their Connexion; whereby men register their Thoughts; recall them when they are past; and declare them one another for mutuall utility and conversation . . .[2]

It seems likely, then, that the consequences of our current transition will not be fully understood until scholars of future generations can look back on our time and see how mass communications changed human life.

What may be helpful is to take just such a backward perspective and look at the slow development of certain principles of communication that have come forward from antiquity. We may not now be able to look backward at our contemporary communications systems to see precisely how they operate or exactly how they are changing our lives. However, we can sort out more timeless principles of communication that have been uncovered in the past and see if these can be of help in understanding the consequences of communication in an age of mass media.

One area in which this approach may be of particular help is with regard to the way in which human beings develop understandings of the physical and social world around them. Before the time of language, this may have been largely a matter of personal experience, such as trial-and-error learning, with some elements of understanding obtained from the signs and signals of others. This method was not much different from the ways in which other complex animals mastered their environments.

Language provided a more effective means of conceptualization, and obviously a greatly increased ability to obtain knowledge from others. However, for millennia the acquisition of knowledge on the part of the individual had to be done without mediated communication. The oral societies had little but language and the human voice with which to bridge the gap between the objective realities of nature and the individual's subjective internal world of meanings.

The question of how individuals come to know the world around them, talk to each other about it, and agree on interpretations remains central to an understanding of how human beings differ from animals. That surely was one of the very first problems that was pondered, even around the cooking fires of prehistoric times, as human beings gained the capacity to abstract, reason, and analyze. Perhaps for that reason, it was one of the central issues addressed in relatively sophisticated ways in the earliest known teaching of Western philosophers. By the time writing was in use, making it possible to record such teachings, the problem of how people grasp internal understandings of the world external to themselves was already an ancient one.

Since communication is still the central process by which people obtain subjective understandings of objective reality, that process remains a timeless topic of study whose principles are yet to be fully revealed. The part played by *mediated* communication in that process becomes increasingly important as contemporary human beings make increasing use of the mass media. For that reason, the remainder of this chapter is devoted to the way in which understandings of the relationship between external reality and internal constructions of that reality evolved over a number of centuries. The purpose of such an analysis is not simply to show that the problem is an ancient one, but to indicate how some of the principles of human understanding uncovered in past centuries are linked to central issues of the impact of mass communications today. In a very real sense, then, our grasp of many of the indirect influences of contemporary mass communications rests upon an intellectual foundation of ancient origin.

THE ANCIENT QUESTION: HOW DO WE KNOW REALITY?

We suggested above that it is very likely that even during prehistoric periods critical questions were being raised about the major features of the physical world, the origins of humankind, the basic nature of human beings, and the way to design a just social order. Unfortunately, we have no record of the conclusions reached on these issues before the emergence of philosophy. The term "philosophy" itself comes from the Greek words for "love" and "wisdom."

Philosophers before Plato did not leave a heritage of written works, although we know some of the teachings of earlier philosophers through ideas attributed to them by later writers. It is clear that they were concerned with the study of principles that underlie the nature of *being*, that is, existing in reality, and *knowledge*, or the subjective counterpart of that reality.

The study of "being" provided the early foundations of the physical sciences because it addressed the nature of reality itself. Understandings were sought of the substances of which things were composed, the workings of the sun, moon, and stars, the nature of animals, and so forth. The problem of "knowing" eventually led to what we now call psychology and to all of our contemporary social sciences, because it was concerned with the relationship between internal and subjective representations of reality (meanings) and the influence that knowledge had on human conduct. Thus the relationship between knowing and doing was *the* critically important issue to the Greek thinkers because it was the foundation on which conceptions of *virtue* and justice could be developed. They understood that when a person acquires internal knowledge of the nature of things, that knowledge provides the basis for determining appropriate modes of behavior toward those things. This is particularly true of social relationships. Only if the basic social nature of human beings can be known will it be possible to get them to act virtuously toward each other. If that can be achieved, then plans for organizing society can be developed so that justice can prevail in human life. These very basic questions about nature, and human nature, then, were fundamental concerns thousands of years ago. They were the beginning points of science, psychology, and the study of politics—timeless pursuits with which we still struggle today.

In many ways, systematic philosophy begins with Plato. His *Republic* was the first complete book on philosophical analysis that survived. Plato was the student of Socrates, whose teachings provided the foundation for many of his important ideas. From his teacher, Plato adopted the Socratic method as a means of analyzing ideas: He posed a significant question and then tried to reach answers in group discussions with his students. Our contemporary graduate seminars use this approach.

Socrates convinced Plato that certain principles had to be used to develop knowledge. For example, he stressed the importance of *definitions*. That is, he assumed that to *know* something, one had not only to name it, but to define it in precise terms and use that meaning *consistently* in discussions. Only by beginning with clear and concise definitions, and then following rules that specified their meaning in standardized ways, maintained Socrates, could one reason logically from premises to conclusions so as to reach truth.[3] Even today we remain firmly committed to these principles of concepts, meanings, and conventions as the foundations of logical analysis.

But how can we develop meanings on which people can agree? That became a question of overwhelming importance to Plato. In fact, the question of how human beings obtain internal, subjective interpretations of the objective world of reality was the most central issue of philosophy for thousands of years, and it remains of overwhelming importance because it addresses the most fundamental issue of human communication. If we could not develop, label, and agree upon subjective meanings for aspects of objective reality, we could not communicate about them as we do—and we could not function at a human level. The question of the mind versus reality, and how the one knows the other, then, is at the heart of human existence. The Greek philosophers understood this idea completely.

Essentially, there are three issues that are embodied in the ancient problem of "how we know." One is the problem of dividing up the world we contact with our senses into mentally manageable segments and providing a label for each. Inseparable is the associated problem of sorting out in our memories specific clusters of inner experiences that we can label and repeatedly recognize as the meaning attached to the label. These provide our personal definitions corresponding to some specific thing, condition, or state of affairs in the physical or social environment to which we have applied a label. The term *concept* refers to both of those elements of knowing taken together.

An inescapable part of the development of concepts is that of agreeing on rules that a particular label will be associated with a specific definition that embodies the meaning of the concept. This is not individual behavior alone, but a kind of social agreement. Such rules provide our *conventions* of meaning and definition, standardizing the connections between our words for aspects of our environment and the subjective experiences of meaning that they arouse.

Finally, the knowledge we have about some aspect of our environment provides the basis for how we act toward it. Therefore the issue of *consequences* is embodied in the ancient question of the relationship between mind and reality. This is a very complex issue, and in many ways it is the most important one of all. Knowledge may be worth pursuing for its own sake, but it is from our understanding of both the physical and social world that we obtain our guidelines as to how we should live. It was this issue that led the Greek philosophers, and an ever-lengthening list afterward, to propose various systems of government and society so as to make life as equitable as possible for all of their members.

These three issues—conceptualization, conventions, and behavioral consequences—have long been central to the analysis of human knowledge and the human social condition. They are also the foundation of the relationship between language and behavior. For that reason, the ways in which they have been analyzed and understood by some of the great thinkers of the past need to be briefly reviewed.

Concepts: The Foundations of Knowledge

Plato set forth a sophisticated analysis of "meaning" in his Theory of Forms. If we had to rename his analysis today, we might call it a theory of "concepts." Plato was addressing the most fundamental problem of knowledge—how we define and understand things that exist outside our subjective experience. This is the first issue that must be addressed in trying to solve the problem of how we know reality. Plato maintained that human knowledge is developed on the basis of *universals,* or general ideas about the principal characteristics of each category of things that human beings come to think about. He called those general ideas *forms,*[4] and he believed that the reality itself was composed of such forms. They did not have to be things that had hard existence, like a stone, a tree, or an animal; they could be abstractions, like a triangle, justice, or beauty.

Plato maintained that by developing a grasp of the essential attributes of some definitive class of objects, real or abstract, we could easily identify, understand, and discuss any *particular instance* of that category. Thus if we know the essential elements that separate a cat from a crocodile, or a circle from a square, we can recognize specific instances of each, regardless of variations in color, size, or other nonessential attributes of those particular examples. The meaning of an object, then, consists of its form—the configuration of essential attributes that distinguish one category of objects from another.

Later philosophers and other scholars had a lot of trouble with Plato's theory of forms. In contemporary times in particular, approaches to definition and meaning have taken several other routes, especially in fields of science.[5] Nevertheless, when schemes for classification have to be developed, even in scientific work, critical characteristics that set off one class from another become important. Or, when ordinary people have to explain meanings of concepts that they use in informal conversations, they often do so in terms of what they believe to be their essential attributes—the central idea of Plato's approach to the link between mind and reality.

Whether one likes Plato's analysis or not, it is significant to understand that by 400 B.C. the foundations of a theory of human knowledge were already in place. Those foundations were based on the idea of concepts as sets of meaningful attributes of some aspect of reality identified by a term or label that was a part of the language. That principle was not invented by Plato. It probably extends as far back into antiquity as language itself. The significance of Plato's work is that he set forth a systematic analysis, using the alphabetical form of writing that had recently been standardized in Greece. His works remain our major source for understanding the level of sophistication at which the question of knowledge was being addressed at this important turning point in human development. By any measure it was impressive.

Concepts, then, are the foundations of knowledge and the beginning point for a theory of human communication. They represent our way of relating ourselves to reality by providing for our internal subjective experiences of things, conditions, and relationships in our physical and social environment.

Conventions: The Basis of Communication

Whatever system is used for arriving at a definition of an object, condition, or state of affairs, there remains the problem of using that meaning *consistently*. This is a social more than a psychological issue. It is a matter of collective agreement on the rules that link concepts and their meanings. This was a matter of critical importance to Plato. He used the method of Socrates—systematic discourse and debate (communication) among a learned teacher and his students—to arrive at a definition of a concept. After examining all aspects and attributes of the idea, they would achieve agreement on its meanings. Doing this made it possible to spell out its implications or consequences for human conduct, such as the organization of social life. Plato's *Republic*, for example, opens with the question of "what does Justice mean?"[6] The analysis proceeds by describing an imaginary discussion between Socrates and a group of students and associates, leading to a full description of all aspects of the concept. With those meanings in mind, Plato goes on to describe an ideal social system that would provide a maximum of justice for its citizens.

It seems clear that the importance of conventions of meaning—namely, that the subjective interpretation of reality is a *social* as well as an individual matter—was well understood at the time of Plato. Knowledge of the world in which we live, he maintained, depended upon not only what we personally perceived with our senses, but what we agreed upon with our fellows as the shared meanings for the world out there. Modern scholars have come to refer to this idea as the "social construction of reality," but a better term might be "social agreement on meanings." Plato's insights into the role of conventions in structuring meanings are revealed by his well-known Allegory of the Cave.[7]

"Imagine," said Plato, "the condition of men who had always lived deep within a sort of cavernous chamber underground, with an entrance open only to the light and a long passage all down the cave." He then asked the reader further to imagine that the men had since childhood been chained in such a way that they could see only straight ahead. Behind them is a wall, with a parapet built along it. The men cannot see it because they are facing the other way. Just behind the parapet is a parallel road or track along which people move carrying various objects, like figurines of animals and men, that can be held just above the top of the wall. Behind that is a fire burning very brightly so that it glows strongly against the opposite wall of the cave. Such an arrangement will cast shadows of the objects held up by the people as they move along, producing a kind of phantasmagoria, like a puppet show of shadows that can be observed by the chained men. They can talk about the shadows, but they cannot see the actual figurines or the people who are responsible for moving them.

Plato added sound to his shadow show. Suppose, he said, that the people carrying the objects talked freely but that the prison had an echo from the wall on which the shadows were cast, so that the chained men could only suppose that the voices they heard came directly from the shadow images.

The lesson he was posing was this: How would such men construct meanings for the shadows that they perceived with their senses? In every way, Plato maintained, such prisoners would believe that the shadows *were* reality. He believed that they would build their lives around shared rules for interpreting those meanings. They would have names for the different kinds of shadows. They would honor and commend the man with the keenest eye for the passing shapes and the best memory for the order in which they passed. They might give prizes for the one who could best predict what shadows would appear next.

Now, suggested Plato, suppose that one of them was suddenly set free, and he was allowed to see the wall, the walkway, the people, the objects, the fire—the whole of objective reality from which the shadows had been created. He could be told that what he formerly had seen was but an illusion and what he was now experiencing was the true meaning of his former world. In time, of course, he could be retrained and would come to recognize and understand that the new world to which he was now exposed was indeed the objective nature of reality.

But try to predict what would happen if the man were now taken back to the cave, to be seated again in his former place. Try also, Plato asked, to predict what would happen when he tried to explain to his former companions that what they were all seeing was not reality at all, but mere shadows of the real world. How would the others react? Plato was convinced that they would reject his explanations as the ravings of a madman, they would laugh at him, and, if he attempted to set them free to experience the new reality he had found, they would kill him.

Transporting ourselves to the world of today, are we the counterparts of those men in the cave? Does the information shown to us by our television sets or in the movie theater where we view projected shadows on the screen (or even receive in print) lead us to construct shared meanings for the world of reality that have no actual counterparts in that world? It is an ancient idea with a startlingly clear compemory application. Furthermore, there are ample grounds for predicting that we do indeed construct conventionalized meanings for reality on the basis of what our media present!

Modern discussions of the nature of communication continue to stress the importance of linking labels and meanings through social agreements. Language *conventions* refers to the socially agreed-upon rules for interpreting words that are developed within a speech community that shares a particular language. Conventions link a particular word (a specific set of orally produced sounds) to the internal subjective experiences (aroused by contact with reality) that members of the speech community mutually agree will correspond to that word. For communication to be possible, those meanings must be the same, or at least very similar, from one person to the next who shares in the conventions. More simply put, words have meanings that can be shared because of rules or conventions linking the two.

In contemporary times we have somewhat broadened the idea of named concepts and conventions by noting that we develop conventions of meaning not only for orally produced words, but for many other kinds of symbols. Thus language extends beyond oral expressions. Nonverbal gestures often serve as words. So do material objects that play a part in communication. Examples would be waving a clenched fist, or thumbing one's nose at someone. Our conventions are fairly clear about the meaning of such gestures. We use hundreds of objects that have language-type conventions of meaning. Thus, the two silver bars on the collar of an army officer "means" that the individual holds the rank of Captain. The mink coat worn conspicuously "means" that the woman is not from a poor level of society. Other examples of nonverbal symbols would be traffic lights, the skull and bones on a bottle of poisonous liquid, and well-known company logos. Words, of course, remain the largest and most important category of symbols for which we develop and share language conventions.

While we owe much to Plato and his counterparts, we have discovered principles of knowledge in recent times that would have troubled the Greek philosophers. That is, concepts and conventions need have little to do with "truth." The fact that we have a convention that links a particular word (or other symbol) and some agreed-upon meaning says nothing about whether the meaning is "correct" or "accurate." People are able to link consistently virtually *any* word and *any* meaning to develop a concept whether or not it is an accurate representation of the real world. Thus we have words for such concepts as ghosts, flying saucers, Bigfoot, and the Bermuda Triangle. People have internal meanings for these ideas regardless of whether there is any reality "out there" that corresponds to them.

We noted earlier that language conventions linking symbols and meanings provide the foundation of human communication. Obviously, when we converse, read the paper, listen to the radio, or watch television, the parties involved use symbols and their rules for interpretation to arouse internal subjective meanings in the receivers of the messages. That, in fact, is a definition of *human* (but not necessarily animal) communication: meaning-arousal in others. Two important principles of that process were understood long ago, although ways of discussing the issues were very different. First, concepts (labels and their meanings) are the foundation of our personal knowledge of reality (and sometimes unreality). Second, we can communicate because we develop social rules, that is, language conventions, that require consistent linkages between labels and their meanings.

Conduct: The Consequences of Knowing Reality

Another great principle that was well established in early times was that knowledge shapes action. That is, one of the most significant consequences of knowledge is the choice between alternatives in behavior. It was through considering how knowledge shapes behavior that philosophers came to be concerned with the nature of the virtuous life and with justice in human relationships. This concern led to the problem of what kind of a social order would maximize those qualities for the majority of citizens. Codes of law, such as that of Hammurabi, Justinian, and others, sought to make the rules specific.

Later, as Christianity came to dominate Western thought, both moral philosophers and theologians came to address such issues as the nature of "free will." The choice between *good* and *evil* behavior was a matter of the most critical concern. Powerful injunctions and lists of commandments were included in all of the scriptures of the great faiths as guidelines for choosing the one and avoiding the other.

Even in more secular theories of government and power, the problem of how human beings choose deviant rather than conforming behavior has been linked for centuries to the ancient problem of knowledge. The legal systems of Western nations have long assumed that human beings *know* the behavior required of them by their society and that if they deviate from that they do so in a deliberate, willful, and malicious manner. The phrase "ignorance of the law is no excuse" is one form in which that principle can be recognized. Until recent times, when it became recognized that an individual's knowledge could be impaired and that behavior could thereby be caused by factors beyond the person's control, the assumption was made that any criminal "knew the right and chose the wrong to do."

The issue of the relationship between knowledge and behavior remains central in understanding contemporary life. Common sense tells us that our beliefs about the nature of reality set the stage for our decisions regarding action. For example, if we are planning a camping trip in certain parts of the country, we can worry about Bigfoot and the creature's attributes. We can discuss the problem with others if they share our meaning convention and assess the likelihood of an attack. We can also fervently believe in the Bermuda Triangle and avoid sailing into such treacherous waters if we and others share the belief that the danger is a reality.

The principle here is that in shaping our overt behavior as well as our thoughts it is our *shared* convictions that count—our subjective knowledge shaped by the conventions of meaning that we maintain with others—and not the nature of reality itself. If some words have no counterparts in the objective world, but we *believe* that they do, we can still use them to think and communicate. Those beliefs take on a truly compelling significance when we know that others believe as we do (e.g., that Bigfoot *does* exist, or that the Bermuda Triangle really *is* a dangerous area). When such beliefs support a particular interpretation of reality, all who share in the system come to understand that reality according to those shared definitions of meaning.

The Lengthy Search for the Principles of Knowledge

The paths to understanding have never been simple or consistent. For example, between the ninth and the thirteenth centuries, philosophy evolved into a search for quite different truths from the concerns that had been dominant in earlier centuries, yet, as we shall see, it was still focused on the ancient problem of knowledge—what is the ultimate nature of reality, how do we come to know it, and what are the consequences of having that knowledge.

It was a time of consolidation of religion. Greece was but a faint memory. Rome had fallen centuries earlier, and Christianity was the universal Church in the Western world. Scholarly efforts were pursued in the protected environments of monasteries and schools initially set up by Charlemagne. (The great medieval universities eventually developed from them.) Because of their association with these centers of learning, the philosophers of the time have come to be called the Scholastics. Their writings were devoted to a merging of theology and philosophy. The most important knowledge that they sought was that of God and the nature of His social plan for humanity. If knowledge of God's plan for the virtuous life could be discovered, then the true route to moral salvation would be revealed.

The Scholastics had an advantage. They already knew that God existed! Their deep religious convictions could lead them to no other position. So, in their own minds, they already had the most important truth in hand even before they undertook the search. However, they had other truths to seek. At the time there were three ways in which knowledge could be obtained. One was through *revelation and faith,* which they had in abundance. Another was *authority.* There was no science to uncover the nature and workings of the physical universe. The third was through the application of *metaphysical reasoning*—logic that was not dependent upon physical premises, considerations, or limitations. Metaphysical reasoning and the conclusions reached by that method, coupled with the revelations of truth that they already had through their faith, would be their route to valid knowledge.

The Scholastics preferred metaphysical logic to observation of the physical world as a means to obtain trustworthy conclusions, for two reasons. First, they really were not much interested in worldly matters; the important issues were theological. Furthermore, the supernatural could not be observed in any case. Second, they felt that they already understood everything one needed to know about the physical world, because they had the teachings of a great authority. The Scholastics had been reintroduced to the writings of Aristotle, whose works had been brought to the attention of Europeans by the Moors who invaded Spain. Aristotle's ideas had been all but lost to Western society for centuries but kept alive by Arabic scholars. About 95 percent of Aristotle's writings were about the world of nature and he came to be regarded as the final source on such matters. They called him "The Philosopher," or "The Master" and he was regarded as the absolutely final source of truth on all matters pertaining to the natural world. Their principal concern was with the supernatural.

From Aristotle the Scholastics had inherited a sophisticated system of reasoning based on the *syllogism*. Its classic form includes two propositions called the premises, with a common middle term, and a conclusion that necessarily follows from the first two. The classical form is often given as:

Omne animal est substantia
Omnis homo est animal
Ergo: omnis homo est substantia.

Complex versions of this system of reasoning would serve as their means of demonstrating through pure logic the existence of God (just in case anyone did not want to accept it on faith). With that accomplished, they could discover from scriptures and metaphysical reasoning His plan for the virtuous life. With this, they could verify their conclusions about the just society—the rules for living taught and enforced by their Church.

Thus from revealed truth in biblical accounts, plus the reasoning systems of Aristotle, the Scholastics developed a comprehensive body of knowledge consisting of interpretations of theology and guides to human conduct. Their central conclusion was that the teachings of their Church were *infallible* and had to be followed. Those who did not accept those teachings were heretics who had to be vigorously rooted out of society. That activity came to be pursued rather enthusiastically.

As the centuries moved on, other philosophers sought other kinds of knowledge, proposed other ways of establishing truth, and showed other consequences for human life that their conclusions revealed. The issue of the just society continued to be at center stage, but new understandings about the nature and role of language were an important part of the intellectual heritage. These were important in developing insights into human nature. If the true nature of human beings could be understood, that knowledge would show the way to develop the political system that would best serve humankind.

The great figures of the sixteenth and seventeenth centuries were philosophers like Thomas Hobbes and John Locke, both of whom were deeply concerned with the nature of language and how it was related to the mental life of the human being. Hobbes, for example, in his essay on speech saw that it was through words and language that we developed the ability to think and remember:

> The general use of Speech, is to transferre our Mentall Discourse, into Verbal; or the Trayne of our Thoughts, into a Trayne of Words; and that for two commodities; whereof one is, the Registering of the Consequences of our Thoughts; which being apt to slip out of our memory, and put us into a new labour, may again be recalled by such words as they were marked . . . Speciall uses of Speech are these; First, to Register, what by cogitation we find to be the cause of any thing, present or past; and what we find things present or past may produce, or effect; which in summe, is acquiring of Arts. Secondly, to shew to others that knowledge which we have attained; which is, to Counsell, and Teach one another. Thirdly, to make known to others our wills, and purposes, that we may have the mutuall help of one another. Fourthly, to please and delight ourselves, and others by playing with our words, for pleasure or ornament, innocently.[8]

Clearly, by the mid-seventeenth century the principle that thought depends on the self-directed use of language was well understood. The role of words in memory was also evident, as well as the entire idea that knowledge of the objective world, including its causes and consequences, was embedded in speech and language.

John Locke took these principles a step further and made language the basis of the social order as well. He described a relationship among words, internal meanings, and the role of language as a basis of both mind and society:

> God having designed Man for a sociable Creature made him not only with an inclination, and under the necessity to have fellowship with those of his own kind, but furnished him also with Language, which was to be the great Instrument and common Tye of Society. *Man* therefore had by Nature his Organs so fashioned, as to be *fit to frame articulate Sounds*, which we shall call Words. But this was not enough to produce language; for Parrots, and several other Birds, will be taught to make articulate Sounds distinct enough, which yet, by no means are capable of Language.
>
> Besides articulate Sounds therefore, it was further necessary that he be able to use *these sounds*, as Signs of Internal Conceptions; and make them stand as marks for the Ideas in his own Mind, whereby

they might be made known to others, and the thoughts of Men's Minds be conveyed from one to another.[9]

The idea of society as a set of understandings based on symbolic interaction brings together the ancient principle of knowledge as concepts, the principle of language as a social construction of conventions of words and meaning, and the idea that communication is the basis of the social order—"the great Instrument and common Tye of Society." All of those propositions would be greatly elaborated in later centuries within the social sciences.

One of the great debates that was pursued between the sixteenth and eighteenth centuries was the value of *rational* versus *empirical* knowledge—that is, whether true understanding of objective reality could be obtained only through the exercise of reason, or whether it was obtainable through sensory contact with objective reality. Some held that the senses were not a reliable guide to knowledge and that the resulting impressions that were made on the mind were untrustworthy and misleading. It was a very important debate during the time when science was being vigorously developed. What kind of knowledge was this that these new kinds of philosophers were producing? They insisted on *observation* and *experiments* to make those observations more systematic.

The great model for rational knowledge was mathematics. Mathematical truths could be reached by reason alone, and it was an impressive kind of knowledge because of its exactness and precision. Yet others insisted that reason was not enough; it was necessary to look at the world in a very objective way, to count, measure, and experiment. Only by that empirical approach, they maintained, would true knowledge be revealed. As the debate between the rationalists and the empiricists continued, writers like Descartes, Hume, Berkeley, and Kant offered different theories explaining how human beings grasped their mental constructions of reality. One line of thinking, the idealists, rejected both approaches and maintained that we can develop no grasp at all of the true nature of the external world—all we know are the ideas in our own minds.

Slowly, however, the interpretations of the *empiricists* came to dominate philosophy. The world, they said, was perceived through the senses, and internal images and understandings were developed in the human mind. That mind, they believed, was clearly separate from the objective world out there, but it could construct representations of reality and it was necessary to assume that the meanings of one person were more or less the same as those of others. In other words, internal subjective realities were similar from one person to another, making possible interpersonal exchange of meanings through language. That was a very important consensus.

Later this same question of how human beings know the true nature of the external objective world became the most central issue in the philosophy of science. It was critical to the development of a new approach to understanding based on *both* reason and observation. The task of these great pioneers who began the use of the scientific method—like Bacon, Galileo, Copernicus, and Kepler—was to reveal the workings of the *physical* world. It would be long after their time that science would eventually expand to explore the psychological and social worlds.

On the basis of what criteria, however, should the answers revealed by the scientific method be accepted or rejected? The need for an adequate *epistemology* was paramount—a theory of knowledge by which investigators could decide on the truth or falsity of conclusions that they had reached through empirical observation. By the nineteenth century, one of the major answers to that question became *probability*. If a condition could have been produced by chance, even if only rather rarely, it could not be concluded that it was brought about by causal factors under study. It was a new and unusual answer to the ancient question of how we know reality, but it had profound consequences.

If the complex ideas discussed in the preceding sections can be represented by a simple diagram, it might be that in Figure 9.1. During centuries of philosophical analysis and debate, five great principles about human existence had been addressed. Debate continues on all five, but they can be summarized as follows: (1) There is a reality in which we live (including both an objective world of nature and a supernatural one about which we lack consensus); (2) human beings develop some form of mental representations that provide meanings for that reality; (3) there is an intervening process by which individuals construct subjective meanings for reality; (4) our subjective meanings and interpretations guide our personal conduct; and (5) humankind's patterns of conduct are such that a controlling social order of just rules is required. That order, in turn, influences conduct.

The central issue for the present analysis is the process by which we know—the box second from left in Figure 9.1. What is that process by which we obtain our meanings for reality? We have shown that by the beginning of the nineteenth century many answers to that ancient question had been proposed. Some of those who had worked on the problem through the ages claimed that the most important knowledge of all was how we know God and His plan for our personal behavior and the social order. That could be obtained by the application of rigorous

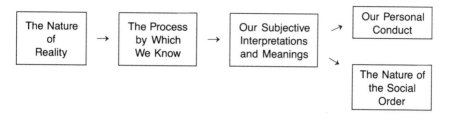

Figure 9.1. The Centuries Old Answer to the Relationship Between Reality, Knowledge, Personal Conduct, and the Social Order.

logic. Other knowledge, about the world of nature, was readily available from authority, from Aristotle who was referred to as The Philosopher, who had long ago worked out all we really needed to know. Later analysts insisted that we obtain our subjective interpretations and meanings through the exercise of reason. We need not be concerned with objective aspects of reality as they actually exist; it is our internal images of it that really count. Some went so far as to claim that there was no external reality; everything that existed did so only in our minds.

Eventually the more modern conclusion was advanced that knowledge is based on empirical contact with objective reality. The critical link between the human mind and the meanings it derives are the senses. Therefore, our images, ideas, and interpretations—our meanings—are subjectively constructed from sensory impressions. That view became especially important to those who wanted to gain knowledge about the nature of the physical world through experiments and controlled observations. As science matured, complex criteria based on probability considerations were invented for deciding whether knowledge reached by that means was trustworthy.

In spite of the almost overwhelming accumulation of knowledge that was produced between the time of Plato and the beginnings of the nineteenth century, however, little was known about how ordinary people acquired and verified *their* knowledge. The world's populations were made up of people of humble origins, who lacked the great learning of the philosophers, who had no access to the logical systems of Aristotle, who knew little or nothing of science and its epistemological theories. Yet, in farm, factory, and city, people in all walks of life still had to come to grips with reality. How did *they* attach meanings to concepts that label various aspects of reality? How were their conventions established to link labels in standardized ways to subjective interpretations of the world outside? Furthermore, what were the behavioral consequences of the unique concepts and conventions of meaning that existed in their particular system? The answers to those questions would come slowly in an uncoordinated manner from new branches of philosophy that would be established during the nineteenth century. They were called the social sciences.

CONTEMPORARY ANSWERS: SOCIAL CONSTRUCTION THEORIES

Each of the social sciences broke away from the central body of philosophy during the nineteenth century. They carried the ancient question of how human beings develop knowledge of reality into their specialized disciplines. Each developed its own concepts, assumptions, theories, and methods of investigation. Starting in the early part of the century the science of linguistics was established.[10] Today linguists probe the structure and semantics of language. During the last half of the century the broad and inclusive field of anthropology emerged, studying everything from ancient bones and the ruins of great civilizations to the cultures of primitive contemporaries. One branch of the field was devoted to understanding how the languages of various people uniquely shape their subjective experiences of the physical and social environment.[11] After initially resisting such subject matter, psychologists came to study how people acquire meanings and how language influences perception, memory, and social behavior. Sociology broke from philosophy early in the century to focus on broad patterns of social organization and change in society. By the beginning of the present century branches of sociology undertook the study of the way that meanings and knowledge emerge from social interaction based on language, and how this process shapes personal and social life.[12]

While each of these disciplines has developed somewhat independently of the others, they clearly have focused on a number of common problems. In particular, each has studied how individuals construct internal subjective meanings for the objects and events of reality, how that knowledge enables human beings to communicate with each other in ways different from those of other creatures, and how that fact shapes both individual and social behavior. In short, they continued the study of the ancient problems. A brief review of some of the major concepts of each discipline will provide an overview of how each has addressed the general principle that the meanings people use are socially derived constructions.

Linguistics: Knowing Reality through Language

Early in the nineteenth century it became increasingly clear that there was a close relationship between the organization or structure of a language and the way in which people use it to arouse meanings in each other. It seemed essential, then, to make a specialized study of the different languages that were in use so as to understand common principles as to how meanings were conveyed by sounds, words, and patterns of words. The field of linguistics began with the comparative study of languages. This quickly led to attempts to reconstruct ancient languages. Later, linguistics became a complex discipline that was concerned not only with origins, but with the organization, patterns of change, and comparative characteristics of contemporary languages the world over.

The search for the earliest language achieved interesting results. Linguists who specialized in comparative studies soon discovered common characteristics and significant differences among and between contemporary languages. However, certain families of languages had many similarities, implying that they might have been derived from a common source. Linguists worked ever backward in time. Painstaking analyses were made of the things that were named and the rules for arranging words together in the most ancient languages for which even fragments of written records remain. By that means, linguists were able to reconstruct at least some aspects of a very old mother tongue, from which languages known in the ancient world seem to have been derived. For example, that parent language contained words for plants, animals, and conditions of climate that characterized life in a rather harsh northern environment. Just such an environment existed during the last Ice Age in areas lying between what is now northern Europe and the western part of the Soviet Union. It was the same area in which CroMagnon people began the first great period of cultural innovation that we have linked to the transition into the Age of Speech and Language.

Whatever the origins of language, its use spread long ago to all peoples of the world. Each has a complex oral system for describing, understanding, and coping with the environment. It is to those systems that linguists turned to expand their studies. Essentially, linguistics today consists of the systematic investigation of three major aspects of language that help understand how people use it to communicate meanings. One area is concerned with *phonology*, the sounds that are used to make up words. Another is concerned with *syntactics*, the rules by which people use patterns of words to convey meanings beyond those associated with each. Finally, *semantics* is concerned with the linkages between words (or other symbols) and their referents, that is, the aspects of reality for which they are substitutes, and the meanings that they arouse if the speaker follows the established conventions of his or her speech community.

These three areas of linguistic study have greatly advanced our understanding of the ways in which people link various kinds of symbols with physical and social referents so as to arouse conventionalized meanings that can be used in communication. For one thing, it is clear that the selection of a particular symbol to use as a label for some referent, some aspect of physical or social reality, is a purely *arbitrary* matter. There is no natural connection between a particular word, sound, written mark, or object and that which it signifies in our world of experience. The conventions people construct to arouse meaning with particular gestures, words, or objects are just that—constructions.

An interesting conclusion from such considerations is that aside from snob appeal, there is no inherently "correct" language. The "right" meanings for words and "proper" grammar become a matter of whatever agreements speakers currently share in the matter of what symbols or patterns should arouse what meanings. If consensus erodes, of course, communication becomes impossible. Therefore there is an understandable tendency to preserve the conventions over time in the form of dictionaries and grammar books. Nevertheless, language is a constantly changing social construction of symbols, referents, syntax, and meanings.

As the specialty of semantics developed, some enthusiasts began to believe that many of the world's ills were caused by the arousal of the wrong kinds of meanings in others by people who were trying to mislead or manipulate voters, consumers, or followers. The field of *general semantics* was developed by reformers who undertook to limit such activities. General semantics is a more mission-oriented field than semantics as such, which remains a more technical study of labels, referents, meanings, and the conventions that link them.

In any case, the study of meaning is incomplete without an understanding of the contributions of linguistics. In many ways, the discipline focuses on the same behavior as that studied by other social sciences. All are extensions of the efforts of the philosophers who attempted to sort out how we know and what difference it makes in the conduct of human affairs.

Anthropology: Cultural Relativity in Constructing Meanings

Anthropologists often define their discipline as the study of human beings, their origins, human societies, and their cultures, both past and present. If that is correct, it is a very broad discipline, with concerns that overlap to a considerable extent those of other social sciences. One of the early offsprings of the field was actually linguistics. Since language is a critical part of human culture, it was natural for early anthropologists to foster its study. Thus it is sometimes difficult to distinguish between linguistics as a separate technical specialty and the study of language and culture within anthropology. Actually, it really doesn't matter. The important issue is what has been discovered and not the disciplinary label of the discoverer.

One of the pioneers in the study of language and culture was Edward Sapir, who in the first decade of this century undertook studies of the languages of various American Indian tribes. Later he expanded his investigations to include languages of many parts of the world, both ancient and contemporary, primitive and modern. By the 1920s Sapir's studies had led him to the realization that not only were the languages of each group different, but the groups' understandings of the physical and social worlds also differed. In other words, it was not simply that each language group had different names for the same set of objects, conditions, and situations in a more or less uniform reality; what seemed to be the case was that people who used different languages were actually experiencing quite different realities! Their words, language conventions, and meanings were shaping their shared constructions of the very meaning of reality, providing each group with distinctive subjective guides as to the characteristics of the world in which they lived.

Sapir's thesis is very clearly summed up in an oft-quoted passage that sets forth the basic ideas and their implications:

> Language is a guide to "social reality." . . . language powerfully conditions all of our thinking about social problems and processes. Human beings do not live in an objective world alone, nor in the world of social activity as ordinarily understood, but are very much at the mercy of the particular language which has become the medium of expression for their society. It is quite an illusion to imagine that one adjusts to reality essentially without the use of language and that language is merely an incidental means of solving specific problems of communication or reflection. The fact of the matter is, that the "real world" is to a large extent unconsciously built up on the language habits of the group. No two languages are ever sufficiently similar so as to be considered as representing the same social reality. The worlds in which different societies live are distinct worlds, not merely the same world with different labels attached.[13]

The discoveries of Sapir, and somewhat later conclusions of Benjamin Whorf, who extended the concepts into the study of perception and thought, have come to be called the *Sapir-Whorf hypothesis*, or the *linguistic relativity principle*.

The implications of this set of ideas for understanding the nature and sources of human meanings are far-reaching. They represent a truly significant extension of the older generalizations from philosophy, namely that we know reality through our senses and that such empirical experience provides the basis for developing meanings for the external environment. That certainly remains true, but *the unique communication processes of which the individual is a part* are now seen as an additional complex of factors that shape and influence the way in which realities are experienced.

Sociology: Symbolic Interaction and Conceptions of Reality

We saw earlier that Plato made an intriguing analysis of the relationship between language, meaning, and reality. That analysis obviously had nothing to do with mass communications, but it is a timeless illustration of the principle that language conventions linking meanings with words have a powerful influence on people's behavior. That principle has emerged in sociology as a major way of analyzing how people can acquire shared definitions for the meaning of things, including the rules of social living and even their own personal nature, by interacting with others through language—or as sociologists like to phrase it, through *symbolic interaction.*

There are two somewhat separate threads that developed around the idea of social interaction and shared meanings as a basis for individual interpretations of the objective world. One came from early social psychology at the beginning of the century. Charles Horton Cooley became convinced that people are able to relate to each other not on the basis of their objective characteristics as they truly exist in reality, but only through the *impressions* that they create of each other through their interactions. He called these sets of impressions "personal ideas." We develop a personal idea for each individual we know, and more general ones for people in different categories taken as collectivities. The personal idea, then, is a construction of meaning, a set of imagined attributes that we project on each of our friends and acquaintances as interpretations of their actual *personae.*

Cooley was convinced that it is only because we can develop these counterparts of actual people in our own minds that we can engage in social interaction with them. We use the personal idea that we entertain for each as a basis of predicting their behavior. We also use such impressions to predict the behavior of others who seem to be like them. Needless to say, they do the same with us:

> So far as the study of immediate social relations is concerned the personal idea is the real person. That is to say, it is in this alone that

one man exists for another, and acts directly upon his mind. . . . *The immediate social reality is the personal idea;* nothing, it would seem could be much more obvious than this. . . .

Society, then, in its immediate aspect, *is a relation among personal ideas.* In order to have society it is evidently necessary that persons should get together somewhere; and they get together only as personal ideas in the mind.[14]

What is not included in the above quotation is one additional element that Cooley discussed as an essential ingredient of social interaction: We must also have a detailed "personal idea" of *ourselves.* This provides us with important knowledge that helps define how we should act in relationship with other people. The knowledge that we are male or female, fat or thin, dull or bright, handsome or ugly, old or young, is critical in forming our responses to others about whom we have personal ideas. Knowledge of ourselves is also obtained in social interaction based on language.

Cooley called our knowledge of ourselves by the colorful name of "looking glass self," because he maintained that we obtain the impression of what we personally are like as a human being by watching the actions of others. There is a kind of social mirror in which we see people accept or reject us, admire or dislike us, and approve or disapprove of the actions we take. It is from these data that we form conclusions of our self nature.

Each to each a looking glass
Reflects the other that doth pass.[15]

Thus, the social construction theory of Cooley was a kind of "psychic organicism" that conceived of human groups and society as a system of personal ideas, plus a personal idea of self, that each person developed as internal and subjective constructions of meanings.

The theory of the personal and social consequences of symbolic interaction was greatly elaborated and systemized during the early part of the century by George Herbert Mead.[16] Even though he was by discipline a philosopher, he had a profound influence on sociologists who were seeking to understand the relationship between individual thought, personal behavior, and the social order. Mead used the term *mind* to refer not to some ethereal entity but to the human capacity to learn and use symbols whose meanings are shared with others. He held that only because of that capacity can people communicate through language based on conventionalized meanings.

The ability to communicate with others was also said to be the key to individual human thought. Mead considered the act of thinking to be an internal response to self-directed symbols. Because human beings have this capacity, they can construct conceptions of self, along the lines suggested by Cooley, and they can learn to anticipate both the actions of others and what they will regard as socially acceptable behavior.

Mead pointed out that in order to relate to other people we have to "take their role." That is, we have to learn the requirements of playing all of the specific parts in a group and then use these conceptions to anticipate how other people in particular roles will respond to our actions. At first we do that in our immediate family as children. Later we expand our conceptions to include the larger society around us in a more general sense. This construction is what Mead called the "generalized other." Mind, self, and society, then, are all constructions—personal assessments and role definitions that we obtain through symbolic interaction.

A contemporary extension of the symbolic interactionist perspective of Cooley and Mead is what sociologists call *labeling theory*. This formulation is particularly relevant to the study of deviant behavior. The basic idea is that a person who violates the law or transgresses some other significant norm is officially "labeled" by an agency of the society. That label, then, becomes a major identity or public meaning for the person, restructuring how others respond to him or her and eventually bringing about changes in the person's self-concept. For example, such labels as "mental patient," "juvenile delinquent," and "prostitute" evoke powerful meanings and cause a person so labeled to be treated in negative ways by the community. It is difficult to escape from such labels, even though the events that brought them down on one's head may have been only a fraction of one's total life. Furthermore, they can be very unfair. For example, people can recover from mental illness, reform their delinquent ways, and refrain from disapproved sexual behavior; but once a mental patient (or whatever), always a mental patient, at least in the eyes of the public, even with full recovery. Thus the meanings people attribute become guides to their behavior toward the individual who bears the label. A dramatic contemporary example is what happens when a person becomes known as an "AIDS victim."

A somewhat independent construction theory that developed in sociology addresses the broader problem of knowledge in general. One branch of the discipline is called "the sociology of knowledge," a term coined in the 1920s in the form of *Wissenssoziologie* by the German philosopher Max Scheler.[17] Its roots, however, lie farther back and indeed could be traced to the same origins in classic philosophy that were discussed earlier. Its principal thesis is that knowledge of *any-thing* that is developed in a society is shaped and limited by the culture that prevails at the time. This is an important idea for assessing both past and present sets of beliefs about "truth."

Of particular concern to sociologists are those forms of knowledge that shape the nature of society. These come in the form of ideologies, religions, scientific explanations, and of course magic and superstition. Each of these at one time or another has been shared by large populations as the only truth to be tolerated about the nature of the social world. The treatment of people within social orders is shaped by such knowledge and can have a profound effect on the quality of human life.[18]

Social Psychology: Schemata as Meanings for Reality

In more recent times social psychologists have turned their attention in force to the problem of human constructions of meaning and how they influence behavior. The terms that they use to label the issues are different from those of other disciplines, but the underlying concerns are very similar. In this line of research, the dedication of psychologists to the experiment remains, as does their general uneasiness with "mental" explanations of human conduct. They tend to avoid such words as "mind," and "thought," and use terms like "cognition," "impression formation," and "information processing," which somehow seem safer.

An important recent symposium was held on such issues and some eleven papers on *social cognition* were presented. In this symposium, which summarizes virtually all of the studies of social psychologists on social cognition up to 1981, nearly two thousand references to research reports (mainly of other psychologists) were cited. The vast majority were published during the last three decades, indicating a sudden resurgence of interest in the issue of meaning and behavior.[19] While little attention was paid to mass communication in this particular symposium, it provides an excellent summary of recent evidence accumulated by psychological experimentation concerning the ancient problem of the nature of human knowledge and its implications for conduct. As we have indicated earlier, that problem remains critical to an understanding of the significance of mass communications in modern society.

"Social cognition" is an umbrella concept that is said to link "cognitive structures" and "processes underlying social judgment and social behavior."[20] Social behavior includes communication, which was treated in terms of a formulation called "the communication game." Other disciplines have traditionally referred to this as "interpersonal communication." Other topics from related disciplines also appear, such as what George Herbert Mead called "role taking," now labeled "communication rule 1," and what Cooley called "personal ideas," now termed "cognitive representations of persons." There was only one reference to a Greek philosopher among the many citations (Aristotle) and the name was misspelled.

In spite of these different orientations to research strategies, labels for concepts, and appreciation for the thinkers of the past, a number of important lines of research have been developed that parallel those of other social and communication disciplines. In particular, the nature of memory and its functions in interpersonal relationships is probed in depth. Perhaps more important, psychologists have rediscovered *language* and its role in social interaction.

The foundation idea around which most social-psychological research on social cognition is organized is the concept of *schemata*. It was introduced in 1934 by British psychologist Frederick C. Bartlett.[21] He studied interpersonal communication of folktales among various African groups in an effort to gain insights into the functioning and limits of human memory. Unfortunately, the term has dozens of definitions today, but it generally refers to the way in which human memory is psychologically structured and how this structure makes possible perception, communication, and social behavior:

> A schema is a cognitive structure that consists in part of the representation of some defined stimulus domain. The schema contains general knowledge about that domain, including a specification of the relationships among its attributes, as well as specific examples or instances of the stimulus domain. As such, one of the chief functions of a schema is to provide answers to the question "what is it?" The schema provides hypotheses about incoming stimuli, which includes plans for interpreting and gathering schema-related information. It may also provide a basis for activating actual behavior sequences of expectations of specific behavior sequences, i.e., scripts for how an individual behaves in a social situation.[22]

If he could have penetrated the psychological jargon, Plato would have understood the idea of schemata very well. Essentially, they are *personal organizations of subjective meanings* for objects, situations, or events perceived through the senses. They are the social psychologist's way of talking about the stored form of human knowledge—internal responses that are aroused by perceiving something directly, or when using words to communicate with others about that reality. A simple example is the idea of a "house." Within the individual's memory is a set of attributes, representations, traces of experience, or whatever one chooses to call them, that enable the person, on being confronted with an actual house, to recognize the corresponding sensory input as consistent with previously stored experience of "house." The organization of those experiences in memory is the schema. That schema works not only in the perception of an actual house, but as the basis for assigning meaning when someone *says* "house" in interpersonal communication. Presumably it also works when the individual wants to express the idea to someone else and uses the term "house" to do so. In addition, the schema enables the person to engage in meaningful imagination or thought about houses and provides an important part of shaping personal and social behavior toward houses or in house-related situations.

Thus contemporary social psychological research is confirming what has long been maintained by philosophers, anthropologists, sociologists and others. There is a critical relationship between the knowledge that we acquire from learning in society and the way we react toward the physical and social world. Schemata, which bear many similarities to Plato's idea of *forms,* provide an understanding of the psychological functioning of memory, perception, thinking, and communication.

Consistent with much previous thinking about the nature of meanings and behavior is the idea that schemata are *constructions* acquired in a social process of learning. Obviously, people are not born with such internal processing structures; they come to the individual as a result of what other disciplines refer to as socialization, within a particular society that has its unique rules for the structuring of meaning. In brief, then, emerging from the experiments of the social psychologists is additional confirmation of the deeply established principles that remembered meanings are the basis of knowledge; that such meanings, along with their labels and conventions, are the basis of communication; and that communication, in turn, is the foundation of the social order.

The most fascinating aspect of our thumbnail sketch of some of the central concerns of four contemporary disciplines is that in many ways they are pursuing the same basic topics but in different ways; they use different vocabularies, and they use dissimilar epistemologies. Unfortunately, however, what is taking place in one is often unknown to researchers in another. The contemporary social science disciplines tend to become intellectual ghettos, where people live and work in isolation from what is happening elsewhere. Also, unfortunately, contemporary researchers often seem unaware of major insights into the human condition that have accumulated over several centuries of social thought and that are directly relevant to the topics they are currently studying. Perhaps for these reasons there is a considerable amount of reinventing of conceptual and theoretical wheels. Swept up in their narrow empirical studies and blissfully unaware of their own intellectual heritage, many modern researchers are what sociologist Pitrim Sorokin called "new Columbuses," rediscovering and renaming, in each discipline, what has long been known. Nevertheless, the contributions of these contemporary lines of investigation can be critical and there is no doubt that they are moving forward the edge of understanding.

MASS COMMUNICATIONS AND THE INFLUENCE OF MEDIATED REALITY

Scholars and researchers who study the process and effects of mass communication have developed several formulations that are founded on the principle that meanings and interpretations of reality are socially constructed. More and more it is becoming clear that, like the men in Plato's cave, we are incrasingly experiencing a mediated world rather than reality itself. Unlike Plato's shadow show, however, our current media expand rather than reduce what comes to our eyes and ears. Still, what we perceive are representations and not reality, and that fact must surely have some impact on us. One of the major features of our current transition into the Age of Mass Communications, then, is that increasingly we are in contact with *mediated representations* of a complex physical and social world rather than only with the objective features of our narrow personal surroundings.

Communication researchers and theorists have tried to develop lines of research and explanation that probe the implications of our current transition into a media society. In some cases, their formulations and explanations have been built upon the intellectual heritage outlined in this chapter. In other cases, theories in communication have simply paralleled those of other social sciences and ignored principles discovered in earlier times. In any case, communication scholars have developed four more or less contemporary formulations that are in some way versions of, or derivations from, what we are calling the general *meaning paradigm*. That paradigm is based on the principles of knowledge, language, and conduct that have accumulated since the members of our species first started the intellectual struggle to understand their own nature and how they were different from their fellow creatures. The paradigm, then, is in part an intellectual heritage that has been examined and reexamined through centuries of philosophical analysis and debate. It is also, in part, the contribution of contemporary social sciences.

It is difficult to capture so many ideas in any simple list of statements, but essentially the meaning paradigm incorporates the following interrelated propositions:

1. Human memory makes possible the development of *knowledge*.
2. Knowledge exists in the form of *concepts*, which are named or labeled structures of meaning remembered by individuals.
3. Meanings for concepts can be developed by a person either by direct *sensory contact* with various aspects of reality, or through *symbolic interaction* in a language community.
4. *Language* is essentially a set of symbols (verbal or nonverbal) that label agreed-upon meanings.
5. Conventions standardize the links between symbol and meaning, making *communication* possible among those who adhere to the rules.
6. The language symbols and conventions agreed upon and used by a particular people shape their *perception* of, *interpretation* of, and *conduct* toward their physical and social world.

In one way or another, the above are the principles that must be taken into account in the development of theories of mass communication that will aid in an understanding of how media content plays a part in the social construction of meaning. Actually, that understanding has not yet advanced beyond a few preliminary formulations that deal with more or less specific aspects of mass communications. Nevertheless, at least four can be identified that address the issue of how the media shape meanings, and the implications that this has for conduct: (1) the *meaning-construction function of the press*, as outlined initially by Walter Lippmann in the 1920s; (2) *cultivation theory*, which grew out of George Gerbner's analyses of television's influence on public fears about violence; (3) the *agenda-setting function of the press*, developed by Donald L. Shaw and Maxwell McCombs as a means of understanding how the public ranks the importance of political issues covered in the news; and (4) *language-shaping function of the media*, which was initially formulated by Melvin DeFleur and Timothy Plax.

The Meaning Construction Function of the Press

Walter Lippmann's classic work, *Public Opinion*, first published in 1922, compiled many examples of how the factual features of the world often have little relationship to the beliefs that people entertain about that world.[23] It also discussed how the press's interpretations of events can radically alter people's interpretations of reality and their consequent patterns of action. He cited the example of Europe in 1914, at the outbreak of World War I. Many people did not hear about the opening of the war for several days (news moved more slowly at the time). All over the world, he said, people continued to manufacture goods that they would never ship, buy goods abroad that they would never import, plan careers, and contemplate enterprises that would never be realized. They were living, in other words, in a world whose depiction would be radically changed once the news of the war arrived.

Lippmann's major point, however, was that the depictions of the press were often *spurious* in that they were very misleading, creating distorted or even completely false "pictures in our heads" for the "world outside." For example, when on November 6, 1918, the press falsely reported an armistice (five days before it actually became a reality), people were rejoicing on the basis of a falsely constructed depiction of reality. Meanwhile several thousand young men died on the battlefields.

Lippmann concluded that people act not on the basis of what truly is taking place or has occurred, but on the basis of what they think is the real situation obtained from depictions provided to them by the press—meanings and interpretations that often have only a limited correspondence to what has happened. These can lead to inappropriate actions and behavior that have little relationship to the true nature of "the world outside."

Lippmann did not name his formulation. However, it is clearly a construction of meaning theory that focuses on the influence of mediated reality. It is totally consistent with the meaning paradigm discussed earlier. Its importance is that it is one of the earliest statements of the role of mass communications in the construction of meanings that provide a basis for human action. However, it was very clearly concerned with the news industries that existed in Lippmann's time. That is, it is a theory restricted to the *press* in a traditional meaning of that term. Therefore, Lippmann's account of how people acquire knowledge from the media points to a *meaning construction function of the press*.

The news media do not set out deliberately to create illusions or to deceive anyone, at least in most Western societies. On the contrary, the ethical codes of journalism stress being "objective," "fair," "thorough," and "factual." But it is a losing game before the players begin. Selectivity and distortions in the news are products of factors beyond the control of reporters, editors, producers, and publishers. The depictions of the "world outside" presented by the press are consequences of antecedent conditions, such as the limited resources that journalists have at their disposal to study firsthand any particular event. They are also consequences of constraints in the process of preparing the news to fit the requirements of a particular medium. Space and time are dear, and all news accounts must be summaries. There is an inevitable loss of detail in any report that attempts to focus on the central facts and ignore others. Furthermore, there is the problem of capturing and maintaining attention in media industries that are dependent upon advertising as their main source of revenue. Those stories and facts that are likely to raise circulations, which leads to attention to advertisements, which in turn leads to profits, must inevitably have a strong claim to scarce space or time.

Therefore the windows on reality that are provided by our press are shaped in part by the nature of the capitalistic basis of the news industry itself. A press functioning in a socialist or communist society is shaped by economic and political factors of a different type, but for many of the same reasons, they also distort pictures in the heads of their audiences.

What Lippmann could not anticipate in 1922 was that his theory would apply equally well to new media that would present the news in the last half of the twentieth century. As radio, and then television, became part of the "press," they also created pictures in the heads of the people who attended to their presentations. Inevitably, and for the same reasons that operated with the newspapers during World War I, those pictures were distorted constructions of reality rather than accurate representations.

A classic study showing how television provides its audiences with interpretations of an event that depart significantly from the actual facts was done during the early days of the medium. Kurt and Gladys Lang made a detailed comparison between the portrayal of an event on television and the actual event as it occurred.[24] The topic was the MacArthur Day parade in Chicago in 1952. General Douglas MacArthur, one of America's great heroes of World War II, was finally coming home. He had led the ground forces in their war against Japan and had remained in the country after the conflict to administer the American occupation. When the Korean War broke out, he was placed in charge of the military operation. Finally, it was time to return to the United States. After his extraordinary services to his nation, it was fitting to honor him, and many communities did so. Chicago, for example, observed MacArthur Day, complete with a huge parade to pay homage to the general.

While thousands of people went to see the parade in person, additional thousands stayed home to view it on television. Here, then, were two versions of the same set of real events—the parade as it took place on the streets of Chicago and the parade as it appeared on the screens of viewers. The Langs sent one body of observers to see the parade in person and to prepare detailed accounts of the reality that they had experienced. The other body of observers viewed the parade on television and also prepared such accounts. Like the men in the cave who saw only shadows, versus the one who was shown what was really going on, the two groups encountered different worlds. The parade on television was lively with constant action. Viewers got the impression of huge, enthusiastic crowds. The general was shown constantly surrounded by admiring people. It was an exciting experience. In contrast, those who actually attended the parade found it rather boring. They waited along the street with a few other people. They saw no huge crowds. The general moved swiftly by in a car. He waved, went on, and that was it! The Langs concluded that television presents a "unique perspective," selecting scenes and using camera angles carefully so as to maximize the excitement for viewers.

Other research has confirmed that the real world and that presented in the media may be substantially different. People in other countries often form their images of the United States on the basis of crime and detective shows, soap operas, and other dramas that American media distribute to markets overseas. We ourselves undoubtedly form conceptions of reality about *their* societies, as well as our own, in a similar manner. Lippmann's belief, then, that the press creates pictures in our heads—illusions—and that these serve as knowledge of reality that shapes our conduct, seems consistent with what we know today.

Cultivation Theory

Another recent construction theory discussing the influence of mediated reality is the work of George Gerbner and his associates. The formulation grew out of the national concern with the effects of violence that characterized the 1960s and 1970s. The study of televised violence became almost an obsession, perhaps as a result of two major federal efforts to understand the issues. One was the appointment by President Johnson of a Commission on the Causes and Prevention of Violence.[25] The second was the authorization by Congress of a large-scale research effort, the well-known Surgeon General's Report.[26] Each included an elaborate inventory of the amounts and forms of violence portrayed on television during the period. The content analyses, conducted by George Gerbner,[27] were not intended to be theoretical; they were numerical accountings of how much of several kinds of violence were being shown on the television screen. The conclusions were that it was a lot. Widespread public interest in the violence issue continued, so Gerbner and his associates did an annual assessment during the 1970s and 1980s, reporting the amount of violence shown on television in terms of a yearly Violence Profile.[28]

In recent years Gerbner and others have developed both a theoretical framework and an empirical strategy for studying the impact of televised violence on people's beliefs. They extended the scope of their interest to include not only the portrayal of violence but other forms of behavior shown on television. Their central proposition is a time-honored one, namely that such portrayals influence behavior by shaping people's beliefs.

The Gerbner group has coined new terms to refer to the idea— hardly a new one—that mediated reality can influence beliefs and thereby conduct. They call it "mainstreaming." In terms of television, they suggest that its content "cultivates" people's beliefs. It is not clear that the introduction of new terms has added much. Their formulation lies squarely within the ancient traditions of the meaning paradigm and social construction theories discussed earlier.

In any case, in their study of "cultivation effects," Gerbner and his associates have been concerned in particular with how violence shown on television exaggerates the fears people have about crime in their neighborhoods. To provide empirical evidence that this is the case, they devised a measuring procedure, called the "cultivation differential," which is essentially a forced-choice procedure for constructing and using questionnaire items. For example, an item is posed for a subject, such as "During any given week, what are your chances of being involved in some type of violence (in your neighborhood)?" Factually speaking, that chance is small—certainly less than one in a hundred, even in a relatively high-crime neighborhood. However, if the respondent has watched a lot of television, and if this experience has shaped that viewer's beliefs that high levels of violence are to be encountered in reality, the chances of being victimized may appear subjectively much higher (e.g., one in ten). Thus, "one in ten" can be posed as a *television* answer to the questionnaire item, while "one in a hundred" can be the *reality* choice. The prediction of the theory is that if the viewer's beliefs have been "cultivated" by violence shown on television, he or she will choose the television answer. It is an interesting strategy. While it rests upon all of the limitations of survey research that were discussed in Chapter 7, it does focus attention on very specific forms of behavior and link them to very specific forms of media content.

Data assembled with the cultivation differential approach seem to show that at least some people who view television frequently have exaggerated fears about the level of violence that they expect to encounter in their neighborhoods. Unfortunately, this type of research thus far has raised a number of methodological questions. Investigators who have attempted to replicate the findings have not found their data in support of the hypothesis that television has shaped people's fears of their neighborhoods. Rather, the actual level of crime in the area seems to be a more important factor.[29]

In spite of the controversies it has generated, and regardless of whether or not it is more than a reinvention with new labels for well-established theoretical wheels, cultivation analysis is a promising effort to pursue the ancient question of how we gain knowledge and how that knowledge serves to guide our conduct. Hopefully, such assessments of people's beliefs will help to show how mediated reality influences our meanings for the objective world.

The Agenda-Setting Function of the Press

An additional effort to understand the implications of mediated reality is the hypothesis of the *agenda-setting function of the press*. The basic idea is that there is a close relationship between the manner in which the news media (the press in a broad sense) present issues during a political campaign and the order of importance assigned to those issues by those exposed to the news. This construction theory is specifically focused on political news as opposed to the broad spectrum of media content in general. In addition, it is focused on one type of internal meaning or set of beliefs that result from media portrayals—the rank order of importance attributed to a set of political issues that are discussed in the press. Nevertheless, it is consistent with the broader meaning paradigm, and it is a social construction issue relating mediated reality, the development of subjective meanings, and their influence on conduct.

The basic hypothesis was put together in researchable form by Maxwell E. McCombs and Donald L. Shaw during the late 1960s. It became the central formulation for a small-scale study of the news about the presidential campaign of 1968 and how people perceived the importance of the issues.[30] A content analysis was made of how television, newspapers, and news magazines presented political news about the candidates and the issues over an extended period, and a small survey was conducted to assess the beliefs of respondents about the differential importance of the issues that had been covered by the media.

Essentially, what was found was a high level of correspondence between the amount of attention given to a particular issue in the press and the level of importance assigned to that issue by people in the community who were exposed to the media. This did not mean that the press was successful in swaying their audiences to adopt any particular point of view, but it was successful in bringing people to regard some issues as more important than others. The agenda of the press did become the agenda of the public. In this sense, there was close correspondence between the world outside and the pictures in the heads of the voters studied.

The success of the first study in establishing this relationship led the researchers to conduct a larger investigation of the 1972 presidential election,[31] and this effort generally confirmed what had been found the first time. The scope of the research was much larger, the campaign issues were not the same, and the site of the study was different. Nevertheless, the general hypothesis was confirmed. The agendas (levels of attention given to issues) set by the media were closely related to the rankings of importance assigned to the issues by their audiences. In addition, the researchers studied a large number of intervening variables to understand differences between the media, the role of individual differences, and the influence of social categories on the agenda-setting process.

The study of agenda setting has now become a well established research tradition. What is important about this line of theory development and research is that it represents something of a "back to basics" movement for communication researchers. It follows the established traditions of the role of the press in elections and it explores the "power of the press" to help shape public thinking about the political process and the problems it addresses. As it develops further, the results of agenda setting may be more fully addressed, and its importance in the broader democratic process may become increasingly clear. For example, if people come to regard a particular set of issues as having greater or lesser importance, will this emphasis influence the way they vote for particular candidates? Will that public agenda lead politicians to emphasize issues at the top of the public's list and ignore those at the bottom? No clear answers are available on such questions, but they broaden the importance of the agenda-setting hypothesis from a descriptive formulation to one that has potential significance for the dynamic relationship between press, public, and politicians.

The Speech and Language Functions of the Media

As the transition to the media society continues, a larger and larger proportion of the ordinary citizen's daily communication activities are spent with the mass media. Our principal means of communicating is still, and probably always will be, talking face to face. Yet the amount of time that people spend with media has increased dramatically over the last several decades. By 1985 the television set in the typical household in the United States was turned on some seven hours and ten minutes every day, a substantial increase from four hours and fifty-one minutes in 1955. Radio set ownership during the same period increased from three sets per household to nearly six. The use of print in the form of magazines, books, and newspapers has also increased.[32]

As the proportion of our total communication activities that are devoted to attending to mass communications grows, media presentations can be expected to have an increasing influence on the ways Americans speak, the words they use, and the meanings conventionally associated with their symbols. We will refer to such influences as the *speech and language functions of the mass media.*

There are two ways in which the media modify our entire range of communication activities. One is through their influence on our patterns of speech—our pronunciation, grammar, and syntax. The other is on language more generally through vocabulary expansion and modification. By so doing, the media serve as a kind of marketplace of competing forms for influencing our communication. Those influences tend to change and stabilize speech, language, and meanings.

To a certain extent, books did this for written language from their beginnings, and newspapers performed the same function when they became popular. They may still do so daily presenting printed versions of our vocabulary, consistent rules of grammar, and styles of written expression that are fairly similar from one part of the country to another. Television appears to serve a parallel function in oral communication. Actors and actresses in daily soap operas, crime-detective stories, or popular situation comedies all pronounce their words in about the same way and use the same general rules of grammar. The same is true of individuals who present morning shows or the evening news. They do so with a general American accent typical of relatively affluent and educated populations from the midwest. It would be unusual to hear such programs offered by people using regional pronunciations or the speech forms typical of poorly educated strata in American society. While media speech styles have by no means replaced accents, grammar, or syntax used in various local regions, among different ethnic groups, or among people at lower economic levels, they may eventually tend to smooth out such variations.

As mass communications become a larger and larger proportion of our entire communication process, it can also be anticipated that they will have an increasing influence on vocabulary—the symbols we use, the meanings we associate with those symbols, and the conventions we agree upon to link the two. It is already clear that the mass media have greatly expanded our vocabulary. Hundreds of new words have been added that probably would not have found their way into the language without being rapidly presented and diffused by the media. Who, for example, heard of "crack" as a type of dangerous narcotic before 1985?

Before that date, it was used as a slang term among drug users in certain urban areas to refer to cocaine in a particular form, but for the majority of Americans it aroused only its traditional meaning. Then suddenly it appeared in news reports that swept the country. Today Americans share a new and more sinister meaning for "crack." Everyone "knows" that it is a concentrated and dangerous form of cocaine used in "freebasing," readily available to the youth of the nation, among whom its use has spread, posing a new threat to an already troubled society.

The problem with that media-created meaning is that it is factually incorrect. There is no insidious crack "epidemic" sweeping through the youth of America. However, in this case we know how that frightening interpretation of reality was created and how it spread. James Inciardi, one of the nation's leading authorities on illegal drugs, traced it back to an article that appeared in the *New York Times* on November 17, 1985. The word "crack" was used for the first time in that news report as a term to describe what was said to be a new form of cocaine with sinister implications. From there it spread to other papers. Six months later information on crack had appeared in some 400 newspaper reports on drug abuse. Then within a few months CBS did a major prime-time presentation on the dangers of crack, reaching an estimated 15 million viewers. NBC quickly followed with another major exposé. The term "crack" was by then a deeply established term in the American vocabulary with a new and dreadful meaning. Public opinion polls showed that worries about crack became the number one concern of Americans during the period immediately following this publicity.[33]

The media, then, have important influences on our language and meanings. They do so in several ways: They *establish* new words with associated meanings; they *extend* the meanings of existing terms; they *substitute* new meanings by displacing older ones; above all, they *stabilize* existing conventions of meaning for the vocabulary of our language.[34]

The establishment function of the media can be illustrated easily by the constant flow of new words and associated meanings that they present to their audiences. A decade ago very few Americans would have understood the meaning of such terms as "wimp," "couch potato," and "jazzercise." Today few have difficulty in responding subjectively to these terms as labels for a meek individual, a lazy viewer of a great deal of television, and a vigorous form of exercise done in time with music. That is not to say that new terms are constantly invented by media personnel and deliberately introduced to the public. They are simply spread quickly and efficiently on a nationwide basis because media have large audiences.

The extension function of the media is somewhat different. Many words that already have well-established definitions are given additional elements of meanings through media presentations. For example, the term "ecology" was at one time a technical term used mainly by a restricted scientific community to refer to a system of balanced relationships between organisms in a local environment. Its popularization by the mass media has added more general and less technical meanings, vaguely implying a concern about protecting the physical environment from degradation.

We noted above, with the case of crack, the substitution function of the media. It was a simple word, with a rather clear meaning. Then through an almost frenzied use of the term in a way that substituted new meanings for old, the media created a totally new interpretation. Such substitutions take place constantly. Another example is the term "gate." If asked today what the term "Watergate" means, most Americans will refer to a political scandal (assuming reasonable acquaintance with recent history). At one time, however, it referred merely to a fashionable hotel and apartment complex beside the Potomac River in Washington, D.C. Massive publicity about misdeeds associated with the Nixon administration transformed its meaning to refer to scandalous events. At present, the term "gate" can be conveniently attached to any name to suggest the same interpretation. For example, in recent years political issues related to swaps of arms for hostages brought "Irangate."

Finally, the stabilization function of the media is that they reinforce existing usages. In spite of the changes noted above, most meanings in our language remain relatively constant. Furthermore, as we noted above, regional and class differences are not perpetuated by the media. On the contrary, in both spoken and written form, the media remind us daily of the standardized and shared meanings for our words. As people read their newspapers, listen to the radio, attend the films, and watch television, they get daily lessons and practice in the language conventions of our society.

Overall, the contribution of mass communications to our system of shared meanings is both complex and profound. In this sense, the functions of the media in modifying the behavior of their audiences are long range, subtle, and accumulative. In addition, the media are so interwoven with all other forms of communication in our society that their effects are almost impossible to isolate and examine.

Our review of the meaning paradigm in this chapter has shown its ancient origins. From the very earliest times of recorded social thought, and probably before that, human beings have been concerned with the issue of knowledge, that is, the meanings we subjectively construct for the external world. Deep concern over that issue was generated because it is the source of individual decisions about conduct. That is, people's actions are shaped by their meanings for the physical and social world. Early philosophers and theologians saw in this issue the need to understand the rules for containing human conduct—the ideal social order that would result in justice and a triumph of good over evil. Although many routes were followed and many conclusions reached in seeking understanding of the nature of knowledge and how we attain it, consensus around certain principles was slowly achieved. Insights into knowledge and its relation to conduct did accumulate through the centuries. When the specialized social sciences split away from philosophy, they continued the search for understanding, studying the construction of meaning in language, culture, symbolic interaction, and memory schemata. Today those efforts have been supplemented by the study of mass communications in the search for the ways in which mediated reality provides a basis for constructing meanings.

NOTES

1. W. Barnett Pearce and Vernon E. Cronen, *Communication, Action, and Meaning: The Creation of Social Realities* (New York: Praeger, 1980), pp. 13–14.
2. Thomas Hobbes, *Leviathan* (New York: E. P. Dutton and Company, 1950), pp. 21–22. First published in 1651.
3. A. E. Taylor, *Socrates* (New York: Anchor Books, 1960).
4. J. A. Stewart, *The Philosophy of Plato* (New York: Oxford University Press, 1909).
5. Among these were *pragmatism*, which holds that both the meaning and truth of an idea are a function of its practical outcome; and *operationism*, which specifies that the meaning of a concept consists of the steps that one must take to observe or measure it.
6. Stewart, *The Philosophy of Plato*, p. 1.
7. *The Republic of Plato*, trans. Frances MacDonald Cornfield (New York: Oxford University Press, 1958). See pp. 227–35.
8. Hobbes, *Leviathan*, p. 23.
9. John Locke, *An Essay Concerning Human Understanding* (Oxford: Clarendon Press, 1975), p. 402. First published in 1690.
10. An outstanding summary of the issues and concepts addressed by modern linguistics can be found in Stephen W. Littlejohn, "Theories of Language and Nonverbal Coding," in *Theories of Human Communication* (Belmont, CA: Wadsworth Publishing Company, 1983) pp. 77–86.
11. The most important founders of anthropological linguistics were: Edward Sapir, *An Introduction to the Study of Speech* (New York: Harcourt Brace, 1921); and Benjamin Whorf, *Language, Thought, and Reality* (New York: John Wiley and Sons, 1956).
12. Pioneers in these efforts were: Charles Horton Cooley, *Human Nature and*

the Social Order (New York: Schocken Books, 1964) first published in 1908; and George Herbert Mead, *Mind, Self, and Society* (Chicago: University of Chicago Press, 1934).

13. Edward Sapir, "The Status of Linguistics as a Science," *Language* 5 (1929), 209.

14. Charles Horton Cooley, *Human Nature and the Social Order* (New York: Charles Scribner's Sons, 1902), pp. 118–19.

15. Ibid. p. 184.

16. George Herbert Mead, *Mind, Self, and Society: From the Standpoint of a Social Behaviorist,* ed. Charles W. Morris (Chicago: University of Chicago Press, 1934).

17. Max Scheler, *Die Wissenssoziologie und die Gesellschaft* (Bern: Franke, 1960). First published in 1925.

18. Peter L. Berger and Thomas Luckman, *The Social Construction of Reality: A Treatise in the Sociology of Knowledge* (New York: Doubleday, 1963). For essays that combine the perspectives of the sociology of knowledge and symbolic interaction, see Aaron V. Cicourel, *Cognitive Sociology: Language and Meaning in Social Interaction* (New York: The Free Press, 1974).

19. E. Tory Higgins, C. Peter Herman, and Mark P. Zanne, eds., *Social Cognition: The Ontario Symposium* (Hillsdale, N. J.: Lawrence Erlbaum Associates, 1981).

20. Ibid. p. ix.

21. Frederick C. Bartlett, *Remembering* (Cambridge: Cambridge University Press, 1934).

22. Shelley E. Taylor and Jennifer Crocker, "Schematic Basis of Social Information Processing," in Higgins, Herman, and Zahne, *Social Cognition,* p. 91.

23. Walter Lippmann, *Public Opinion* (New York: Macmillan, 1922).

24. Kurt Lang and Gladys Engel Lang, "The Unique Perspective of Television and Its Effect: A Pilot Study," *American Sociological Review* XVII, pp. 3–12.

25. See *To Establish Justice, to Insure Domestic Tranquility,* Final Report of the National Commission on the Causes and Prevention of Violence (New York: Award Books, 1969).

26. Surgeon General's Scientific Advisory Committee on Television and Social Behavior, *Television and Growing Up: The Impact of Televised Violence* (Washington, D.C.: U. S. Government Printing Office, 1971).

27. George Gerbner, "Violence in Television Drama: Trends and Symbolic Functions," in G. A. Comstock and E. A. Rubinstein, eds., *Television and Social Behavior, Vol. I, Media Content and Control* (Washington, D.C.: U.S. Government Printing Office, 1971).

28. George Gerbner and Larry Gross, "Living with Television: The Violence Profile," *Journal of Communication* 26 (Spring 1976), 173–99.

29. Anthony N. Doob and Alen E. MacDonald, "Television Viewing and Fear of Victimization: Is the Relationship Causal?" *Journal of Personality and Social Psychology* 37, no. 2 (1979), 170–179.

30. Maxwell E. McCombs and Donald L. Shaw, "The Agenda-Setting Function of the Mass Media," *Public Opinion Quarterly* 1972, pp. 176–87.

31. Donald L. Shaw and Maxwell E. McCombs, *The Emergence of American Political Issues: The Agenda-Setting Function of the Press* (St. Paul, Minn.: West Publishing Company, 1977).

32. Melvin L. DeFleur and Everette E. Dennis, *Understanding Mass Communication* (Boston: Houghton Mifflin, 1988). See especially Chapters 1 and 2, pp. 4–86.

33. James A. Inciardi, "Beyond Cocaine: Basuco, Crack, and Other Coca Products," paper presented at the 1987 Annual Meeting of the Academy of Criminal Justice Sciences, St. Louis, Missouri.

34. These functions of the media were first developed in Melvin L. DeFleur and Timothy G. Plax, "Human Communication as a Bio-Social Process," paper presented to the International Communication Association, Acapulco, Mexico, 1980.

CHAPTER 10

Theoretical Strategies for Persuasion

In Chapters 8 and 9 we reviewed a number of theories of mass communication that were drawn from either basic paradigms in the social sciences or from much older analyses of topics that have long been of concern to philosophers. From those theories it was possible to explain how people selectively attend to media content, perceive its meaning, acquire knowledge from the content to which they are exposed, and use that knowledge to respond to their social and physical environment. The issue was never raised about the *deliberate* use of media content to shape or control those responses. It is to precisely that issue that this chapter is addressed.

We will show how the same formulations that serve as foundations for understanding the incidental, unwitting, and long-range acquisition of influences on behavior from mass communication can provide a basis for developing explanations of how *deliberate* influences can be achieved. That is we will review alternative strategies for designing mass communicated messages, or media content used in conjunction with other kinds of information, for persuasive purposes.

The basic idea of *persuasion* has ancient roots. Long before the Age of Mass Communication, the term *rhetoric* was used to refer to the art of using language to influence the judgments and conduct of others. During a time when the human voice was the *only* medium of communication that could be used to persuade people to change beliefs and actions, it was an important skill indeed. As societies became increasingly sophisticated, the art of oral persuasion flowered. In Greece, and later in Rome, for example, it was a valuable skill in winning in courts of law and in presenting proposals before political forums.

This type of persuasion remains important today. Contemporary researchers often study the principles of persuasion outside the context of mass communications.[1] However, we will focus our analysis on the premeditated use of media messages to influence the *actions* of individuals. In the present context, then, persuasion refers primarily to the use of the mass media to present messages that are deliberately designed to elicit specific forms of action on the part of audiences. Typical of such actions are *voting* for a political candidate, *buying* a consumer product, *donating* to a worthy cause, or otherwise *complying* with requests for action that a communicator wants to elicit. Obviously, there are many forms of conduct that can be influenced by persuasive messages, but we are referring here to overt and observable behavior rather than to internal psychological changes.

Some communication theorists might find this emphasis on overt behavior as the dependent variable overly rigid; after all, there are other ways to define persuasion. For example, some definitions emphasize changes in an individual's subjective beliefs, opinions, or attitudes as a sufficient criterion as to whether persuasion has been successful.[2] Such definitions are usually based on the assumption that if subjective factors of this kind are changed, modifications in action will surely follow. For some purposes, conceptualizing persuasion in this manner may be important. In this chapter, however, we will regard *actual modification of behavior* as the goal to be achieved, as the dependent variable in theoretical formulations designed to explain it, and as the criterion for deciding whether or not the process has been successful.

There are two reasons for conceptualizing persuasion in this relatively hard-headed manner. One is that it introduces *comparability* into the process of developing and evaluating theories. That is, in constructing competing explanations of the same thing, alternative sets of independent variables have to be defined, described, and synthesized into systems of propositions that link them to some dependent variable. Obviously, each can have very *different* sets of independent variables but they must focus on the *same* dependent variable. Otherwise it would be the theoretical equivalent of trying to compare apples and oranges.

A second reason for emphasizing overt behavior as the criterion of successful persuasion is that *action* is the significant factor in the pragmatic world of advertising, political campaigning, financial solicitation, public health entreaties, and so on. It may be nice to change people's ideas and feelings and let it go at that, but such outcomes pale in importance compared with overt conduct in attempting to stimulate buying, voting, donating, or otherwise complying. The question is, then, can any of the theoretical analyses described in the previous chapters be used as underlying strategies in designing successful persuasion campaigns where the goal is to promote some specific type of behavior?

Admittedly, at this point, we really don't know exactly why most advertising efforts, election campaigns, or other kinds of promotions succeed or fail. Sometimes they do—even spectacularly. Then, again, sometimes they do not, and are dismal failures. Predicting when one persuasion strategy will be a winner and another a failure is a risky business at best. Understanding how to achieve persuasion consistently has been slow in coming. We know little more today than we did twenty years ago. Karlins and Abelson summed up the situation as it was two decades ago:

> Persuasion as an *art* has been practiced for centuries. The emerging *science* of persuasion is a product of the 20th century, and is still in its infancy. . . . Based on current information, then, "it is still too early to be sure" seems the most appropriate answer to the question, "Has science created persuasive appeals that can control human behavior?" Even so, it is reasonable to assume that, as techniques of persuasion evolve from art to science, their effectiveness in controlling behavior will be enhanced. *How effective* remains to be seen.[3]

Today, the situation remains much the same. It is still "too early to be sure" whether theories can be devised and supported by scientific research to a point where the persuasion process can be adequately explained, let alone used at will to manipulate people. Contemporary scholars continue to emphasize the lack of theoretical progress in understanding persuasion. Some have even given up!

> Despite the vast number of pages written and the countless studies undertaken about persuasion, many students of communication find it impossible to shake the uneasy feeling that we have precious little reliable, socially relevant knowledge about it. Laments regarding our collective ignorance about persuasion are commonplace, and more than one communication researcher has been heard to characterize persuasion research as a scholarly dead end.[4]

Even in the face of this dismal assessment, it is important to continue trying to understand this complex and often frustrating activity. One way to press on is to set forth formulations that are relatively unstudied candidates for explaining persuasion. Such candidates then become the focus of research that will eventually sort out which ones work, to what degree, under what circumstances, with what kinds of people, and so on.

In the sections that follow, therefore, three quite different theoretical strategies for persuasion will be described. Each is directed toward the same dependent factor—overt action. It must be recognized that these strategies in themselves are not actually carefully articulated theories set forth in formal postulates and theorems. They are at best guidelines that indicate what kinds of factors and variables can and should go into more detailed explanations of persuasion. In any case, we will try to show how these three strategies are related to the basic paradigms, philosophical conclusions, and theories of mass communication that have been set forth in previous chapters. Specifically, we will outline strategies of persuasion that have been derived from the *cognitive paradigm*, from the theory of *social organization*, and from the *meaning paradigm*, all of which have been discussed previously in some detail.

THE PSYCHODYNAMIC STRATEGY

The foundation assumptions of psychology are incorporated within the expression S–O–R, which we reviewed in Chapter 8. This expression indicates a general sequence of psychological events that are assumed to be involved in determining directions in behavior. First, stimuli are received and detected by the senses from the external environment. Second, the characteristics of the organism shape the type of response that will be made. Finally, some form of behavior follows. Since we are concerned not with "organisms" in general, but with human beings exclusively, we can proceed with the assumption that the intervening factors include (1) some set of human biological characteristics or processes that are inherited; (2) another set of factors that may be based partly in biology and partly in learning, such as emotional states and conditions; and (3) a set of acquired or learned factors that make up an individual's cognitive structure. Thus, for human beings, the intervening O in the expression is a complex structure of biological, emotional, and cognitive components of personality that give direction to R, or conduct.

Among those three categories, strategies of persuasion must focus on either emotional or cognitive factors; it is obviously impossible to modify an inherited biological factor (height, weight, race, sex, etc.) with mass communicated messages. It is possible to use mass communicated messages to arouse an emotional state, such as anger or fear, which can then be important in shaping a response. Indeed, some persuasive strategies do try to link emotional arousal with specific forms of behavior.

While emotions represent an obvious basis for persuasive strategies, they can be used only in a limited number of situations. A far more frequent game plan in designing persuasion campaigns has been to try to manipulate cognitive factors. The assumptions behind this are logical enough. Since most cognitive factors are *acquired* in a process of socialization, they are prime targets for campaigns that try to promote new learning so as to modify them in ways desired by the communicator.

The second assumption is that cognitive factors are major influences on human behavior. Thus, if cognitive factors can be changed, then surely behavior can be changed. This assumption holds out the tantalizing possibility that cleverly designed information provided by mass communications can be used effectively to gain control over human conduct. That potential control has long been a fear of critics of the media and an urgent goal for those who want to use mass communications for this purpose. It is like the ancient vision of the philosopher's stone that could turn baser metals into gold. If the secret of controlling people with clever messages could be discovered, riches, power, and prestige would be within grasp. This vision has for decades driven the search for the magic message content and structures that will reliably accomplish the task. Yet, nagging questions remain. Is behavior controlled mainly by cognitive factors? Many students of human behavior believe that it is.

Cognitive Factors and Behavior

The belief that human action is given direction by internal subjective processes within the individual is so well established that the idea seems virtually axiomatic. One need look no further, it is widely assumed, to understand the mainsprings of behavior. Among the internal processes that are said to be the determinants of behavior is a rich set of concepts—needs, drives, beliefs, interests, anxieties, fears, values, opinions, and attitudes. Dozens more could be added, depending on one's preference for particular psychological writers. Whatever their theoretical genealogy, though, some of these processes or forces are said to be inherited, such as basic needs, or to be learned, such as attitudes or anxieties. It is the learned ones that seem to hold the greatest fascination.

A good example of an acquired internal psychological state that is said to influence behavior is *cognitive dissonance*. According to Leon Festinger, who advanced this idea in 1957, the need to experience a consistent world is a strong motivating factor that shapes our behavior.[5] If we detect inconsistencies in our beliefs, attitudes, or behavior, we suffer from a strong sense of uneasiness (cognitive dissonance), and this acts as a drive to change what we are doing so as to restore consistency. For example, if a friend asks for help in cheating on an exam, and if we believe that such cheating is wrong, we are placed into a state of cognitive dissonance. To reduce that uneasiness, we have to do something.

In this case there would be three choices. We have to either reject our friend, convince him or her to abandon the cheating plan, or modify our committment to the belief that cheating is wrong. One of these changes will reduce cognitive dissonance. The one actually chosen will depend on how much we value the friendship, or how strongly we feel about cheating. In any case, the dissonance—an internal psychological state—acts like a drive. It motivates us to change something, either our behavior or our belief.

Motives and motivation are important concepts in understanding persuasion. The terms "need" and "drive" have long been psychological favorites in explaining influences on behavior, and they need brief explanation. A *need* is essentially a state of deprivation. The "organism" is deprived of some essential substance, such as food or water, that is required for adequate functioning. Or it may be an activity, such as sex or exercise, that is supposedly required by the body to continue normal activities. The state of deprivation brings about an arousal of energy to obtain that which will satisfy the need. That state of arousal is the *drive*. Some needs are products of our biological nature. Others are products of learning in a social environment. Psychologists have discussed a long list of our acquired needs. These include needs for achievement, affiliation, being dependent, exercising power, conforming, having social approval, providing nurturance, engaging in play, being orderly, greedy, and deferent, to mention only a few. All of these are candidates for persuasive strategies on the assumption that they can be modified.

While the concepts above are important, the internal psychological factor that is most often discussed in regard to shaping complex behavior through persuasion is *attitude*. Since the concept was first advanced early in the century, and especially after sophisticated attitude scales came into use, there has been a deeply established conviction that many categories of behavior are directly linked to attitudes. It has been assumed that if one knows a person's attitude toward a particular topic, category of people, or issue, it is possible to predict that individual's overt behavior toward that attitude object. We noted in previous chapters that this assumption is not supported by the substantial body of literature that has probed the issue. Nevertheless, the assumption has taken on a life of its own, and many writers who discuss persuasion ignore the research and continue to make the assumption that attitudes and behavior are closely correlated.

Generally, then, the psychodynamic view of behavior stresses the powerful influence on conduct of factors, conditions, states, and forces within the individual that shape behavior. The cognitive approach as a strategy for persuasion emphasizes that internal structuring of the psyche is a product of *learning*. It is this emphasis that makes it possible to use mass communications to modify that structure so as to change behavior.

Modifying Cognitive Factors to Influence Behavior

The essence of the psychodynamic strategy is that an effective message has properties capable of *altering the psychological functioning* of individuals in such a way that they will respond overtly (toward the item that is the object of persuasion) with modes of behavior desired or suggested by the communicator. In other words, it has been assumed that the key to effective persuasion lies in new learning, on the basis of information provided by the persuader. This presumably will modify the internal psychological structure of the individual (needs, fears, attitudes, etc.) resulting in the desired overt behavior.

There have been many versions and variants of this general approach to persuasion, based on the particular psychological factor being manipulated, and upon the presumed dynamic relationship thought to prevail between the psychological process and the overt behavior patterns it supposedly activates. We noted earlier that extensive use has been made of persuasive messages aimed at individual *attitudes* under the assumption that there is a close relationship between an individual's attitudinal position—positive or negative—and the way in which such a person will behave in a social situation—accepting or rejecting. A common example would be a mass communicated campaign aimed at reducing ethnic discrimination (overt behavior) by attempting to reduce ethnic prejudice (negative attitude purporting to lead to discrimination).

Fear is a factor that has been widely used in advertising and other persuasive efforts. A frequently seen example is the promotion of the purchase of a patent medicine (overt action) by posing a health threat if the substance is not used. Also common is advocating the use of a product to reduce the fear of being socially offensive.

An almost endless list of psychological factors have been provided as bases for persuasive strategies on the assumption that if they are

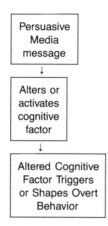

Figure 10.1. The psychodynamic persuasion strategy.

modified, then desired actions are likely to follow. In simple graphic terms, the psychodynamic persuasion strategy can be diagrammed in Figure 10.1.

One of the nagging problems with this strategy is that it really doesn't seem to work consistently and no one knows why. It seems so logical. Common sense dictates that this is the way in which media have to be used to achieve persuasion, in spite of the lack of supporting evidence. For example, John Phillip Jones, who spent twenty-five years as an advertising executive before becoming a communication researcher, has commented on this point:

> Learning, attitudes, and behavior are all influenced in some way by advertising, but to understand how advertising works, we need to know the order of events. . . . The earliest theory was based on a simple chain of causality described by Charles Raymond as "learn-feel-do." In this theory, people receive factual knowledge about a brand. As a result, their attitudes toward the brand change and they develop a preference for it. Then they buy it.[6]

Jones goes on to point out that "there have been only limited attempts to validate this theory, with results falling short of conclusive."[7] While advertisers have looked at other promising theories, the *learn-feel-do* approach remains at center stage.

Everett Rogers and J. Douglas Storey have reviewed the persuasion strategies of information campaigns aimed at achieving change in some socially significant forms of pro-social behavior, including a broad spectrum of individual and collective actions ranging from birth control to the adoption of more efficient farm technology. As is the case with advertising, some campaigns achieve their objectives and some do not, and no one quite knows why. As these two authors put it:

> A survey of the campaigns literature reveals a large body of research tenuously linked by a few general principles but without many overarching generalizations or theories.[8]

The tenuous grip maintained by the "change-attitudes-to-change-behavior" formulation has been noted recently by Gerald Miller, who has reviewed the research on persuasion that has accumulated over several decades, both in mass communication and other contexts. He also notes the limited theoretical accomplishments of scholars in this area, and the continuing commitment to attitude as a key factor. He concludes that, in spite of its lasting popularity, the evidence simply does not support the cognitive strategy as a reliable approach to achieving behavioral change through persuasion, especially with attitude as the key variable:

> Several obvious considerations account for this continuing widespread allegiance. Intuitively, modeling persuasion as a process in which symbolic stimuli (persuasive messages) trigger internal evaluative predispositions (attitudes) that subsequently motivate desired overt behaviors (compliance with persuasive objectives) makes sense. After all, the argument goes, how can people be expected to behave in prescribed ways if they are not favorably inclined toward the prescriptions?[9]

Thus, in spite of the lack of supporting scientific evidence, and indeed in spite of evidence to the contrary in some cases, the persuasion strategy shown schematically in Figure 10.1 has become institutionalized as part of our commonsense knowledge. It seems beyond question to many practitioners that mass communicated persuasive messages can capture the hearts and minds, and, so they hope, the dollars, of those who receive information designed to change feelings and thereby change behavior. The only thing left to do, such people believe, is to discover just what information will do the job.

Unfortunately, after decades of intensive research, those magic message characteristics have not yet been revealed. Therefore, further evidence is needed to support the validity of the psychodynamic strategy. Until that research task has been accomplished, this explanation of persuasion must remain tentative.

THE SOCIOCULTURAL STRATEGY

While the foundation assumptions of psychology are based on the idea that behavior is controlled from within, those of other social sciences assume that a great deal of human conduct is shaped by forces *outside* the individual. Anthropology stresses the powerful impact of culture on behavior; economics points to impersonal processes of monetary policy and trends; political science emphasizes structures for governance and the exercise of power; sociology studies the influence of social organization on group behavior. All of these approaches have merit, and each in some way provides a legitimate basis for predicting the nature of human action.

Explanations of human behavior that consider factors outside the individual have played a much smaller part in developing strategies for persuasion than has the cognitive strategy, which looks within. However, they offer a rich basis on which to develop alternative theories. To develop such theories, however, one needs to have a clear grasp of how human behavior can be guided by considerations *other* than the internal biological, emotional, and cognitive factors with which psychologists have been concerned.

Social Expectations and Behavior

It is not difficult to show the powerful ability of culture to control human conduct. One can easily point to examples of dramatic actions that are difficult to explain in other terms. The powerful Bushido Code that was instilled into Japanese military personnel during World War II led individuals to commit acts that were all but incomprehensible to American troops who opposed them. Kamikaze pilots eagerly took off in aircraft heavily loaded with bombs, with only enough fuel to reach their targets, and deliberately crashed them on American naval vessels. Japanese submarines regularly launched large torpedoes guided by human navigators who deliberately sacrificed themselves as they drove into the sides of Allied ships.

These people were not crazy. They were behaving very normally within the requirements of their culture. Even ordinary ground troops threw themselves off cliffs, blew themselves up with hand grenades, or gutted themselves with knives to avoid capture. It was not that they feared mistreatment as prisoners. It was the shame of surrendering to an enemy, deeply instilled by socialization in the Bushido beliefs, that made capture or surrender beyond what they could bear. Self-inflicted death was an honorable solution and a much preferred alternative.

An endless list of such behaviors that is entirely inconsistent with what *we* believe is right could be assembled. They would include the practice of *sutee* in traditional India—the duty of a faithful wife to throw herself on the funeral pyre of a dead husband; American Indian rites of passage in which individuals seeking manhood underwent self-inflicted tortures; and traditional Eskimo practices of making dependent elderly parents, no longer capable of producing for the group, leave the shelter to freeze to death on the ice. All of these practices were both normal and honorable within the groups in which they occurred.

Even within our own society, forms of behavior can be identified that might seem to others to be exotic, irrational, or dangerous to health. The wearing of high-heeled shoes on the part of females would have to make the list. The consumption of alcohol so as to dull the senses and produce a hangover in the morning could be added. Listening to rock music at decibel levels high enough to impair hearing is another candidate. The fact is, however, that these are culturally established forms of normal behavior among the relevant categories in our society.

In our review of the social expectations theory in Chapter 8 we saw that the components of *social organization* represent another very powerful set of influences on individual conduct. Because of these influences, people can choose courses of action that are opposite to their inner feelings and predispositions.

Consider, for example, the graduate student who wants to complete an advanced degree in communication or one of the social sciences. To do so, the student is often required to take courses in statistics. If we looked to cognitive variables, such as attitude, to understand how the typical student feels about this subject matter, we would find a rather negative picture. Few graduate students seem to have strong positive attitudes urging them to study statistics. Yet year after year cohorts of such students grit their teeth, calm their nerves, and sign up for such courses. Quite clearly, their actions do not fit the learn-feel-do formula.

The fact is, of course, that such behavioral choices have little to do with attitudes or preferences. The explanations lie elsewhere. The social expectations of the high-ranking members of their group—their graduate professors—dictate the required pattern of behavior. The norms are clear-cut. The graduate student role includes mastering such courses. Successful movement upward in rank from degree candidate to degree recipient is contingent on completion of the work. If students do not conform, they will be banished from the group, and such banishment has long been a significant form of social control. The effective sequence, then, is not learn-feel-do, but *learn-conform-or be punished!*

A case could be made that far more of our behavior is controlled by social expectations existing within social systems in which we interact with others than by our internal predispositions. Every group to which we belong—a family, a school, a group within which we work, a club, or just an informal clique of friends—exerts a strong set of controls over us. In some groups we may dislike every minute of the experience, but if we want to remain members we must adhere to the norms of the group, play the role that is assigned to us, submit to the ranking system, and agree to the system of social control. It is these *external* factors that shape our conduct—the social expectations and demands of others— and not just internal feelings, preferences, or attitudes.

There is little doubt, then, that both social and cultural factors provide guidelines that shape human behavior. It is the individual's understandings and acceptance of culturally approved forms of conduct and the behavioral expectations of others that determine how he or she will act in a social context. For this reason, such external factors can provide a basis for persuasion, presuming that their definitions for the individual can be shaped or controlled.

Modifying Social Expectations to Influence Behavior

Whereas the psychodynamic strategy has been studied for years, far less research has been devoted to the sociocultural approach to persuasion. In fact, existing theories of persuasion that have reviewed the part played by culture and social organization have concentrated on ways in which such factors are *obstacles* to achieving behavioral change. For example, in the literature on the adoption of innovation as a result of information campaigns, resistance to change is often described as being due to institutionalized cultural practices that are contrary to the use of the proposed change.

What an effective sociocultural strategy requires is that persuasive messages *define* for the individual the rules for social behavior, or the cultural requirements for action, that will govern the activities that the communicator is trying to elicit. Or, if definitions already exist, the task becomes one of *redefining* those requirements.

This strategy has been used for many decades in the advertising world to reshape thinking about a product. One of the classic illustrations was cigarette advertising just after World War I, when it was socially unacceptable for women to smoke. Designing an advertising campaign to get women to take up the habit was a tough assignment, because it was a widely established stereotype among the public that women who smoked had loose morals. Nevertheless, cigarette advertisers realized that half of the population was not buying cigarettes, and if they could redefine the norms to get women to smoke, their sales would soar.

It took a while, but obviously they did it. One of the famous advertisements of the period was a scene with a nicely dressed man and a lovely woman sitting on a grassy bank. He was puffing away on a cigarette with a contented look on his face. The woman was leaning toward him with a look of longing, saying "blow a little my way." Only a short time later the ads began to show "nice" women smoking in public, and the transformation was under way.

An established strategy, then, is to depict the social expectations of the group within which the action is to take place, providing cultural definitions of what conduct is appropriate. The key is that the message must provide the appearance of consensus. That is, it must be shown that the definitions provided are supported by the relevant group and failing to follow them would constitute unacceptable deviant behavior. Represented schematically, this strategy for developing a theory of persuasion would look like Figure 10.2

The sociocultural strategy is often used in conjunction with interpersonal pressures to conform. This means a combination of media messages and individual exchanges. This multilevel strategy can be illustrated in concrete terms if we examine the tactics of a very successful campaign with which almost everyone is familiar.

Many communities have an annual charity drive, commonly called the United Appeal, Community Fund, or something similar. Such funding drives incorporate a variety of efforts to reach their goals, but the sociocultural strategy is often at the heart of the effort.

In order to illustrate the contrast with the psychodynamic approach, we will assume a hypothetical set of citizens who prefer *not* to make their charitable donations in this manner. They have favorite charities to which they give annually, and they prefer to do so anonymously. Thus we can start with a negative attitude toward the behavior that the communicators will try to elicit as well as preference for anonymity in giving to any cause. As we will see, however, they will be very likely to make a donation in a very public manner to the United Appeal in spite of their contrary feelings.

The first step in the typical United Appeal solicitation is an announcement (via the mass media) that the community has set up the drive and that it has a specific quota of dollars that must be reached this year. Thus, a group *goal* is defined with the suggestion that this has widespread approval among the members of one's community. In fact, this goal has been arbitrarily formulated by the organizers of the drive and does not necessarily flow from grass-roots sentiment on the part of community members as a whole. Nevertheless, it is very likely to go unchallenged. Goals have a rather compelling quality in themselves if it is believed that they have wide support (consensus). Organizers can

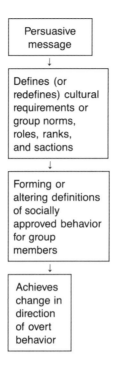

Figure 10.2. The Sociocultural persuasion strategy

create such an impression by getting socially prominent persons (high rank) in the community to participate in the announcement of the quota. Many persons are eager to confirm their high status publicly by participating in such events. And, of course, the media always obligingly give full coverage to such a ceremonial event, thereby validating its importance.

Another significant step is to announce to the community that the "fair share" for citizens is some specified percentage of their earnings. This concept will be given ample coverage by the media. The idea of a "fair share" is socially meaningful. It is compelling to the individual because it appears to be an approved and shared *norm*. Who wants to be identified as "unfair" and thus *deviant* from approved social definitions? If individuals are led to believe that others are in fact giving according to this norm, they will feel pressure toward conformity.

At the heart of the persuasion campaign is the task of creating *role systems* that are linked to the fund drive within community work and neighborhood groups. In stores, factories, schools, and as many other organizations as possible, a "chairperson" for the drive is appointed

with attendant publicity. Chief executive officers of large business organizations feel particularly compelled to cooperate in this type of
effort because of the need to maintain the public relations image that
the organization operates in the interest of the community. The chairperson usually appoints "collectors" for various divisions of the organization if it is at all large. The rank-and-file member of the group must
play a *counter-role* to that of the collectors. When one is asked for a
donation personally by another worker, it is awkward to refuse.

A tactic sometimes used in this sociocultural strategy is to distribute to members a *card* with their name already printed on it and
with a place to mark how much they are "pledging" (to be collected
later). This signals that they are under surveillance, possibly by powerful bosses. Persons who choose not to pledge anything must signify
their deviancy by signing the card to indicate refusal. In addition, they
may have to tell the group collector personally that they will not make a
donation (and are therefore out of step).

If our hapless individuals, who really wanted to give their funds to
another cause, have not been persuaded by these strategies, they will be
confronted with another compelling situation when they get home. The
organizers of the campaign appoint "volunteer collectors" in each
neighborhood to call on residents in their immediate area and request a
donation. Here we have the role of *good neighbor* and that of *good
citizen* (both of which include helping the less fortunate). These roles
are locked into a reciprocal social control system in miniature. It is
embarrassing to refuse a neighbor a reasonable and socially approved
request for a modest donation. Potential negative sanctions underlie
such refusal, to say nothing of a degradation of status. Who wants to be
known to neighbors as a tightwad who would refuse to donate a modest
sum to a community-supported charitable cause?

Therefore, in spite of their negative attitudes and contrary preferences, our friends at this point reach into their pocket for some folding
money, and possibly grit their teeth a little while they smilingly conform. However, for their good behavior they will be given a reward,
intended to provide positive reinforcement. They will get a little button
to wear in their lapels, or at least a card to place in their windows, that
will indicate to others what good citizens they have been.

The sociocultural strategy has been widely used to promote commercial products in ways that parallel the fund drive situation. Two
examples will illustrate how cultural definitions, social expectations,
and all of the components of social organization provide a conceptual
foundation for designing an effective strategy for selling goods. One is
the case of a line of unbreakable plastic kitchen containers. The other is
a line of cosmetics that are distributed through home sales.

The manufacturer of a well-known brand of durable plastic kitchen containers makes use of some media advertising, but the firm's principal means of promotion is through the use of "parties" in private homes. It is a variant of the sociocultural strategy with more emphasis on interpersonal rather than mass-mediated messages. However, it offers useful insights into the dynamics of this strategy for persuasion. Here is how it works.

A representative of the company selects a homemaker in a neighborhood and offers her a "free" gift of the kitchen ware if she will be the hostess for a "party" in which the wares can be demonstrated. Many agree to do this and invite their friends to this social function. At the gathering, the representative displays the products, explains the nice gift that the hostess will receive for sponsoring the event, and demonstrates the line of containers in a variety of ways. The hostess serves snacks and beverages, and the event does have a "party" atmosphere. The guests understand the nature of the gathering but enjoy the social contacts it provides. The main feature is that after the demonstrations are complete, the guests are "invited" to purchase items from the line. And, since everyone has had a good time, this seems the least that one can do for the hostess. Various articles are obligingly bought.

This little social drama depends on cultural definitions, norms, role requirements, and systems of social control, just as does the fundraising system described earlier. Our culture places value on the skill of the housewife to manage her kitchen effectively. The product sold at the gathering is defined as an important aid in doing this. The "party" concept has its own cultural definition, which carries with it many positive elements. The norm is that when invited to a party, one is expected to accept. If one does so, another norm is to refrain from behaving rudely while there. Furthermore, being in the home of another under such circumstances implies a significant role relationship between hostess and guest. Behavior that transgressed these requirements would be seen as more than ungracious.

All of this translates into a virtual *obligation* to buy something the representative is selling. It would dishonor the hostess if one did not. If even her own friends refused to support her, her social standing would be drastically reduced. Sensitive people do not do that to their friends. Therefore, the party is held, goodies are eaten, gossip is exchanged, polite attention is given to the sales pitch, and (above all) goods are purchased. No other outcome is realistically possible. It would be unthinkable for a "guest" to jump up suddenly, be rude to the hostess, denounce the product line, insult the representative, and storm out in a fit of anger because of having been pressured to buy. That may be precisely what one's inner attitudes and preferences may call for, but such unseemly urges are kept under control by the social requirements of the situation.

A number of manufacturers use a version of the sociocultural strategy that could (perhaps with tongue in cheek) be called the *epidemiological variant.* This too is based more on interpersonal than mass communication, but those who use it also provide for supportive mass communications as backup advertising. A good example is a line of cosmetics that is sold out of the home of a dealer who is a direct representative of the manufacturer.

The strategy begins when a neighbor or acquaintance is invited to the dealer's home with the promise of receiving a free "facial." The term refers to a rather complex procedure for cleaning the skin and applying various cosmetics to enhance the individual's facial appearance. Powerful cultural definitions underlying the concept of feminine beauty and its importance in our society make this free facial treatment a significant reward.

When the subject arrives, the line of cosmetics is brought out and placed on a brightly colored tablecloth, and each bottle, can, box, and tube is discussed. The subject is allowed to see, smell, and feel each substance. Then the facial proceeds. Old cosmetics are removed with a "cleanser." A stimulating liquid is then spread on to "condition" the face. A "foundation" is applied. After that, various layers are added, such as "blush," and powder. Finally, "shadow," and "mascara" are used to emphasize the eyes, and lipstick finishes the job. At this point, after nearly an hour of interaction, the subject has no recourse but to buy some of the product.

But this would be an inefficient way to sell cosmetics if it were not for additional steps that will come later. The facial treatment cements a friendly social bond between representative and consumer. Her name goes on a list, and regular calls are made to suggest resupply and to call attention to new cosmetics. The husband is called well before special gift-giving dates (birthday, wedding anniversary, Mother's Day, Christmas, etc.). Such customers also are asked to get together a group of their friends to receive facials, expanding the base of the operation. Even more important is the solicitation of the subject to join the "team" (sometimes refered to as the "family"), to become a cosmetic entrepreneur in her own right. The representative who signs up such new dealers gets special rewards and recognitions from the company. Thus, the proliferation of cosmetic salespersons may follow an epidemiological pattern.

This is an effective way to sell goods. It might not work with many products, but it has been particularly successful with cosmetics. In one way or another similar strategies have been used in the sale of magazines, household cleaning products, encyclopedias, and vacuum cleaners.

While these rather complex illustrations of the sociocultural strategy are not based on mass communications exclusively, they occupy a central place in the activities of the persuaders. The entire persuasive effort is sometimes handled by the media alone, however. If there is any doubt that the sociocultural strategy is widely used in media advertising, the reader is invited to spend an evening before the TV set viewing commercials within the perspective of this strategy. Smiling and happy people act out little dramas concerning beer, laxatives, deodorants, and denture paste. They define for their viewers approved and disapproved norms, acceptable role behavior, how to gain or maintain status, and what social controls might come down on one's head if one deviates from the system. It is made abundantly clear that to be caught with the wrong beer, a detectable body odor, inactive bowels, or loose dentures places one far outside the pale of social acceptability.

THE MEANING CONSTRUCTION STRATEGY

A third approach to persuasion is provided by manipulations of meanings. We saw in Chapter 9 that the link between knowledge and behavior was realized as far back as recorded history can take us. For centuries of human existence, knowledge—that is *meanings* for the world of objective reality—was shaped for individuals through processes of socialization based solely on oral transmissions. People learned the accepted meanings for symbols, for the events in nature, and for the complexities of their social order. Later, writing brought new avenues to the acquisition of meanings. Print expanded those enormously. Now, in an Age of Mass Communication, the media provide ready channels to huge populations for the purpose of the deliberate structuring of meanings. Those channels are obviously used by an overwhelming number of competing sources of information that want to mold, monitor, or modify the meanings that people experience for everything from commercial products to political policies.

Constructions of Meanings and Behavior

The proposition that *knowledge shapes action* was the first great postulate of what we now call behavioral science. It was established a long time ago, probably even before the beginning of recorded philosophy. Certainly the relationship between subjective meanings and conduct was an accepted cornerstone of the analysis of human nature during the time of Plato and Aristotle. We noted in Chapter 9 that the link between knowledge and conduct continued as a fundamental principle of human behavior through the time of the Scholastics, through the Renaissance, and on into modern times as the scholars of each century sought to establish how conduct should be shaped by knowledge of either a religious faith or a secular system of government.

More recently, as each of the social sciences emerged from philosophy, that principle was rediscovered by contemporary writers. Anthropologists found that meanings are linked to language and that each provides a unique way of understanding and acting toward the external world. Sociologists discovered that our internal conceptions of (knowledge of) the social order provide us with "definitions of the situation." And, if we believe a situation to be real, we will act as though it were real. Psychologists also rediscovered the ancient principle with their concept of *schemata* as meanings for reality and the strong influence such structures of meaning have on human behavior.

Still more recently communication scholars have incorporated this ancient principle into their formulations to explain how mass communication content influences the behavior of their audiences. The press shapes the "pictures in our heads" and influences the ways in which we act toward the public issues of the day. Media "cultivate" our beliefs about the real world and influence our conduct. The press helps us arrange internal meanings in the form of an "agenda" of topics to think about and a hierarchy of how important they are. Finally, mass communications establish, extend, substitute, and stabilize meanings for words in our language. These modifications of meaning influence our responses to the things and issues that are labeled.

There is little doubt, then, that the relationship between knowledge and conduct remains as a foundation principle of human behavior. Meanings do shape our actions. The validity of that proposition has survived for thousands of years.

Modifying Meanings to Influence Behavior

The meaning construction theories discussed in Chapter 9 outline ways in which the behavior of media audiences can be influenced without deliberate intent. That is, those who gather, edit, and disseminate the news are not doing so with a plan in mind for creating pictures in our heads, or even setting our personal agenda. Those who write violence into their scripts and bring it to the television screen are not trying to make people afraid of their neighborhoods. Similarly, extensive television coverage of an issue like "crack" is not broadcast for the purpose of establishing new meanings in our language. These are unintended influences that are probably neither understood nor wanted by those who manage the media.

But if mass communications can modify meanings and influence behavior unintentionally, there are adequate grounds for looking to a meaning construction strategy for the purpose of *deliberately* changing conduct. Mass communicated information should be as effective as any other kind in changing the meanings people assign to some thing, product, cause, candidate, or issue. If such changes can be achieved, modifications of behavior toward that target of persuasion should follow.

This is a relatively simple idea: knowledge influences behavior. What is missing are elaborate assumptions about internal predispositions and processes, such as attitude change, cognitive dissonance, or even complex social or cultural expectations. In simple terms, this strategy could be characterized as *learn-do*, as opposed to the learn-feel-do and the learn-conform approaches discussed earlier.

While the term "meaning construction strategy" may be new, the approach itself is hardly new. A good example of how significant this strategy has been in the past can be seen in a major change in automobile advertising that took place in the mid-1920s. Up to that time, auto makers like Henry Ford, William Durant, the Dodge brothers, Walter Chrysler, and dozens of others used a rather sensible approach. Their advertising copy stressed the mechanical reliability, safety, economy, and durability of their products. That changed overnight, however, when an early automobile manufacturer discovered the meaning construction strategy.

The story concerns Edward S. Jordan, the founder of the Jordan Motor Car Company. His factory was producing the Playboy, an uninspired open car of relatively poor mechanical qualities. It wasn't selling very well, and Jordan realized that something had to be done. Then, during the summer of 1923, he was traveling in his private railway car from Detroit to San Francisco. As the train was pulling slowly out of a Western town, he looked outside and saw a sight that stirred him greatly. A beautiful young woman was cantering her horse beside the train. She was tanned, athletic, and seemingly uninhibited as her hair flowed behind her in the breeze. Jordan could hardly take his eyes away, but he turned and asked a companion where they were. The reply was, "Somewhere west of Laramie."

The whole incident, and especially the phrase with which his companion replied, so impressed Jordan that he had his advertising people begin promoting his car in a new way. Soon ads appeared in magazines and newspapers across the nation showing the automobile superimposed in the middle of a large, romantic-looking drawing of a beautiful woman galloping on a powerful horse with hair streaming behind. The ad read:

> Somewhere west of Laramie there's a bronco-busting, steer-roping girl who knows what I am talking about . . . the PLAYBOY was built for her.
>   Built for the lass whose face is brown with the sun when the day is done of revel and romp and race . . .
>   There's a savor of links about that car—of laughter, and lilt and light—a hint of old loves—and saddle and quirt . . .
>   Step into the PLAYBOY when the hour grows dull . . .
>   Then start for the land of real living with the spirit of the lass who rides, lean and rangy, into the red horizon of a Wyoming twilight.[10]

That was it! There was no information on horsepower, number of seats, cylinders, cargo capacity, or even the number of wheels. But the "meaning" of Jordan Playboy came through loud and clear. It was, above all, *exciting*. To buy the Playboy was to associate with meanings of laughter, freedom, adventure, and perhaps just a hint of uninhibited sex. The sale of Jordan's car rose sharply and continued long after the design should have been junked. As even the most casual viewing of contemporary television commercials reveals, automobile advertising has been deeply dependent upon this strategy ever since.

The use of meaning in campaigns, advertising, and other attempts at persuasion continues full force. In recent years we have seen a little old lady ask, "Where's the beef?" to provide meaning for a particular fast-food sandwich. Airplanes now fly "friendly" skies. Certain laxatives and acid-stomach products "mean relief." Political candidates urgently seek brief, slogan-like expressions that can attach positive meanings to their mass communicated images (New Deal, Fair Deal, War on Poverty, Great Society, New Beginnings, New Ideas, and so on).

A diagram of the meaning construction strategy hardly seems necessary. Its assumptions are much simpler than those discussed earlier. Nevertheless, such a diagram would have the components shown in Figure 10.3.

Does this learn-do formulation work? The world of practical advertising seems to think so. On the other hand, the technical journals of social science and communication research provide few answers. In spite of its ancient origins, relatively little research has been done on meaning construction strategies for persuasion.

This chapter has shown that the psychodynamic strategy for persuasion held center stage in advertising, information, campaigns, and other forms of persuasion for decades. Of late, however, serious questions are being asked about whether or not it can reliably produce

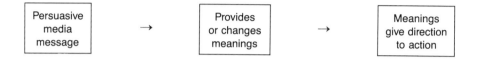

Figure 10.3. The meaning construction persuasion strategy.

results. Sometimes it seems to work, but many times it does not, and no one is sure why. Sociocultural strategies, on the other hand, have never been as popular, either in terms of stimulating research or as a basis for actual advertising or other forms of media persuasion. There is some evidence that they can be very effective, but their success may require using media information along with interpersonal persuasion. Meaning construction strategies remain even less well understood. This strategy appears frequently in contemporary advertising, but whether it works reliably to trigger desired responses is not known.

One thing is very clear. It is difficult to adapt and apply principles that seem to characterize the ability of mass communication content to influence behavior in a nondeliberate way to practical tasks such as selling goods, candidates, or pro-social conduct. In spite of the intense efforts made to find the theoretical bases of effective persuasion strategies, they remain elusive.

NOTES

1. See Gerald R. Miller, "Persuasion," in Charles R. Berger and Steven H. Chaffee, eds., *Handbook of Communication Science* (Newbury Park, Cal.: Sage Publications, 1987), pp. 446–83.
2. Victoria O'Donnell and June Kable, *Persuasion: An Interactive-Dependency Approach* (New York: Random House, 1982), p. 9. See also Charles U. Larsen, *Persuasion, Reception and Responsibility* (Belmont, Cal.: Wadsworth Publishing Company, 1986), p. 8
3. Marvin Karlins and Herbert I. Abelson, *Persuasion: How Opinions and Attitudes Are Changed* (New York: Springer Publishing Co., 1970), p. 2.
4. Miller, "Persuasion," pp. 447–48.
5. Leon Festinger, *A Theory of Cognitive Dissonance* (Stanford, Cal.: Stanford University Press, 1957).
6. John Phillip Jones, *What's in a Name? Advertising and the Concept of Brands* (Lexington, Mass.: D. Heath and Company, 1986), p. 141.

7. Jones, *What's in a Name?* p. 142.

8. Everett M. Rogers and J. Douglas Storey, "Communication Campaigns," in Berger and Chaffee, *Handbook,* p. 841.

9. Miller, "Persuasion," p. 453.

10. The incident and the significance of this change in advertising strategy are described at length in Robert Lacey, *Ford: The Man and the Machine* (New York: Ballantine Books, 1986), pp. 297–99.

PART III

The Media
in Contemporary
Society

CHAPTER 11
Media System Dependency Theory

A considerable variety of theories have been discussed in the previous chapters, and their links to various theoretical paradigms from sociology and psychology have been examined. It is clear that the study of mass communication suffers from an embarrassment of theoretical riches rather than from an insufficiency of explanatory formulations. As the field has developed, this surfeit has been both helpful and problematic. Each of the theories we have examined has served to guide important research in its time and has led to increased understanding of media effects. Yet it is not at all clear which of the competing theories best explains the relationship between the mass media and the people who make up the societies in which they disseminate messages. No single explanation predicts that relationship fully. Furthermore, some of the theories openly contradict each other. One says that there will be immediate, universal, direct, and powerful influences on audience members from exposure to mass communications; another says that such influences will be long term, indirect, selective, and limited.

The dissimilarity among contemporary theories of mass communication exists because each focuses on different configurations of independent and dependent variables and therefore each uses different assumptions in unique ways to make predictions about influences on people and society. For example, one focuses on beliefs, attitudes, and behavior at an individual level while another attempts to explain shared conventions of meaning and their influence on social organization, society, and culture.

For that reason, it would be illogical and premature to assume that one theory is "correct," or even "complete," while others are completely "wrong" or should be abandoned. The massive research base needed to identify the "best" theory remains to be assembled. In fact, the time may be a long way off when one general theory stands out in mass communications, subsuming or synthesizing all competitors, as, say, Einstein's theory of relativity does in the field of physics.

Meanwhile, all of the theoretical approaches that have been examined here remain *potentially* viable explanations of at least *some* kinds of media influences. At the same time, it cannot be denied that some earlier theories now seem considerably less attractive than once was the case. Few scholars today would maintain that the "magic bullet" theory provides adequate explanations of how the media influence people. The accumulated research evidence has failed to support its claims. Other earlier formulations have similarly started to come into question. Yet most of the theories still remain as sources of important research hypotheses, and until totally convincing data have been gathered it is not yet time to dismiss them completely.

In spite of the number of theories that are already available, still more are needed! As we have indicated, none of the existing theories has been shown to provide a full analysis of *all* of the influences of mass communications. In fact, we are not sure at this point what influences actually exist! Each new theoretical perspective has uncovered new factors. For instance, the earliest theories ignored individual and social differences and the selective influences that they brought about. Theories stressing selective influences did not discuss long-term socialization. Theories addressing socialization influences did not try to explain the role of the media in the construction of meaning, and the part played by such constructions in shaping behavior. Each new theoretical perspective, then, has broken new ground by bringing research attention to new categories of independent and dependent variables.

That process of discovery is not yet complete. It is not unreasonable to assume that there remain influences of and on the mass media in our society that have yet to be identified. For that reason, theoretical development must continue its probe beyond the limits of our current understandings of the processes and effects of mass communication.

In line with this situation, another theoretical formulation that can be proposed at this point is a *media system dependency theory,* a complex formulation that attempts to link into a single configuration a number of the ideas that have been explored in previous chapters.[1] It draws upon several of the general theoretical paradigms discussed in Chapter 1. It is appropriate to begin our discussion by looking back briefly at certain features of the general paradigms that provide the intellectual roots of mass communication theories, because these features also provide a foundation for media system dependency theory.

THE ROOTS OF MEDIA EFFECTS THEORIES

Theories that ask questions about the general and powerful effects of the mass media tend to be based on three of the paradigms that were discussed in Chapter 1: the structural functional, the conflict, and the (social) evolutionary perspectives. As was made clear, these formulations are not restricted to the study of mass communication. They are widely used by social scientists for the study of virtually *any* large-scale social institution or process. Generally, sociologists use these three paradigms as conceptual frameworks for *macro* analysis, that is, for the study of large-scale social systems, such as complex formal or bureaucratic groups, whole societies, or for the assessment of very general social processes, such as stability, conflict, and change. For example, in discussions of the earliest attempts to develop theoretical interpretations of the effects of mass communication (Chapter 6) a macro analysis was made of the nature and origins of the "mass" society. The analysis drew upon several macro conceptualizations of social structure and processes of sociocultural change, providing the "big picture" of the conditions of social life within which the new mass media were thought to be all-powerful. For instance, Durkheim made use of the structural functional paradigm in his (macro) analysis of the consequences of increasing societal complexity. He pointed out how increasing specialization, resulting in a vastly differentiated division of labor, leads to a decrease in social consensus. This brings about a reduction in effective interpersonal communication and an increase in confusion concerning the guiding norms of the society. He called that condition (structural) *anomie*. This, in turn, leaves individual members of such societies in a state of psychological confusion (personal anomie), because their subjective conceptions of societal norms are correspondingly ambiguous. Such a situation reduces close and intimate ties between people, restricting significant influences from interpersonal communication, and leaving such individuals increasingly open to influences from other sources.

Early media theorists picked up on Durkheim's logic in formulating the view that it is a combination of societal complexity, limited consensus, normlessness, personal confusion, and psychological alienation or isolation that can make mass communications powerful. Under such "lonely crowd" conditions, it was believed, people could be easily swayed by the media. Thus the structural functional paradigm used at a macro level of analysis led to specific conclusions about the nature of society. This in turn provided corollaries concerning the explanation of media influences.

In contrast, a *micro* level of analysis is concerned with very specific units. In social sciences this usually means the *individual*. Whereas sociologists focus on groups and societies, psychological theories of media effects are formulated at the micro level, focusing on specific variables and processes that affect individuals. The most common micro theories are rooted in the cognitive paradigm, discussed in Chapters 1 and 7.

Psychological theories of media effects, then, ignore the societal "big picture" and the way that long-term or large-scale social forces can affect the likelihood of individuals being influenced by mass communications. They are also limited to examinations of relatively immediate consequences of short-term exposure to the content of mass communications. Of course one of the attractions of such an approach is that it allows theorists and researchers to focus on simpler variables, to exercise more control, and to be very specific. The effect of the individual's needs, attitudes, values, and interests upon how they selectively expose themselves to media, perceive message content, and selectively retain information can be examined without one's having to consider influences from the social systems within which the person lives (Chapter 7). Similarly, psychodynamic theories of persuasion are concerned with internal psychological processes that can supposedly be activated with media messages in order to get people to buy products or behave in other desired ways.

Somewhat more general are theories of media effects coming from *social* psychology. They do take into account at least some social relationships that influence people, such as the theories of selective influence (Chapter 7), theories of indirect media effects (Chapter 8), and meaning construction strategies of persuasion (Chapter 10). Such approaches tend to combine elements of the cognitive paradigm with aspects of the structural functional paradigm. For example, the processes of selective exposure, perception, and retention are combined with the structural functionalist's emphasis upon stability and order. In this case, individuals are assumed to live in stable interpersonal environments, not in the unstable social milieu of a mass society. Individuals' interpersonal networks and group bonds are said to provide them with stable norms and beliefs—as opposed to conditions of anomie—that insulate them against arbitrary media influence. Specific attitudes and forms of behavior are examined in an attempt to demonstrate that these are the result of interpersonal influence, not of media influence. The sociocultural model of persuasion (Chapter 10) is based upon similar thinking. The decisions of an individual to contribute to an organization, buy a product, or vote for a candidate are conceptualized as products of both personal characteristics (needs, attitudes, etc.) and social pressures to conform to significant group or community norms.

Meaning construction theories, which were examined in Chapter 9, are closely linked to the symbolic interactionist paradigm. As we noted, formulations of this type are becoming increasingly popular in the study of media effects. Such construction theories attribute more power to the media than do selective influence theories, although that power is said to be long range and indirect.

The fact that meaning construction theories attribute considerable power to the media has not escaped the attention of a group of media scholars who are sometimes called "critical" theorists. They point out that using communications to shape the meanings people share is a very effective strategy for gaining and maintaining social, political, or economic control. This idea is scarcely a new one. The old adage that the pen is mightier than the sword speaks to the belief that whoever controls ideas—that is, the production of knowledge—can potentially control people's behavior without ever having to use force. If Karl Marx were writing today, he would undoubtedly make much of the fact that the mass media provide a constant flow of information that can shape meanings. He would undoubtedly conclude that those who own or control the economic means of production would also be strongly motivated to control the nature and dissemination of mass communications as a means of preserving their interests and maintaining their positions of dominance. Thus, controlling the *economic* means of production would require control of the means of *mental* production in order to entrench meanings favorable to their continued exercise of power.

It would come as no surprise to Marx to discover that our contemporary media—newspapers, magazines, books, radio, movies, and television—are all characterized by similar patterns of ownership: large chains, syndicates, conglomerates, and corporations own America's media. The day of the crusty editor-owner of the local newspaper, or the family-owned book publishing firm, faded into history long ago. At the same time, it would be difficult indeed, in a society of complex markets characterized by diverse demographics and psychographics, to show that concentrated ownership leads to any significant control over the beliefs, attitudes, opinions, or meanings broadly shared in our society.

Whether one is attracted or repelled by Marxian interpretations, control of information can be important. There seems little doubt that information that can shape meanings is a critical resource in today's society for many specific purposes. We showed in Chapter 10 how attempts are made to shape beliefs and behavior, not only in the marketplace but across a spectrum of social institutions: dependency on information control exists also in education, family life, religion, and especially politics. Candidates for political office constantly struggle to convince people that *their* versions of what should be done are the correct subjective interpretations of reality that will lead to the best consequences. Similar dependency links can be postulated for other social institutions. Obviously, a theory is needed that takes these linkages into account.

Contemporary theories of mass communication tend to be at the micro level and have not focused on dependencies at a macro level. Each begins with different assumptions, flows from its own configuration or underlying postulates, incorporates a particular pattern of independent variables, and provides explanations and predictions for a unique set of dependent variables. None is completely wrong, but certainly none addresses the way in which various components of the overall social structure are linked to the existence of a deeply institutionalized media system within the society. Therefore, as we noted above, a serious limitation in the contemporary study of mass communication is that few attempts have been made to bring theories together into a more integrated form. Media system dependency theory, discussed in the remainder of this chapter, represents such an attempt.

CONCEPTUALIZING MEDIA DEPENDENCY RELATIONSHIPS

A major aim of media system dependency theory is to explain why mass communications sometimes have powerful and direct effects and at other times have indirect and rather weak effects. To do this, the theory draws upon the central issues of each of the five general paradigms that were set forth in the first chapter: the structural functionalist concern for societal *stability,* the *change* focus of the conflict paradigm, the emphasis on social *adaptation* of the evolutionary paradigm, the concentration on *meaning* construction in the symbolic interactionist perspective, and the explanation of *individual* factors (motivations, values, attitudes, and behavior) drawn from the cognitive paradigm.

One way to describe media dependency theory is to say that it is an "ecological" theory (in the original meaning of that term): it focuses on relationships between small, medium, and large systems and their components. An ecological theory views society as an organic structure; it examines how parts of micro (little) and macro (big) social systems are related to each other and then attempts to explain the behavior of the parts in terms of those relationships. The media system is assumed to be an important part of the social fabric of modern society, and it is seen to have relationships with individuals, groups, organizations, and other social systems. These relationships may be conflict-ridden, or cooperative; they may be dynamic and changing or static and orderly. They also may range from being direct and powerful to being indirect or weak. Whatever the particulars of the relationship, it is the *relationship* that carries the burden of explanation.

As the name of the theory suggests, the key relationship around which the logic of this approach is based is one of *dependency*. These relationships may be with the media system as a whole or with one of its parts, such as the television, radio, newspaper, or magazine industries.

Media dependency relationships rest upon *goals*, on the one hand, and *resources*, on the other. Part of what it means to live in a society is that in order for individuals, groups, and large organizations to attain their personal and collective goals, they have to rely upon resources that other people, groups, or systems control, and vice versa. The media system is seen as an information system in control of three types of "dependency-engendering" information resources, to which others have to have access in order to attain their goals. The first resource is information *gathering* or *creating*. Reporters, for example, gather information about people and events that we need to know or are simply interested in knowing. Script writers create information about real or imaginary events that allow us to fulfill the goal of playing or having fun with other people by going to the movies. The second resource, information *processing*, refers to the transformation of raw information that has been gathered or created. An editor, for example, processes the reporter's raw information so that it can fit into a story; a director processes the information created by a screenwriter, making it into a film. The third resource controlled by the media system is information *dissemination*, or the capacity to get information out to a mass audience. The primary job of the television news anchor, for example, is to broadcast the information gathered by the reporter and processed by the editor. The movie distributor's business is to get the film that the screenwriter and director have created and processed out to the movie-going audience.

The term "information" is used here in a general way to refer to the production and distribution of *all* types of messages. Conventional distinctions that suggest that "news" is informational whereas "entertainment" is not, are misleading. Such distinctions suggest that people glean the information that guides their constructions of meanings and their actions primarily from news. There are at least two important limitations to this way of thinking. First, it ignores the ways in which people utilize entertainment content to understand themselves, their world, or the many worlds beyond their direct experience, and to orient their own actions and their interactions with others. Limiting the idea of information to news would, for example, suggest that what people learn from entertainment has no important consequences for the meanings they construct and act upon or upon their socialization.

Second, by removing entertainment from the realm of information, we diminish the role of play in personal and social life. Despite psychological and anthropological wisdom to the contrary, play is generally, and mistakenly, treated as an unimportant dimension of human motivation. Nevertheless, play is, in many important respects, "serious." It is, for example, serious in child development (e.g., language acquisition and identity formation) and in the form of ceremonies, contests, and celebrations that contribute to social solidarity. For these reasons, we prefer the broader conception of information, in which all messages are considered to have potential for affecting how people think, feel, and act.

The Two-Way Nature of Media Dependency Relationships

The media system's power lies in its control over scarce information resources that individuals, groups, organizations, social systems, and societies depend upon to attain their goals. The goals–resources dependency relationship determines the relative degree of media power in any particular situation and is the key variable in whether the question being asked is about large (macro) social units or small (micro) units.

This dependency relationship is not one way. The power of equation involves not only how others depend upon the resources of the media to attain their goals, but also how the media system depends upon the resources controlled by others. The media system too has goals, and in order to attain these goals, it requires access to more than just the resources under its control. The media system can be conceived in terms of relationships between its many parts, including its print (e.g., newspapers) and electronic (e.g., television) forms, all of the cross-media organizations involved in information gathering/creating, processing, and dissemination (e.g., Associated Press, advertisers, or production companies), professional associations, unions, and other organizations that participate in the production of mass communication products.

To illustrate the two-way nature of media dependency relations, we can look at the relations between the media system and the political system. In a manner reminiscent of the structural functionalist paradigm, we call the relationship that the media system has with the political (or any other) social system, a *structural dependency relation*, because it concerns *repetitive patterns of interdependence* between macro units of analysis—in this case, social systems.

Some resources under the control of the political system are necessary for the attainment of media system goals. The primary goal of the media system in modern capitalist societies is to make a *profit* (Chapter 5). Another important goal is *legitimacy* or the willingness of others to grant the media the right to certain freedoms, such as of the press, and the right to play certain social roles such as surveillance and investigator roles. Other goals include economic expansion and stability. The political system controls legislation, regulative agencies, and tariff and trade policies that affect the profitability, expansion opportunities, and economic stability of the media system. It also controls the more subtle legitimacy resource. The political system endorses the media system by granting it constitutional and other legal rights to operate as an information system on the grounds that the media are essential to the conduct of a democratic society. If the media system were denied access to these resources, its stability and economic welfare would be severely jeopardized.

The structural dependency relation between the media and political systems is elaborated in later sections, when the contributions of structural functional, conflict and evolutionary paradigms to media dependency theory are discussed. In general, it is assumed that the relative degree of power of the media system vis-à-vis another social system, whether it be the political, economic, religious, family, educational, military, recreational, or legal system—is a product of the distribution of resources and dependencies of each system (i.e., the structural dependency relation). An advantage of media system dependency theory is that we can use the same basic concepts that apply to the abstract macro relations between systems to examine the more concrete (and micro) relations between individuals and the mass media.

Dependencies between Individuals and Media Systems

Individuals, like social systems, develop dependency relationships with the media, because individuals are goal directed and some of their goals require access resources controlled by the mass media. The types of dependency relations that individuals develop with the media are

Figure 11.1. Typology of Individual Media System Dependency Relations

Understanding	Orientation	Play
Self-understanding e.g., learning about oneself and growing as a person	Action orientation e.g., deciding what to buy, how to dress, or how to stay slim	Solitary play e.g., relaxing when alone or having something to do by oneself
Social understanding e.g., knowing about and interpreting the world or community	Interaction orientation e.g., getting hints on how to handle new or difficult situations	Social play e.g., going to a movie or listening to music with family or friends

presented with examples, in Figure 11.1. We assume that survival and growth are fundamental human motivations that impel individuals to achieve three important goals: *Understanding, orientation,* and *play.* Human beings are motivated to understand themselves and their social environments. They use these understandings in orienting their actions and interactions with others. Play is considered to be an equally essential goal. It is a feature of all societies and is more than just escape or tension release; it is also a way in which we become "social," learning roles, norms, and values by playing with others. Moreover, in our play we express ourselves and our cultures, such as in dance, sport, ceremony, and celebration.

Social understanding dependencies develop when individuals utilize media information resources to comprehend and interpret people, cultures, and events of the present, past, or future. *Self-understanding* refers to media relations that expand or maintain individuals' capacities to interpret their own beliefs, behavior, self-concepts, or personalities. Questions of meaning and knowledge are basic to both understanding dependencies, with the object of understanding being external to the individual in the case of social understanding, and internal in self-understanding. Central to the orientation dependencies are questions of behavior. *Action orientation* refers to a multitude of ways in which individuals establish dependency relations with the media in order to obtain guides to specific behaviors of their own. Some are mundane behaviors concerned with everyday life events of getting up in the morning, making it through the day, and getting to sleep at night. Others are more consequential such as political (voting), economic (buying a house), religious (supporting or opposing tele-evangelism), legal (going to small claims court), medical (exercising or giving up smoking), or crisis problem-solving behaviors (coping with a natural disaster). *Inter-*

action orientation dependencies require that the object of action be one or more persons. When individuals glean media information about the kinds of behavior (including communication behavior) that are appropriate or effective in dealing with their personal relationships (lovers, siblings, or parents) or with occupants of social or professional positions (an employer, law enforcement agents, or clergy), they are exhibiting an interaction orientation dependency. Another common example of this kind of dependency occurs when individuals look to the media for cues on how to behave toward "out-groups," such as ethnic, socioeconomic, or disabled groups with whom one has little experience or contact.

Finally, the same personal versus social distinction is made with types of play dependencies. *Solitary play* dependency refers to instances when the aesthetics, enjoyment, stimulation, or relaxation properties of the media content itself are the attraction. Other people may be present but their presence is secondary as, for example, when one is listening to a symphony or watching a movie. In *social play*, in contrast, the dependency relation is based upon the capacity of the media to provide content that stimulates play between people; in this case the content is secondary to friends, family, or others getting together as co-participants in media behavior. For example, two persons in a budding romantic relationship may go to movies where the aesthetic quality of the movie is less important than their movie-going together.

A fact of "social" life is that understanding, orientation, and play cannot be easily achieved without access to the resources of others, and information is one of the more essential resources. In Chapter 1 we saw that power holders tend to control access to key information resources, such as written language or books, and, by restricting access, making the resources scarce and therefore prized. In premodern societies where no media system existed, the most prized and, therefore scarce, information resources were usually under the control of leaders in the political/military sphere (tribal chiefs and kings, for example), the religious/medical domain (shaman/medicine man), or kinship systems (the elders). In modern societies, the media control some of the scarce information resources, including those that individuals require to achieve their basic understanding, orientation, and play goals. It is partly for this reason that we usually conceive of the media as an information system. We also assume that whatever power the media system has with respect to its effects on individuals' beliefs, perceptions and behavior is, in the final analysis, a consequence of control over scarce and prized information resources. As a practical matter, it would simply be more difficult for individuals to achieve all of their understanding, orientation, and play goals without access to media information resources.

We should not, however, overstate the importance of the mass media. They do make it easier to attain understanding, orientation, and play goals, but they are not the only way to attain such goals. Individuals are, after all, connected to interpersonal networks of friends and family as well as to educational, religious, political, and other systems that also help people to attain their goals. Media dependency theory does not share the mass society idea that the media are powerful because individuals are isolated, without group bonds. Rather it conceives of media power as lying in control over certain information resources that individuals require to attain their personal goals. Furthermore, the more complex the society, the broader the range of personal goals that require access to media information resources.

The typology presented in Figure 11.1 is intended to capture the range of basic dependency relations that individuals—singly or collectively, in audiences—develop. It should also be applicable to particular social categories of individuals. For example, men and women may seek to attain different kinds of goals through their relations with the media; older people may depend on the media more for solitary play than for the social play that may dominate dating-age people's relations with the media. Also we can expect to find the kind of individual differences that psychologists attend to, with some individuals relating to media primarily for play, others for understanding, and still others for orientation. In any case, we can use the same typology and the same dependency conception to describe and analyze whole audiences, large social categories, and individuals.

We can also use this typology to describe individuals' dependency relations with a particular medium. For example, audiences might depend heavily on books or magazines for social understanding (e.g., nonfiction stories) or for self-understanding (pop psychology books), while they might come to depend upon radio more for orientation to action (traffic and weather bulletins) or to interaction (talk shows about love and sex). We do not expect, however, that one type of mass medium would engender only one type of dependency relation. In fact, Ball-Rokeach, Rokeach, and Grube[2] found that television is implicated in all the types of dependency listed in Figure 11.1. Not surprisingly, they found social understanding to be the most common type of television dependency relation, but, more unexpectedly, they found that self-understanding dependency is also very important. These findings suggest something important about individual audience relations with television; people seek to attain more than just play through television use. Television media have the information resources that individuals find necessary to the attainment of understanding and orientation as well as play goals.

In addition to using the dependency typology to describe individuals' relations with the media system in general or with a particular medium, we can also use the typology to describe the dependency relations that they have with specific media products, such as a genre of television programs or even a particular TV program, movie, or magazine. Reserachers are, for example, trying to determine the kinds of dependencies that viewers of home shopping programs develop.[3] Discovering such dependency relations can provide an insight into how new forms of television programming are incorporated into individual lives.

People construct their own media systems. From the many alternatives available to them—newspapers, radio, television, VCR and theater movies, compact discs and stereos, books, magazines, newsletters and pamphlets, and so on—people put together their particular combinations of media and their particular relationships with these media.[4] People differ not only in the combinations of media that form their media systems, but also in the nature of the dependency relationships that they establish with any particular medium. Radio, for example, may be part of some peoples' and not other peoples' media systems, and it may serve primarily social understanding dependencies for some and primarily play dependencies for others. There are predictable situational variations as well. The media system that we construct for ourselves changes as the situation in which we find ourselves changes. For example, during a crisis, we construct the kind of media system that will best serve the personal goals that are most important at the time. When the crisis is over, we may return to our everyday media systems, reestablishing our dependency relations with media that are germane to the attainment of our everyday goals.

We should not overstate individuals' freedom to construct media systems. There are constraints on the choices they can make, and shared constraints account for similarities between individuals' media systems. Technological and organization differences between the media make some media better suited than others for play, understanding, or orientation. For example, it is in the nature of movie making and book publishing that movies and books are less timely than television and radio. This difference puts important limitations upon the utility of movies and books for the attainment of everyday or crisis goals that require prompt information. Another important constraint that shapes the general contours of individuals' media systems is the tendency for media to specialize in their content, specializations that affect the kinds of goals they are likely to serve. The peculiar combination of music, news, traffic weather reports, and talk shows is likely to suggest "radio," while grocery, car, clothes, and appliance ads combined with news are likely to suggest "newspapers." Media also vary in the diversity of content that they produce, with VCRs and compact discs being very specialized in content, and television and books being very diverse.

Thus individuals differ in the media systems they construct because they have different goals and interests, but at the same time, the organizational, content, and technological characteristics of different media constrain individual choice and these restraints result in a similarity of their media systems. Moreover, while individuals can differ in their personal goals, they also tend to share some personal goals and this fact also contributes to the similarities between their media systems. For example, some people are "news freaks" who just have to know what is going on at all times, while most are content to learn the news when they get up or get home from work. Both types of individuals nonetheless share the goal of understanding their environments and will therefore have to employ one of a limited set of mass media—newspapers, television, or radio, as opposed to movies, VCRs, compact discs, or stereos. The fact that more than 70 percent of the American people say that they get most of their national news from television suggests considerable similarity of at least this feature of people's media systems.

BASIC PARADIGMS AND MEDIA SYSTEM DEPENDENCY THEORY

It was noted earlier that a number of the basic paradigms for conceptualizing human behavior and social relationships that were set forth in Chapter 1 provide an important foundation for media system dependency theory. The sections that follow address some of the ways in which the central concerns of the cognitive, symbolic interactionist, conflict, and structural functional paradigms provide perspectives for interpreting patterns of dependency among individuals, media, and society.

Contributions of the Cognitive Paradigm

We are interested in more than just describing individuals' dependencies. We are also interested in demonstrating how these dependency relationships help us explain the effects of exposure to media messages upon individual beliefs and behavior. This is a focal concern of those who use a cognitive approach to explaining the effects of mass communications upon their audiences. In media dependency theory, the key to explaining when and why individuals *expose* themselves to the media and the *effects* of that exposure upon their beliefs and behavior is to account for the ways in which people employ media resources to attain their personal goals.

People who have developed dependency relationships with television to attain social understanding, for example, should select different types of television programs from persons who depend upon television primarily for play. Or, if there are two persons watching the same television program, one to attain primarily understanding goals and the other to attain primarily play goals, they should get different things out of the program and therefore be affected by it in different ways. In their study of the effects of exposure to a television program designed to affect political beliefs and behavior, Ball-Rokeach and her colleagues[5] provide evidence to support this way of thinking about selective exposure and media effects. They found that people did selectively expose themselves on the basis of their established dependency relations with television and that viewers who had certain kinds of dependency relations were affected differently from those who did not.

Media system dependency theory envisions a *cognitive* psychological process that increases the likelihood of one's being affected by particular media content, such as a program, story, or a genre of programs or stories. The process, diagrammed in Figure 11.2, begins with either an individual who scans the media to decide actively what he or she wishes to listen to, watch, or read, *or* one who more casually comes into contact with media content.

In step one, *active selectors* expose themselves to media content that they have reason to expect will help them to achieve one or more of their understanding, orientation, or play goals. Their expectations are based upon (1) their prior experience, (2) conversation with their interpersonal associates (friends and co-workers), or (3) cues obtained from media sources (advertising or reviews). *Casual observers* encounter media content incidentally with no preformed expectations (e.g., walking into a laundromat where the TV is on). Some, during the course of exposure, may find that one or more dependency is activated that motivates them to continue exposure. Others may not experience dependency activation and can be expected to terminate exposure when the situation permits. In cases where the content is not connecting with the individual's motivations, continued exposure would be due to situational demands, such as conventions of politeness or an inability to escape the exposure situation, as in public bars with video screens or

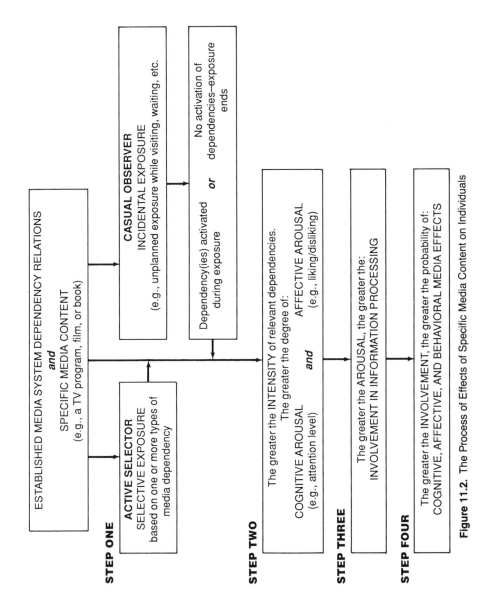

Figure 11.2. The Process of Effects of Specific Media Content on Individuals

STEP ONE

ESTABLISHED MEDIA SYSTEM DEPENDENCY RELATIONS
and
SPECIFIC MEDIA CONTENT
(e.g., a TV program, film, or book)

CASUAL OBSERVER
INCIDENTAL EXPOSURE
(e.g., unplanned exposure while visiting, waiting, etc.

No activation of
dependencies—exposure
ends

ACTIVE SELECTOR
SELECTIVE EXPOSURE
based on one or more types of
media dependency

Dependency(ies) activated
during exposure   *or*

STEP TWO

The greater the INTENSITY of relevant dependencies.
The greater the degree of:
COGNITIVE AROUSAL   AFFECTIVE AROUSAL
(e.g., attention level)   *and*   (e.g., liking/disliking)

STEP THREE

The greater the AROUSAL, the greater the:
INVOLVEMENT IN INFORMATION PROCESSING

STEP FOUR

The greater the INVOLVEMENT, the greater the probability of:
COGNITIVE, AFFECTIVE, AND BEHAVIORAL MEDIA EFFECTS

blasting radios in a park, bus, or subway or on a beach. Most people are active selectors much of the time and casual observers some of the time.

In step two, other aspects of dependencies become important. Not all people who selectively expose themselves to certain media content will do so with the same degree of dependency, nor will all people who have their dependencies activated during incidental exposure. Variations in intensity of individuals' media dependencies will be a function of differences in (1) their personal goals, (2) their personal and social environments, (3) expectations with regard to the potential utility of the specific media content under consideration, and (4) ease of access to that content. Variations in individuals' goals often reflect variations in their environments.[6] When those environments are full of ambiguity or threat, for example, individuals' media system dependencies should be quite intense. This is so because access to media information resources is often necessary to the resolution of their ambiguity and the reduction of real or potential threat. Another example of how variations in people's personal and social environs affect the intensity of dependency concerns serious health problems. People who are, themselves, or who have loved ones who are seriously ill often develop strong media dependencies in order to gain access to relevant information that might contribute to their finding the best medical and support services. They should, for example, be particularly responsive to relevant health information presented in talk shows, dramas, health news columns, and the like.

People's expectations about the helpfulness of a particular show, story, or other type of media content should vary as well. The active selector clearly has higher expectations than the casual observer. Active selectors will also vary according to whether past media experiences have led them to expect that exposure will satisfy their goals; others may have received cues from their friends or from media advertising that affect their expectations. Of course, the more that people expect to receive helpful information, the more intense their dependency should be—as long as they are not disappointed. Finally, there are some media that, while widely available, are not equally available to all. These include expensive media and programs that have limited availability, such as those that are carried only on closed circuit television or are not carried nationwide.

No matter what the source of the variation in the intensity of the dependency, we can hypothesize that the greater the intensity of relevant media dependencies, the greater the degree of (1) cognitive arousal (catching and maintaining people's attention) and (2) affective arousal (arousing their emotions). (See Figure 11.2.) For example, in the study conducted by Ball-Rokeach, Rokeach, and Grube, high-dependency viewers reported that they were highly attentive while watching the TV program and that they liked the program and its co-hosts. When people's dependency upon a TV program is low or nil, we would expect to find them talking or doing other things while the television is on, and therefore be unlikely to feel strongly (positively or negatively) about the program.

In step three, a key concept is *involvement*. The politician who says "love me or hate me, but don't ignore me" is speaking to the importance of audience involvement. Involvement, in the present conception of the effects process, refers to more than arousal; it refers to active participation in information processing. Our hypothesis is that people who have been cognitively and affectively aroused will engage in the kind of careful processing of information that will allow them to recall or remember the information after exposure. Research suggests that high involvement is a particularly important consideration in successful public health media campaigns designed to get audiences to change their beliefs or behavior, such as to stop smoking, start exercising, or get medical checkups.[7]

The fourth and final step in the media system dependency effects process should now be obvious: Individuals who have become intensely involved in information processing are more likely to be affected by their exposure to media content. Most media effects research concerns *cognitive* effects, or effects on perceptions, attitudes, knowledge, or values. *Affective* effects, such as feelings of fear, happiness, sentiment, or hatred, receive far less attention.[8] It is difficult to see how cognitive and affective dimensions can be separated in reality. Most attitude changes, for example, carry with them some change of liking or disliking of an object or situation. Less obvious is the connection between cognitive and behavioral effects dimensions. There has been a tendency to abandon efforts to demonstrate media effects on behavior, largely because the attempts to show that attitude change produces change in behavior have been disappointing. Another reason is the rigorous and expensive research design required to demonstrate convincingly long-term media effects on behavior (e.g., research that is conducted in a "natural media exposure situation,"[9] rather than in a laboratory). Nonetheless, in the major empirical test of media dependency theory, Ball-Rokeach and her colleagues were able to demonstrate that high media dependency increased the probability of both cognitive and long-term behavioral effects. The research was conducted in such a way as to preserve the "natural media exposure situation" and concerned political values, attitudes, and behaviors.

Thus, the media system dependency hypotheses about exposure to specific content and the effects of exposure on individuals' beliefs, feelings, and behavior, as we have outlined them in Figure 11.2, have received some research support. Unfortunately, not all mass media effects are effects of particular media contents, nor are they effects upon individuals. In order to account for more complicated effects, such as the effects of cumulative exposure to many types of media content or effects upon organizations, systems, or whole societies, we have to go beyond the psychological paradigm to other paradigms of social thought.

Contributions of the Symbolic Interactionist Paradigm

The construction of meaning, a primary concern of the symbolic inter-actionist, is also a central concern in media system dependency theory. Of particular interest is how the world created by the media affects the ways in which individuals and groups interpret their interpersonal and social worlds. We who live in modern complex societies are dependent upon the information resources of the media system to tell us about a great variety of events, places, and people that we never encounter directly.

Our interpersonal networks of friends, family, and co-workers are also dependent on media information resources. People who serve as our "opinion leaders," for example, often have no more direct experience with important events than we do. Our opinion leaders develop strong dependency relations with the media so that they can understand what's going on in the world, the nation, or even those aspects of community life that are beyond their direct experience. There are so many things that we and our interpersonal associates have to understand in order to know how to act in this complex and ambiguous world. Our knowledge problems vary from the most specific matters, such as the weather, traffic conditions, matters of health and safety, or the latest fashion, sports, and the arts, to the most general of concerns such as the changing worlds of politics, power, and economics, ecological relations between human and nonhuman societies and their physical and chemical environments, or value and lifestyle changes underlying generational and religious conflicts.

Ambiguity, Threat, and Social Change. The symbolic interactionist's view that the social world is held together by fragile subjective understandings of reality is reflected in the emphasis given to ambiguity, threat and social change in media dependency theory. We assume that individual and group media dependency relations become more intense when the social environment is ambiguous, threatening and/or rapidly changing.[10]

Ambiguity is "the inability either to define a situation or to choose between competing definitions of a situation."[11] Under such conditions, knowledge is problematic. This is so because ambiguity is primarily an information problem; people lack enough information to create stable meanings of events. In those numerous instances where neither we nor our opinion leaders can directly experience or observe the events that we seek to understand, the mass media become the primary information system that has the resources to create meanings. There are times when ambiguity is accompanied by clear threat. Such times include economic crises, natural disasters, political upheavals, and open conflict between groups in our community. When such events occur, individuals and their opinion leaders alike typically look to the media system to provide the information required to figure out what is going on, why it's happening, and what people can do to reduce threats to personal and collective welfare.

Equally, if not more, important are the less obvious ways in which individuals and groups depend on media information resources to attain everyday understandings. In a society, such as ours, where change is the order of the day, where social life is always in some degree of flux, there is a chronic ambiguity that leads people to develop ongoing dependency relations with the media. This is a very different condition from that of many societies of the past, where people could count on things staying the same from day to day, even from generation to generation! The changing nature of our social and physical worlds creates a constant and tiring condition of ambiguity. Because the media system is not only accessible to most people, but is also the information system that is best situated to gather/create, process, and disseminate relevant information, we naturally develop dependency relations with it to help us, individually and collectively, to resolve the chronic ambiguities of daily life.

Knowledge and Meaning Effects. These ongoing dependency relations with the media open the door to media effects upon our beliefs and behaviors. If, out of habit or necessity, we incorporate the media system as a major vehicle for understanding, then the media system takes on a certain power to influence how we think, feel, and act. In this case, that power is akin to the information-based powers of parents vis-à-vis young children or teachers vis-à-vis their students. Ultimately the question we are addressing is the creation and control of *knowledge*. The cultivation theory (Chapter 9) that the media create culture, and the indirect influence idea (Chapter 8) that the media socialize audiences, rest on this most basic idea that the media system is actively involved in creating shared knowledge. Indirect influence theorists who emphasize the symbolic interactionism paradigm locate the origins of such powers in linguistic and cognitive processes activated by a media "text" or message. Cultivation theorists and, more generally, "critical theorists," locate the origins of this power in elite control of the "means of mental production," where media create knowledge that serves the elite's interests.

From the view of media system dependency theory, the origins of knowledge construction powers include but go beyond these views. The media system dependency theorist looks to the consequences of dependency relations generated by the media system's control over scarce and prized information resources. These include the micro dependency relations of individual and small interpersonal networks and how they are shaped by the dependency relations that the media have with larger parts of the social fabric (i.e., structural dependency relations).

Direct and Indirect Knowledge Effects. A central "ecological" assumption in media dependency theory is that micro dependency relations of individuals and groups cannot be understood without an understanding of structural (macro) dependency relations. Individuals and groups do not just decide to depend upon the media for their knowledge of themselves and their worlds. An important part of the answer to the question of why individuals and groups develop their dependency relations with the media concerns the roles and functions of the media system in the larger society. This idea can be illustrated if we consider the political system and focus upon citizens' voting decisions.

Whereas many people might like to make their decisions to vote for candidates for national, state, or local office on the basis of direct interpersonal contact, most citizens do not have the opportunity to talk directly with candidates. The election process is structured in such a way that candidates must, whether they like it or not, depend upon the media as the primary communication vehicle with citizens. The media system is more than just a neutral channel of communication. It uses its information resources to gather, process, and disseminate campaign information. The content of that information or political knowledge is not under the complete control of the candidates, much less the citizen.

Both direct and indirect effects of the media can be seen in this illustration, including direct effects upon the "boundaries of knowledge"—the range of things that citizens can know—and indirect effects upon the choices that people make in voting for particular candidates. The two-step flow process of opinion leadership may occur with respect to particular voting decisions. At the same time, however, opinion leaders generally have no more control over the boundaries of knowledge constructed about the candidates than do others in their networks. In fact, we assume that it is meaningful to speak of *interpersonal networks* as having dependency relations with the media system. That is interpersonal networks—such as friends, co-workers, and family members—are stable groups that can be meaningfully characterized in terms of their media dependency relations.

There are at last three forms of media influence that can occur in such groups: (1) indirect influence, such as political socialization, that occurs as a result of members' cumulative media exposure over long periods of time, (2) indirect influence through the two-step flow process whereby opinion leaders are influenced by the mass media and then pass along their interpretations of media messages to other group members, and (3) direct influence of the mass media upon the membership of the group. The last form of influence is most likely to occur when neither opinion leaders, nor the general membership of a group have political knowledge based on either direct experience or a stable interpretation of the issues.

There are many other spheres of life—economic, health, recreational, legal, educational, military, familial, and religious—in which the same kind of analysis could be made about direct and indirect effects of the mass media.

No theory bounded by the limits of the psychological paradigm or the symbolic interactionist paradigms, can, however, account for the wide range of media effects upon the workings of organizations, social systems, culture, and society. In order to account for these kinds of macro effects, we have to consider aspects of media dependency theory that are rooted in the conflict, structural functional, and evolutionary paradigms of social thought.

Contributions of the Conflict and Structural Functional Paradigms

The goals–resource dependency relation so pivotal to the explanatory frame of media system dependency theory is, in a sense, a double-edged sword. On the one side, it is a conflict relation and, on the other, it is a relation of functional interdependence. The dependency relation, then, draws upon both conflict theory and structural functional analysis. Similarly, both the change emphasis of conflict theory and the stability emphasis of structural functional analysis are incorporated into media dependency theory. This integration of the two paradigms does not, however, represent a wholesale adoption of the assumptions of both paradigms. Probably the simplest way to demonstrate the contributions of both is to specify the assumptions of media dependency whose origins can be traced to the conflict paradigms and those traced to the structural functional paradigms.

In accord with structural functional analysis, it is assumed that society has an "organic" structure that can best be understood in terms of the interdependence of its parts. A media system is a necessary component of modern complex societies. Mass communication is essential to the social organization of societies that have become so complex that the conduct of essential activities, such as production and integration, cannot be organized solely on the basis of interpersonal communication. The media dependency relation is, by definition, a relation of interdependence; the media and other social systems are the parts and they need each other in order to survive and prosper. Specifically, they need access to each other's resources in order to achieve their respective goals.

Interdependent relations between the parts produce both *cooperation* and *conflict*. The emphasis in structural functional analysis is upon the necessity for cooperation between the parts, based upon their mutual recognition that the survival and welfare of one part is dependent upon the survival and welfare of other parts. This kind of "organic solidarity" between the parts (Chapter 6) is said to create a mutuality of interests that ensures the stability of the larger society; no part wants to destroy the social order because to do so would mean its own destruction. In contrast, conflict theory emphasizes consequences of interdependence that produce strain and tension between the parts.

Both points of view are represented in the media dependencey framework. We have described, for example, a cooperation between the media and the political systems that is rooted in their mutual dependence. Equally true, however, is the fact that the media system controls scarce and prized resources that others would prefer to capture so as to reduce or remove their media dependency. While interdependence can be accepted, and thus produce cooperation, it also produces an underlying conflict. Conflict, or a "struggle over scarce resources," may remain dormant for long periods, emerging only at opportune times. In other words, it is assumed that media, political, and other systems will seek to gain control over each other's resources when the conditions would enable them to do so without endangering their own welfare. That such attempts will be made is an expectation made on the basis of another assumption taken from conflict theory: All groups (including interpersonal networks, organizations, and systems) are motivated not only to maintain, but also to enhance themselves. They are, in other words, *interest groups.*

Those who conceived of the media system as a Fourth Estate recognized this incipient conflict between interest groups when they anticipated that the other "estates"—the legislative, executive, and judiciary—would not only try to capture each other's powers by gaining control of each other's resources, but would also seek to capture the resources of the media system. The revolutionary idea of an independent media system whose control over its resources was ensured constitutionally was not a denial of the interdependence between the media and other social systems; it was based upon the assumption that whenever the media control resources that the political system has to have access to in order to survive, and vice versa, there will be conflict.

Examination of two related assumptions reveals some of the areas of disagreement between media system dependency theory and purely functionalist or purely conflict paradigms. *Asymmetric* media dependency relations are more likely to produce conflict, and *symmetric* media dependency relations are more likely to produce cooperation. Asymmetry and symmetry here refer to the relative power of the media in its relations with other social systems, asymmetry signifying a power imbalance and symmetry signifying a balance of power. In our previous description of media–political relations we described a rather symmetric dependency relation. Both systems depend upon each other's resources to about the same degree, such that neither system is much more powerful than the other. In this situation, their relative equality of resources and dependencies serves to increase the likelihood that they will cooperate. However, when one system acquires more scarce resources that the other needs, then an asymmetry develops: one is more dependent (less powerful) and one is less dependent (more powerful). In this situation, conflict is more likely than cooperation, and that conflict should emerge from both sides of the relationship, one seeking to increase its dominance even further and the other seeking to restore its position.

Many conflict theorists would fundamentally disagree with this mode of analysis. They would challenge the very idea of an independent media system in control of scarce and prized resources. They regard the media, not as a social system in its own right, but as a tool employed by ruling elites to further their interests. From this point of view, it would make no sense even to discuss relationships with the media because the media are only resources controlled by "capitalists," the "military industrial complex," or some other economic elite.

Classical structural functional analysts, on the other hand, would reject the media dependency way of thinking for entirely different reasons. They would reject the assumption that there is always a conflict side to media relations with other social systems. Because functionalists do not share the assumption that conflict is a normal and inevitable consequence of interdependence, they tend either to ignore examinations of conflict or to regard conflict as an aberration that threatens the stability of the social order. In media dependency theory, however, conflict is regarded not only as a normal state of affairs, but also as a major force in creating social change, particularly change in the nature of media system dependency relations.

Thus media dependency theory draws upon some but not all of the major concerns and assumptions of the conflict and structural functionalist paradigms. In summary, the media are best understood as a system in control of scarce and prized information resources that engender interdependent relations with other systems, relations that produce cooperation motivated by mutual interest, conflict motivated by self-interest, and change toward greater symmetry or asymmetry of dependency.

ACCOUNTING FOR CHANGE IN MEDIA DEPENDENCY RELATIONS

We assume that there are two basic sources of change in the nature of media dependency relations, one being *conflict* and the other being *adaptation*. As we suggested above, the media, like other systems, seek opportunities to maximize their resource control and minimize their dependency, that is to create asymmetric relations in which they are more powerful. Of course, other systems try to do the same thing by decreasing their dependency upon media resources and increasing the media system's dependency on *their* resources. This struggle is akin to that of children seeking to reduce their dependency upon the resources controlled by their parents by developing their own financial resources, or to the struggle of people trying to gain autonomy in their jobs by gaining a position in the organization where they control more of the resources that others depend upon. As children and employees know, there are costs to waging such struggles; for example, they can get thrown out of the house or lose their job. Thus the *desire* to lessen dependency (increase power) is one thing and the *capacity* to do it and still prosper is another. This fact serves to constrain many media system attempts to increase its resource base.

Contributions of the Evolutionary Paradigm

The second source of change, adaptation, is the primary concern of the (social) evolutionary paradigm. Evolutionary theorists postulate that social systems never stay the same but are always evolving into more complex forms. Like the evolutionary theorist, we assume that interdependent relations between the media and other parts of the social organism must undergo change in order for societies to survive in the face of changing environments. Such adaptive changes are usually slow and are often unplanned, and so they are difficult to perceive at the time they are occurring.

We can see an example of this kind of change in the political–media system relation. An important environmental change has been a decline in the power of political parties and the rise of the primary election as a vehicle for selecting candidates for national, state, and local office. At the same time that these changes were going on, the media system was evolving. Not only was it becoming more complex by the addition of new forms of mass communication, such as cable and satellite delivery of television, but other innovations afforded new ways to make information gathering, processing, and dissemination even more rapid and realistic. Such developments are discussed in detail in the next chapter.

These changes in the political environment and in the media system have progressively altered the media dependency relation. At the very least, the relation has become more intense. As is evidenced by the decline in candidate "whistle stops" or "coffee klatches," and dramatic increases in the proportion of campaign budgets devoted to media advertising, it is virtually impossible to hold an election today without the mass media. The political system has become, at least in this way, more dependent on the resources of the media system than it was when political parties were powerful and mass communication was only incidental. No matter how angry that state of affairs may make candidates or how frustrated it may make citizens, they cannot do too much to alter it. It is a structural fact that shapes the election process.

The Ripple Effect of Change

These changes in the macro political–media system relation have had a ripple effect upon smaller political units, such as political organizations. Research has demonstrated that candidates and their campaign organizations have little control over definitions of what the election is all about.[12] They can and do put out position papers, but they must depend upon the media to get these issues and statements on the public agenda. Some campaign organizations are better than others in achieving such goals, but the structural fact of their substantial dependency upon the media information resources remains.

On the other hand, the media system is not so powerful as to be able to act arbitrarily vis-à-vis the political system and its organizations. The media's dependency upon resources controlled by the political system is also a structural fact. This fact has a similar ripple effect upon media organizations, affecting what they do and, equally important, do not do. Such organizations are, for example, unlikely to attack the legitimacy of the election or more general political processes, because to do so would bring down the full weight of the political system to limit the media system's control over information resources. Recent history is replete with attempts on the part of angry politicians to place limits on the press or to use regulatory agencies to undermine the economic welfare of offending media corporations. The heightened media dependency on the political system thus carries with it real conflict potentials that media organizations and even individual mass communicators may seek to avoid by not overstepping certain boundaries.

As Figure 11.3 illustrates how changes in media dependency relations produce what we have referred to as *ripple* effects, beginning at the top of the funnel with the media system's position in society, and spiraling down through its dependency relations with other social systems, with organizations, with interpersonal networks, and finally with individuals. Changes that occur at higher levels will affect dependency relations at all lower levels. Thus changes in the societal roles of the media system, such as its increasing importance to the stability and integration of American society since the days of the penny press, have ramifications upon all other levels of social action. This change in role had the effect of increasing the media dependencies of social systems, organizations, interpersonal networks, and individuals.

Change in systems, however, is not only from top to bottom or from big to small. Although changes that occur from top to bottom (macro to micro) probably ripple down more quickly, changes can also occur in micro dependency relations that may, over time, ripple up (micro to macro). For example, if, as some thoughtful observers of the American scene fear, individuals come to expect the media to produce information designed to serve social understanding in a way that also entertains or serves play goals, they may turn away from any "serious" information that is not also "fun." The ramifications of individuals changing their media dependency relations from a time when social understanding was a sufficient goal itself to a time when such a goal must be combined with play dimensions would be felt at the level of organizations and, ultimately, the society as well. Systems and organizations dependent on the media to communicate with their clienteles would, for example, have to develop new media or public relations talents and departments to create informative—but entertaining—messages. In the process, they

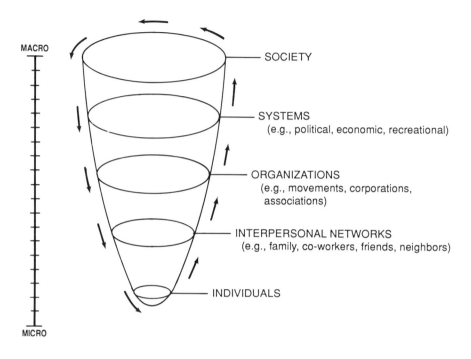

Figure 11.3. Ripple Effects of Change in Media System Dependency Relations

would become more dependent on the media system. When one surveys the political, religious, and other spheres of our contemporary life, one wonders if this effect has not, in fact, already occurred.

MEDIA AND SOCIETY

In Chapter 1 we charted the ages of communication and saw how each new age brought with it the capacity of human beings to enrich their processes of thought and to organize themselves into more and more complex societies. Just as the advent of language opened new doors for people to escape the limits of time-bound and place-bound communication and to organize themselves accordingly, the advent of mass communication and its development into complex systems of communication allows human beings today to organize themselves on a more global scale.

Through its complex web of dependency relations with individuals, interpersonal networks, organizations, and social systems, the media system has evolved from its status in the 1830s as an experimental curiosity to its contemporary status as an information system essential to the continuation of contemporary society as it is currently organized. The specific societal roles that the media play vary from society to society, because the media system has a different ecology of dependency relations in different societies. In American society the historical growth in the media system's importance to societal functioning can be charted in terms of increases in the number and intensity of media dependency relations. Such increases inform us about the expanding societal roles of the media in the central institutional domains of social life. The primary dependency relations in the 1830s, for example, were with the economic and political systems, with the media's capacities for advertising and news construction being its major information resources. At first, these resources were neither scarce nor extremely prized. Word-of-mouth was still regarded as the most viable channel through which to spread economic and political information.

The more complex American society became, the more such things changed. Most important were the limits of the interpersonal communication system that had once made word-of-mouth viable. The organizational requirements of an increasingly complex society were less and less capable of being met with interpersonal communication alone. Over time, the system of mass communication filled the breach, becoming more and more necessary to the attainment of societal consensus, coordination of national political and economic activities, mobilization of the citizenry in times of threat or crisis, and other societal goals. In other words, the information resources of the media system became increasingly important and prized.

As time passed, the insinuation of media resources into the goal-attainment efforts of other institutions emerged and it continues to intensify. In the recreational or leisure institution, for example, the information resources of the media system have become essential to activities that almost define American sport, such as the World Series or the Super Bowl. The now intense media dependency of the recreational system can be most easily seen in the modification of the values and norms of sport culture[13] and the remaking of the rules of tennis, basketball, and every sport that seeks to prosper via access to media resources. In every other sphere, whether it be the military, educational, family, religious, or science and health systems, we can see increases in dependency on the media. Similarly, as the media system itself has evolved into more complex form, it must establish new relationships that become more or less essential to its welfare and survival.

In order to appreciate what an important system the media have become, it is instructive to imagine what would happen to the organization of personal and social life if for some inexplicable reason all of the forms of mass communication that we have today suddenly vanished. How would people be able to understand the world they live in, act in, and play in if all of the media were gone? How would groups and organizations accomplish their understanding, acting, and recreational goals? How would order and stability be maintained, social change occur, community or national conflicts be waged or resolved, adaptations to changing environments be made? And how would we sustain the shared meanings that make our complex society possible? How, in short, would our society, as we know it, survive?

NOTES

1. For a review of media system dependency theory, see: S. J. Ball-Rokeach, "The Information Perspective," paper presented at the Annual Meeting of the American Sociological Association, Montreal, 1974; S. J. Ball-Rokeach and M. L. DeFleur, "A Dependency Model of Mass Media Effects," *Communication Research* 3 (1976); 3–21; S. J. Ball-Rokeach, M. Rokeach, and J. W. Grube, *The Great American Values Test: Influencing Behavior and Belief Through Television* (New York: Free Press, 1984); S. J. Ball-Rokeach, "The Origins of Individual Media System Dependency: Sociological Framework," *Communication Research* 12 (1985); 485–510; S. J. Ball-Rokeach and M. G. Cantor, eds., *Media, Audience and Social Structure* (Beverly Hills, Cal.: Sage, 1986).
2. Ball-Rokeach, Rokeach, and Grube, *The Great American Values Test.*
3. K. Guthrie, A. Grant, and S. J. Ball-Rokeach, "Media Dependency, Television Shopping and Television Shoppers: Theoretical Significance and Empirical Test," ICA paper, 1988.
4. This is a dimension of the "active audience" that deserves more attention.
5. Ball-Rokeach, Rokeach, and Grube, *The Great American Values Test.*
6. See Ball-Rokeach, "Origins of Individual Media System Dependency," for a fuller discussion.
7. D. S. Solomon, "Health campaigns on television." In D. Pearl, L. Bouthilet, J. Lazar (Eds.), *Television and Behavior: Ten Years of Scientific Progress and Implications for the Eighties*, Vol. 2, pp. 308–21 (Rockville, MD: NIMH (1982).
8. P. Tannenbaum, ed., *The Entertainment Functions of Television* (Hillsdale, N.J.: Erlbaum, 1980).
9. For a discussion of the characteristics of a "natural media exposure situation," see Ball-Rokeach, Rokeach, and Grube, *The Great American Values Test*, Chapter 4.
10. See Ball-Rokeach, "Origins of Individual Media System Dependency."

11. S. J. Ball-Rokeach, "From Pervasive Ambiguity to a Definition of the Situation," *Sociometry* 36 (1973): 378–89.

12. P. Clarke and S. Evans, *Covering Campaigns: Journalism in Congressional Elections* (Stanford, Cal.: Stanford University Press, 1983).

13. J. L. Sewart, "The Commodification of Sport," in Ball-Rokeach and Cantor, *Media, Audience, and Social Structure*, 1986, pp. 174–88.

CHAPTER 12

Emerging Media Systems

In the decades following the development of television we witnessed the emergence of an impressive number of communications technologies that have excited the imagination of those seeking to use them to create new media systems. We know that only some of the visions of new media systems will actually evolve to become our mass media of the not-too-distant future.

We begin this chapter with a discussion of the information technologies that are most likely to be incorporated in new media systems. Some of these, such as personal and mainframe computers, are already familiar features of our environment but have not yet been successfully transformed into national media systems. Others, such as basic and satellite-delivered cablevision, are already developed and have significance for the future because they may be adapted to serve new uses in new media systems. Still others, such as two-way television and videotex, represent a more revolutionary genre of interactive communication technologies that may or may not be successfully transformed into media used not only by wealthy or powerful organizations, but also by ordinary people in the course of everyday life.[1]

Just as our contemporary mass media systems are the products of social forces that determined which technologies survived and how they were developed into media systems, so too will our future mass media be the products of political, legal, and other social forces. Not knowing all of the social forces that may be unleashed puts us in an uncertain situation. We think we know what technologies will be employed, but we don't know which handful of the millions of possible combinations and permutations will actually emerge as mass media.

We therefore conclude this chapter where we began this book: by examining paradigms of social thought and how they may inform us in our effort to predict the media systems of our tomorrow.

THE INFLUENCE OF COMPUTERS

The ever-increasing pace of development of technologies into new communication systems is a hallmark of our time. Whereas it took three centuries after the invention of the printing press for the newspaper to emerge as a significant medium of communication, it was only thirty-three years (from 1888 to 1921) between Hertz's discovery of radio waves to the beginning of regular broadcasting in the United States. Similarly, although the first electronic computer was built in 1946 (based on vacuum tube technology), the microchip, which is the essential component in today's small but powerful computers, was not available until 1971 (when it was invented by Marcian Hoff, Jr.). It is this now familiar "desktop" or "personal" computer that may be a key component in at least some communication systems of the future. The degree to which the pace of development has increased can be emphasized again by our noting that mass marketing of personal computers did not begin until 1975!

In the early days, only corporations, governments, or other agencies with a lot of money and space could use huge mainframe computers based on vacuum tube technology. At the time, these machines seemed wondrous; they could store and process what was then a truly amazing amount of information with equally amazing speed. They also seemed strange. For example, scientists accustomed to spending weeks, even months, deriving an equation or conducting statistical analyses were suddenly faced with having to change their way and pace of work. To do in minutes what used to take weeks, and to remain competitive with other scientists, they had to learn how to use an information machine that looked as if it came out of a science fiction movie.

Personal Computers

The period of the bulky vacuum tube mainframe was a short one. Rapid advances in miniaturization and mass production of component parts produced incredible reductions in the amount of space and money needed for computer ownership. Also rapid advances in software made computers more "user friendly." By the mid-1980s approximately 15 percent of American households had a microcomputer.

Along with a speedy diffusion of the microcomputer—from 0 to 15 percent of American households in approximately a decade—we have seen a rapid increase in its memory or storage capacity. Storage capacity of individual numbers, letters, or other characters went from 1,000 bytes, or individual characters of information (1K in computer jargon), in the initial versions to several million characters (several megabytes of RAM) in the late 1980s. Thus the homeowner or small business operator now can have a desktop machine whose capacities and speed exceed those of the mainframes that were thought of as wonders of high technology only a couple of decades ago.

This trend will undoubtedly continue. Soon personal computers will have memories that will handle far more than any possible amount of information that could be generated by a homeowner. Still, such increases remain important, particularly if the devices are to be used in sophisticated interactive systems of information exchange. Generally speaking, the greater the internal memory of a computer, the greater the number of communication and information tasks it can perform. And, the greater the number of tasks that can be handled simultaneously, the greater the versatility. Therefore the utility of the device increases as a function of its speed and memory capacity, up to a point.

There is evidence that once a computer is acquired, even one with substantial memory, pressures soon develop for the purchase of one or more additional machines. In many cases others living in the household want to do work they have brought home from the office, or want to perform household accounting, correspondence, shopping, or banking tasks. Children want the computers for homework or for recreation. A single microcomputer, regardless of its speed or capacity, cannot handle all of these demands. Multiple computer families are thus becoming increasingly common.

Along with the unfolding reality of a mass market for personal computers has come a lower cost per unit of computer memory. While high-capacity PCs are not currently cheap, the pattern of steady cost reduction suggests that they will be more affordable in the not-too-distant future. One important factor is the copycat computer or "clone." After a new system is developed by IBM or one of the other major American developers, dozens of cheap copies appear, largely from Third World countries. They can produce them cheaply not only because of much lower labor costs, but also because they did not have to make the initial investment in research and development. The end result is either good or bad, depending on one's perspective. The major manufacturers suffer, but rather powerful clone computers are available to families or businesses that otherwise could not afford them.

All these developments strongly suggest that the microcomputers' rapid rate of diffusion will continue, and with it the increasing prospect that computers will become the cornerstone of future modes of mass communication. Thus there is general agreement that at least some of the successful mass communication technologies of the future will be based upon personal microcomputers owned and operated by ordinary people who are not computer specialists. The current 15 percent of American households with a personal computer is still a minority compared with those owning television and radio receivers. However, the curve is climbing, and projections seem realistic that a *majority* of American households will have a computer within a decade or so.

Just as the average person in the nineteenth century had to develop the ability to read in order to use the newspaper, people today must become "computer literate" before computer-based mass media can emerge and succeed. And just as the development of the public education system was crucial to people learning to read, so is today's public education system essential to the development of mass computer literacy. The level of skill required to use computer-based media, like the level of reading and writing ability required to use newspapers, is really quite minimal. People do not have to become computer programmers any more than readers of newspapers have to become reporters or editors.

Despite such low skill requirements, it is often frightening for people, especially adults, to have to learn new ways of doing things. Because many children are gaining familiarity with the use of micro-computers in the course of their elementary and secondary school education, an age-role reversal between adults and their children develops. The traditional case of parents being more skilled than their children in the crucial information technologies of work, play, and survival is often turned upside-down. Children not only acquire the psychological comfort that comes with knowing how to use computers before their parents do, but so do younger children before their older sisters and brothers. The frustration of these "out-of-sync" relations is evident on the faces of many college students who, when home for vacation, suffer the indignity of being treated like dinosaurs by their computer-literate younger sisters and brothers. Such disjunctions of family and work life are common, but temporary, features of communication revolutions.

Computers in the Service Economy

While ownership of personal computers has by no means reached its highest point on the diffusion curve, computer transactions have in one way or another become a part of everyday life for virtually all members of modern society. Modern societies are commonly called "information societies," a label that summarizes a massive transformation of the economy, with the industrial society, characterized by mass production of tangible goods such as cars or steel, giving way to a society whose economy is based upon the production and distribution of intangible information services. Information services include legal, governmental, travel, recreational, medical, managerial, financial, and, of course, scientific and educational services. Computer-based communication and information systems, both microcomputers and mainframes, have been important in the development of this information service economy.

A large proportion of our population comes into daily contact with mainframe computers whether they realize it or not. These contacts with "mass" communication systems are not in the traditional sense of one-way transmission of news, entertainment, and so on, but involve huge numbers of people who transmit and receive various kinds of information related to business and services. Throughout the society, commercial establishments, industries, government agencies, education institutions, and other organizations either operate their own mainframe computer systems or participate in time-share systems.

Time-share is an arrangement to use a mainframe computer along with many other customers. In many respects it is a name that is becoming outmoded. As computer memory and operating systems of large computers become ever more sophisticated, a given company can be assigned a particular part of the memory for its files (data base). It can also perform its operations without having to do them in a particular time slot. With the use of modems, which are devices that make it possible to utilize telephone lines or fiber optic cable to send and receive messages, users now have only to install or rent a transmission-reception terminal that links them to their space in the central computer.

For "on-line" transmission and reception, the user sends messages to the mainframe computer by typing them on the keyboard of a terminal. At the same time that the information is received by a mainframe located some miles away, even in another city or country, the information is also displayed on the user's video monitor. Travelers, for example, have become accustomed to dealing with airline reservation agents connected to a mainframe computer that is usually located in another city. Ticket agents type in their information on a terminal connected by phone lines, a microwave system, or even satellite transmission, to the computer which then sorts through all the schedule information it has stored to see if there is space remaining on the desired flight. If the agent has transmitted the request properly, a speedy reply is sent from the computer and visually displayed on the agent's monitor. When the traveler reaches the desired destination, contacts with computers will almost surely continue. A credit card phone call to home or office may be made; a rental car may have been reserved and the customer's credit checked through a computer, and even a subway to the hotel may be computer-operated. The hotel clerk will similarly verify the reservation and conduct a credit card check, and when the traveler is comfortable in the hotel room, he or she may order a movie or arrange for a wake-up call by talking to a computer.

It is not only travelers who have frequent contact with service personnel who process information through their organization's computer or a shared system. An ever-increasing number of routine aspects of everyday life involve such contacts—activities as varied as going to the supermarket, making a department store credit card purchase, getting a traffic ticket, voting, obtaining a license for a pet, receiving a paycheck, banking, or registering for a college course.

Rapid diffusion of this kind of indirect relationship to a variety of small, medium, and large computers represents a major change in the communication processes by which the business of daily life is conducted. A little more than a decade ago people depended primarily on other people to handle transactions transmitted via paper records, within organizations or through the mails. Now individuals, organizations, and whole societies must frequently depend on other people in new information occupations who depend on their networks of terminals and computers. This growing dependence of economic and social life on computer-based information services becomes painfully clear when activities come to a halt because a computer is malfunctioning.

These dramatic developments in the growth of computerized networks to send, receive, and store information do not represent *mass* communication in the traditional sense. In many ways they are simply electronic replacements for other forms of information transmission, storage, and recovery, those based on paper transactions, forms, files, internal shuffling of written records, or the use of the mails. Nevertheless, the new networks *are* a part of our society's communication systems and they deserve the closest possible attention on the part of scholars and researchers. This transformation in social communication systems has influences on both individuals and the society as a whole, even though they are not what media scholars usually think of when pondering the "effects" of communication.

One clear influence of these significant changes in information processing in our society—its higher speed, greater accuracy, and lower costs—has been a major change in the composition of the labor force. While this may not seem to be an immediate "effect" of communication, it is a clear outcome of the changes taking place. One such effect is *structural unemployment,* or unemployment caused by permanent loss of industries and occupations. In this case, workers are not simply laid off until better economic times return; rather, their jobs or occupations vanish altogether, never to return.

Because far fewer clerks, for example, are needed to prepare and process paper records, numerous lower-level white collar jobs have simply disappeared. There are many other examples that are less obvious or visible. The depletion of the white collar clerical labor force in America has had very real consequences in such seemingly unrelated industries as retailing (which must now accommodate to new income distributions), manufacturing (which may have to cut back on production of consumer goods formerly purchased by those displaced), entertainment (which now may be a luxury to those of reduced means) and so on. Such economic displacements indirectly influence many parts of the social system, including the fashion industry, various imports of cheaper clothing and foreign-made consumer goods, and even educational institutions that are responsive to changing income distributions in the society.

The structural unemployment trends created, at least in part, by the growth of computer networks are part of the transition to an information service economy. Highly paid blue collar workers felt the impact first as they lost their jobs in the old steel mills and auto industries. They are now finding fewer and fewer employment opportunities because their jobs have been exported, so to speak, either to lower-wage workers in the industrializing nations of the Third World or to nations that are more advanced in their efficient use of computer-based technologies. The loss of spendable income has not only created a class of unemployables left behind in the dust of change, but has also created difficulties for all businesses that used to cater to their needs and tastes.

On the other side of the coin, new professional specialties have developed around the computerized management and processing of business, industrial, and commercial transactions and data bases. People in those specialties find their prospects ever brighter and their incomes increasing. That growth, in turn has indirect influences on businesses, including media organizations that supply goods and services to more upscale clients. Thus while one type of business may be losing customers, others are gaining.

While all these influences may be difficult to trace out, they are very real in their consequences. At the individual level, a person certainly feels the influence—anger, frustration, and loss of self-esteem—when he or she is fired because a computer now performs the job. On the other side, for an individual who has obtained advanced degrees in computer information studies and gets a highly paid job because of increasing computerization, there is a very visible "effect."

Such influences are less visible at the societal level. To understand them, the communication scholar needs to see the society as a social system in transition. To do this, a structural functional perspective is helpful. That is, the structure of society (labor force, stratification system, economic institution, etc.) is undergoing change as new information/communication systems replace older forms. The functions or patterned activities of the new systems create at least some disequilibrium or societal instability during the time of transition (unemployment, expansion and contraction of various businesses and service agencies, increasing impersonality in human relationships, and changes in various social indicators). Yet, at some point equilibrium is restored as the society adapts to the changes and as individuals find their niches in the new system.

In other words, analyses of these kinds of indirect effects can be approached within a structural functional framework to discover the nature of the emerging parts of the changing system, where dysfunctions are occurring, how they are being handled, and what contribution is made to the society as a whole by the new communication media.

In such an analysis, even deviant behavior needs to be assessed. Changes in our communication system for basic information processing have not uniformly brought conformity and conventional behavior. Durkheim and other classic scholars would predict that a certain amount of deviance is inevitable. In fact, one does not have to look far to discover it. Clever "hackers" with a sophisticated understanding of computers have been able to break into electronic files for a variety of purposes. This activity has created calls for a number of new laws, giving lawyers even more to squabble over! Aside from such examples, however, far too little is understood about how our new computer networks are changing us. Our body of communication scholars remains preoccupied with more traditional questions concerning the established media.

Computers and the Mass Media

Will the rising use of personal computers by individuals at home, and the extensive use of computer-based information systems in society, be enough to create new mass media? This does not seem likely. In order to have a new system of *mass* communication, the average person would have to have both the hardware and the skills to be able to use computers in daily life as we now use other media. Even if computer literacy were to become universal, and even if every household had a personal computer equipped with a modem so that it could be hooked up to vast networks, it is difficult to see how a new system of mass communication could develop from this base alone.

The essence of mass communication as we now know it is that professional communicators operate the media for profit by disseminating content to large and heterogeneous audiences on a more or less continuous basis. A computer network in which people send messages to each other is a different kind of process altogether. It is difficult to visualize how such a system could be used by the majority of our citizens, how it would be supported financially, or even what services it would provide for large and heterogeneous audiences. In many ways having people type out messages to each other via their home computers would have few advantages over the telephone network that we already have. In business settings, however, where records of memos, messages, and transactions are important, it would have advantages. In fact, intraorganizational systems of this kind (e.g., computer-based electronic mail) are already in use. But for the casual user who initiates messages to greet relatives, exchange gossip, ask for a date, or inquire about the price of rhubarb, a vast network would seem to have few advantages over the existing telephone.

A more likely prospect is that new mass media will develop by *coupling* computers to modern variants of cable television. In fact, experimental media using this technology have already come into use.

BASIC CABLE TELEVISION

We saw in Chapter 4 that community antenna television (CATV) had developed by 1950 as a way to improve reception in rural communities that, for reasons of topography (such as mountain ranges) or geographic remoteness, had limited over-the-air television reception capabilities. Development of cable television was a relatively inexpensive and simple technical matter. Receiving antennae were installed atop mountainous areas to increase the range of reception, and transmissions were sent via cable from the antenna to subscriber homes. Channel capacity and picture fidelity were improved because cable transmissions were relatively unaffected by the air-space limitations and interference problems of conventional over-the-air television. The initial cost of connecting households with the CATV antenna was made relatively modest by piggybacking coaxial cable lines on existing telephone pole routes and by using the household TV set as the receiver.

Despite the advantages of cable television, subscription rates did not exactly soar. In 1975, a quarter of a century after its invention, only 12 percent of American households subscribed to one of the 3,550 cable television systems. As the large number of companies operating cable systems suggests, many analysts expected cable TV to spread much more rapidly than it did. We noted in Chapter 4 that many people were disappointed with the content of cable.

The conflict paradigm helps us to understand an even more basic reason for its slower than expected rate of diffusion. Interest groups who were threatened by the emergence of cable were able to throw political, legal, and regulatory impediments in the way of its development. Cable TV was, for example, a potential threat to the economic welfare of the three major commercial networks. A number of people were trying to make cable TV a vehicle for local community programming by offering free community access to cable production facilities and air time. The commercial networks, fearing increased pressures to provide their own community-based programming, as well as increased competition for audiences, sought to limit the development of cable television. These and other social factors that effectively slowed the diffusion of cable were overridden in more recent years by two subsequent developments: the social invention of extra-fee or pay cable in 1972, and the joining of communication satellite technology with cable technology in 1975. These two events lie at the heart of certain developments that may influence our future media, and they merit brief discussion.

Satellite-Delivered Cable TV

In the belief that cable TV could become very popular if more channels carrying interesting and unique content were available to subscribers, Time, Inc. initiated the Home Box Office (HBO) pay cable channel. The corporation's analysts put their faith in the popularity of feature films for HBO's content. The first few years of HBO were disappointing, however. It proved difficult to obtain the most attractive films, and problems with broadcast quality created poor reception in the home. As a result, subscription rates failed to rise as much as hoped. What turned the situation around was the high-risk decision to use communication satellites to transmit HBO programming to subscribing cable TV systems.

The era of commercial communication satellites in the United States began in 1974 with the launching of WESTAR I. In the span of a decade, satellites became fundamental to virtually every mass communications industry, including newspapers, telephone, and the electronic media. It costs millions of dollars (currently $75 million) to launch a communication satellite. That initial investment quickly pays off, however, because each satellite has about two dozen transponders aboard that can be leased to users (like HBO) for about a million dollars a year per unit. (A *transponder* is an electronic device that receives a transmission from one location on the surface of the globe, instantly converts it to an appropriate frequency, amplifies it, and sends it back as a high-quality television signal to a designated location.) The antenna required to receive a satellite transponder signal comes in the form of a large "dish," examples of which can be observed around most contemporary communication facilities. By the use of satellites, transponders, and dish antennas, television programs can be transmitted instantaneously, and with high signal quality, from virtually any place in the hemisphere to any other. With the use of specialized satellite systems, transmissions can span the oceans or even be sent around the world.

The importance of communication satellites to the advancement of modern telecommunications is analogous to the importance of the telegraph to the development of the newspaper. Both the telegraph and the satellite dramatically overcame the limits of distance, thus permitting a broader reach for both information gathering and dissemination. Since satellite systems came into operation, the saying, "it's a small world," has taken on dramatic new meaning: reporters are now able to provide coverage of stories along with televised video directly from the scene. These can be transmitted to a satellite from virtually any point on the globe and then sent down instantaneously to central facilities where they can be relayed on (perhaps again via satellite) to media audiences of unprecedented size and distribution.

As an example of the evolution of media systems, satellites have begun to alter the venerable newspaper industry in its constant struggle to cope with its competitors in a changing environment. For example, satellites made the development of national newspapers, such as *USA Today*, far more practical. Previously, newspapers could send their page formats and contents from one central point to several receiving points, but the time and money costs in overcoming long distance made a national newspaper economically impractical. Satellite transmission changed all of that.

Another change in the newspaper industry provides an additional example of the process of adaptive evolutionary change: the use of satellite-delivered wire services. In Los Angeles, for example, a video news service analogous to the United Press (UP) and Associated Press (AP) print news services is now in operation. Reporters from subscribing newspapers watch the news on video screens operated by the news service just as they would read the AP or UP Telex messages in order to gather stories. It is still too early to know if this invention will succeed or what the consequences may be on the quality and depth of newspaper coverage. It is, nonetheless, a good example of a new industry that has evolved as a result of communication satellites. It also illustrates how our oldest form of mass communication has found ways to utilize new technologies to survive in a world dominated by newer electronic media.

At the time that new technologies emerge, it takes imagination and a willingness to take risks to transform them into better or more adaptive media systems. As we noted earlier, Time, Inc. advanced the development of cable television by making the considerable financial investment required to lease a satellite transponder and having the imagination to see how this technology could be used. This was a particularly bold move when you consider that HBO was losing money at the time. Transmission by satellite did provide greatly improved broadcast quality over the previous microwave delivery modes. The combination of better and more recent films with better transmission quality probably accounts for the rise in HBO's success since 1975. Ted Turner, another bold innovator, and owner of an Atlanta TV station, demonstrated that not only could pay cable produce a profit, but it could do so with the news programming of his successful Cable News Network. Doubt about the possibility of pay cable succeeding in a market accustomed to receiving "free" TV were thus put to rest.

The success of extra-fee pay cable television fueled the rate of diffusion of basic subscriber cable. Two factors seem to have created the positive effect of the extra-fee services. One was the attractiveness of a variety of high-quality programming uninterrupted by commercials. The desire to gain access to this programming motivated increasing numbers of rural and urban residents to hook up to basic cable and become extra-fee service subscribers. The other factor was the increased profitability of cable TV generally. This provided cable companies with the necessary capital to lay more and more cable and, thus, expand the size of their potential subscriber population. As a result, many more households were ready and able to make the change to cable from simple over-the-air reception.

As we noted, it took almost twenty-five years for basic cable to be adopted by 12 percent of American households. After the social invention of satellite-delivered extra-fee cable, it took only ten years (1975–1985) for this percentage to triple. The graph in Figure 12.1 shows this dramatic rise in the rate of diffusion of cable TV. By 1986 close to 50 percent of American households had become cable subscribers, there were about 40 extra-fee cable services one could buy, and there were as many as 70 to 100 cable channels available in some (but by no means all) areas. Generally, then, the coming of the long-awaited surge of cable television has brought increased choice to audiences and

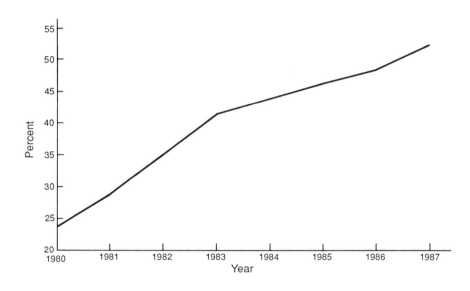

Figure 12.1. Cable Households: Percentage of U.S. households with cable television. Source: Cabletelevision Advertising Bureau Inc., as adapted from the Wall Street Journal.

has provided a greater number of outlets to companies that produce movies and other content that can be shown on television.

Direct Broadcast Satellite Systems

In addition to the advantages of communication satellites for cable and network television, users (including many businesses) have also benefited through what are called direct broadcast satellite systems (DBS). The American landscape is increasingly dotted with satellite dishes in yards or on rooftops of American homes (about a million in 1985). The primary advantage of having direct access to satellite transmissions is that one can pick up an enormous number of broadcast channels (120 at last count) without having to pay a cable company or anyone else for transmission services.

Both the size and the cost (approximately $2,500 in 1985) of home dish antennas are dropping, making it likely that the number of DBS households will increase. However, the "free ride" may not last. The economic interests of broadcasters, who must pay to rent satellite transmission services, are threatened when dish owners receive their broadcasts for free.

The conflict paradigm once again comes into play as a way of analyzing struggles between broadcasters, DBS system operators, and audiences. First, the broadcasters made an unsuccessful effort to prohibit people legally from being able to tap into television satellite transmissions. Failing to win this battle in the courts, broadcasters are seeking to turn back the tide of satellite dish proliferation by scrambling their transmissions so that dish owners cannot receive them without purchasing or renting a de-scrambler device. How this scrambling will affect the rate of household satellite dish diffusion remains to be seen, but basic conflict theory would predict that some modification of the broadcast industry will emerge from these struggles.

The development of satellite cable and direct broadcast satellite systems presents many new problems and turmoil in the regulatory and economic sectors of the media industry. In many ways it is reminiscent of the early days of radio. Fundamental questions have arisen, such as: Who owns satellite transmissions? How can actors and other members of the media industry equitably receive rewards for their work or creations in the form of residuals or other economic benefits? Will the traditional dominance of the three commercial networks be undone? Will ownership of the media system become more or less centralized in the future? Because both cable and satellite systems continue to change, these and many other questions are not likely to be answered in any enduring manner in the near future.

INTERACTIVE COMMUNICATION SYSTEMS

Another significant advance that may help shape our future media is the development of interactive communication technologies.[2] Interactivity generally refers to processes of communication that take on some of the characteristics of interpersonal communication. In interpersonal communication, sender and receiver alternately share the role of communicator, and each partner receives immediate and full feedback in the form of verbal and nonverbal messages. Conventional mass communication is not interactive, because the flow of one-way communication does not permit audience members to provide, or mass communicators to receive, full and immediate feedback. The mass communicator does not know what the audience is doing, thinking, or feeling, and the member of the audience cannot express puzzlement, sadness, anger, excitement, or any other reaction back to the source. Traditionally this has been one of the major characteristics of mass communication.

Interactivity also means mutual control over the flow of communication content. For example, in interpersonal communication partners can affect the nature of a conversation by changing the subject or by showing disapproval of what the partner is saying. No "new" mass communication technology yet comes even close to this rich interactivity of interpersonal communication, but to a certain extent the distinction is beginning to blur.

Telephone-Based Systems

There are a number of telephone-based technologies presently in use by corporations, universities, and other residential and professional communities that are designed to allow people to confer while seeing pictures of each other. Another way of linking people is by messages that are sent back and forth by parties who type messages into computer terminals. These technologies are seen by many as improvements over conventional telephone, because they allow more than two people in more than two locations to communicate with one another. Audio teleconferencing (which is not new) requires that the parties all be available at the same time. In computer teleconferencing, however, messages can be sent and received without all communication partners being present at their respective locations at the same time. Video teleconferencing, of course, allows two or more parties engaged in communication to see and hear each other simultaneously.

Each of these systems uses a somewhat different technology. Telephone lines connect people in an audio teleconference, and such lines linked to computers connect users in a computer teleconference. Video teleconferencing is more complex: it requires cable-linked studio-type rooms equipped with a television monitor, microphones, and a camera. These requirements make it very costly and, understandably, this communication form is not widely disseminated in the general population. Moreover, there is evidence that many people would resist a technology (such as the videophone) that allows others to see them—especially when partially or poorly dressed or otherwise in an "unpresentable" state. Thus, the simple telephone is likely to be with us for the foreseeable future.

Television-Based Interactive Media

Of the interactive media intended for use by large and diverse groups comparable to the audience of conventional mass media, two-way cablevision has been the most visible. Two-way cablevision is an extension of the conventional one-way or monological cable television system discussed earlier in this chapter. It has not only promoted the hopes and fears of social analysts, but it has also been tried out in a number of cities around the world.

The development of two-way cablevision, like that of its one-way predecessor, has been slow. The technology is simple but relatively expensive. Two household cable lines are installed, one to receive transmissions (as in one-way cable) and one to send transmissions. The first two-way cablevision system in the United States, "Qube," was developed in 1977 by Warner-Amex and installed in Columbus, Ohio, offered as an option along with a basic cable television. It was not really very sophisticated. Each subscribing household had an electronic keypad. After a request from the station for viewer input (e.g. to indicate how much a previous broadcast was liked or disliked, a selection can be made from a limited number of options seen on the screen (somewhat like an elaborate multiple choice test item) and thereby send a message back to the central computer. The return messages were rapidly processed so that viewers could learn the outcome. In a typical operating situation, connected customers were told how to record their opinion or preference by punching in a number from 0 to 9. Once tallied by the computer, responses might be displayed back to Qube households or could be treated like a preference poll for selection of future programming material.

A more provocative feature of this novel form of two-way communication was that it was equipped with a monitoring device capable of determining what program was being received in the homes of Qube customers when the set was turned on. This feature made it possible to obtain virtually instantaneous information to compute program *ratings* (i.e., of all Qube households, the percentage watching a program) and program *shares* (i.e., of all Qube households watching TV at that time, the percentage watching a program).

Monitoring of this kind undoubtedly provided economically useful information to Warner-Amex, but it also had a darker side. It raised a very real concern about the privacy of people's activities in their own home. Analysts concerned about the political and social consequences of new technologies saw it as the first step along the path of communications technologies being employed to gather information that subscribers may wish to keep private. Subscribers could not avoid monitoring except by turning off the television set. Warner-Amex promised their Qube customers that individual household information would not be made available to anyone else, including mass communication scholars, and they appear to have kept that promise. However, firm ethical resolve can soften in the face of an opportunity to make a profit. It doesn't take much imagination to see how even this limited type of information could be misused—for example, to identify viewers of "pornography," or to build and sell mailing lists on the basis of program preferences for sports, fashion, religion, or political orientation.

The Qube experiment was not financially successful. Warner-Amex lost about $30 million between 1977 and 1984. One reason for the loss was that the majority of Qube households would not participate in any of the interactive opportunities offered during an average week. One interpretation of their nonparticipation in what was a novel opportunity to "talk back to their TV set" may be the very limited nature of what they could say. Registering opinions and preferences by punching a number on a keypad when others have control over the questions and response options is akin to being a respondent in endless (and possibly mindless) surveys; registering a desire to ask a question of someone on a TV talk show with whom you might finally talk by telephone is a lot of trouble to go to and does not produce a very rich form of communication. The delay between expressing a desire for, and actually engaging in dialogue, as well as the sensory limits imposed by the technology (e.g., subscribers can only be heard whereas officials can be seen and heard) help to explain the lack of wide appeal of this form of mediated-dialogue. The bottom line for Warner-Amex was that they severely cut back the amount of interactive programming offered on the Qube system.

Not all such systems have suffered the same fate. Two-way cablevision has been installed as a fundamental part of more sophisticated interactive information/communication systems in Japan (1978), England (1982), and France (1984). The more advanced and complex of these systems, such as the one operated by the Ministry of Post/Telephone/Telegraph in Biarritz, France, employ fiber optic cable instead of the copper wire used to make conventional cable connections. Fiber optic cable consists of a number of tiny (like a human hair) malleable glass tubes that transmit pulses of light generated by lasers or light-emitting diodes. Messages sent via such optical means do not interfere with electronic messages employed in television, radio, portable home or car phones, and other electronic communication devices. Because it consists of many strands, rather than a single wire, fiber optic cable can carry a greater volume of messages than can be sent via conventional cable.

Households in Biarritz and other "wired cities" are equipped with a system that combines a color TV, telephone, and a microcomputer. Household members may use the system in a variety of ways—two-way cablevision, videophone, videotex (described below), or teleshopping.

The considerable governmental investment required to install these systems was made with the hope of providing jobs and national expertise in the information-based economies of modern society.

As was the case with Qube, critics soon became concerned about potential political consequences. They feared that such technology could be employed by governments to "watch" private citizens. The common practice of security guards watching customers in stores and visitors to museums or other public places could be extended to the home. The videophone, for example, could be used in a manner reminiscent of Orwell's "telescreen," with Big Brother seeing to it that TV monitors are on at all times for the surveillance of what people are doing in the "privacy" of their own homes.

The monitoring of program selection in the Qube system is taken considerably farther by the prospect of home video screens that cannot be controlled or even turned off by household members. This technological possibility has not, as far as we know, become a reality, because social, political, and legal forces operate against it. What worries some is that such social forces will weaken to the point where these technologies are employed by police, governmental, or other agencies to obtain information about individuals and families that can be used to control their behavior. In spite of these worrisome aspects, it seems almost certain that some form of a "wired" household communication environment will develop, although its specific shape is not yet clear.

Videotex

One system that has already been partially accepted in the United States is videotex. This is not actually a new technology. Videotex is simply a novel combination of some of the technologies that we have already discussed. Mayer (1986) defined videotex as: "any interactive electronic system which allows users to send data to and receive data from computers or other videotex users by means of a terminal capable of displaying text and pictures."[3] The basic hardware or equipment that videotex subscribers require is a TV set with an associated keypad device (or personal computer with a video monitor) that is connected by telephone (or cable) lines to a mainframe computer. Videotex provides for a two-way information flow wherein the user may request and receive information from a menu of information services provided by a videotex company. Subscribers become, in effect, time-share computer users who can, upon request, receive almost immediate responses to their information service requests. The information services from which subscribers can choose typically include news, sports scores, banking records, stock market reports and the weather, and even catalogue shopping. The service menu corresponds to numeric or other types of codes on the subscriber's keypad. Once a request is punched in, appropriate information stored in the central computer is called up for display on the video monitor of the user's personal computer or on the home television screen.

The advantages of videotex—its diversity of information services and its two-way interactive characteristics—led many to predict its rapid diffusion. Some businesses acted on these predictions by making the considerable investment required to start up videotex services (e.g., Knight-Ridder and Times-Mirror). Social and economic factors once again proved the forecasters wrong. Because of the way that videotex systems have been designed for the American market, the advantages to a user of being able to control the timing and the content of information received have been outweighed by the disadvantages of becoming a videotex subscriber.

One obvious disadvantage and obstacle to videotex adoption has been the cost of subscription. In American videotex systems, for example, subscribers have to buy a special receiver costing hundreds of dollars. This obstacle has been overcome by some videotex companies (such as H&R Block's CompuServe) that use the household PC as the receiver. It should be recalled, however, that only 15 percent of American households presently own a personal computer, and many of these lack the modem needed for linking their PC via telephone lines to the videotex system.

Another way to overcome the cost problem would be simply to provide people with receivers free of charge, a tactic successfully employed by the French government. The government-owned French videotex system, Teletel, has been a success largely because the government subsidized it to the tune of $2 million to $3 million a year. The government not only provided the free equipment, but also invested money and effort to link its videotex system with the telephone system, which is also government owned. The French boosted public use of their system by converting their telephone directory into a videotex service. It was hoped that people's fear of using computers would be reduced as they acquired the low level of skill required to locate a phone number via the videotex directory. Once over this hurdle, the public was more likely to use other videotex services. Widespread use of these additional services could amortize or pay back the costs of the original investment and, in the long run, make a profit for the French government.

While the verdict is not completely known, it appears that the French government's gamble is paying off. Only four years after the program began, the base income provided by use of the videotex directory assistance service, plus the revenues from use of three additional videotex services, has led officials to predict full recovery of the costs of giving away almost 2 million videotex terminals. The failure of videotex to take off in the United States and in other national contexts (such as in England, where videotex was first tried) may be due to the lack of the kind of economic support provided by the French. In other words, a key social factor in the development of videotex is the receptivity of governments to new media systems.

As a communication form, videotex also has some physical drawbacks that may lead people to resist adoption even if they did not have to pay a substantial sum for the necessary equipment. For example, users must stay in front of the receiver to call up and to receive information. Aside from economic considerations, if the same information is available from a more portable medium, such as a newspaper or radio, people may decline the use of videotex, despite its interactivity. They may opt for media that may be used anywhere inside or outside the home.

Another difficult problem to solve before videotex is likely to be adopted on a mass basis in the United States concerns the fine lines between information that is too general and that that is too specific. Videotex offers the advantage of a personalized information service in the sense that users can request only what they want from a broad array of information bases; they may have far more *control* over the content that they receive than in the conventional one-way mass communication situation. However, much of the available information may never be of interest to a user (e.g., stock market reports, football player injury reports, or the latest jokes). Or, the information that is of interest may not be given in sufficient depth to meet their needs. People who could afford to adopt videotex may be more likely to do so if offered a service tailored to their specific information needs, both in the range of available content and in its depth. The problem here is that specialized information services cannot exist without sufficiently large numbers of people who are willing to pay for them. There may be so few who need a particular type of information that maintaining the data base is not economically feasible. For example, a data base providing the latest information on trout fishing opportunities and chances of success in various areas of the country would find enthusiastic use among those dedicated to this sport, but the total number of users nationwide might be only a few thousand, while the costs of obtaining and updating the information might be expensive indeed.

There is no clear answer to this problem short of some alternative way of financing specialized information data bases. At present, the largest videotex service in the United States, CompuServe, still has only

275,000 subscribers, and many of these are businesses rather than households.

Transforming Interactive Technologies to Media Systems

One of the more difficult problems in trying to assess the significance of new technologies is to make accurate predictions about their chances of being transformed into mass communication systems. A technological innovation does not in itself ensure that a communication system will be built around it. Some that seem destined to lead to elaborate communication systems that would be quickly adopted by the public have not achieved popularity. For example, technological possibilities led observers to predict a much more rapid diffusion of two-way cablevision and videotex than that which has occurred to date in the United States.

Both business people and communication scholars try to figure out why some technologies are successfully developed as mass communication systems while others never catch on. They also seek to understand the conditions that lead to slow or rapid adoption. The newspaper and the telephone took a long time to develop, whereas film, radio, and television spread rapidly. What was there about those particular media, and the conditions of the society at the time, that led to these different rates of adoption?

Generally, then, it is clear that our newest technology will or will not be transformed into systems that come into wide use because of the influence of the family, the political system, economic considerations, schools, the requirements of the military, and other conditions that have also shaped our present-day mass media systems. This conclusion points once again to one of the critical questions in the study of mass communication that was posed in Chapter 1: *What is the impact of a society on its mass media?* Only through the intensive study of the social milieu and the way it shapes media will it be possible to forecast which technologies are likely to become full-fledged mass communication systems.

In trying to forecast the workable media systems of the future and how they will incorporate some of the technological developments reviewed above, we can be fairly confident of only a limited number of conclusions. One is that the personal computer will very likely play an increasing role in whatever interactive systems develop. A second, however, is that until the content of such systems can be made to parallel more closely the interests, needs, and personal goals of large numbers of ordinary citizens, and at the same time remain financially viable, it is unlikely that videotex or its near relatives will grow rapidly. In addition, satellites will find increasing uses. Coupled with cable, they promise to expand the number of channels available to the ordinary household. The problem here is content, not cost. If over a hundred channels *were* available to every television set, what would be shown? With a few rare exceptions, cable currently is a mix of programs ranging from low to lower aesthetic quality. It is disconcerting to many thoughtful observers of the American system of mass communication to realize that the brilliant new technologies that are being developed will probably be used to double or triple the amount of wrestling, quiz games, rock video, and soap operas available to the average family.

There is every reason to believe that the successful media of the future, whatever their technological base, will operate on the same principles as the ones of the past. In a society in which the profit motive is valued highly, and the basic economic system is capitalism, radical change from that base seems unlikely. The new media will probably be supported either by advertising (as is the case with newspapers, radio, and television today) or by direct fees for content (as is now the case for cable, extra-fee services, books, and the movies). This means that their content has to deliver either an audience of millions that advertisers will pay to reach, or a smaller audience of people who see the content as so essential to their personal goals that they will be willing to pay.

All of these considerations point directly to the individual media dependencies discussed in the previous chapter. The challenge for developers of new technologies is to design media systems that not only serve individuals' understanding, orientation, and entertainment goals, but do so in a way that is superior to more traditional media alternatives. It is not easy to "build a better mousetrap." Successful media systems of the future will have to offer a better combination of content, convenience, cost, and accessibility than people already have in televisions, radios, movies, stereos, newspapers, books, and magazines. Designers of new media must also take into account institutional constraints. They have to design systems that are compatible with prevailing economic, political, and other institutional orders.

Government-subsidized media, for example, can work in some societies (e.g., videotex in France) but not in others. American institutional traditions create a resistance to government involvement in the ownership and operation of media systems, so that solution appears unlikely in the United States. Thus, whatever the future brings in the way of new hardware, emerging media systems will undoubtedly bring forward most of the features of our mass media of the past. In other words, a society does indeed shape its media, regardless of the sophistication of the technology that is available at any given point.

At a more theoretical level, the paradigms discussed in Chapter 1 also aid in understanding why some of the potential mass communication systems will become realities and others will not. They also sensitize us to different types of social forces that are likely to affect the chances of a technology's being transformed into a media system.

From the point of view of structural functional analysis, the technologies that should survive and prosper as media systems are those that serve societal needs for stability, integration, and efficient production. Thus, technologies that facilitate cooperation between the various parts of our society and that aid in controlling threats to stability or equilibrium (e.g., conflict and deviance) are functional and should therefore develop into mass communication systems.

The conflict paradigm offers a quite different view, namely, the technologies that will develop into mass communication systems are those that result from the clash of powerful groups. In other words, the way in which such technologies are transformed into communication systems is through a dialectical process of conflict between groups, each promoting the system that best serves its economic and political interests. This process is evident in the historical struggles between promoters of cable and network television, or even in the present struggles between owners of direct broadcast satellite dishes and owners of cable TV stations.

From the perspective of the evolutionary paradigm, technologies that best serve the adaptation needs of our society will develop into new media systems. For example, as our society becomes more and more complex, it is increasingly difficult to hold it together with traditional modes of interpersonal and mass communication; thus new media systems will have to be developed to fill this void and ensure survival. New media systems may succeed, for example, by contributing to the solution of problems created by the fundamental transition to an information service economy or equally fundamental changes in world economic order. The question is which of the various new media best facilitates our ability to adapt to our changing domestic and world environment. Which, for example, provides the kind of international communication and exchange systems necessary to the welfare of an increasingly complex world, one in which the survival of the species is made problematic by nuclear weapons, scarce natural resources, and poor communication among peoples.

When new media do become firmly established communications systems, the older mass media will face their own adaptation problems. As we have seen in the historical development of newspapers, movies, radio, and television, once "new" media become "old" media, their survival depends upon their ability to find new ways to provide services that audiences will buy or governments will support.

The symbolic interactionist paradigm also sensitizes us to questions of change, but the concern is more with individuals than with the societal or global concerns of evolutionary theorists. A major consideration for a symbolic interactionist would be how well new media systems assist individuals in their collective efforts to create meaning in an ambiguous and changing world. In the previous chapter we discussed the significance of our complex, ambiguous, and ever-changing world in the development of individual dependency relations with the mass media. For the symbolic interactionist, the most important of these is the chronic dependency upon media to keep our subjective realities up-to-date so that they keep pace with the changing world around us. Individuals would thus be expected to develop the strongest dependency relations with new media systems that do the best job of helping them keep up with what is going on and, more important, what it means. In other words, developers of new technologies who design communication systems that serve individuals' *understanding dependencies* have a good chance of succeeding.

A related consideration is the capacity of new media to create the shared meanings and shared symbolic cultures that are essential to effective communication among diverse peoples and nations. The fact that national economics are giving way to a world economy means that powerful groups and nations will seek new communications media that provide a world communication system, a new "world information order." Many conflict theorists who contemplate such developments incorporate symbolic interactionist concerns when they point out that the worldwide symbolic cultures and social realities that could be constructed and disseminated by such communication systems could also be more important than military force. The old adage that "the pen is mightier than the sword" is the classic symbolic interactionist premise that those who control the communications media that we depend upon to construct our subjective realities can also control our behavior. It remains to be seen if those who control new media can and will employ them to create world harmony or world domination or both.

Finally, the cognitive paradigm draws attention to the effects of new media systems upon individuals' beliefs, feelings, and behavior. Presumably, those technologies that have "desirable" effects, as judged by the individuals themselves and by power holders, are most likely to be developed into communication systems. In societies, for example, where the media are dependent upon advertising as their source of income, a technology is more likely to become a media system if it can be used by large numbers of people to attain their personal goals. In societies where the media are owned and operated by governments, the more important determinant may be the effects that potential communication systems can have in shaping individuals' beliefs, feelings, and behavior toward the state. This would be especially true in tightly controlled political systems.

In many ways, then, these classic social and behavioral paradigms give us at least some guides to the factors that need examination in order for predictions to be made about which of the many new technologies will constitute the media systems of the future. The extent to which these technologies are diffusing or are being adopted is of considerable interest to communication scholars.

The challenge that lies ahead is to do the kind of theory-based research that is required to predict accurately which technologies will and will not emerge as new forms of mass communication. An even more challenging problem is to determine which general paradigms have the most validity in accurately identifying the social factors that affect the likelihood of a technology's developing into a mass media system.

NOTES

1. For a detailed description of the new technologies and their contemporary uses in American society, see Melvin L. DeFleur and Everette E. Dennis, "The Continuing Revolution in Technology," in *Understanding Mass Communication* (Boston: Houghton Mifflin, 1988), pp. 245–267.
2. For an extensive analysis of the significance of these "new" forms of communication, what these authors call *telelogic* communication forms in contrast to the dialogic form of interpersonal communication and the monologic form of traditional mass communication see S. J. Ball-Rokeach and K. K. Reardon. 1988. "Telelogic, dialogic, and monologic communication: A comparison of forms." In R. P. Hawkins, S. Pingree, and J. M. Wiemann (Eds.), *Rethinking Communication Research*. Beverly Hills, CA: Sage.
3. Mayer, R. M. 1986. The French videotex system: Success story of "Edsel" of the eighties? Unpublished paper. Family and Consumer Studies, University of Utah.

Index